My Dearest Elizabeth,

Bet you find something in this book about our lovely old home!

ILY,

-M-

Forgotten Philadelphia

Forgotten Philadelphia

Lost Architecture
of the Quaker City

THOMAS H. KEELS

 TEMPLE UNIVERSITY PRESS | PHILADELPHIA

Publication of this book was made possible by a grant from
FURTHERMORE: A PROGRAM OF THE J. M. KAPLAN FUND

Additional support generously provided by the
CLANEIL FOUNDATION INC.

TEMPLE UNIVERSITY PRESS
1601 N. Broad Street
Philadelphia, PA 19122
www.temple.edu/tempress

Text design by Kate Nichols

This book is printed on acid-free paper for greater permanence and durability.

Library of Congress Cataloging-in-Publication Data

Keels, Thomas H.
    Forgotten Philadelphia : lost architecture of the Quaker city / Thomas H. Keels.
        p.   cm.
    Includes bibliographical references and index.
    ISBN-13: 978-1-59213-506-6 (cloth : alk. paper)
    ISBN-10: 1-59213-506-4 (cloth : alk. paper)
    1. Lost architecture—Pennsylvania—Philadelphia. 2. Historic buildings—
Pennsylvania—Philadelphia. 3. Philadelphia (Pa.)—Buildings, structures, etc.
4. Philadelphia (Pa.)—History. I. Title.

NA735.P5K44 2007
720.9748′11—dc22

                                                                    2006102654

2 4 6 8 9 7 5 3 1

CONTENTS

ACKNOWLEDGMENTS

Since the scope of *Forgotten Philadelphia* was so broad, I was truly fortunate to be able to draw upon a variety of archives and collections that captured the rich diversity of Philadelphia architecture, existing and vanished, over the past 350 years.

I am deeply grateful to those individuals who generously shared their private collections with me, particularly James Hill Jr. and Robert M. Skaler. Christopher Lane and Don Cresswell graciously opened up their treasure trove of rare prints at the Philadelphia Print Shop, allowing me to select the ones I wanted for this book.

Denise Scott Brown, John Izenour, and Kevin Kaminski of Venturi, Scott Brown and Associates, Inc.; Robert Gutowski of the Morris Arboretum of the University of Pennsylvania; and Dr. Thomas McClellan of St. Mary's at the Cathedral, all provided access to their organizations' archives and reviewed relevant sections of my manuscript. Dr. Jeffrey A. Cohen, Dr. David R. Contosta, Stephen G. Hague, and Richard S. Lee offered sage advice on the structure and focus of the book, while Dr. Michael J. Lewis and Dr. Page Talbott kindly shared their own research with me.

Among archival institutions, special thanks must go to Bruce Laverty, Michael Seneca, Jill LeMin Lee, and Ellen Rose at the Athenaeum of Philadelphia; to Phil Lapsansky, Charlene Peacock, and Sarah Weatherwax at the Library Company of Philadelphia; and to Margaret Jerrido and her staff at Temple University Libraries, Urban Archives. All of these dedicated and considerate people worked closely with my assistant, Anne Swoyer, and me to locate research and graphic materials that vividly illustrated the rise and fall of the buildings in *Forgotten Philadelphia*.

I am also grateful to the following individuals for their help: Geraldine Duclow and Karen Lightner at the Free Library of Philadelphia; James M. Duffin at the University of Pennsylvania Archives; Joseph Elliott; R. A. Friedman and Jack Gumbrecht at the Historical Society of Pennsylvania; Gregory Heller of the Ed Bacon Foundation; Elizabeth Jarvis and Tina Gravatt of the Chestnut Hill Historical Society; Gary Jastrzab of the Philadelphia City Planning Commission; Edward Lawler Jr. of the Independence Hall Association; Valerie-Anne Lutz of the American Philosophical Society; Douglas Muth; and William Whitaker of the Architectural Archives of the University of Pennsylvania.

Micah B. Kleit, my editor at Temple University Press, took my idea for a book about lost Philadelphia architecture and made it a reality, providing encouragement at every step of the process. Dr. Paul M. Puccio of Bloomfield College reviewed my manuscript in detail, polishing and refining my writing and ensuring a smooth and consistent tone and viewpoint. Anne Swoyer, my research assistant, spent many hours scouring Philadelphia libraries and institutions, tracking down the perfect illustrations for this book.

Finally, I offer my deepest gratitude to my partner and friend, Lawrence M. Arrigale, who inspired this book with his gift of Nathan Silver's *Lost New York* at Christmas 2003. As with all my endeavors, his support, advice, and assurance were essential to the success of *Forgotten Philadelphia*.

City Neighborhoods
PAST and PRESENT

BUCKS COUNTY

MONTGOMERY COUNTY

MORELAND

BYBERRY

FAR NORTHEAST

LOWER DUBLIN

DELAWARE

CHESTNUT HILL

MOUNT AIRY

GERMANTOWN

ROXBOROUGH

PHILADELPHIA

LOGAN/OLNEY

OXFORD CIRCLE

FRANKFORD

MANAYUNK

BRIDESBURG

COUNTY

NORTH PHILADELPHIA

RICHMOND

BELMONT

KENSINGTON

SPRING GARDEN

NORTHERN LIBERTIES

WEST PHILADELPHIA

CENTER CITY

BLOCKLEY

SOUTHWARK

MOYAMENSING

SOUTH PHILADELPHIA

PASSYUNK

CHESTER COUNTY

KINGSESSING

River

Delaware

Schuylkill River

Wissahickon

Tacony Creek

Pennypack Creek

Poquessing Creek

Cobbs Creek

Market St

Ridge Ave

Broad St

Germantown Ave

Lancaster Ave

Belmont Ave

Girard Ave

Baltimore Ave

Passyunk Ave

Penrose Ave

Roosevelt Blvd

Pennsylvania Turnpike

SCALE IN MILES
0   1   2

Forgotten Philadelphia: Selected Landmarks
COUNTY MAP

1. Benjamin Rush Birthplace
2. Blockley Almshouse
3. Boulevard Pools
4. Budd Company Red Lion Plant
5. Cannon Ball House
6. Carlton
7. Compton
8. Cooper and Union Volunteer Saloons
9. Horticultural Hall
10. J.F.K. and Veterans Stadiums
11. Liberty Bell Park
12. Monument Cemetery
13. Mower U.S. Hospital
14. Moyamensing Prison
15. Municipal Airport
16. Naglee House
17. Pennsylvania Hospital for the Insane
18. Townsend's (Roberts) Mill
19. Sears Distribution Center
20. Sedgeley
21. Sesqui-Centennial Entrance
22. Shibe Park/Connie Mack Stadium
23. Woodside Park

OLD CITY Circa 1780

0   500 feet

Vine   St

North-East Square

Sassafras   St

Mulberry   St

High   St

Chestnut St

State House Square

Walnut   St

South-East Square

Locust St

Spruce St

Pine St

Lombard St

N 7th St
N 6th St
N 5th St
N 4th St
N 3rd St
N 2nd St
N Front St
N King St

S 7th St
S 6th St
S 5th St
S 4th St
S 3rd St
S 2nd St
S Front St
S King St

Dock Creek
Dock St

William Penn's Landing Site

Delaware River

Windmill Island

Islands removed in the 19th c.

Center City Today

with Historic Street Names in Italic

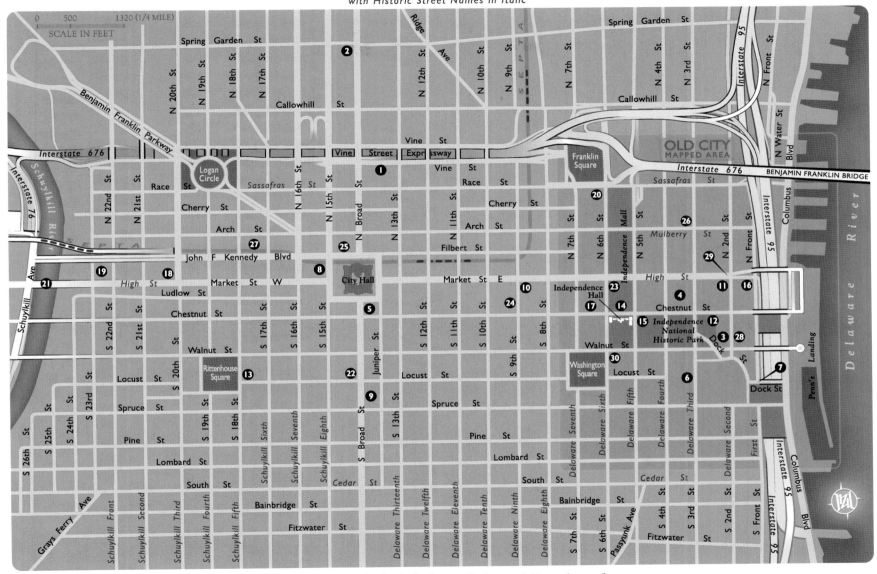

Forgotten Philadelphia: Selected Landmarks

CENTER CITY and OLD CITY MAPS

1. AFL Medical Plan Building
2. Baldwin Locomotive Works
3. Bank of Pennsylvania
4. Benjamin Franklin House
5. Betz Building
6. Bingham Mansion
7. Blue Anchor
8. Broad Street Station
9. Broad Street Theatre
10. Gimbels Department Store
11. Great/Greater Meeting Houses
12. Jayne Building
13. Joseph Harrison Mansion
14. Liberty Bell Pavilion
15. Library Hall
16. London Coffee House
17. Marble Arcade
18. Mastbaum Theatre
19. Municipal Gas Works
20. Pennsylvania Hall
21. Permanent Bridge
22. Philadelphia Art Club
23. President's (Masters-Penn) House
24. Presidential Mansion (unused)
25. Reyburn Plaza
26. Second Presbyterian Church
27. Sheraton Hotel
28. Slate Roof House
29. Town Hall and Court House
30. Walnut Street Jail

Introduction

I repeat your glory, BROAD STREET STATION!
The proper shrine, the true Main Line,
Of Immortality the Intimation;
Such offsteam blowing,
Such bells, and hells of coming and going,
Suburban cowcatchers' dainty snouts,
Beautiful barytone All abooaard shouts,
Drive wheels, and firebox glowing. . . .
Goodbye, Goodbye! No wonder I
Preserve in pure imagination
My memory of BROAD STREET STATION.

CHRISTOPHER MORLEY
"Elegy in a Railroad Station: Obit for Broad Street, Philadelphia, 1952"

Facing page: **C**rowds wait for the departure of the Philadelphia Orchestra Special at Broad Street Station on the evening of April 27, 1952. At far right, behind the entrance gates, the orchestra serenades the throng of passengers and well-wishers. (Temple University Libraries, Urban Archives, Philadelphia.)

At 9:57 PM on Sunday, April 27, 1952, the last train rolled out of Philadelphia's venerable Pennsylvania Railroad Station, better known as Broad Street Station. Although regular service had ended the day before, an eighteen-car train, the Philadelphia Orchestra Special, was scheduled as part of the closing ceremonies for the landmark that had dominated the northwest corner of Broad and Market streets for seventy years.

Seven hundred passengers presented souvenir tickets to ride the Special as far as North Philadelphia Station. Among them was eighty-four-year-old Mrs. Henry P. Baily of Overbrook who, on Opening Day, December 5, 1881, had boarded a train out of the new station, its exterior bright red brick and shiny terra cotta, the glass panes of its vaulted train shed clear and unclouded. Besides the passengers, 3,000 observers packed the station floor and boarding platform on that rainy April night in 1952, catching their last glimpse of the landmark before demolition began.

Eugene Ormandy and the Philadelphia Orchestra, who had treated the crowd to a special concert, were guests of honor on the eponymous train. As orchestra members played "Auld Lang Syne" from the rear platform of the observation car, passengers and spectators sang along, filling the vast station with their voices. After the train departed along the elevated viaduct known as the Chinese Wall, heading west to Thirtieth Street before turning north for its final trek, the now-silent witnesses disappeared into the rainy night, leaving Broad Street Station dark and deserted.

This ceremony was the culmination of a long farewell to the station, a prolonged mourning for a soon-to-be-razed building unique in Philadelphia history. Even though an agreement to demolish Broad Street Station had been in place since 1925, the destruction of the building (postponed by the Depression and World War II) took countless Philadelphians by surprise, much like the death of an elderly but vital aunt whom one had assumed would live forever. Philadelphians' sorrow transcended the loss of a familiar, lifelong locale, the scene of countless memorable meetings, arrivals, and departures.

Many mourned the loss of an important symbol in their city's life. Broad Street Station represented the Pennsylvania Railroad—known simply as "the Railroad" to the consternation of its older competitor, the Reading—when that company reigned supreme as the largest and richest corporation in the world. The Railroad employed thousands of Philadelphians, enriched thousands more through its rock-solid bonds and stock, and provided comfortable bourgeois enclaves with its development of the Main Line, Chestnut Hill, and other suburbs. The Railroad was the epitome of what sociologist E. Digby Baltzell called "a very Proper Philadelphian business enterprise."[1]

The Railroad's presence was a talisman clutched by Philadelphians as their city stumbled through the treacherous postwar world. Its technological and industrial prowess reinforced Philadelphia's status as the Workshop of the World, while the city's employers fled, leaving their empty factories to decay. As the largest and busiest passenger terminal in the United States, Broad Street Station reassured Philadelphians that their city was a major crossroads, even as it gained a reputation as a provincial backwater. As long as the Railroad's iron tentacles stretched from Broad Street to cover the United States east of the Mississippi, Philadelphians knew they exerted influence over the nation, even as they fell further behind New York, Chicago, and even, God forbid, Los Angeles. While Broad Street Station stood, the stable, secure, soot-covered Philadelphia of the past century—with its immutable fixtures of Rittenhouse Square, the Union League, the Girard Bank, the Assemblies, the *Bulletin*, and a solidly Republican City Hall—remained intact.

Perhaps it was the realization that this late Victorian city was already in its death throes that led even the most nostalgic Philadelphians to accept Broad Street Station's destruction as inevitable. Aside from a few wistful letters to the *Bulletin* and *Inquirer*, no organized attempt was made to preserve the station, unlike later campaigns to save the Jayne Building and other nineteenth-century landmarks. The day the last train pulled out of Broad Street Station, an *Inquirer* editorial called the terminal's closing "a new chapter in civic progress," noting that this event opened the way not only for the redevelopment of Center City, but for the consolidation of train service at the modern and commodious Thirtieth Street Station.[2]

The following morning, Monday, April 28, 1952, Mayor Joseph S. Clark expressed the city's general ambivalence when he told reporters: "I'm sorry to see the station go, in a way, but it's in the interest of progress. What else can I say without sounding corny?"[3] Then, as press cameras flashed, Clark and Matthew H. McCloskey Jr., whose demolition firm would raze the station, smiled as they wedged a crowbar into a terra cotta railing atop the rain-swept roof of the building and pried out a brick. Below, workers ripped up rails from the Chinese Wall, removed brass stairway railings, and began to dismantle the massive clock that stood over the main entrance at Broad and Market streets.

McCloskey was smiling because his firm was being paid $157,500 to demolish Broad Street Station, plus all the materials it could salvage and sell. Clark was smiling because, less than four months after taking office as the first Democratic mayor in decades, he was clearing the way for one of the largest urban renewal projects in U.S. history. Broad Street Station and its Chinese Wall would give way to Penn Center, a modern complex of office blocks, parking garages, sunken terraces, and pedestrian walkways. Narrow Filbert Street, crowded with warehouses and express offices, would become expansive Pennsylvania Boulevard, lined with gleaming glass-and-steel towers like New York's Park Avenue.

In the minds of progressive (and Democratic) Philadelphians, Clark was liberating the city from its corrupt (and Republican) past. To them, the Railroad represented not power and prestige but political chicanery (including the scheme that had rammed the Chinese Wall, 2,000 feet long and 55 feet wide, through the center of the city), inefficiency (trains had to back out of the stub-end station, slowing travel time, to a more modern and comfortable station less than a mile away), and corporate indifference.

By exorcising the ghosts of his city's past, Clark was bringing Philadelphia into the twentieth century only fifty-two years late.

Less than twelve hours after the Philadelphia Orchestra Special pulled out, Mayor Joseph S. Clark and Matthew H. McCloskey Jr. deliver the first blow to Broad Street Station. (Temple University Libraries, Urban Archives, Philadelphia.)

With that crowbar, Clark struck a blow against the Dickensian city of smoke-belching locomotives, soot-encrusted brick, endless miles of decrepit rowhouses, sweaty laborers, and crooked ward bosses. In its place would rise a bright new world, where white-collar professionals would drive shiny automobiles from neat suburbs along modern expressways to sparkling, glass-walled offices, generating taxes to enable an army of competent, scrupulous bureaucrats to move the city closer toward perfection.

And after the bulldozers finished with Broad Street Station, Clark and his planning czar, Edmund N. Bacon, would have them cross the street to City Hall and raze that symbol-encrusted Victorian pile (except for its tower), replacing it with a public plaza to further symbolize Philadelphia's new transparency, modernity, and civic virtue.

The divergent emotions triggered by the destruction of a venerable landmark like Broad Street Station—grief over the loss of an irreplaceable historic and architectural gem, versus a strong faith in progress and pride in the embrace of the modern and new—is one of the central themes of *Forgotten Philadelphia: Lost Architecture of the Quaker City.* It is a theme that reverberates throughout Philadelphia history, from the filling in of the caves along the Delaware that sheltered the area's seventeenth-century settlers, causing older inhabitants to sigh over the loss of their village's innocent ways, to the 2006 dismantling of Romaldo Giurgola's Liberty Bell Pavilion,

viewed by some as a masterpiece of modernist architecture and by others as a dated eyesore.

Modern Philadelphians—motivated by nostalgia, aesthetics, architectural appreciation, historical awareness, or a combination of these factors—look at the destruction of a Broad Street Station or a Slate Roof House and wonder how their forefathers could have been so shortsighted or self-centered as to permit the loss of such relics. Greed and myopia certainly played a major role in the death of many buildings in this book. In other cases, however, the destroyers were driven by a sincere desire to substitute a functional and

modern structure for one rendered obsolete by population growth and movement, technological advances, changes in the size and scale of enterprises, evolving social needs, or some other shift.

By studying the stories of Philadelphia's demolished structures, *Forgotten Philadelphia* explores the symbiotic relationship between the city's architecture and the political, economic, and social forces that have shaped the city since its founding. While many books describe the reasons behind the creation of memorable buildings, far fewer examine the factors leading to their destruction (the most notable being Nathan Silver's 1967 classic, *Lost New York*). Instead of simply offering a nostalgic glimpse of things that aren't there anymore, *Forgotten Philadelphia* attempts to define the changes in the city's history capable of turning a building from landmark to landfill, often in only a few years.

As the first book to focus specifically on Philadelphia's demolished architecture, *Forgotten Philadelphia* also challenges the relatively static architectural image of our city. Mention Philadelphia to most Americans, and the first images that come to mind are Independence Hall and the Liberty Bell, possibly followed by Carpenters Hall, the

By November 1952, demolition of the station was well under way, and the ornamented columns of the Frank Furness–designed waiting room were exposed to the sky. (Temple University Libraries, Urban Archives, Philadelphia.)

Betsy Ross House, and Christ Church. Thanks to these structures and to the city's possessing, in the form of Society Hill, the largest American collection of existing colonial and Federal buildings, there is a perception that Philadelphia has never torn down a single building. Unlike its dynamically destructive neighbor New York, Philadelphia is seen as preserved intact, like a prehistoric insect in a lump of amber.

In reality, Philadelphia has destroyed as many notable buildings by important architects as has any other world-class city. Its explosive and continuous growth during the first 250 years of its existence —from a few thousand inhabitants in 1700 to over two million in 1950—made widespread destruction inevitable, just as it did in most older U.S. cities. As architectural historian George B. Tatum pointed out in 1961 (when official Philadelphia was busy obliterating the city's Victorian heritage), such destruction cleared the ground for constant invention and innovation:

> However much we must regret the continuing destruction of important structures that has gone on almost from the founding of the city, there is something heartening in this steadfast refusal of earlier Philadelphians to content themselves with preserving the architectural monuments of their illustrious past. . . . Because they were not afraid of new ideas, whether in the field of politics, social reform, or the arts, Philadelphians were among the first to try new architectural forms and theories. They produced the most advanced hospitals, the most progressive prisons, several of the most ambitious churches, and some of the earliest and most beautiful municipal parks. Their bridges were longer, wider, and deeper than others of their day. Whenever a new style made its appearance in America it was apt to be found in Philadelphia first; here were a number of the earliest and finest Federal buildings, the first examples of the Greek and Gothic styles, the first and most numerous Egyptian structures, and one of the largest and handsomest buildings in the Moorish manner.[4]

Selecting fewer than 200 structures to profile out of the thousands Philadelphia has lost over the past 350 years meant making choices that may appear random and arbitrary. The structures that I finally selected for *Forgotten Philadelphia* all met at least one of the criteria in the National Register for Historic Places guidelines, freely adapted:

- *They were outstanding examples of American architectural design.* Admittedly, this is a very broad and subjective standard. Few architectural historians, however, would dispute the importance of such works as Latrobe's Bank of Pennsylvania, Johnston and Walter's Jayne Building, and Furness & Hewitt's Guarantee Trust and Safe Deposit Company.

- *While not necessarily noteworthy structures, they were designed by noted architects.* The original Library Company was one of the few local structures by William Thornton, the amateur architect who would design the first U.S. Capitol. Oskar Stonorov's Schuylkill Falls Apartments attempted to adapt Le Corbusier's utopian principles to U.S. public housing, with mixed results. Louis I. Kahn's Medical Services Plan Building represented a transition between his earlier work and his later designs for the Alfred Newton Richards Medical Research Building and Jonas Salk Institute.

- *They introduced major architectural or technological innovations.* The Chestnut Street Theatre was the first U.S. playhouse illuminated by gas. The Permanent Bridge over the Schuylkill River, completed in 1805, was the longest wooden covered bridge in the world at the time and opened the way for the city's westward development. The Pennsylvania Hospital for the Insane featured an echelon design that became standard in nineteenth-century U.S. hospitals.

- *They played an important role in the city's political, industrial, economic, or social history.* The caves and cabins dug into the banks of the Delaware by early inhabitants are not traditional architecture, but they represent an early foothold by European settlers in Penn's Woods. The former blacksmith's shop where Richard Allen formed the Bethel Church gave birth to the African Methodist Episcopal Church. The ramshackle warren of buildings that housed Palumbo's served as the social and political center of Italian American life in Philadelphia for most of the twentieth century.

- *They were associated with notable Philadelphians.* The Slate Roof House, Benjamin Rush birthplace, Breintnall/Benezet House, and Fairhill were more important for their association with famous Philadelphians of the colonial era than for their architecture. The Peter A. B. Widener mansion on North Broad Street was remarkable not just for Willis Hale's over-the-top German Renaissance design, but as an embodiment of the social aspirations of the foremost robber baron of Philadelphia's Gilded Age.

- *They were representative of a class of structures that played a major role in the city's history.* When the construction of Interstate 95 obliterated hundreds of eighteenth- and nineteenth-century structures on the Delaware waterfront, much of Philadelphia's maritime heritage disappeared. The Baldwin Locomotive Works and Stetson Hat Factory, while undistinguished architecturally, represented Philadelphia's manufacturing supremacy during the nineteenth century.

- *Their life and death illustrated important shifts in the history of the city.* Samuel Sloan's mansion for Joseph Harrison marked the emergence of Rittenhouse Square as an enclave for the wealthy; its demolition for a club in the 1920s indicated changes in twentieth-century residential patterns. The swanky Sheraton Hotel on Pennsylvania Boulevard and Holiday Inn on City Avenue symbolized Philadelphia's hopes during the heady 1950s and 1960s, while their gradual decline paralleled the city's financial constrictions during the shaky 1970s and 1980s.

These broad guidelines allowed me to cast as wide a net as possible, capturing not only buildings, but also caves, cemeteries, utilities, bridges, airports, athletic fields, and other edifices that illustrate important facets of Philadelphia's history. Since one can tell as much about a society by its unfulfilled plans as by its physical reality, the final chapter ("Projected Philadelphia") presents fifteen structures that might have changed the face of the city had they ever been constructed.

As I write this introduction in September 2006, Philadelphia is experiencing an unprecedented building boom that is transforming the city once again, with dozens of luxury condominiums, office towers, and casinos proposed or under construction. In the midst of this growth, Philadelphia—in 1954 the first U.S. city to pass a municipal preservation ordinance—attempts to maintain the delicate balance between preservation and stagnation, creation and destruction.

Should Philadelphia preserve a 1950s pastiche of a Federal house because its owner, the late Richardson Dilworth, helped establish Society Hill, or should it allow a new condominium designed by world-famous architect Robert Venturi to either replace or overshadow Dilworth's home? Is it worth destroying Philadelphia's aging but architecturally significant public schools—150 of which are on the National Register of Historic Places—to provide up-to-date but spartan facilities for the city's children? Can Philadelphia realistically expect poor, inner-city congregations to preserve their elaborate Victorian churches, relics of a more prosperous era, or should the congregations be allowed to demolish or develop their properties as they see fit?

Despite such complex questions, Philadelphia is uniquely poised among U.S. cities to learn from its mistakes and, by combining its best older buildings with new and original designs, to create an architectural mosaic that will enrich the lives of its inhabitants while attracting new residents, businesses, and visitors. In this context, a thoughtful and consistent policy of historic preservation makes sense not only aesthetically, but also financially and commercially. Since we can learn as much about our heritage from the buildings we have lost as from the buildings we have saved, it is my hope that *Forgotten Philadelphia* will not just entertain readers but help inform future decisions about the preservation of historic structures in this city.

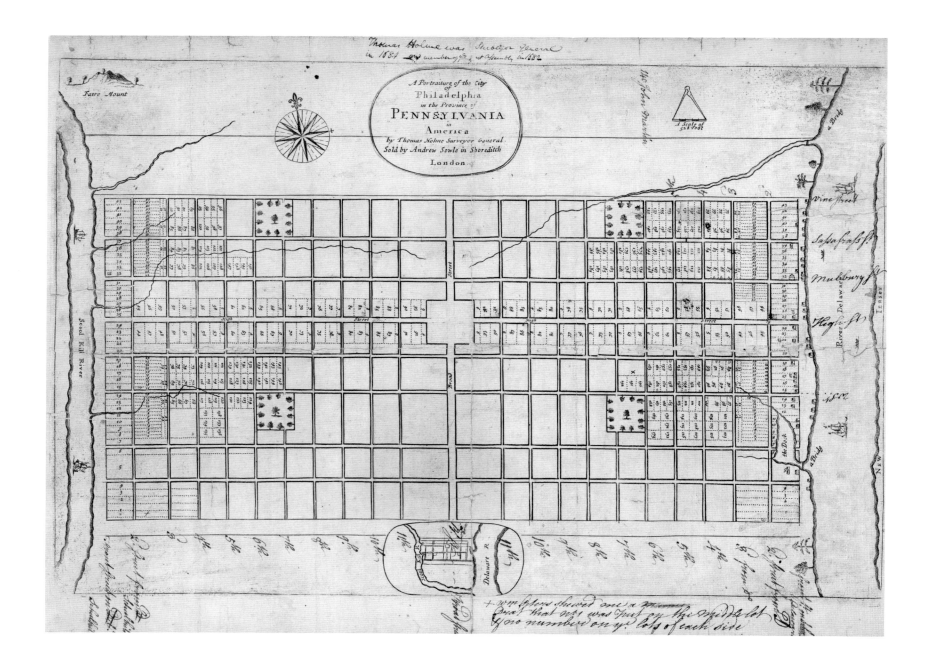

A Portraiture of the City of Philadelphia in the Province of PENNSYLVANIA in America by Thomas Holme Surveyor General. Sold by Andrew Sowle in Shoreditch London

A Scale of 528 foot

Faire Mount

Scool Kill River

Delaware R.

CHAPTER 1

Penn's Green Country Town

(1682 to 1775)

William Penn had a clear vision for his great town well before it existed. Six months after a royal charter made him lord proprietor of 45,000 square miles in America, Penn sent his three commissioners a detailed layout of Philadelphia. They were to set aside 10,000 acres along the Delaware River for a large town of widely spaced houses stretching fifteen miles along the waterfront. Penn's own house would stand in the middle of town, near the main wharf and commercial buildings. With memories of London's great plague and fire of 1665–66 in mind, Penn recommended: "Let every house be placed, if the person pleases, in the middle of its plot as to the breadth way of it, that so there may be ground on each side for gardens or orchards or fields, that it may be a green country town, which will never be burnt and always be wholesome."[1]

Like all visionaries, Penn soon ran headlong into reality. His commissioners reached Pennsylvania to find much of the province's riverfront already occupied. Instead of 10,000 acres, they had to settle for 300 acres along the Delaware, a few miles north of the mouth of the Schuylkill River. Penn was able to acquire a mile of river frontage along the Schuylkill parallel to his Delaware property. This still left him with a rectangle of 1,200 acres, only 12 percent of the space he had expected. Penn was forced to juggle the land grants promised to the First Purchasers, giving them liberty lands north and west of the city to compensate for their reduced city lots. Penn also assigned less desirable lots along the Schuylkill River to the First Purchasers who did not emigrate immediately.

Thomas Holme, Penn's surveyor-general, reworked Penn's original layout to accommodate the 1,200-acre rectangle. Holme's 1683 map "A Portraiture of the City of Philadelphia" shows the familiar grid of streets between the two rivers, bordered by Vine Street at the top and Cedar (today South) Street at the bottom. The grid was divided into four quadrants by two arteries a hundred feet wide, the north-south one named Broad, and the east-west one named High (today Market). Placed in the middle of each quadrant was an open square meant to serve as public land

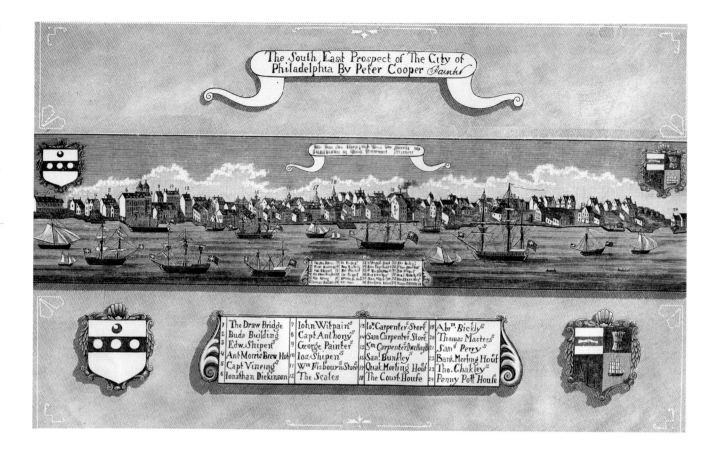

for the surrounding community. A central square at the intersection of Broad and Market streets would serve as the town's municipal and religious center.

Even before Holme's map reached potential buyers in London, reality interfered with Penn's plans once again. Penn had expected the first Philadelphians to settle equally along both the Delaware and Schuylkill rivers, gradually moving toward the center of town. Instead, they clung to the Delaware, leaving the Schuylkill nearly deserted. The Quaker meetinghouse that had been boldly built on the central square was abandoned, while another meetinghouse was hastily constructed farther east.

With Delaware waterfront property at a premium, wharves and warehouses soon covered Penn's projected riverside promenade. The sizable lots were quickly subdivided, bisected by alleys and crowded with houses, a far cry from Penn's dream of spacious, green grounds. While Penn may have mourned his lost town, he could hardly complain: Philadelphia might have been his vision, but it was also a real estate investment: "Though I desire to extend religious freedom," he wrote in 1681, "yet I want some recompense for my trouble."[2] Penn needed to sell land to cover his mountain of debts, and what was good for Philadelphia business was good for Penn.

Unrestrained growth offered other compensations. When Penn first viewed his future city in 1682, he saw a few cleared acres and a handful of houses around a sandy inlet, surrounded by an endless vista of forest, thicket, and swamp. On Penn's second visit in 1699, he found a bustling town of 5,000 souls, with 400 houses, at least six churches and the same number of taverns, three breweries, an open-air market, a brickyard, four shipyards, and numerous wharves and warehouses. Before he returned to England in 1701, Penn gave Philadelphia a new charter that, among other benefits, raised its status to that of city.

Aside from a few downturns, Philadelphia's growth continued unabated during the first three-quarters of the eighteenth century. Its mercantile wealth made it home to the grandest and most innovative buildings in North America, such as the State House, Pennsylvania Hospital, and Christ Church. The small brick houses of early days gave way to gracious Georgian town houses, while the surrounding countryside was peppered with the estates of the town's elite.

Not surprisingly, construction and architecture became leading occupations in the fast-growing city. The Carpenters' Company of the City and County of Philadelphia, the oldest builders' organization in the United States, was founded in 1724 "for the purpose of obtaining instruction in the science of architecture and assisting such of their members as should by accident be in need of support."[3] Gentlemen-designers like John Kearsley and Andrew Hamilton worked closely with master carpenters like Edmund Woolley to create the city's great public buildings. By the end of the colonial period, professional builder-architects like Robert Smith, capable of managing both design and construction, had begun to emerge.

The rapid expansion and increasing prosperity of Philadelphia guaranteed that its earliest buildings would soon be at risk. While the city was spreading in all directions, its densest development continued to be in the blocks surrounding the Delaware River. This concentration of residential, commercial, and municipal functions within a small area triggered the cycle of demolition and replacement that would characterize Philadelphia and other older American cities. By 1760, larger, more modern structures had superseded older buildings like the Great Meeting House, the original Christ Church, and the Court House and Town Hall.

In 1774, Philadelphia was the largest, richest, and most centrally located city in the American colonies. It was the obvious meeting place for the Continental Congress convened to determine how to handle the growing governmental crisis with Great Britain. As the congressional delegates arrived in the metropolis of 16,500 inhabitants and 6,000 houses and viewed the imposing tower of the State House, they may have felt for the first time the apparently limitless possibilities of being American.

Old Block House/First Swedes' Church

Location: 916 South Swanson Street, near Columbus Boulevard
(site of current-day Gloria Dei Church)
Completed: ca. 1666 (converted to church 1677)
Demolished: 1698
Architect/Builder: Unknown

Decades before William Penn landed in America, Swedish, Dutch, Finnish, and English settlers lived along the banks of the Delaware and Schuylkill rivers. The Dutch explorer Cornelius Hendricksen had established a trading post and stockade on the future site of Philadelphia by 1623. Beginning in 1638, Swedish immigrants established outposts at Fort Christina (Wilmington), Upland (Chester), Tinicum Island, and Wicaco, a former Indian village located nearly a mile south of Dock Creek. As Sweden's dreams of an overseas empire faded, its colonists peacefully accepted Dutch and then English control of their province.

For protection from attack by Indians and other Europeans, the Swedish pioneers at Wicaco built a square, one-story blockhouse around 1666. Made of tree trunks notched at the end and cross-laid, this common Scandinavian structure would be the model for other early buildings in the region. Instead of windows, the Old Block House had narrow slits from which defenders could fire on attackers. The blockade stood on a bluff overlooking the Delaware River, a short distance from the log cabin of Sven Sener, the settler who donated the land for the structure.

The Block House was also used for Lutheran religious services, with Pastor Lars Lock paddling upriver from Upland each Sunday to preach. As the threat of attack receded, the Block House was converted to a full-time church in 1677 with the addition of a pavilion roof and a central spire or steeple. The former fortress became the first church within the region that is present-day Philadelphia. The same year, the Swedes' Church received its first resident ordained minister, Jacobus Fabritius, a Dutchman. Fabritius proved less than satisfactory, due to his shaky command of the Swedish language, his near-blindness, his temper, and his drunkenness.

When Fabritius's successor, Andrew Rudman, arrived from Sweden in 1697, he found the Swedes' Church neglected and time-worn. After much discussion, Wicaco was chosen as the location for the main church for all Swedish settlers in the region, beating out Tinicum and Passyunk. Under Rudman's guidance, the Old Block House was dismantled, and a one-story brick church with a wooden steeple was erected on its site. The new church was dedicated on July 2, 1700. Near the waterfront at Columbus Boulevard and Christian Street, Gloria Dei, or Old Swedes' Church, still stands, the oldest extant church in the city of Philadelphia.

A conjectural drawing of the Swedish blockhouse after its conversion to a church. (Reprinted from J. Thomas Scharf and Thompson Westcott, *History of Philadelphia, 1609–1884, in Three Volumes* [Philadelphia: L. H. Everts, 1884], vol. 2, 1024.)

Original Caves and Cabins on the Delaware River

Location: Front Street, between Market and Spruce streets
Constructed: ca. 1680–85
Demolished: By 1687
Architect/Builder: Various

Some of Philadelphia's earliest inhabitants were cavemen. When Penn's first settlers arrived in 1681 and 1682, they found only a few crude huts and cabins, most clustered in the clearing around the Dock Creek inlet. Faced with the need to create shelters quickly in the wilderness of Penn's Woods, these pioneers burrowed into the soft soil of the high bluffs overlooking the Delaware River.

While an illustration from John Fanning Watson's *Annals of Philadelphia* depicts men in sizable caverns just above the waterline, the reality was less dramatic. Usually, the caves consisted of holes three to six feet deep, dug in the ground at the top of the riverbank along Front Street. The settlers lined the holes with low walls of sod and brush and covered them with roofs formed of tree limbs overlaid with sod or bark. They built chimneys of stone and river pebbles mortared with clay and grass.

Primitive as they were, these caves provided warmth and protection to the early settlers, who often sold them to later arrivals. Francis Daniel Pastorius, one of the original founders of Germantown, described his first home in America: "The caves of that time were only holes digged in the Ground, Covered with Earth, a matter of 5. or 6. feet deep, 10. or 12. wide and about 20. long; whereof neither the Sides nor the Floors have been plank'd. Herein we lived more Contentedly than many nowadays in their painted and wainscotted Palaces, as I without the least hyperbole may call them in Comparison of the aforesaid Subterraneous Catatumbs or Dens."[4]

A true case of *nostalgie de la boue*.

This drawing by Edward W. Mumford, prepared for the 1844 edition of John F. Watson's *Annals of Philadelphia*, shows caves on Front Street in 1685. (The Library Company of Philadelphia.)

As soon as possible, hard-working Philadelphians traded their "Subterraneous Catatumbs" for sturdier housing. At first they built square, one-room log cabins modeled on those of the Swedes. By 1685, however, two- and three-story brick houses were rising along the riverfront. The abandoned caves were usurped by the town's "lower sort" to be used for taverns and other unwholesome purposes. Soon caves of ill repute sprawled along the Delaware, such as the Crooked Billet, Owen's Cave, and Townsend's Court.

By 1685, William Penn, dismayed by the reports of Sodom-on-the-Delaware reaching England, directed the provincial council to purge the caves of their inhabitants and admonished the city fathers to "let vertue be cherisht." Penn might have been more concerned with land values than with virtue, since he still retained ownership of the riverfront and was anxious to lease the land for development.

The provincial council reacted quickly, directing the town constables and undersheriffs to "forthwith pull down & demolish all emptie Caves as they shall find" on Front Street.[5]

In April 1687, the provincial council ordered all remaining cave dwellers to "provide for themselves other habitations, in order to have the Caves Distroy'd."[6] By this time, Front Street was crowded with the wharves and warehouses of Samuel Carpenter, Robert Turner, and other merchants. Within a few years, the rapid development of the Delaware riverfront had obliterated all traces of Philadelphia's Barbary Coast.

A later drawing by Charles H. Stephens, while highly romanticized, provides a more accurate depiction of early riverfront dwellings. (Collection of the author.)

Blue Anchor Tavern

Location: Northwest corner of Front and Dock streets
Completed: ca. 1682
Demolished: 1828
Architect/Builder: Unknown

Before Penn established Philadelphia, the land where Dock Creek (today Dock Street) met the Delaware River was home to about forty Dutch, Swedish, and English families. The hub of their settlement was the Blue Anchor Tavern, located 146 feet north of Dock Creek, in the middle of current-day Front Street. The Blue Anchor stood on a bluff overlooking the Swamp, a tidewater basin formed where the Dock, a natural harbor in the Delaware River, flowed inland to become Dock Creek. From the Swamp, various branches of Dock Creek extended north to Market and Fifth streets, west to Washington Square, and south to Pine Street.

The date of the founding of the Blue Anchor is uncertain. Some historians place its erection as early as 1671. Others, including John Fanning Watson in his *Annals of Philadelphia*, state that the tavern was still under construction when Penn first visited Philadelphia in autumn 1682. According to early accounts, the Blue Anchor was a one-story brick building, about twelve by twenty-two feet, with ceilings about eight and a half feet high. The building was set on a lot measuring sixteen feet on Front Street by thirty-six feet on Dock Creek. According to tradition, the Blue Anchor Tavern was the first building Penn entered in Philadelphia, after disembarking on a sandy beach nearby.

Besides being "Victuallers and Tappers of strong drink" with sturgeon and sea turtle on its menu, the Blue Anchor became Philadelphia's commercial exchange and transportation hub.[7] Watson called the tavern "the proper key of the city, to which all new-comers resorted."[8] At the Blue Anchor, goods were traded from all ships anchored in the Dock. Ferries carried passengers to New Jersey, to Windmill Island where a windmill ground their grain, and across

Dock Creek to Society Hill. Farmers tied their boats to the trees lining the Swamp and sold their produce to local housewives.

A 1691 citizens' petition asking that the Blue Anchor's landing be made a free harbor signified its pivotal role in early Philadelphia. Penn obliged by designating the Blue Anchor wharf one of two permanent public landings in his 1701 city charter. By this time, unfortunately, Dock Creek was changing from open water to an open sewer, polluted by the waste of nearby tanneries, lumberyards, and slaughterhouses. (Between 1767 and 1784 the entire creek was covered over to create Dock Street.)

When the city was laid out in 1683, the Blue Anchor was moved to what is now the northwest corner of Front and Dock streets. About 1690, the tavern was purchased by Thomas Budd, who made it the southernmost of a row of ten houses he constructed along Front Street known as Budd's Long Row. At this time, the original tavern was rebuilt as a two-story, half-timbered structure to fit in with the rest of the Long Row. As the city's center shifted toward Market Street, the Blue Anchor's role as an exchange passed to newer hostelries like the London Coffee House. Renamed the Boatswain and Call, it continued to serve waterfront denizens well into the eighteenth century.

According to Watson, the much-altered tavern survived until the 1820s, when it was "pulled down to build greater" and replaced by a tobacco warehouse. Watson preserved some of its timbers as relics, as he did with other historic buildings destroyed during his lifetime. The warehouse was replaced in turn by a four-story brick building, the Garman House, which housed a hotel named the Blue Anchor during the late nineteenth century. (During this period, another Blue Anchor Tavern operated on Walnut Street.) In the early 1960s, the Garman House and nearby buildings were demolished as part of the Washington Square East redevelopment project. Today, I. M. Pei's Society Hill Towers stand on the original site of the Blue Anchor Tavern.

Townsend's (Roberts) Mill

Location: Church Lane and Lambert Street, East Germantown
Completed: 1683
Demolished: 1874
Architect/Builder: Unknown

ozens of streams and creeks once threaded through Philadelphia's landscape. This was especially true of the settlements
ringing Philadelphia, from Kensington southward to the Falls of
Schuylkill. Germantown, founded in 1683 by Francis Daniel Pastorius and thirteen families from the German province of Krefeld, was
especially rich in waterways. Besides the Wissahickon Creek along
its southern border, the Wingohocking, Cresheim, and dozens of
smaller creeks flowed through the Township. Beginning in 1683 with
the founding of Townsend's Mill, Germantown quickly emerged
as one of the region's milling centers.

   Richard Townsend, a Quaker who sailed on the *Welcome* with
William Penn in 1682, brought a disassembled mill with him from
London, which he set up along the Chester Creek. The following
year, he established a second mill north of Germantown, shortly
after the township was laid out. The gristmill was located along
Wingohocking Creek, which ran east through Germantown until
it merged with Tacony Creek in what is now Northeast Philadelphia. The fieldstone mill with its overshot wheel and pond stood on
the north side of Church Lane (also known as Mill Street), one mile
northeast of Germantown's Market Square. Writing in 1727, Richard
Townsend recalled the isolated, primitive community that his mill
served: "As soon as Germantown was laid out, I settled my tract of
land, which was about a mile from thence, where I set up a barn and
a corn mill, which was very useful to the country round. But there

The Roberts Mill as it appeared shortly before its destruction in 1874. (Collection of
the author.)

being few horses, people generally brought their corn upon their backs, many miles. I remember, one had a bull so gentle, that he used to bring corn upon his back."[9]

Thanks to the Townsend Mill and others like it, Philadelphia became the colonies' breadbasket. Between 1730 and 1745, Pennsylvania's production of flour grew from 38,750 barrels to nearly 166,000. A pound of flour cost nine shillings and sixpence in Philadelphia, compared to fifteen shillings in New York and twenty-eight in Boston.

After Townsend retired from milling, his mill passed through a number of owners before being acquired by the Roberts family in 1811. Renamed the Roberts Mill, it continued to operate until 1858. By then, modern mills run by steam engines could grind more grain in a day than the colonial-era mill could in months, and as Germantown had developed, the Wingohocking Creek had grown too shallow to power the millwheel.

The Roberts Mill remained in place until 1874, a decaying reminder of Germantown's water-powered past. Hugh Roberts, its last owner, sold it to an "improvement association" (real estate developer), which drained the millpond and tore down the mill. A mansion built around 1812 by the first Roberts to own the mill stood until 1904, when it too was demolished. Today, two-story row houses stand on the site of Philadelphia's first gristmill, while the Wingohocking Creek flows beneath them through sewer pipes.

High Street Market Sheds

Location: Center of High (Market) Street, from the Delaware waterfront to Seventeenth Street.
Completed: ca. 1683–1835
Demolished: 1859
Architect/Builder: Unknown

Within a year of Philadelphia's founding, an open-air market was established at Front and High streets where farmers and fishermen could offer the bounty of the surrounding river and country to the fast-growing town. On Wednesdays and Saturdays, vendors drove their wagons in from Germantown and Frankford, or rowed their boats across from New Jersey, to sell produce, meat, and fish. A bell tower at Second and High streets announced the opening of market. Soon, wooden stalls stretched down the middle of hundred-foot-wide High Street from Front to Second Street.

In 1707, a brick head house was erected at the head of the market at Second and High streets. While its upper stories served as the Town Hall and Court House, its arched ground floor became the first permanent market building in Philadelphia. Behind the new municipal center, more sheds soon stretched to Third Street. Philadelphia's market was such a hub of activity that High Street acquired the nickname "Market Street."

In 1720, the town councils resolved to replace the wooden market stalls with brick arcades, designed to harmonize with the Town Hall. The spacious new sheds, consisting of square columns supporting a gable roof, let both shoppers and fresh air circulate. Each shed was roughly twenty feet wide and sixteen feet long, separated by a four-foot space from the next shed. Lanterns hung from the high arched ceilings. Vendors displayed their wares on shelves placed between the columns, hanging meat or fish on hooks suspended overhead. Wide projecting eaves sheltered vendors and customers from bad weather.

market house was erected in High Street between Schuylkill Eighth and Seventh (Fifteenth and Sixteenth) streets. Architect William Strickland submitted a cutting-edge design with iron columns and a low-pitched metal roof. All subsequent market houses were built in metal rather than brick.

On December 8, 1853, Philadelphia City Councils gave High Street the official name of Market Street during a major street renaming campaign.* By this time, ironically, the market sheds were on their way out. During the second quarter of the nineteenth century, High Street had changed from a residential boulevard to a commercial thoroughfare lined with stores and warehouses. Since the 1830s, the Columbia and Pennsylvania Railroad had run down both sides of Market from Eighth to Third streets. Merchants and business owners lobbied to have the sheds removed to relieve the snarl of wagons, drays, omnibuses, and railcars on Market Street.

In 1859, the City Councils ordered all market buildings on Market Street to be demolished, from the Jersey Market on the water-

In addition to being user-friendly, the High Street Market was orderly and well run. A clerk of the market was appointed as early as 1693 to regulate sales and keep conditions wholesome. Vendors were forbidden to sell their goods before market hours or on their way to market. For buyers' convenience, sellers of meat, fish, and produce were grouped in specific locations.

As Philadelphia's population spread westward, so did its market. The sheds reached Third Street by 1759, Fourth Street by 1786, Sixth Street by 1810, and Eighth Street by 1821. By then, the market boasted a separate structure for fishmongers, denoted by a shad on its gable, and for Jersey produce farmers, whose head house was a round clock tower decorated with cornucopias. In 1834, a

*As part of the same campaign, Mulberry became Arch Street, Sassafras became Race, Cedar became South, and all streets west of Broad Street were renumbered, from Schuylkill Eighth (Fifteenth Street) to Schuylkill Front (Twenty-second Street).

front to the newer iron sheds that reached Seventeenth Street. To replace them, private developers built large, enclosed markets throughout the city. Although many of these ventures failed, the Philadelphia Farmers' Market at Twelfth and Market streets proved so popular that when the Reading Railroad Terminal replaced the Samuel Sloan–designed market house in the 1890s, it incorporated the Farmers' Market into its building, where it remains today.

Today, the New Market head house and market sheds on South Second Street, constructed between 1745 and 1804 to service Society Hill, offer a truncated version of High Street Market during its eighteenth-century glory.

Market Street looking east from Sixth Street in 1859, shortly before the sheds' removal. The oversized hat extending from the building at right advertises a men's hatter. (Collection of the author.)

Slate Roof House

Location: Southeast corner of Second and Sansom streets
Completed: ca. 1684
Demolished: 1867
Architect/Builder: Attributed to James Porteus

By the end of the seventeenth century, multistory brick houses began to replace the caves and cabins of the original settlers. One of the first great houses built in the frontier town was the Slate Roof House, which served as William Penn's home during his second visit to Philadelphia. In the nineteenth century, its threatened removal prompted one of the first coordinated, widespread efforts to preserve a historic structure in Philadelphia. Unlike an earlier campaign that saved the State House from destruction, the Slate Roof House effort ended in failure.

In 1684, Samuel Carpenter acquired land that stretched from Front to Second Street along a narrow alley, Hatton Lane (later known as Norris' Alley and then Sansom Street). Carpenter, who had arrived in Philadelphia from Barbados only the previous year, quickly became one of the town's largest landowners. Besides the first and largest wharf on the Delaware, his holdings included warehouses, a tavern, a limekiln, farms in the Northern Liberties, and mills in Bucks and Chester counties.

After acquiring his town lot, Carpenter commissioned James Porteus, a cofounder of the Carpenters' Company, to design a house on the Second Street end of the property. Porteus produced a modified-H design, similar to one in Stephen Primatt's book *The City and Country Purchaser,* published in London in 1667. The two-story brick house featured two projecting wings, or "bastions," framing a recessed entryway, which gave it a fortresslike appearance. The house's most prominent feature, a hipped roof covered with slate, gave the house its nickname. (Slate roofs were relatively rare in seventeenth-century Philadelphia.) Since Carpenter occupied a town house on the eastern end of his lot, he may have intended to use the Slate Roof House for rental income.

The Slate Roof House's first resident was proprietor and governor William Penn, who rented it from Carpenter for eighty pounds a year during his second visit to Philadelphia. Penn, his second wife, Hannah, and his daughter Letitia moved into the house in January 1700. Less than a month later, the house witnessed the birth of John Penn, known to early Philadelphians as "the American." During Penn's occupancy, the Slate Roof House served as the de facto seat of the provincial government, where Penn met with the council and other leaders. There, Penn composed the Charter of Privileges, a guarantee of religious and civil freedom for the inhabitants of his province that would influence the writers of the Constitution.

Besides the Penns, the Slate Roof House was home to James Logan, Penn's secretary and successor as governor. After the Penns

returned to England in 1701, Logan lived at the house until 1704, when Carpenter sold it to William Trent (founder of Trenton, New Jersey) for £850. By 1708 it was on the market again, but the asking price of £900 was too high for the financially strapped Penn.

Instead, Isaac Norris purchased the property. The Norris family owned the Slate Roof House until 1864 but did not live there after 1732, when Isaac Norris Jr. moved to his country estate, Fairhill. By the 1770s, it had become a "superior" boarding house, patronized by John Adams and other members of the Continental Congress, as well as by British officers during the 1777–78 occupation.[10]

During the late eighteenth century, as the waterfront district became heavily commercial, the Slate Roof House began a slow decline. In 1801, its ground floor was occupied by the shops of engravers, watchmakers, and silversmiths; by the 1860s, dealers in secondhand clothes and used furniture had replaced the artisans. An oyster cellar operated in the basement of one of the wings, and a sign painter used the second floor as a workshop. The area between the two wings was filled in to create more commercial space.

Appalled, some Philadelphians attempted to rescue the Slate Roof House from oblivion. During the 1820s, John Fanning Watson commissioned the artist W. L. Breton to paint the house as it had appeared in its early glory. When Watson published his *Annals of Philadelphia*, he included a lithograph of Breton's painting and beseeched his readers to honor Penn's memory by restoring the house.

Spurred by Watson's plea, the Historical Society of Pennsylvania attempted to purchase the Slate Roof House for $10,000 in 1844, but the Norris family refused to sell. In 1864, Charles and Anna Knecht bought the house for $20,000

W. L. Breton's 1836 watercolor of the Slate Roof House as it appeared in colonial days indicates the extensive gardens behind the house. (The Library Company of Philadelphia.)

and announced their plans to demolish it. The Historical Society offered the Knechts $30,000 for the house, but unfortunately, opponents of the purchase within the society forced a withdrawal of the offer. Despite efforts by private citizens, newspapers, organizations, and the City Councils, the Slate Roof House was demolished in August 1867. The house was studied, sketched, photographed, and measured before its destruction, in one of the first systematic efforts to document an endangered building.

The Commercial Exchange Building erected on the site burned within a year of its construction. Its replacement, designed by James Windrim, stood on the site from 1870 until its demolition in 1976, housing the Keystone Telephone Company and its successor, Bell of Pennsylvania. The National Park Service, which acquired the site that year, considered constructing a replica of the Slate Roof House on it.

Instead, the Friends of Independence National Historical Park commissioned the firm of Venturi, Rauch & Scott Brown to create a memorial to William Penn in 1982 on the 300th anniversary of his founding of Philadelphia. Today, a miniature version of the Slate Roof House stands atop a pedestal in Welcome Park.

Benjamin Rush Birthplace

Location: Intersection of Keswick Road and Rayland Drive,
north of Red Lion Road, Torresdale section of
Northeast Philadelphia
Completed: ca. 1690
Demolished: 1969
Architect/Builder: Various

Dr. Benjamin Rush, signer of the Declaration of Independence, delegate to the Continental Congress, abolitionist, medical pioneer, father of American psychiatry, director of the U.S. Mint, and a fervent if misguided advocate of bloodletting as a panacea, was born at the family farm in Byberry Township on January 4, 1746.* The farm on the Poquessing Creek had been established by Rush's great-great-grandfather, who arrived in Pennsylvania in 1683—John Rush, a horse trooper under Oliver Cromwell.

The two-and-a-half-story fieldstone farmhouse, built around 1690, housed five generations of the Rush family. When Benjamin Rush was five, his father John died. His mother, Susanna, was forced to sell the 500-acre Byberry farm, along with other property of her late husband's, and move with her six children to Philadelphia. There, she opened a grocery shop and liquor store, the Blazing Star, which was successful enough for her to send Benjamin first to West Nottingham Academy and then to the College of New Jersey (later Princeton University).

The early loss of his childhood home remained painful for Rush throughout his illustrious career. In July 1812, a year before his death, Rush visited his former homestead and viewed the upstairs room where he was born, the apple orchard his father had planted, and the family graveyard where four generations of

*December 24, 1745, in the old-style or Julian calendar, which was replaced by the Gregorian calendar in England and the American colonies in September 1752.

Rushes rested. Later, Rush described his visit to his friend John Adams:

> The building, which is of stone, bears marks of age and decay. On one of the stones near the front door, I discovered with some difficulty the letters J.R. Before the house, flows a small, but deep creek, abounding in pan-fish. The farm consists of ninety acres, all in a highly cultivated state. I knew the owner to be in such easy circumstances, that I did not ask him his price for it; but begged, if he should ever incline to sell it, to make me or one of my surviving sons the first offer, which he promised to do.[11]

The house Rush visited was much changed from the one he had left sixty years earlier. Sometime around 1765, a stone addition doubled the size of the dwelling, changing it from a square, two-bay

Benjamin Rush's birthplace in the early twentieth century, with the nineteenth-century additions to the right. (Collection of the author.)

house to a rectangular, four-bay, center-hall house. During the nineteenth century, a three-story frame addition was built on the north side, a porch was run along the front of the house, and the floors, joists, and stairways were replaced.

The area of Northeast Philadelphia where the Rush birthplace lay remained fairly rural and isolated until the mid–twentieth century. By the 1960s, time and urban sprawl had caught up with the dilapidated homestead, and abandoned cars filled its garden.

Through a series of bureaucratic blunders, the Benjamin Rush birthplace was slated for restoration by one city agency and condemned by another. In early 1969, a bulldozer knocked down the only historic structure in the far Northeast. At the time, some fragments were reportedly transferred to the Philadelphia State Hospital for the Insane (Byberry) for safekeeping.

In June 2002, a state historical marker was erected at the site of Benjamin Rush's birthplace. Rush is also commemorated in his native Northeast by the Benjamin Rush State Park, a large tract of meadows and woods on the former grounds of Byberry Hospital, where some historians hope to rebuild his house from the remaining fragments stored on the hospital grounds.

Great Meeting House

Location: Southwest corner of High (Market) and Second streets
Completed: 1695
Demolished: 1754
Architect/Builder: Unknown

Greater Meeting House

Location: Southwest corner of High (Market) and Second streets
Completed: 1755
Demolished: 1804
Architect/Builder: Unknown

For the Quakers who established Philadelphia, one of the first requirements was a meetinghouse for community worship and discussion. Holding their early meetings in private homes, they began construction on houses at Front Street above Sassafras (Race), near the banks of the Delaware, and at Centre Square (today the site of City Hall). Neither was a success. The first decayed quickly and was removed by 1698, while the second was too far from the riverfront for regular use.

For their third try, the Quakers chose a site in the middle of town: High and Second streets, across from the busy market. The Great Meeting House, the largest gathering place for Friends at the time, was erected in 1695. The simple square structure stood fifty by fifty feet and had a sloping roof topped by a square glass cupola to light the interior. It was designed to resemble a residence rather than a church, which the Quakers disdainfully called a "steeple-house."

Among the notable Philadelphians who entered the Great Meeting House was then unknown Benjamin Franklin on his first day in his adopted city in October 1723. After gorging himself on penny rolls, exploring the town, and spying his future wife in a doorway laughing at him, he returned to High Street:

Thus refreshed, I walked again up the street, which by this time had many clean-dressed people in it, who were all walking the same way. I joined them, and thereby was led into the great meetinghouse of the Quakers, near the market. I sat down among them, and, after looking round awhile and hearing nothing said, being very drowsy thro' labor and want of rest the preceding night, I fell fast asleep, and continu'd so till the meeting broke up, when one was kind enough to rouse me. This was, therefore, the first house I was in, or slept in, in Philadelphia.[12]

The Second or Greater Friends' Meeting House at left, in an 1840 watercolor by W. L. Breton commissioned by John F. Watson. At right is the Town Hall and Court House, with market sheds extending behind it. The proximity of the Friends' Meeting House to the seat of civil government indicated their early prominence in the administration of Philadelphia. (The Library Company of Philadelphia.)

By 1754, when a survey of the Great Meeting House revealed the need for major repairs, the Quakers decided to replace it with a larger structure. Their decision may also have reflected trepidation over the Anglicans' rebuilt Christ Church farther north on Second Street. When the Great Meeting House and the original Christ Church were erected in the 1690s, the Quakers were the dominant group in Philadelphia, and their brick building outshone the Anglicans' small wooden church. By the 1750s, Quakers constituted only about a quarter of Philadelphia's population, while Anglicans were its wealthiest and most socially powerful segment. A grander meetinghouse may have represented the Quakers' attempt to reinforce their presence in the face of the Anglicans' new church, the most elaborate steeplehouse in the colonies.

In 1754–55, the Great Meeting House was replaced by the Greater Meeting House, a two-and-a-half-story brick building measuring seventy-three feet along High Street and fifty-five feet along Second Street. Although considerably larger than the Great Meeting House, it was still a simple structure with few architectural details. Among those who worshipped there were such Quaker Saints as the antislavery crusaders Anthony Benezet and John Woolman.

By the turn of the nineteenth century, the area around High and Second streets had become a noisy commercial district, far from conducive to the Quakers' quest for the light within. In 1803, the decision was made to tear down the Greater Meeting House and sell the land, using the profits to build a new meetinghouse on the south side of Arch Street between Third and Fourth, on the outskirts of town. The following year, the Greater Meeting House was dismantled and the property sold for $76,000. Despite this substantial return, the thrifty Quakers recycled materials from the Greater Meeting House into their new structure. Today, Arch Street Meeting House is still the city's principal meetinghouse and the site of the Philadelphia Yearly Meeting of the Religious Society of Friends.

Naglee House, Germantown

Location: 4518 Germantown Avenue, Germantown
(between Berkley Street and the SEPTA R8 tracks)
Completed: Before 1708
Demolished: 1965
Architect/Builder: Unknown

Built in the early eighteenth century, the Naglee House stood across the Great Road to Philadelphia (Germantown Avenue) from Stenton, the Logan family mansion, and was reputedly one of the oldest buildings in the district. Its use over the years as a farmhouse, tannery, coal yard, and florist's shop, and its final replacement by a gas station, mirrors Germantown's transition from an independent agricultural community to a bustling commercial and industrial district, and finally to a declining urban neighborhood.

Land records show a house on the site by 1708, when Peter Keurlis sold 120 acres of farmland to George Gray. In 1727, the Germantown farmer John Naglee (whose name also appears as Neglee, Nagley and Negley) purchased the property for £285. The land lay just within the southern boundary of Germantown Township, near the Great Road to Philadelphia. Originally, the fieldstone house consisted of one room, roughly fifteen by twenty-six feet, with an attic. It was a typical example of early Germantown architecture, a utilitarian design notable for its small size, low ceilings, and roughhewn masonry and woodwork. According to early Germantown historian Naaman H. Keyser, James Logan lived in the Naglee house during the construction of Stenton across the Germantown Road from 1727 to 1734, although no documentation exists to support this claim.

By 1752, when John's son Jacob insured it with the Philadelphia Contributionship, the house had been enlarged to two stories and four rooms, with a cellar. The property now included a number of outbuildings, as well as "Tan Yards Tan Pitts Vatts, etc.," since Jacob was a tanner.[13] The location of the Naglee house in an isolated area

The Naglee House in 1903. The front addition housed the florist's business run by the Kulp family, owners from 1895 to 1964. (The Library Company of Philadelphia.)

south of the center of Germantown would have been appropriate for a smelly business like a tannery. The house stood at the base of Naglee's Hill, a lonely and densely wooded place plagued by highwaymen and reputed to be haunted. For many years, the house served as the threshold to ancient Germantown.

The first railroad in Philadelphia, completed in 1831–32, ran from Ninth and Poplar streets to Shoemaker's Lane in German-

town. Just south of the Naglee house, a bridge conveyed the railroad over the Germantown Road. With the advent of the railroad, the Naglee's Hill neighborhood grew largely industrial. By the 1870s, the Wayne Junction Station of the Pennsylvania Railroad stood about a hundred feet from the house's south side, and Berkley Street had been cut through on its north side. In 1885, the New Glen Echo Mills carpet factory went up on land behind the Naglee house. By then, the house was occupied by the yard and office of Lee and Shallcross, sellers of "Lehigh and Schuylkill coal, sand, lime, plaster, cement, plastering hair, building material general."[14]

In 1895, the Kulp family purchased the house and used it as the office and greenhouse for their florist business for about the next seventy years. In 1964, after the family sold the property, the Sun Oil Company announced plans to demolish the Naglee house and expand an adjoining Sunoco gas station. The City Historical Commission, the National Park Service, and the Germantown Historical Society all protested the destruction of what some historians considered the oldest house in Germantown and the third oldest in Philadelphia. They recommended renovating the property as "the gateway to historic Germantown" and using it as a visitors' center for the proposed Germantown National Historic District.[15]

Despite the efforts of city and private agencies, no funds were available to acquire the property. The Naglee house was demolished in April 1965. According to one observer, demolition took several days, since a bulldozer pulling a steel cable was unable to tear down the sturdily built walls. Despite Sun Oil's promise to build a "colonial" gas station, a modern building with blue and white porcelain panels stood on the site by February 1967.

Breintnall House/Benezet House

Location: 325 Chestnut Street (today the northwest corner of
   Chestnut and Orianna streets)
Completed: ca. 1700
Demolished: 1818
Architect/Builder: Unknown

A brick town house at 325 Chestnut Street (historically 115 Chestnut) built for the wealthy Quaker merchant David Breintnall was one of the first substantial houses in Philadelphia. Above the two-story structure, eighteen-and-a-half feet wide on Chestnut Street and twenty-six feet long, a hipped gable roof formed an attic. A pent roof extended over the first story, and eaves extended over the second story in a similar fashion.

According to Watson's *Annals,* Breintnall considered the house "too fine for his plain cloth and profession" and rented it to the governor of Barbados, who was visiting Philadelphia to recover his health.[16] A branch of Dock Creek ran across Chestnut Street along the path of current-day Orianna Street, so the governor could be rowed from the Delaware River to his own front door. After Breintnall's death in 1731, his widow moved back into the house, where she ran a tavern, the Hen and Chickens.

In 1753, the house was acquired by Anthony Benezet, a French-born Quaker educator and philanthropist who has been called "America's first great humanitarian reformer, the epitome of all that was comprehended in the phrase 'the good Quaker.'"[17] Benezet convinced the Philadelphia Yearly Meeting of Friends to take an official position against owning and trading slaves and in 1775 organized the first meeting of the Society for the Relief of Free Negroes Unlawfully Held in Bondage. He also formed a society called the Friendly Association for Regaining and Preserving Peace with the Indians by Pacific Measures.

Benezet established schools dedicated to teaching African Americans, Native Americans, and poor females, which he ran out

William Strickland's drawing of the Anthony Benezet House, dated March 4, 1818. (The Philadelphia Print Shop.)

of his Chestnut Street house until his death in 1784. In his will, he left his house and lot, as well as the remainder of his estate, to the support of "a religious-minded person, or persons, to teach a number of negro, mulatto, or Indian children to read, write, arithmetic, plain accounts, needle work, etc."[18]

Despite the terms of Benezet's will, a succession of small businesses rented his house, including a bonnet maker, a broker, and a currier (leather processor), reflecting the transformation of lower Chestnut Street from a residential to a commercial district. In 1816, Joseph Keen bought the Benezet house and announced his intention to demolish it and replace it with a three-story office building.

Roberts Vaux, a prominent Quaker who had edited the memoirs of Anthony Benezet, wished to create a memorial to the late Quaker Saint and commissioned architect William Strickland to draw the street elevation of the Benezet House before its demolition in March 1818. Strickland's drawing appeared as a frontispiece in the October 1818 edition of the *Port Folio of Philadelphia.* The accompanying article, while misjudging the age and uniqueness of the Benezet House, confirmed that some Philadelphians realized how quickly their architectural heritage was vanishing: "It is but a few months since one of the oldest, if not the first brick house erected in Philadelphia, was torn down, to give space to a more spacious structure, and we believe that edifice to have been the last specimen in this city, toward which the curious inquirer in these matters, might have been directed."[19]

Today, a 1954 office building houses the Philadelphia Maritime Museum on the site.

London Coffee House

Location: 100 Market Street (southwest corner of Market and Front streets)
Completed: ca. 1702
Demolished: 1883
Architect/Builder: Unknown

Selling liquor was one of the great growth industries in colonial Philadelphia. The number of taverns increased from 7 in 1683 to 117 in 1758, with more than 20 on Second Street alone. At the top of the social ladder were coffeehouses, genteel establishments that served coffee, tea, and lemonade in addition to wine, beer, and spirits. Popular in England since the 1650s, the first coffeehouses opened in Philadelphia in the early eighteenth century. Like their British counterparts, and like the earlier Blue Anchor Tavern, coffeehouses became centers of commerce and politics.

In 1754, to fill the gap left by the retirement of Widow Roberts, whose coffeehouse on Front Street below Blackhorse Alley was the city's most popular, more than 200 Philadelphia merchants subscribed £348 to finance the London Coffee House. As its proprietor, they selected William Bradford, a well-respected printer and publisher, who promptly applied to the governor and council for a liquor license.

The London Coffee House opened in April 1754 at the southwest corner of Front and High streets in a three-and-a-half-story brick building built as a private residence in 1702. Its most noticeable feature was its roof, with two high-pitched hipped gables intersecting at right angles. The first floor held the bar and a large public room where British and American newspapers were available. The upstairs held smaller rooms for private meetings.

Thanks to its corporate sponsorship and a location near the docks and market, the London Coffee Shop quickly became the city's commercial and financial exchange. Crops, carriages, horses, houses, and human beings were bought and sold under the shelter of its

Edward Mumford's depiction of the London Coffee House during the colonial era, with a slave auction in progress along its Market Street front. To the right stands the printing house of *Pennsylvania Journal* publisher and London Coffee House proprietor William Bradford. (The Library Company of Philadelphia.)

wide, wraparound awning. The coffeehouse hosted frequent slave auctions, like this one advertised in the July 18, 1765, edition of the *Pennsylvania Gazette:* "TO BE SOLD, On Saturday the 27th Instant, at the London Coffee House, TWELVE or Fourteen valuable NEGROES, consisting of young Men, Women, Boys and Girls; they have all had the Small Pox, can talk English, and are seasoned to the Country. The Sale to begin at Twelve o'Clock."

Before long, the London Coffee House was home to the Philadelphia Board of Brokers, forerunner of the Philadelphia Stock Exchange. The house also functioned as the Palm Restaurant of its day, where the governor, council, ship captains, merchants, bankers, and other power brokers met at noon in their regular stalls to drink and cut deals.

Before the American Revolution, the London Coffee House was a hotbed of anti-British agitation. William Bradford, a leader in the Sons of Liberty, opposed the Stamp Act and other forms of British taxation, as did many of his profit-minded investors and customers. In 1765, bonfires burned before the Coffee House, fueled by parchment and paper bearing the hated stamp.

As the rift with Britain widened, the coffeehouse was where royal officials were burned in effigy and where Tories were forced to acknowledge their sins publicly or risk being tarred and feathered. When the Continental Congress was in session, John Adams, Robert Morris, Benjamin Rush, and other revolutionary leaders met there to discuss strategy. On July 8, 1776, after the Declaration of Independence was publicly read for the first time, the royal arms were ripped down from the supreme court chamber at the State House, carried to the coffeehouse, and burned before a cheering mob.

When the Revolution began, William Bradford closed the coffeehouse and joined the Continental Army. Badly wounded at the Battle of Princeton, he never fully recovered from his injuries. He returned to Philadelphia in 1778 to find his establishment's role as business exchange usurped by the City Tavern, a more modern and elegant facility that had remained in business during the British occupation. Opened in 1773 on Second Street between Walnut and Chestnut, the City Tavern (later the Merchants' Coffee House) would function as the city's exchange until the 1830s. After competing against the City Tavern for two years, Bradford relinquished his proprietorship to the building's owner in 1780 and retired.

The London Coffee House closed its doors in 1793. After serving as a dry goods store, the building housed a tobacco shop from 1817 until 1883, when the owner demolished the historic but outmoded structure, replacing it with the five-story office building that currently occupies the site.

Court House and Town Hall

Location: Center of Market Street, on west side of intersection
with Second Street
Completed: 1710
Demolished: 1837
Architect/Builder: Samuel Powel, carpenter

The Court House and Town Hall did triple service as the political, judicial, and commercial center of Philadelphia. Built in 1707–10 between Christ Church and the Great Meeting House, the brick building combined the city's market head house with its courthouse, an ancient British tradition. It served as the seat of government for the city and county of Philadelphia, as well as for the province of Pennsylvania, until these functions were transferred to the State House in 1748.

The impetus for the building came in 1706, when the provincial assembly threatened to leave the city for either Bucks or Chester County unless Philadelphia built them a more suitable meeting place than the alehouse they were obliged to use. After much wrangling, the Court House and Town Hall was erected at the eastern end of the High Street market shed between Second and Third streets. It stood on the site of the town bell, which was rung to open and close the market and to announce proclamations.

The Great Towne-House, or Guild Hall, was the first piece of civic architecture in the young city. Modeled on the medieval market/courthouses of England and Scotland, the brick building stood two-and-a-half stories high, with its steeply pitched gable roof forming a garret. The town bell was relocated to a wooden steeple in the

middle of the roof, which gave the structure a churchlike appearance. The arcaded first floor, one arch wide on Second Street and three arches long on High Street, housed the town jail as well as market stalls. The second floor and garret became the seat of the city, county, and provincial governments, and the meeting place of the provincial assembly, legislature, municipal council, mayor's court, county court, orphans' court, and supreme court.

Outside stairways on the north and south sides of the building snaked around to the Second Street façade, joining at a covered balcony on the second floor, the site of public announcements and speeches, as well as elections. Enfranchised freemen ascended the stairs to vote or blocked them to keep their opponents from casting their ballots. In an October 1742 election between the Proprietary and Governor's parties, supporters of the royal governor enlisted sailors to hold the stairs. Proprietary partisans, mostly Quakers, used fists, sticks, stones, and clubs to drive the sailors back to their

A copy of an 1855 drawing by C. A. Poulson Jr. of the Town Hall and Court House as the building appeared upon completion. In the background at left is the Great (or First Friends') Meeting House, replaced by the Greater Meeting House in 1755. (The Library Company of Philadelphia.)

Workmen toss debris down upon unsuspecting passersby in this William L. Breton drawing of the Court House during its 1837 demolition. The commercial structures on the left have replaced the Quaker Meeting House. (The Historical Society of Pennsylvania.)

ships. Perhaps to discourage similar brawls, the outside stairs were removed before the Revolution.

When the new State House (now Independence Hall) was completed in 1748, it became the site of all judicial and governmental functions for the city, county, and colony. The old Court House survived for nearly another century, its space occupied by market stalls, an auction gallery, and shops. In June 1828, *The Casket* magazine noted with condescension: "This once venerable building, long diverted of its original honours, had long been regarded by us and others, as a rude and undistinguished edifice. . . . This structure, diminutive and ignoble as it may now appear to our modern conception, was the chef d'oeuvre and largest endeavor of our Pilgrim Fathers."[20]

Responding to tradesmen's demands for more market space, the city passed an ordinance for "doing away with the Court House" on September 1, 1836. Despite the opposition of John Fanning Watson and other early preservationists, the Court House was dismantled in March and April 1837. In its place rose one of the modern iron market sheds designed by William Strickland, which would itself be demolished in 1859.

Bleakley House/Cannon Ball House

Location: Penrose Ferry Road, South Philadelphia
Completed: ca. 1715
Demolished: 1996
Architect/Builder: Unknown

The Bleakley, or Cannon Ball, House stood in Kingsessing Township, in the far southern reaches of the city. The two-and-a-half-story brick farmhouse had some features associated with Swedish vernacular architecture, including a steep, hipped gable roof, a wooden pent roof across the gable ends, and a flat, elongated chimney. The original house stood nearly thirty-six feet long by nineteen feet wide; a later kitchen wing added to the back, measuring twenty-six by twenty feet, transformed it into an L-shaped structure. At one time, it was thought that the house dated from the mid–seventeenth century and belonged to a Swede named Peter Cock. More recently, historians have placed the date of the house's construction at 1715–20, despite some features that seemed to belong to an earlier period.°

By the time of the Revolutionary War, ownership of the property had passed to John Bleakley. In October 1777, the British navy laid siege to Continental forces at nearby Fort Mifflin, who were preventing their ships from sailing up the Delaware to supply the king's forces in Philadelphia. The British built a land battery in the rear of the Bleakley house, placing it in the direct line of fire between Fort Mifflin and the battery.

According to legend, the Bleakleys ignored orders to evacuate until November 11, 1777, when a cannonball from Fort Mifflin crashed through the south side of the house and passed over their heads as they sat down to dinner. In fact, the house had already been commandeered by the British, as shown by a diary entry by John Montresor, chief engineer for the British, for that day: "One corporal and two seargeants wounded at Bleakley house, it being in the line of fire."[21] From that time on, the Bleakley house was nick-named the Cannon Ball House. After the Revolution, the cannonball's entry and exit points were bricked over but kept whitewashed as a souvenir of the house's battle service.

During the late nineteenth century, the City of Philadelphia acquired the Cannon Ball House and then forgot about it. The 1937

The south side of the Cannon Ball House in 1937, distinctive for its elongated chimney and whitewashed cannonball hole. (Historic American Buildings Survey.)

°In *Portrait of a Colonial City* (1939), Eberlein and Hubbard stated that the house "could have been built as early as 1657–60, certainly by 1668" (29). The Historic American Buildings Survey PA–134 (August 1937) specified the building period as 1668–1715 on its plans. On the summary report for the same survey, however, District Officer Joseph P. Sims placed the date of construction as "about 1750." Robert Smith, in "Two Centuries of Philadelphia Architecture, 1700–1900" (in American Philosophical Society, *Historic Philadelphia* [1953]), stated that the house "may antedate the founding of the city"; "the greater part of the present structure seems to date, however, from between 1714 and 1720" (289).

Historic American Buildings Survey noted that "the house has long been unoccupied and is in deplorable condition." In 1947, a fire left only its walls standing. The house remained in its semi-ruined state until 1975, when the city needed room to expand the nearby Southwest Sewage Treatment Plant.

City officials spent nearly $200,000 to move the shell to a site near the entrance to Fort Mifflin, a mile away, where it was left to decay on I-beams in a muddy, weed-filled lot for twenty-two years, while the Water Department, Recreation Department, and other city agencies bickered over who should maintain it. In November 1996, workers from the Department of Licenses and Inspections knocked down the ruins. The head of that department insisted that notice of the Cannon Ball House's pending demolition had been submitted two months earlier to the Philadelphia Historical Commission, which denied receiving such notice. Dori McMunn, then executive director of nearby Fort Mifflin, salvaged some bricks, molding, handmade square nails, and other artifacts from the house. The rest of the historic—and supposedly historically protected—structure became landfill.

Fairhill

Location: Marshall Street between York and Cumberland streets, North Philadelphia
Completed: 1717; rebuilt, 1787
Demolished: Original house burned by the British, 1777; rebuilt house demolished, 1885
Architect/Builder: Richard Redman and John Hart

William Penn expected Philadelphia's larger property owners to adopt the habits of England's landed gentry and spend more time at their country estates than at their town houses. Penn himself set the standard by establishing a plantation at Pennsbury Manor in Bucks County, traveling by barge down the Delaware to his rented quarters in town. Men of means followed his lead, creating about 150 country estates within a twelve-mile radius of the city by 1750. Along with the surviving Stenton, Fairhill (or Fair Hill) was among the earliest examples of a Philadelphia country estate.

Isaac Norris Sr., a Quaker planter who moved from Jamaica to Philadelphia in 1693, became a trusted associate of Penn's and one of the city's wealthiest merchants. In 1709, after buying the Slate Roof House, he began to purchase land on the Germantown Road north of the city. By 1713, Norris had assembled 804 acres and had begun to build a mansion, which he named after the nearby Quaker meetinghouse of Fair Hill.

His builders designed an H-shaped structure fifty-six feet wide by forty-five feet deep. The house consisted of a raised basement, a first floor, and a second story or garret under a high-pitched, cross-gabled roof. A recessed entrance led into a central hall, which in turn opened into four rooms, two in each wing. A balcony ran across the top of the recessed central section of the house and a square tower rose from the middle of the central gable. From these vantage points, Norris could enjoy views of the Delaware River and the distant city. Visitors arriving along the tree-lined drive from the

Germantown Road saw an imposing brick façade; the less visible side walls were composed of cheaper rubble stonework.

While many early country houses were little more than cabins, Norris spared no expense on his. He ordered locks, hinges, sashes, and window glass from England, as well as much of the furniture. Black and white marble slabs lined the floor of the front hall, while the front parlors were wainscoted with oak and red cedar. The finishing touch was a large weathercock atop his tower, connected to an interior compass.

Despite its handsome furnishings, Fairhill was a working farm with numerous outbuildings, including a kitchen, stable, brew-house, milk house, smokehouse, granary, greenhouse, corn house, cider house, and barn. An orchard provided various fruits, a kitchen garden produced a variety of vegetables (including English beans, a gift from proprietor Thomas Penn), and an apiary yielded honey.

In 1717, Isaac Norris made Fairhill his year-round home, turning the Slate Roof House over to his son, Isaac Jr. The younger Norris moved to Fairhill in 1742, six years after his father's death. Reflecting the growing wealth and leisure of the colony, Fairhill became less a working farm and more a gentleman's residence under Isaac Jr. The greenhouse was converted to house the largest library in Pennsylvania after James Logan's. Norris added formal

Joseph Pennell's fanciful conception of Fairhill in the colonial era, drawn for the Historical Society of Pennsylvania in 1882. (Collection of the author.)

gardens with parterres and gravel walks and beautified the surrounding woods and waterways according to the picturesque aesthetics of English landscape design.

These improvements continued after Isaac Jr.'s death in 1766, when the house passed to his daughter Mary and her husband, lawyer and politician John Dickinson. After dining at Fairhill in 1774, John Adams wrote: "Mr. Dickinson has a fine seat, a beautiful prospect of the city, the river and country, fine garden, and a very grand library."[22]

Fairhill's halcyon days ended with the American Revolution. Although Dickinson had declined to sign the Declaration of Independence, he supported the American cause and served as a brigadier general in the Pennsylvania militia. The family abandoned the estate during the British occupation of Philadelphia and the surrounding area. In November 1777, the British army burned Fairhill and other country houses as part of a scorched-earth campaign to make the Northern Liberties unusable by American forces. Deborah Logan, granddaughter of the original owner, later wrote: "From the roof of my mother's house, on Chestnut Street, we counted seventeen fires, one of which we knew to be the beautiful seat of Fairhill, built by my grandfather Norris and owned by his family, but in the occupation of the excellent John Dickinson, who had married my cousin."[23]

After the Revolution, the house lay in ruins until 1787, when Isaac Norris III built a simpler, one-story structure incorporating the remains of the original walls. The Norris family used the property as a summer residence until 1841. After that, it became a tavern under such names as the Old Revolution Inn and Fairhill Beer-Garden, where "merry Teutons quaffed the beverage of Cambrinus beneath the fine old trees of the Norris estate."[24] In 1885, Marshall Street was opened through the property and the last traces of Fairhill were destroyed, at length replaced by the endless row houses of North Philadelphia.

Second Presbyterian Church

Location: Northwest corner of Arch and Third streets
Completed: 1752
Demolished: 1837
Architect/Builder: Robert Smith; Thomas Nevell (steeple)

As Philadelphia expanded, so did the variety of sects and denominations enjoying Penn's policy of religious tolerance. Houses of worship increased in number from about six at the start of the eighteenth century to eighteen by the time of the Revolution. Fueled by the growth in Scots-Irish immigration, Presbyterianism surged in popularity during this period; by 1745, there were nearly as many Presbyterians as Quakers in Philadelphia.

In the 1730s, the religious revival known as the Great Awakening created a schism among Philadelphia's Presbyterians. The First Presbyterian Church, at High Street and Bank Alley, was the home of the conservative Old Lights. The New Lights, inflamed by the passionate preaching of the Reverend George Whitefield, sought a faith that was more emotional and fundamental. Many of the New Lights were recent Scots-Irish immigrants, who felt divided from the more established Old Lights on social and economic, as well as religious, grounds.

In 1743, about 140 Presbyterians split from the original church to organize the Second Presbyterian Church. Originally, they met in the New Building on Fourth Street below Arch, later the birthplace of the University of Pennsylvania. When the New Building was sold in 1747, the Second Presbyterian Church was forced to find a new home. The New Lights purchased a lot at the northwest corner of Arch and Third streets and laid a cornerstone on May 17, 1750, for a church designed by Robert Smith, Philadelphia's leading architect-builder. The brick church, measuring sixty feet on Arch Street by eighty feet on Third, featured a classic Georgian façade with a pedimented front door framed by arched windows; a Palladian window on the second floor, also framed by arched

A nineteenth-century recreation of the original Second Presbyterian Church from the church's centennial program. (The Historical Society of Pennsylvania.)

windows; an oculus in the gable; and urns at the gable peak and ends. Inscribed in gilt letters on its eastern pediment were the words "Templum Presbyterianum, annuente numine, erectum. Anno Dom. MDCCL" ("Presbyterian Temple, erected with divine approval in the Year of our Lord 1750").

A notable feature of Smith's design was an imposing steeple, one of the few to compete with the spire then rising over Christ Church on Second Street. It would take eleven years and at least two lotteries to raise sufficient funds to erect the spire. When it was finally completed in 1761, the church elders had discarded Robert Smith's original design for a simpler tower created by Thomas Nevell, as shown in the William Birch print of Arch Street. By this time,

their exertions had prompted one anonymous wit to compose a sneering verse:

> The Presbyterians built a church,
> And fain would have a steeple;
> We think it may become the church,
> But not become the people.[25]

Despite this mockery, the Second Presbyterian Church had been steadily gaining in membership and prestige. After the Revolution, it counted Benjamin Rush, David Rittenhouse, Peter S. DuPonceau, and Elias Boudinot among its members. George Washington worshipped at the church occasionally, in his own President's Pew. In 1789, the first General Assembly of the Presbyterian Church in the United States was held at the Second Presbyterian Church.

In 1802, the church's troublesome steeple was removed, after its wooden supports were discovered to have rotted. A few years later, the building was enlarged and its interior redesigned to accommodate a growing congregation. Despite this overhaul, the need for a new facility was inescapable by the 1830s. Not only was the church too small, but its neighborhood had grown commercial and noisy, especially after the repeal of a law permitting the church to close Arch and Third streets to traffic on Sundays. In 1837, the building was sold and torn down, and the congregation moved to "a beautiful marble front church" on Seventh Street below Arch. It remained there until 1872, when it moved farther west to Walnut and Twenty-first streets. The church, which rejoined the Old Lights in 1949 to become the First Presbyterian Church in Philadelphia, still occupies that site.

John Drinker House/Krider Gun Shop

Location: Northeast corner of Walnut and Second streets
(135 Walnut Street)
Completed: 1751–60
Demolished: 1955
Architect/Builder: John Drinker

According to legend, the first child born to European parents in Philadelphia, John Drinker, arrived on December 24, 1680, in a log cabin along Dock Creek. After a long and varied career elsewhere, he returned to Philadelphia and in 1751 purchased a lot measuring twenty-six by fifty feet at the northeast corner of Walnut and Second streets, a location believed to be either on or near the site of his birthplace. Drinker, who lived to be over a hundred, loved to point out sites where Indians once camped and to reminisce about being taken as a toddler to see William Penn arrive at the Dock. While in England on a diplomatic mission, Benjamin Franklin was asked how long Americans lived. He responded that he could not tell until John Drinker died.

Sometime between 1751 and 1760, Drinker built two adjoining, three-and-a-half-story brick houses on his property. Although he may have intended them to be used as a double house, Drinker sold them separately in 1760. The corner house (135 Walnut Street), measuring forty-six feet along Second Street and thirteen feet on Walnut

Street, was a gable-roofed, two-bay building with a pedimented gable on the Second Street side. At some point, a three-story, flat-roofed addition was constructed in the rear of the house.

After Drinker sold the corner house, it belonged to several owners before being acquired by the McCalla family, who owned it for eighty-nine years. In 1839, a gunsmith, John Krider, rented the back addition, taking over a business that Prosper Vallée had run since 1826. When the McCalla family died out in 1856, Krider purchased the property and moved his gun shop to the front room. Krider's Gun Shop was in the middle of a busy commercial district and close to the Walnut Street wharves, where Cope's Steamship Line brought a fresh flood of passengers to its doorstep every day.

Besides selling guns, Krider dealt in fishing and hunting equipment, sporting goods, and taxidermy. During the Civil War, his gun

Krider's Gun Shop as it appeared ca. 1920. A placard to the left of the Second Street doorway identifies the site as the birthplace of John Drinker. Farther left, a sign hanging from the St. Alban's Hotel directs diners to Bookbinder's Restaurant. (The Library Company of Philadelphia.)

shop also served as a cartridge-loading station. By the 1870s, advertisements described Krider's as a "sporting depot" that provided the same services for Philadelphia's hunting, shooting, and riding folk that Abercrombie & Fitch offered to New Yorkers.[26]

Krider's business occupied the entire house, with the shop on the first floor, a gun-manufacturing room on the second, and fishing equipment on the third. After Krider's death in 1886, the business was sold to his protégé, John Siner, and stayed in the Siner family until the death of John Siner's son Leandro in 1944. As factory-produced firearms flattened the market for custom-made guns, the staff shrank from eleven gunsmiths to one repairman.

After the gun shop closed, the ground floor of the building housed a luncheonette. When the lunchroom owner died in 1952, the National Park Service debated buying the property but was unable to proceed because it was outside the park area authorized by Congress. Instead, John Taxin, owner of Old Original Bookbinder's Restaurant at 125 Walnut Street, purchased both the Krider Gun Shop (133 Walnut Street) and its neighbor (135 Walnut Street) for $15,000. Charles Peterson, resident architect for the National Park Service, asked Taxin to consider rehabilitating the two Drinker houses as a gun museum. Unfortunately, surveys of the structures conducted by the Historic American Buildings Survey and the Department of Licenses and Inspections concluded that they were in poor condition.

In 1955, with the city's permission, Taxin had 133 and 135 Walnut Street demolished to expand Old Original Bookbinder's. Grant Miles Simon, chair of the Philadelphia Historical Commission, designed a structure to house the restaurant's Hall of Patriots banquet room and Signers dining room. His design—a three-and-a-half-story, gable-roofed brick building—was a stylistic salute to the vanished Drinker houses rather than an accurate copy. Today, the recently reopened Old Original Bookbinder's still occupies the site. (Over the years, the Taxin family would continue to clash with preservationists over their demolition of such historic structures as the McCrea houses in 1984 and the Elisha Webb Chandlery in 1993.)

Friends' Almshouse

Location: South side of Walnut Street between Third and Fourth streets
Completed: 1729
Demolished: 1841 (main building); 1876 (cottages)
Architect/Builder: Unknown

First Philadelphia Almshouse

Location: Square bounded by Third, Fourth, Spruce, and Pine streets
Completed: 1732
Demolished: 1765
Architect/Builder: Unknown

Second Philadelphia Almshouse

Location: Square bounded by Tenth, Eleventh, Spruce, and Pine streets
Completed: 1767
Demolished: 1834
Architect/Builder: Robert Smith

Guided by Quaker principles of charity and social responsibility, Philadelphia was a pioneer in public welfare. In 1713, the city's Quakers founded the Friends' Almshouse, the first institution of its type in the American colonies, in a small house on Walnut Street between Third and Fourth. In 1729, the house was replaced by a substantial brick building; behind this central structure, a number of small cottages stood within a central courtyard. The main Almshouse accommodated indigent Quakers for 112 years until its

replacement by offices in 1841. The cottages, known as the Quaker Nunnery for the elderly ladies inhabiting them, survived until 1876, when Walnut Place was run through the block.

By the early eighteenth century, the number of poor and needy in Philadelphia necessitated municipal involvement. In 1730 the mayor and aldermen paid £200 to purchase the square bounded by Third, Fourth, Spruce, and Pine streets. The Philadelphia Almshouse was erected on the site in 1731–32, taking the name Green Meadows from its bucolic setting. Little is known of the brick structure other than that it resembled the Friends' Almshouse, with its main entrance on Third Street and a "great gate" on Spruce, and a porch running around the building. Besides housing and feeding the poor, the Almshouse offered an infirmary and hospital for the sick and insane, their only refuge until the opening of the Pennsylvania Hospital in 1751.

By the 1760s, the Almshouse was overwhelmed, with 220 paupers seeking refuge in a building designed for less than half that number. In 1764, the Overseers of the Poor reported that four to six men were squeezed into a room no larger than ten feet square. The city turned to its citizens for support, raising funds to purchase

Above: **O**ne of the cottages that stood behind the central Friends' Almshouse, before its demolition in 1876. For many years, it was believed that poet William Wadsworth Longfellow reunited his heroine, Evangeline, with her dying lover in one of these cottages in his poem "Evangeline." (Collection of the author.)

Facing page: **T**he Second Philadelphia Almshouse and House of Employment on Spruce between Tenth and Eleventh streets, as depicted by William Birch in 1799. A central pavilion between the two structures was never completed. (The Philadelphia Print Shop.)

a lot on the edge of the city, one block west of Pennsylvania Hospital. The former Almshouse property was sold and subdivided into lots for Society Hill town houses, including the historic Hill-Physick-Keith house.

Robert Smith was hired to design the new facility, which was completed in 1767. The complex featured two buildings: the Almshouse fronting on Tenth Street, and a workhouse, or House of Employment, fronting on Eleventh. The buildings were identical two-story brick structures, L-shaped, 180 feet (on Tenth and Eleventh streets) by 40 feet (on Spruce Street), with four-story corner towers. On the back of the buildings, arched cloisters provided outdoor shelter for inmates. Many early prints, possibly copying Smith's design rather than the actual building, show a central pavilion on Spruce Street connecting the two wings. A later print by William Birch shows no central structure, leading modern historians to conclude that it was never built.

During the American Revolution, the Continental Army appropriated the Almshouse for a hospital for wounded soldiers, and all the inmates were crowded into the House of Employment. When the British occupied the city in September 1777, they forced the managers to vacate the House of Employment as well. Of the 200 dislocated inmates, more than half died before the British evacuation in June 1778. Shortly after the British left, the Almshouse and House of Employment reoccupied the buildings, despite their wretched condition.

By the early nineteenth century, the number of poor, sick, and insane in the growing city had overwhelmed the resources of the Almshouse and House of Employment. The value of the buildings' location had increased as the city moved westward, as had the public desire to remove their inmates from a prosperous residential district. A new almshouse and a bettering house (or workhouse) were built in the open country at Blockley (later West Philadelphia) in 1835. Cypress and Clinton streets were opened through the property and, once again, elegant residences occupied the former refuge of society's rejects.

The Cliffs

Location: Columbia Avenue, near Thirty-third and Oxford streets,
East Fairmount Park
Completed: 1753
Demolished: 1986
Architect/Builder: Unknown

The bluffs overlooking the Schuylkill River, both above and below the city, became a favorite spot for country estates. Wealthy Philadelphians could reach these houses easily from town via a cooling barge ride. Because of their proximity (compared to the rigorous journey to Germantown or Frankford), many river houses, such as Woodford, Ormiston, and the Cliffs, were built on a relatively modest scale.

In 1753, the merchant Joshua Fisher, whose grandfather sailed with William Penn on the *Welcome,* acquired several parcels of property from the Mifflin family on the east bank of the Schuylkill. There he built a two-and-a-half-story country house with a hipped roof, measuring roughly thirty-six by twenty-two feet. The house was built of rubble stone and covered with stucco scored to look like ashlar. The compact structure contained a basement kitchen, parlor, and dining room on the first floor, two bedrooms on the second, and a full attic. Fisher named his house the Cliffs after his grandfather's country seat near Wakefield, England.

The Cliffs was probably meant to be used as a summer house for short excursions from the Fisher city house at 110 South Front Street. Its two bedrooms and attic could not easily accommodate Fisher, his wife, seven children, and servants for an extended stay. Although the use of simple materials, such as the rubble exterior, pine floors, and oak beams, reflected Fisher's Quaker restraint, the Cliffs was elegantly finished, with wood paneling and details such as dadoes and chair rails.

The Fisher family owned the property until 1868, occasionally renting it out to tenants such as Sarah Franklin Bache, who in 1789

The Cliffs in East Fairmount Park, boarded up and abandoned, in January 1975. (Temple University Libraries, Urban Archives, Philadelphia.)

wrote her father, Benjamin Franklin, about "this small, charming house."[27] In 1868, the Fairmount Park Commission acquired the property as part of its campaign to protect the city's water supply, an effort that had the added benefit of preserving a number of early houses.

While housing park employees, the Cliffs served as an important model for the restoration of other historic buildings. The soapstone steps leading to its front and rear doors served as examples for the new steps at Independence Hall in the 1950s, while its interior details guided restoration of the Todd House and Bishop White House. The Cliffs was certified as an historic structure by the Philadelphia Historical Commission in 1956 and added to the Pennsylvania Register of Historic Buildings in 1971.

In 1968, the Fairmount Park Commission vacated the Cliffs, leaving it to the mercy of vandals and the elements. Three years later, opposition from members of the Philadelphia Historical Commission and Independence National Historical Park halted a proposal by the cash-strapped commission to demolish the "obsolete" house. Their actions saved the Cliffs from immediate destruction but failed to produce a long-term solution.

In February 1986, a fire gutted the vacant building, leaving only the walls. Firefighters watched helplessly as flames consumed the house, unable to approach because the mud surrounding the Cliffs would not support their trucks. (Dirt had been brought in to transform a nearby garbage dump into parkland.) A 1987 assessment of the Cliffs and other historic structures in Fairmount Park by Kieran, Timberlake & Harris estimated that stabilization of the remains would cost between $15,000 and $25,000. The Fairmount Park Commission never took action, and today only a few ruins remain.

In evaluating the future of the Cliffs in 1987, Kieran, Timberlake & Harris might have composed its obituary: "The Cliffs testifies both to the grace of Philadelphia's eighteenth-century architecture and the city's neglect of its cultural resources in the twentieth century."[28]

Benjamin Franklin House/Franklin Court

Location: Orianna Street south of Market Street, between Third and Fourth streets
Completed: 1765
Demolished: 1812
Architect/Builder: Robert Smith and Samuel Rhoads

In 1763, fifty-seven-year-old Benjamin Franklin had returned to Philadelphia after a seven-year stint as colonial agent in London. Comfortably retired from his successful printing business, Franklin had become Philadelphia's leading mover and shaker, cofounding the Pennsylvania Hospital, the American Philosophical Society, the Library Company, and a host of other institutions. Having lived in thirteen rented properties during thirty-three years of marriage, he and his wife, Deborah, were ready to settle down in their own house.

Rather than build a country estate, Franklin wanted to stay in the city, near the State House, the commercial district, and the many institutions he had brought to life. The Franklins had assembled a large lot on the south side of High (Market) Street between Third and Fourth, extending nearly to Chestnut Street. Just as construction began, Franklin was appointed agent for the Province of Pennsylvania to the English government, leaving Philadelphia on November 7, 1764. He had no way of knowing that of the remaining thirty-six years of his life, he would spend only seven in his own house.

Before leaving for England, Franklin selected Robert Smith as the master carpenter for the house and appointed his friend Samuel Rhoads as agent to supervise construction. They built a three-story brick structure, thirty-four feet square, with three rooms to a floor and a basement kitchen. A chimney rose at each end of the wood-shingled roof. The house stood in a courtyard about 200 feet back from High Street, to minimize noise from the busy marketplace, and was further shielded by three brick houses fronting on High Street, which Franklin had built to generate rental income.

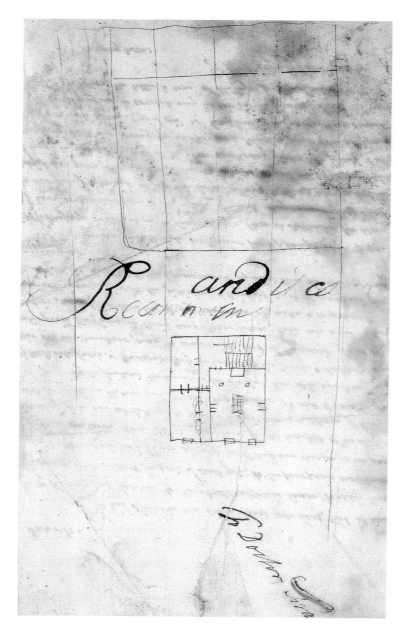

By May 1765, the house was sufficiently completed for Deborah Franklin to move in with her daughter Sarah. The house bore the signs of Franklin's inventive nature, with his own Franklin stoves and lightning rods, a trap door to the roof to facilitate firefighting, a furnace, and in the kitchen "several Contrivances to carry off Steam & Smell and Smoke."[29] Soon its rooms were papered and carpeted, and filled with the elegant possessions Franklin had collected in England.

Franklin did not return to his house until May 1775, after the death of his wife, to live with his daughter and her husband, Richard Bache. In October 1776, with the country at war with England, Franklin was dispatched to France to negotiate a treaty. During the British occupation of 1777–78, General Sir Charles Grey and Captain John André lived in his house. When the British officers decamped, they stole Franklin's books, electrical equipment, musical instruments, and portrait, but otherwise left the residence intact.

Franklin returned to Philadelphia for the final time in September 1785, a hero for his role in winning French support for the American cause. To accommodate his daughter's growing family, he added an extension, eighteen by thirty feet, to the house's eastern end. Along with two bedrooms and two attic rooms, the addition created a long room for Franklin's library and scientific instruments, and a spacious drawing room where Franklin could entertain fellow members of the American Philosophical Society.

During this time, Franklin rearranged his holdings to provide security for his family. He tore down the three houses on High Street and replaced them with two modern rental properties, built another building at the northwestern edge of the property, and added a print shop north of the house for his grandson. For his own

Benjamin Franklin sketched the first floor of his future house, with a central hallway leading to a staircase on the northern end, two smaller rooms on the west side, and a large dining room with a fireplace on the east side. (American Philosophical Society.)

pleasure, he surrounded the house with an ornamental garden, full of shade trees and flowering shrubs. In his later years, the ailing Franklin often held court under a mulberry tree in the rear of the property.

After Franklin's death in 1790, his daughter and son-in-law sold his possessions at auction and rented the house to the Portuguese minister to the United States. Over the next decade, the house served as a boardinghouse, a female academy, a coffeehouse, and the home of the African Free School. After the deaths of Sarah and Richard Bache, their descendants sold the property. In 1812, Franklin's house was demolished, along with the printing shop. Orianna Street was run through the property, with houses lining both sides of the street.

In 1954, the federal government acquired the property as part of Independence National Historical Park. After conducting extensive historical and archaeological investigations on the site, the National Park Service decided to recreate Franklin Court for the nation's bicentennial. The well-documented properties on Market Street were reconstructed by John Milner as the United States Postal Service Museum, the Franklin Print Shop, and the office of the *Aurora,* the newspaper edited by Franklin's grandson. Aside from two rough sketches of floor plans by Franklin himself, however, no authentic image of Franklin's house existed. The only known picture of the house, an early nineteenth-century watercolor by James Thackara, disappeared in 1948.

Faced with this lack of visual documentation, architects Robert Venturi and John Rauch designed "ghost houses"—open steel frames outlining the dimensions of the Franklin house and print shop on their original sites. Beneath the house, an underground museum presented a multimedia history of Franklin's life and contributions. The rest of the courtyard was developed as a small urban park, with plantings, pergolas, and benches evoking an eighteenth-century garden. Franklin Court opened in April 1976, one of the few Bicentennial projects to be realized and to survive to the present.

Franklin Court shortly before its opening in 1976, showing the Venturi and Rauch "ghosts" of the main house in the foreground and the print shop in the middle distance, with John Milner's reconstructed Market Street properties at top. (Temple University Libraries, Urban Archives, Philadelphia.)

FOUNDED MDCCIV   REBUILT MDCXCIV

CHAPTER 2

Athens of America

(1776 to 1820)

For much of the period between 1776 and 1820, Philadelphia was the true center of the new United States, not just politically and culturally, but geographically. From 1769 to 1800, U.S. longitude was calculated from the Meridian of Philadelphia, determined by David Rittenhouse as being 75 degrees, 8 minutes, and 45 seconds west of Greenwich. The Meridian of Philadelphia ran through the observatory in the State House yard from which Rittenhouse first tracked the Transit of Venus in 1769.

In the early days of the Revolution, Philadelphia enjoyed a burst of wartime prosperity as the seat of the Continental Congress and as the hub of American maritime traffic and military provisioning. Its status changed swiftly when the British Army, under General Sir William Howe, occupied the city in September 1778. The army used many of the city's public buildings and churches as hospitals, barracks, or stables and requisitioned its larger houses for officers' quarters. During the harsh winter of 1778–79, Philadelphians desperate for fuel chopped down trees and tore down fences and old houses. Before the British left in June 1779, they demolished, gutted, or vandalized many buildings, leaving behind "a wanton desolation and destruction" filled with "dirt, filth, stench, and flies."[1]

Wartime deprivation left Philadelphia semi-ruined for years after the British left. When the American victory at Yorktown in October 1781 effectively ended hostilities, prosperity began to return to the devastated city. Men like Henry Hill, Robert Morris, and William Bingham, whose wealth had been enhanced rather than diminished by the war, were soon building handsome residences.

When the Constitutional Convention was convened at the State House on May 25, 1787, Philadelphia returned to the national spotlight. Its status was further elevated by the Residence Act, which moved the federal government from New York to Philadelphia while the new Federal City, or District of Columbia, was being created. The act, brokered by Robert Morris, called for Philadelphia to serve as the national capital from 1790 only until the first Monday in December 1800. Many Philadelphians, of course, hoped that after a decade of soft living in their metropolis, the new government would forget about moving to the malarial wilderness of Virginia.

To entice the government to remain, Philadelphia gave itself a much-needed facelift, covering the open sewer that was Dock Creek to create Dock Street and planting trees in the overcrowded Strangers' Burying Ground (today Washington Square) near the State House. The city erected new accommodations for the government, including buildings for the Supreme Court and Congress, a presidential mansion, and facilities for the First Bank of the United States and the U.S. Mint.

These structures were part of a citywide construction boom that included handsome public buildings like the Pennsylvania Hospital and Library Hall, as well as magnificent private residences like the Hill-Physick-Keith House, the Bingham Mansion House, and the Woodlands. Many of these buildings were designed in the Adam brothers' classical manner, imported from Britain to become the Federal style in America. Rows of modest houses spread across the Northern Liberties, which had been subdivided and sold off by the state legislature after the Revolution.

Between 1790 and 1800, the population of Philadelphia grew from 28,500 to over 41,000, making it the second largest city in the United States. While New York had more people, Philadelphia was the center of American politics, finance, trade, industry, and culture to a degree unrivaled by any single U.S. city since then. Even after the federal government departed on schedule, Philadelphia retained its financial, mercantile, and intellectual supremacy for another two decades.

Foreign visitors expecting a provincial backwater were stunned to find a dazzling capital comparable to London or Paris. In 1791, the Vicômte de Chateaubriand wrote of the "elegance of dress, the luxury of equipage, the frivolousness of conversations, the unequality of fortunes, the immorality of banking and gaming-houses, the noise of ball-rooms and theatres."[2] Every day brought an exciting novelty or invention: the first American monthly magazine, the

HORIZONTORIUM.

Toward the end of the period, Greco-Roman architecture began to give way to the Gothic Revival style, reflected in Benjamin Henry Latrobe's 1808 design for the Philadelphia Bank at Fourth and Chestnut streets. (The Philadelphia Print Shop.)

Columbian; the first gaslights, advertised as "a grand fire-work by means of light composed of inflammable air"; even a steam-powered vehicle called the Orukter Amphibolos that traveled unaided on both water and land.[3]

English immigrants like Benjamin Henry Latrobe and John Haviland brought the latest architectural styles and techniques from Europe, which were quickly adopted by native sons like Robert Mills and William Strickland. This first generation of professional architects established new standards of sophistication, innovation, and technical expertise. Despite the conservative influence of the Carpenters' Company, these trendsetters made Philadelphia the undisputed leader in U.S. architectural design. Under their sway, the favored Georgian and Federal modes gave way to experimental styles like Greek Revival and Gothic Revival.

By the early nineteenth century, the city boasted such impressive structures as the Centre Square Water Works, the Bank of Pennsylvania, the Chestnut Street Theatre, and the Pennsylvania Academy of Fine Arts. Philadelphia, a town of plain red brick when this period began, was changing into a city of neoclassical gray marble as it ended. When Benjamin Henry Latrobe, in an 1811 address to the Society of Artists of the United States, foresaw that "the days of Greece may be revived in the woods of America, and Philadelphia become the Athens of the Western world," his words sounded like an accurate forecast rather than a utopian vision.[4]

Philadelphia Waterfront

Location: Front and Water streets and adjacent streets along the Delaware waterfront.
Built: ca. 1770–1830
Demolished: ca. 1839–1980
Architect/Builder: Various

From its earliest days until the mid–nineteenth century, Philadelphia was a maritime city, its commercial life focused on the Delaware River. This was especially true after the Revolution, when Philadelphia emerged not just as the country's leading political and mercantile city, but as the center of U.S. shipping and naval power. Its waterfront bristled with wharves, shipyards, and the masts of sailing vessels. Front and Water streets were jammed with the business of maritime life: warehouses, countinghouses, chandleries, breweries, taverns, and inns.

By the late eighteenth century, many who earned their living from the water lived a little distance from it; most merchants preferred the spacious yet convenient retreat of Society Hill. Those further down the ladder—mariners, sailmakers, coopers, carpenters, rope makers, and riggers—concentrated south of the city, in Dock Ward and Southwark. Front, Water, Catherine, Queen, and Swanson streets were lined with uniform rows of redbrick houses, two and three stories high, with keystone window lintels, white shutters, gable roofs, attic dormers, cellar doors, and white marble steps.

Successive waves of improvements demolished many of these buildings, which themselves had replaced structures erected by earlier settlers. In 1839, the waterfront was extended eastward for the construction of fifty-foot-wide Delaware Avenue (today Christopher Columbus Boulevard) from Vine to South streets. Financed by Stephen Girard's estate, Delaware Avenue was meant to handle the mercantile traffic that had overwhelmed narrow Water Street. Soon, large commercial structures replaced many of the eighteenth- and

early nineteenth-century brick houses between South and Vine streets. From 1897 to 1899, Delaware Avenue was widened to 150 feet and extended north, destroying other parts of the waterfront, especially in previously untouched areas like Kensington. Around 1906, more buildings along Front Street were demolished for an elevated railroad.

The pace of demolition quickened after World War II, when Philadelphia's dormant waterfront fell victim to urban renewal. After the removal of the wholesale food distribution center to Packer Avenue, all structures in the block bounded by Dock, Walnut, Front. and Second streets were demolished in the 1960s. Society Hill Towers (completed 1964) and the Sheraton Society Hill (completed 1984) now occupy much of this space.

The most widespread destruction was triggered by the construction of the Delaware Expressway (Interstate 95) in the 1960s

and 1970s. The federally financed highway cut a gash through three centuries of Philadelphia maritime history, leveling hundreds of structures and thrusting an eight-lane asphalt barrier between the city and its river. Even in Society Hill and Center City, where community and political pressure forced I-95 underground between Delancey and Chestnut streets, the river seems far from the city. In fact, the approaches and bridges built over the sunken portion of I-95 forced the removal of more early buildings along Front and Market streets.

The Southwark district, where a Federal-era waterfront community had remained largely intact for over a century, was especially devastated by I-95. Starting in November 1967, 131 historic houses were demolished, despite a two-year struggle by residents and preservationists. Nearby Queen Village organized to preserve the buildings that remained, forcing the relocation of access ramps to I-95 planned for their area. In 1972, the Southwark Historic District was established, providing some protection for the remaining 600 buildings bordered by Delaware Avenue, Washington Avenue, Fifth, Lombard, Front, and Catherine streets.

Philadelphia's long-term attempts to define and rationalize Penn's Landing—a work in progress since 1967—illustrate its struggle to reconnect with its river heritage. While current plans to erect casinos and luxury condominiums along the area north of Vine Street suggest a waterfront renaissance, these massive structures may place another barrier between the city and the river, except for a few lucky residents or gamblers.

By 1976, construction on Interstate 95 (shown here south of the Benjamin Franklin Bridge) had obliterated hundreds of colonial and Federal structures along the riverfront. (Temple University Libraries, Urban Archives, Philadelphia.)

Walnut Street Jail

Location: Southeast corner of Walnut and Sixth streets
Completed: 1776
Demolished: 1836
Architect/Builder: Robert Smith

As Philadelphia's population exploded, so did its crime rate. With a night watch consisting only of two paid constables and twelve unpaid volunteers, thefts and assaults grew more frequent. The Old Stone Prison at Third and High streets was a poor deterrent; fourteen inmates escaped by scaling its walls between 1729 and 1732 alone. To stop Philadelphia's crime wave, the Pennsylvania Assembly passed a law on February 23, 1773, authorizing the erection of "a commodious, strong, and sufficient gaol, workhouse, and house of correction, with a good yard to each of them, inclosed by a wall of proper height and strength."[5]

The Walnut Street Jail was built between 1773 and 1776 at Walnut and Sixth streets, across from State House Square (Independence Square). The two-story structure, made of gray, rough-cast stone, ran 184 feet along Walnut Street and 32 feet along Sixth. Two perpendicular wings, each about 90 feet long, extended from the rear of the building toward Prune (Locust) Street. Its front elevation, with a projecting center section, bore a strong resemblance to architect Robert Smith's 1754 design for Nassau Hall at the College of New Jersey (today Princeton University). Atop the building stood a cupola with a weathervane in the shape of a gilded key. A two-and-a-half-story stone workhouse stood at the southern end of the lot, facing Prune Street, and a brick wall twenty feet high surrounded the entire lot.

Smith's design introduced numerous innovations over earlier prisons, which thrust inmates into a common, filthy pen. At Walnut Street, prisoners would live in separate cells, each with a privy flushed by a roof cistern. Male and female prisoners would be housed in different wings, and hardened criminals would be separated from lighter offenders. There were dining rooms, baths, and an infirmary. Tile floors supported by stone groin vaults made the prison both fireproof and, supposedly, escape-proof.

The construction of the Walnut Street Jail coincided with the early days of the Revolution. When the jail opened in January 1776, its initial 105 inmates included Tories and prisoners of war in addition to felons and debtors. Later that year, Congress requisitioned the new prison for the confinement of captured enemy personnel and collaborators.

When British forces occupied the city in 1777, the jail became the British provost prison, housing American prisoners of war. Under the sadistic watch of Provost Marshal William Cunningham, inmates were deprived of food, clothing, and blankets. Starving prisoners ate rats, leather scraps, and wood chips; in winter, they shiv-

ered as snow and air poured through the open windows. Hundreds of American soldiers were executed or perished from disease, exposure, and malnutrition. Their bodies were buried in mass graves across Sixth Street in the Strangers' Burying Ground (later Washington Square).

But even after the prison returned to civilian use, it resembled the hellholes it had been designed to replace. In 1787, the Society for Alleviating the Miseries of Public Prisons (today the Pennsylvania Prison Society), organized to inspect and reform the Walnut Street Jail, called it "an Augean stable of filth and iniquity," run by a former tavern owner who prospered selling liquor and collecting bribes from his inmates.[6]

The society agitated to separate the sexes, ban liquor, provide proper food and clothing for prisoners, separate hardened convicts

In this William Birch print, created ca. 1800, two constables armed with clubs lead a group of miscreants to their new lodgings in the Walnut Street Jail. (The Philadelphia Print Shop.)

from untried prisoners, close the dungeons, and introduce religious instruction. By 1810 conditions had improved: No more than thirty men slept in a room, and each had his own blanket.

In 1791, the first penitentiary in the United States was established in the rear of the jail yard. The "penitentiary house" was a rectangular, two-story brick structure, supported on arches to ensure that prisoners would not tunnel out. The building contained sixteen cells, each six by eight feet, with one small window and no beds. In these cells, prisoners were kept alone to meditate upon and repent for their sins. In addition to solitary confinement, the penitentiary pioneered the use of religious study and productive labor to rehabilitate inmates. As part of what would later be called the Pennsylvania System, workshops erected in a half-octagonal structure behind the original jail in 1795 allowed prisoners to work as weavers, shoemakers, tailors, carpenters, and stone carvers; fire destroyed the shops in 1798.

As both the city and its social problems grew, the Walnut Street Jail became densely overcrowded. Between 1791 and 1822, the number of inmates in the main part of the prison jumped from 143 to 804. Escapes and riots grew commonplace. A new prison opened on Arch Street (on the current site of the Municipal Services Building) in 1816, followed by the Eastern State Penitentiary in 1830 and the Philadelphia County (Moyamensing) Prison in 1835.

In 1836, the Walnut Street Jail was demolished and the property sold to John Moss for $299,000. When Moss's proposal to erect a luxury hotel fell through, the lot was cut up into building sites and Adelphi Street run through the property. In 1845, John Notman's Athenaeum was erected on what had been the west side of the prison yard. Ironically, the prison site itself became a string of law offices known as Lawyers' Row. In 1913, Lawyers' Row was demolished for the Penn Mutual Life Insurance Company headquarters, which still occupies the site. The only surviving trace of the Walnut Street Prison is its key-shaped weathervane, which resides today at the Atwater Kent Museum.

Carlton

Location: 2932 Midvale Avenue (south side of Midvale at Stokley Street)
Built: 1780
Demolished: 1948
Architect/Builder: Isaac Tustin

In 1771, wine merchant Henry Hill, whose Madeira was one of Philadelphia's favorite postprandial tipples, acquired a 31-acre tract on the border between lower Germantown and Roxborough Township. Despite the upheavals of the Revolution, Hill expanded his holdings between 1776 and 1792, assembling a 180-acre estate he named Roxborough Plantation. An early eighteenth-century farmhouse there served as headquarters for George Washington before and after the Battle of the Brandywine in August–September 1777. In October 1777, Hessian General Wilhelm Knyphausen occupied the house during the Battle of Germantown.

In 1780, Hill constructed a two-story, stucco-over-stone structure, fifty-two by twenty-three feet, that incorporated or replaced the war-ravaged farmhouse. A tablet placed in a nearby stone wall noted that the house was:

> Ruined by the war of 1777
> Rebuilt more firmly 1780 by
> The trusty Isaac Tustin.[7]

When peace arrived, Hill added a two-story brick structure to the west of his original house, possibly for one of his six sisters. During this period, Hill also built a new city residence on part of the former Almshouse property at 321 South Fourth Street, known today as the Hill-Physick-Keith House. After Hill's death from yellow fever in 1798, Roxborough Plantation was divided among his sisters.

In 1830, John Craig acquired the house and ten acres of land and named his new purchase Carlton, after one of Queen Elizabeth's castles. He added two frame wings on either side of the original structure, connecting the 1780s addition. By 1840, Carlton was a sprawling country house 128 feet long, its original façade sheltered by a wide verandah and graced by a massive Palladian window on the second floor. Craig used the property as a stock farm, constructing a racecourse for his horses.

Carlton survived until 1948, when it was doomed by the demand for affordable postwar housing. During the early twentieth century, the surrounding neighborhood had grown more suburban, as East Falls spread north and Germantown spread south. Carlton's 3.6 acres were one of the few large parcels of open land in the area. In February 1948, a real estate developer demolished Carlton and its colonial barn to erect three apartment buildings as part of the Queen Lane Manor housing project. An *Evening Bulletin* article detailing Carlton's destruction bore the headline, "Germantown Mansion Bows to March of Progress."

The north façade of Carlton, also known as the Carlton-Smith Mansion, in 1913. (The Library Company of Philadelphia.)

Bingham Mansion House

Location: West side of South Third Street between Walnut and Spruce streets
Completed: 1787
Demolished: ca. 1850
Architect/Builder: John Plaw

When Philadelphia shone as the brightest star in the young American galaxy, its domestic architecture achieved new magnificence. Wealthy merchants and entrepreneurs like Robert Morris and Henry Hill competed in building extravagant city houses. The acknowledged winner, however, was the Bingham Mansion House on South Third Street, the most lavish residence in Philadelphia and possibly in the new nation.

Starting as an agent for American privateers, William Bingham became a successful banker, land speculator, and politician who married the lovely heiress Anne Willing. After the Revolution, the Binghams spent four years in Europe, where they grew enamored of English styles and status. When they returned home in 1786, they decided to build a larger version of the London house of the Duke of Manchester on Third Street, the most fashionable thoroughfare in Society Hill.

The three-story Mansion House stood forty feet back from Third Street, shielded by a brick wall and reached by a circular carriageway. One of the first Philadelphia structures built in the full Federal style, the symmetrical mansion featured a massive front entrance framed by a rusticated stone arch, topped by a Palladian balcony window on the second floor. A large lunette window on the third floor mirrored the fanlight over the front door. Carved marble plaques decorated the space above the slender side windows on the second floor. Matching two-story wings topped by marble balustrades framed the central structure.

But the Mansion House's true glory lay in its interior design. Visitors entered a soaring center hall with a marble floor in a mosaic pattern, the first of its kind in the country. Passing the banqueting room and ballroom, they ascended a self-supporting staircase to the *piano nobile*, a high-ceilinged suite of public rooms on the second floor. After a liveried servant announced their names, the dazzled guests entered a drawing room lined with mirror-covered folding doors and lit by glass chandeliers. Tall windows offered a view of the three-acre garden, stretching to Fourth Street, bordered by Lombardy poplars and filled with statues, exotic plants, and parterres. The house was decorated with French carpets and furniture, damask curtains, Italian paintings and sculptures, and arabesque wallpaper by Reveillon.

When Philadelphia became the nation's capital in 1790, Anne Bingham quickly established herself as its leading hostess. Her salons attracted Washington, Adams, Jefferson, and other members of the "Republican Court," along with foreign dignitaries like Talleyrand and La Rochefoucauld. According to John Fanning Watson, the Binghams hosted the first masquerade ball in the United States. William Bingham's magnificent residences at Third Street and at Lansdowne, his country estate, reflected his status as a U.S. senator and a director of the First Bank of the United States.

The Binghams and their mansion also drew censure from visitors who considered both too imperially glamorous for a young republic. In 1789, architect Charles Bulfinch wrote that the Bingham house "would be esteemed splendid even in the most luxurious parts of Europe" but found it "far too rich for any man in this country."[8] (His feelings didn't stop him from copying the house's design for the Benjamin Otis House in Boston.) Peter Markoe wrote a poem lampooning Bingham's ill-gotten wealth, "wrung . . . by arts, which petty scoundrels would abhor," and his mansion, to which "wits and fops repair, to game, to feast, to flatter, and to stare."[9]

After enjoying a glorious decade as America's social arbiter, Anne Bingham was carried from the house in April 1801 suffering from a "serious affection of the lungs."[10] She sailed with her husband for Bermuda, her coffin in the ship's hold, and died the following month at age thirty-seven. The grief-stricken William retired to England, where he died in 1804 at the age of fifty-two.

After Bingham's death, the mansion became the Mansion-House Hotel, the city's most luxurious hotel, charging its guests an astronomical ten dollars a week. From 1813 to 1816, the Washington Benevolent Society, a mutual aid group for the poor and unemployed, occupied the mansion and erected Washington Hall next to it when the house grew too small for its needs. Damaged by a fire in 1823, the mansion reopened as Head's Mansion House, a hotel popular with actors Charles and Fanny Kemble. A second fire in 1847 ruined the mansion beyond repair, and it was demolished around 1850. It was replaced by a row of brownstones built by Michael Bouvier, great-great-grandfather of Jacqueline Bouvier Kennedy Onassis, several of which still stand.

Elegant Philadelphians promenade in front of the Bingham Mansion House in a 1799 print by William Birch. (The Philadelphia Print Shop.)

Library Hall/The Library Company of Philadelphia

Location: 105 South Fifth Street (east side, between Chestnut and Walnut)
Completed: 1790
Demolished: 1887
Architect/Builder: William Thornton

The first circulating library in America was founded in 1731 by Benjamin Franklin and other members of the Junto, young tradesmen and mechanics bent on self-improvement and self-advancement. Unable to afford their own books, the fifty original members each subscribed forty shillings, plus ten shillings a year, to buy books and maintain a shareholder's library. For most of its first sixty years, the Library Company rented quarters in the west wing of the State House (1740–1773) and Carpenters' Hall (1773–1790). With its extensive collection in history, law, and politics, the Library Company served as the first Library of Congress for delegates to the two Continental Congresses and the Constitutional Convention.

In 1789, the directors of the Library Company purchased land on Fifth Street, directly across from the American Philosophical Society's newly opened Philosophical Hall on State House Square. They announced a competition for a new building that would be seventy by forty-eight feet, two stories, and "as elegant as the unavoidable frugality of the Plan will admit."[11] The winner was William Thornton, a physician who would later design the Capitol in Washington, D.C. Sounding like the epitome of an eighteenth-century gentleman architect, Thornton later recalled: "When I traveled, I never thought of architecture, but I got some books and worked a few days, then gave a plan in the ancient Ionic order, which carried the day."[12]

Thornton created a simple yet elegant Palladian brick structure with a hipped roof. Four white pilasters with Ionic capitals supported a central projecting pediment on the front façade. A balustrade decorated with urns extended on both sides of the pediment, while a curving double flight of steps led to an imposing doorway. The cornerstone—with text mostly composed by the Library Company's most illustrious founder, Benjamin Franklin—was laid on August 31, 1789. Franklin did not live to see Library Hall open on January 1, 1791. In his honor, a marble statue of Franklin in a toga was placed in a niche above the doorway in 1792. Carved by Francesco Lazzarini, the statue was donated by William Bingham at a cost of more than 500 guineas.

Between 1792 and 1794, an east wing was added to Library Hall to house the Loganian Library, formerly located on South Sixth Street. James Logan, William Penn's secretary and later governor of Pennsylvania, had left his private collection to the public as the Loganian Library, the first free library in America, after his death in 1751. Logan's sole descendant and trustee arranged for the Library Company to take custody of the older library's 4,000 volumes and to ensure that it was kept intact and separate within its new home.

By the 1860s, Library Hall—also known as the Old Philadelphia or Franklin Library—contained nearly 100,000 volumes, as well as the 10,000 books of the Loganian Library. In addition, the building held such treasures as William Penn's desk and grandfather clock, James Logan's library table from Stenton, and a huge bust of Minerva that had once graced the House of Representatives at Sixth and Chestnut streets.

By this time, shareholders were concerned about the building's age, small size, and flammability. In 1869, Dr. James Rush (son of Benjamin Rush) left the Library Company a million dollars for a large, fireproof building at Broad and Christian streets. A decade later, the Library Company moved into the Parthenon-like Ridgway Library (today the Philadelphia High School for the Creative and Performing Arts). Since many members objected to traveling so far south to borrow books, the Library Company commissioned Frank Furness to design a modern, angular version of its original

building as a branch at Juniper and Locust streets. (This building was demolished in 1940.)

Shortly after the Furness branch opened, the Fifth Street property and building were sold. In 1887, Library Hall was replaced by the Drexel Building, which was in turn torn down for Independence National Historical Park in the 1950s. In 1954, the American Philosophical Society commissioned the firm of Martin, Stewart and Noble to recreate the 1789 design on the original

site, complete with a replica of the Lazzarini statue of Franklin, for its own library.

Today, the original Franklin statue resides in the latest home of the Library Company of Philadelphia, a 1964 Carroll, Grisdale & Van Alen building at 1314 Locust Street. The Library Company still houses the books ordered from London in 1732, along with 500,000 books and printed volumes, 75,000 graphics, 160,000 manuscripts, and a priceless collection of early American art and artifacts.

United States Mint

Location: 37–39 North Seventh Street (east side, between Arch and Filbert streets)
Completed: 1792
Demolished: 1911
Architect/Builder: Unknown

One of the first priorities of the central government established by the 1787 Constitutional Convention was the creation of an American currency. After the Revolution, trade was conducted not only in Continental dollars, but in "Pennsylvania pounds," English pounds, French livres, Spanish pieces of eight, and other European currencies. Merchants and tradespeople had to memorize a dozen different exchange rates, and currency conversion manuals were best sellers. Besides causing confusion, the lack of a strong single currency helped fuel the monetary inflation and speculation that plagued the new country.

In February 1791, the Bank of the United States was chartered as the country's national bank. As the next step, an act passed in April 1792 established a national mint that would produce coins using the decimal system, rather than the British method of pounds, shillings, and pence. President George Washington appointed astronomer and inventor David Rittenhouse as its first director.

Rittenhouse purchased two lots on Seventh Street north of Sugar Alley (later Farmer Street and then Filbert Street). Within a few months, the three structures of the U.S. Mint were in place. The main building, a three-story brick double house fronting on Seventh Street, contained offices, precious metal vaults, an assay laboratory, and rooms for deposits and weighing. Behind it stood the two-story coinage house, where the coins were struck. At the rear of the lot stood a one-and-a-half-story smelting house, where

An idealized view of the first U.S. Mint in its prime, painted ca. 1911 by Edwin Lamasure. The watercolor was commissioned by Frank H. Stewart, the man responsible for the mint's destruction. (Courtesy of Robert M. Skaler.)

a furnace purified metallic ore and a rolling mill produced metal sheets. These were the first public buildings authorized by the U.S. government.

In November 1792, with George Washington present, the U.S. Mint struck its first coins, half-dismes (five-cent pieces). The first coin actually circulated by the mint was the 1793 copper "chain cent," with the Goddess of Liberty on the front and a chain of fifteen links (for the fifteen states) on the reverse. By 1795, the mint was producing a full range of coins, from copper halfpennies to ten-dollar gold eagles.

Unfortunately, the mint was unable to meet the growing demand for coinage. With only men and horses to power its mills and presses (the first steam engine was installed in 1816), production was limited. Yellow fever epidemics shut down the mint repeatedly. It was forced to buy metals at above-market rates, meaning that a coin's raw materials often cost more than its face value. To cope, merchants used British currency in tandem with U.S. coins until November 1800. Congress, unhappy with the mint's erratic productivity, introduced bills to abolish it in 1800 and 1802.

When the federal government moved south, the U.S. Mint stayed in Philadelphia—partly to placate the city for its loss of status, but primarily to help the cash-strapped government save money. In 1828, an act of Congress guaranteed that Philadelphia would keep the mint "until otherwise provided by law." The mint remained on Seventh Street until 1833, when it moved to a larger, modern facility at Chestnut and Juniper streets. In 1836, the government sold the Seventh Street property at auction for $8,100. After housing the Apprentices' Library, the buildings were occupied by a series of shops and businesses. One of its last owners painted the words "Ye Olde Mint 1792" on the main building's façade.

In 1907, Frank H. Stewart purchased the property, demolished the smelting house, and announced plans to destroy the remaining structures for an office building to house his electrical supply business. In 1911, Stewart offered the main and coinage buildings to the City Councils, provided that the city move them from his prop-

The Seventh Street façade of the U.S. Mint, photographed shortly before the building's demolition in 1911. (Collection of the author.)

erty. Since Stewart made his offer in July, when the councils were on vacation, it was no surprise that the city did not act in time to save the buildings.

A month later, Stewart demolished the main and coinage buildings, replacing them with a six-story steel and concrete structure he called The Old Mint Building. The mint's original marble steps and doorsills were smashed, except for the sill to the front door of the main building, salvaged for a lawn ornament by a New Jersey dentist. Stewart later cast himself as the mint's memorialist, writing its history and commissioning a painting of the original complex by Edwin Lamasure.

The Old Mint Building stood until 1968, when it was demolished along with other buildings on its block for the William J. Green Jr. Federal Office Building and the U.S. Courthouse. During the same period, the fourth and current U.S. Mint was constructed on the east side of Independence Mall, two blocks from the site of the first mint.

President's House/Masters-Penn House

Location: 526–530 Market Street (south side, between Fifth and Sixth streets)
Completed: ca. 1768
Demolished: 1832 (some portions survived until 1951)
Architect/Builder: Unknown

Presidential Mansion

Location: West side of Ninth Street, between Market and Chestnut streets
Completed: 1797
Demolished: 1829
Architect/Builder: attributed variously to Pierre Charles L'Enfant, William Williams, and John Smith

During its interregnum as the national capital, Philadelphia had two president's houses (four if you include the Dove and Deshler-Morris Houses in then separate Germantown). The Masters-Penn House was home to the Washington and Adams households from 1790 to 1800. The grandiose Presidential Mansion built for them was never used.

The real President's House at what was then 190 High Street was built by the wealthy Masters family in 1767–68. The three-and-a-half-story brick mansion stood forty-five feet wide on High Street and fifty feet deep. One of the largest and handsomest buildings in the city, it was given to the daughter of the owner on her marriage to Richard Penn, grandson of William Penn and lieutenant governor of the province. During the British occupation of 1777–78, General Sir William Howe commandeered it as his residence and headquarters. After the Revolution, military governor General Benedict Arnold rented the house during the time he began his treasonous arrangement with Great Britain. After Arnold departed,

the French consul lived in the house until a fire burned out the top stories on January 2, 1780.

In 1781, the Penns sold the ruined house to financier Robert Morris, who rebuilt and expanded it. Morris increased the height of the house, adding a steeply pitched roof to create a full attic. A back building connected to the main house by a piazza held the kitchen, washhouse, bedrooms, and a bathing room. Behind the back building stood the stable yard, stable, coach house and ice-house. A walled garden ran along the west side of the lot.

During the Constitutional Convention, George Washington stayed at the house as the Morrises' guest. When he prepared to return to Philadelphia as president in 1790, the city offered him the house for his official residence, and the Morrises moved next door. More alterations were made, including the addition of bow windows in the rear, an enlargement of the servants' hall, and the erection of quarters for the nine African slaves Washington brought from Virginia. Despite this expansion, the Washingtons still found the house far too small for their thirty-person household when they took possession in November 1790.

During Washington's administration, the President's House was one of the centers of Philadelphia social life, with weekly president's levees (formal receptions) and state dinners, in addition to public receptions on holidays. After the Washingtons returned to Mount Vernon in 1797, President John Adams and his family occupied the house until 1800, when they moved to Washington, D.C.

After the Adamses' departure, the President's House became Francis's Union Hotel. As Market Street between Fifth and Sixth

---

Facing page: **T**he President's House at 190 High Street, looking southeast from the north side of Market Street, in a ca. 1830 watercolor by William L. Breton for John Fanning Watson's *Annals of Philadelphia*. Breton's fairly accurate representation of the Masters-Penn House was supplanted by later erroneous conceptions until unearthed by Edward Lawler Jr., Independence Hall Association Historian, whose painstaking research has brought this nearly forgotten structure back to life. (Athenaeum of Philadelphia.)

grew commercial, the house was stripped of much of its architectural detail, the ground floor was converted to shops, and the upper floors became a boardinghouse. In 1832, the building was gutted, leaving only the side walls and foundations, and three stores were fitted into the Market Street frontage. The stores and part of the western wall were demolished between 1935 and 1941. Ironically, the remaining walls of the President's House were torn down in 1951–52 to create Independence Mall, and a restroom was erected on the site in 1954.

In 2000, the National Park Service announced its plans for the new Liberty Bell Center, with an entrance covering the rear of the Presidential Mansion lot on the site of the smokehouse where most of Washington's slaves were quartered. After criticism of these plans reached the U.S. House of Representatives, the National Park Service agreed to revise its design to include a memorial to the house and its residents, including Washington's slaves. In 2007, ground was broken for a $5.2 million President's House memorial, designed by Kelly/Maiello Architects & Planners, which will be the first national commemoration of American slaves.

Three blocks west of the President's House stood the "President's House that never was," authorized by the Pennsylvania Legislature in 1791 as an official presidential residence. Many Philadelphians hoped that building a magnificent mansion, even on the outskirts of town, would persuade the government to remain after the Residence Act expired in December 1800. They might have sensed the futility of their gesture when Washington, anxious to move the government to his native Virginia, skipped the groundbreaking.

The empty Presidential Mansion on sparsely settled Ninth Street, drawn by William Birch in 1799 as the federal government prepared to leave Philadelphia for the District of Columbia. (The Library Company of Philadelphia.)

The mansion was unlike anything ever built in Philadelphia: an immense, three-story, five-bay square edifice of brick trimmed with marble, more than twice the size of the State House. At the center of its hipped roof was a glass dome and cupola topped by a gilded eagle. The façade featured twin Palladian windows on the end bays, and eight Corinthian pilasters rising from a marble belt between the first and second floors.

The first floor consisted of seven large, high-ceilinged public rooms. At its center was a domed, circular hall with double stairs leading to a gallery supported by eight Corinthian columns. The second and third floors contained the presidential apartments. The entire building was decorated with a profusion of carved and painted designs, including acanthus leaves, festoons of fruits and flowers, cornucopias, and other classical motifs.

Completion was delayed for almost three years when the state legislature refused to provide additional funds. When it was finally finished in March 1797 (at a cost of over $110,000), it was offered to incoming President Adams at a rent he might obtain on "any other suitable house in Philadelphia."[13] Despite this handsome offer, Adams declined. The federal government departed as planned, and the Presidential Mansion sat empty for five years.

In July 1800, the University of Pennsylvania bought the Mansion and its sizable lot at auction for $41,650. The university occupied the mansion in 1802, later hiring Benjamin Latrobe to remodel it and build the Medical School next to it. When the school required more space, it demolished the Presidential Mansion in 1829 and commissioned William Strickland to design two new buildings on the site. After the University of Pennsylvania moved to West Philadelphia in 1872, Alfred Mullett's Victorian post office stood on the site from 1873 to 1884, in turn replaced in 1935 by the current U.S. Post Office and Federal Building.

Today, the cornerstone for the President's House, noting that it was laid on May 10, 1792, "when Pennsylvania was happily out of debt," resides in Room 200 of College Hall on the University of Pennsylvania campus.

First Chestnut Street Theatre

Location: 603–609 Chestnut Street (northwest corner of Sixth and Chestnut streets)
Completed: 1794
Demolished: 1820
Architect/Builder: John Inigo Richards (later work by Benjamin Latrobe)

From 1790 to 1830, when New York's Times Square was still a wilderness, Philadelphia was the theatrical capital of America. Thanks to Quaker censure, drama got off to a slow start in Philadelphia. The first players' troupes to visit were either run out of town or forced to perform outside the city limits in Southwark. Yet Philadelphia (or rather its southern border) was home to one of the first American theaters, the Southwark at South and Apollo (Leithgow) streets. On April 24, 1767, the first play by an American writer to be produced on an American stage, Thomas Godfrey's *The Prince of Parthia*, premiered at the Southwark.

By 1791, Philadelphia was the nation's capital, and a far more worldly and wealthy city than it had been before the Revolution. The last law prohibiting plays and players had been repealed in 1789, clearing the way for a theatrical renaissance. Actor-manager Thomas Wignell and musician Hugh Reinagle raised funds by selling shares to Robert Morris, William Bingham, Henry Hill, and about a hundred other leading citizens. With their revenues, they commissioned the Chestnut Street Theatre, the largest and most lavish playhouse in North America. Using the Royal Theatre at Bath for a model, architect John Inigo Richards created a three-and-a-half-story brick structure with a large central Palladian window on the second floor and a pedimented gable decorated with a lunette window. A wooden awning protected theatergoers from the elements.

The theater had a seating capacity of 1,165 in three horseshoe galleries and a thirteen-row parquet. Fluted and gilded Corinthian columns supported the galleries, which were decorated with crimson drapes and pale rose panels. Above the stage, an eagle hovering over a classical figure represented America encouraging the drama; below the painting were the words, "For useful mirth or salutary woe." The stage was lit with oil lamps, which were raised or lowered depending on the mood of the scene.

Begun in 1791, the Chestnut Street Theatre did not open until February 17, 1794, because of the yellow fever epidemic of 1793. A troupe of British actors proved immensely popular in a repertoire that included works by Shakespeare, Richard Sheridan, and John Otway. George Washington and his family were frequent visitors, occupying a stage box decorated with the U.S. seal. On December 23, 1799, the theater presented a special evening of music and drama to mourn its presidential patron, who had died at Mount Vernon nine days earlier.

Soon, other theaters like Rickett's Circus began to compete with Old Drury, as the Chestnut Street Theatre was called. Its managers hired Benjamin Henry Latrobe to freshen up the theater in 1801. Latrobe added a new front entrance, with a Corinthian colonnade running between two projecting marble wings ornamented with sculptured panels. Statues of Comedy and Tragedy, carved by William Rush, were placed in niches on either side of the Palladian window (today they are in the Philadelphia Museum of Art). The

managers' taste exceeded their purse: The Corinthian columns were made of wood and papier-mâché, and four years later Latrobe complained bitterly that he had still not been paid.

In 1816, the Chestnut Street became the first U.S. theater to install gas lighting; the managers noted that audiences would surely appreciate its "superior safety, brilliancy, and neatness."[14] On the evening of Easter Sunday, April 2, 1820, a fire broke out at the theater, possibly caused by a gas leak. Besides Rush's statues of Comedy and Tragedy, the only items salvaged were the green-room mirror, a ship model, and the prompter's clock. In the grand tradition of "the show must go on," the managers were soon selling shares for a new Chestnut Street Theatre designed by William Strickland, which opened on the site on December 2, 1822.

The Chestnut Street Theatre with Benjamin Henry Latrobe's new façade, drawn by William Birch after 1801. William Rush's statues of Comedy and Tragedy were not placed in the niches on either side of the Palladian window until 1808. (The Philadelphia Print Shop.)

African Church of Philadelphia
(African Episcopal Church of St. Thomas)

Location: Southwest corner of Fifth and Adelphi streets
(St. James' Place)
Completed: 1794
Demolished: 1887
Architect/Builder: Unknown

Bethel Church (Mother Bethel
African Methodist Episcopal Church)

Location: 419 Richard Allen Avenue (northeast corner of Sixth and
Lombard streets)
Completed: 1794
Demolished: 1805
Architect/Builder: Unknown

After the Revolution, more free African Americans lived in Philadelphia than in any other U.S. city. In 1787, Richard Allen and Absalom Jones, former slaves and lay ministers at St. George's Methodist Episcopal Church, founded the Free African Society, a mutual aid organization serving the social, financial, and religious needs of their community. While many blacks attended Methodist services because of John Wesley's staunch opposition to slavery, Allen and Jones felt that a distinctly nondenominational church was needed to strengthen the black community. Their movement gained momentum when the white elders of St. George's insisted that its black members sit in a newly built upper gallery and physically removed those sitting downstairs during services.

In response, Allen, Jones, and other black Methodists left St. George's en masse and established the African Church of Philadelphia, which historian Gary Nash has called "the first free black church in the northern states of the new American republic."[15] With the support of the Society of Friends, the Pennsylvania Abolition Society, and private citizens, they purchased land at Fifth and Adelphi streets and began construction.

In his autobiography, Benjamin Rush writes of attending the roof raising of the African Church on August 22, 1793. After Rush and a hundred other whites sat down to dinner at an outdoor table and were served by members of the African Church, they changed places, and the whites served the blacks dinner. Rush offered two toasts to the joyful crowd: "Peace on earth and good will to man," and "May African Churches everywhere soon succeed African bondage."[16] Work on the church was suspended during the yellow fever epidemic that began in September. During the epidemic, Allen, Jones, and other African Church members served heroically

A Sunday-morning view of the African Episcopal Church of St. Thomas in the 1820s, drawn by William L. Breton. St. Thomas's occupied this structure from 1794 until 1887, when it was sold for development. (The Historical Society of Pennsylvania.)

as nurses, gravediggers, and death-cart drivers, under the mistaken belief that blacks were immune to yellow fever.

By spring 1794, the church was finished, a simple yet handsome two-and-a-half-story brick building with a gable roof and a Roman arch door and windows. An Old Testament text, "The people that walked in darkness have seen a great light" (Isaiah 9:2), was etched in marble above the church doors. The church held its first service on July 17, 1794.

At this time, a majority of the church's members decided to affiliate with the Episcopal Church, and the African Church was renamed the African Episcopal Church of St. Thomas. Richard Allen declined the post of minister, saying that he could not leave the Methodist church despite his treatment at St. George's. Instead, his friend and associate Absalom Jones became the first minister. In 1795 Jones was ordained as deacon and in 1804 became the first black Episcopal priest in the new nation.

The church remained in its first home until 1887, when rising property values compelled it to sell its property to a commercial developer. After several moves, the African Episcopal Church of St. Thomas is now located at 6361 Lancaster Avenue, in the former St. Paul's Overbrook church.

After leaving St. Thomas's, Allen used his own money to purchase a wooden blacksmith's shop on the grounds of the Walnut Street Prison and had it hauled to a plot he owned at Sixth and Lombard streets. The converted blacksmith's shop was dedicated on July 29, 1794, less than two weeks after the first service at St. Thomas's. At its dedication, Methodist elder John Dickins prayed that the church might be a Bethel, or house of God, to thousands of souls, giving the church its name, Bethel Church. In June 1799, Allen was ordained as the first black Methodist deacon.

By 1805, church membership had increased to nearly 500, more than twice what the building could handle. It was replaced by a second church called the Roughcast because it was built from rough cinder blocks. In 1816, this building was the site of the formation of the African Methodist Episcopal Church in America, which resulted in the church's being known as "Mother Bethel." A red-brick building similar to St. Thomas's replaced the Roughcast in 1841 and was replaced in turn by the present Romanesque Revival church, designed by Hazlehurst & Huckel and completed in 1890.

Today, Mother Bethel A.M.E. Church, which W.E.B. DuBois once called "the vastest and most remarkable product of American Negro civilization," stands on the oldest piece of property continuously owned by African Americans in the United States.[17] Founder Richard Allen and his wife, Sarah, are entombed in a crypt in the church basement.

An 1829 view of the Roughcast, second home of the Bethel Church, drawn by William L. Breton. The first convention of the Unified African Methodist Episcopal Church was held here, the home of Mother Bethel from 1805 until 1841. (The Library Company of Philadelphia.)

Facing page: In this 1799 William Birch print, teams of horses pull the former black-smith's shop that would serve as the first home of the Bethel Church to its new location at Sixth and Lombard streets, where the current church still stands. (The Philadelphia Print Shop.)

Athens of America | 67

Robert Morris Residence

Location: 714–716 Walnut Street (block bordered by Walnut, Chestnut, Seventh, and Eighth streets)
Begun: 1794 (never finished)
Demolished: 1800
Architect/Builder: Pierre Charles L'Enfant

Many fortunes were won and lost in the rollercoaster economy of the 1790s, with investors speculating wildly on the unseen frontier lands of the new Republic. One of the most dramatic cases was that of Robert Morris, financier of the American Revolution. One of only two men (the other was Roger Sherman) to sign all three of the Republic's founding documents—the Declaration of Independence, the Articles of Confederation, and the Constitution—Morris ended his illustrious career in debtor's prison.

As superintendent of finance for the Continental Congress, Morris was responsible for financing the American rebellion. Besides lending large amounts from his own fortune, he established the Bank of North America as the country's first national bank. As head of the Secret Committee of Commerce, Morris procured, with no oversight, arms and supplies for the Continental Army, cutting deals that made him the wealthiest merchant in America. While many Americans hailed him as a founding father, others reviled him as a self-serving war profiteer.

After the Revolution, U.S. senator Morris vied with William Bingham for the title of wealthiest Philadelphian. The completion of Bingham's Mansion House in 1787 may have inspired Morris to build his own dream house. Morris sold his Market Street holdings, including the President's House, to purchase an entire block of land in the western section of the city for £10,000. As a lover of French culture (his French chefs were the envy of Philadelphia), Morris hired Pierre Charles L'Enfant to design his house, a decision he lived to regret. L'Enfant was an early "starchitect," dismissed by George Washington from his post as planner of the District of Columbia because of his dictatorial manner and cost overruns.

For Morris, L'Enfant designed a two-story mansion in the style of a Parisian *hôtel*. Historian Thompson Westcott estimated that the house stood between eighty and one hundred feet wide on Chestnut Street, and forty to sixty feet deep. A large central doorway framed by columns stood in the center of the Chestnut Street façade, with porticoed entrances at the four corners. Marble window surrounds, moldings, and carvings decorated the brick walls. Two large cupolas were planned but never completed. The mansion featured details borrowed from French urban architecture, including ornamental iron railings and perhaps the first mansard roof in the United States.

Ground was broken in 1794, but construction proceeded slowly. In 1796, when the building was still an empty shell, Morris

Robert Morris's unfinished Chestnut Street house as depicted by William Birch in 1800. After World War II, the Chestnut Street Association placed a tablet at 714–716 Chestnut Street to mark the location of the mansion. (The Philadelphia Print Shop.)

complained bitterly to L'Enfant about the intolerable "delay and accumulation of Expense."[18] Construction ceased completely when the bankrupt Morris went into hiding in 1797 to escape his creditors. Local moralists seized upon "Morris's Folly" as the cause of his ruin. John Fanning Watson later wrote that the ruined Morris "has been heard to vent imprecations on himself and his lavish architect."[19]

While the mansion may have contributed to his ruin, Morris was actually bankrupted by the collapse of speculative real estate investments in Washington, D.C., and on the American frontier. His holdings and possessions were sold to satisfy his creditors, and Morris was imprisoned for debt at the Walnut Street Jail from 1798 until 1801. The only inhabitants of his unfinished mansion were women prisoners from Walnut Street quarantined there during the 1798 yellow fever epidemic.

When no one bought "Morris's Folly" at auction, the white elephant was dismantled and its materials sold separately in 1800, shortly after William Birch had drawn the only existing picture of the structure for his *Views of Philadelphia*. William Sansom, who bought the plot and opened Sansom Street through it, recycled some of the materials into Sansom Row, one of the first planned row-house developments in Philadelphia.

Traces of "Morris's Folly" decorated other local buildings for years. Bas-reliefs of Tragedy and Comedy, carved by Jardella, were added to the wings of the Chestnut Street Theatre during Benjamin Latrobe's redesign. Two marble dogs meant to guard the Morris mansion stood in front of Fritz's Marble Yard on Race Street between Sixth and Seventh streets.

For many years, a beautiful marble plaque from Morris's house decorated a fieldstone farmhouse on Butler Pike near Plymouth Meeting. The four-foot bas-relief showed two cherubs, representing art and literature, supporting a central medallion with a portrait of the Madonna. When the "Angel House" was pulled down in 1927 by the Philadelphia Electric Company for a high-tension line, a company official took the plaque for his Maryland home.

St. Augustine Roman Catholic Church

Location: West side of Fourth Street, between Vine and Race streets
Completed: 1801
Demolished: 1844
Architect/Builder: Nicholas Fagan (later work by William Strickland)

Thanks to the religious freedom guaranteed by William Penn, Philadelphia was the first city in the English-speaking world where eighteenth-century Catholics could worship openly. By 1790, the city was home to one of the largest Catholic populations in the country, and to three Catholic churches, all located south of Walnut Street: St. Joseph's (founded 1733), St. Mary's (founded 1763), and Holy Trinity (founded 1789).

In 1796, Matthew Carr, an Augustinian friar at St. Mary's, called for the establishment of a new church to serve the growing Irish Catholic community in the Northern Liberties. In June 1796, Carr purchased a lot on Fourth Street south of Vine and opened a subscription list to build the first Augustinian church in Philadelphia. The initial subscribers included President George Washington, as well as such prominent Catholics as Commodore John Barry, merchant Stephen Girard, and publisher Matthew Carey. Despite their support, construction dragged on for five years.

When St. Augustine's was finally dedicated in June 1801, it was the largest of the city's four Catholic churches, measuring 62 by 125 feet. Unlike the earlier churches, whose original entrances were set away from the street, St. Augustine's presented a handsome classical façade on Fourth Street. A recessed central pavilion featured a large pedimented door surrounded by tall arched windows and framed by two square corner towers, each of which also had a pedimented doorway topped by Palladian windows.

By 1828, the growing church served several thousand parishioners. William Strickland redesigned its façade, adding a new spire that rose to 188 feet. Above the steeple's clock tower stood a domed

cupola surmounted by a gilded cross. Since Strickland was rebuilding the State House tower at the same time, he may have facilitated the sale of the old State House clock and bell to St. Augustine's. The bell, used to ring the hours after the first bell (later the Liberty Bell) proved unsatisfactory, was called the Sister Bell. The church boasted frescoes and an altarpiece by Nicola Monachesi, and a wooden sculpture of the Crucifixion by William Rush.

On nearby Crown Street stood St. Augustine's Academy, a church school founded in 1811 and the forerunner of Villanova University. Among the school's prize possessions was a 3,000-volume theological library, one of the largest in the country. During an 1832 cholera epidemic, both this school and the Augustinian convent were converted to hospitals, where physicians ministered to several hundred patients of all faiths.

As immigration brought thousands of European Catholics to the United States, resentment toward the newcomers grew among native-born Protestant Americans. The 1840s saw the emergence of the Nativist (also known as Native American or Know-Nothing) party in Philadelphia and other cities. On May 3, 1844, Irish Catholic workers broke up a Nativist meeting in Kensington, touching off a violent, week-long reprisal. On May 8, after burning down a Catholic church, school, rectory, and female seminary in Kensington, Nativists turned their sights on St. Augustine's Church.

Despite the presence of Mayor John M. Scott, Sheriff Morton McMichael, the police, and the First City Troop Cavalry, members of the mob set St. Augustine's on fire. The mob also burned the academy, destroying its priceless library, and smashed gravestones in the churchyard. Within a few hours, nothing was left of St. Augustine's except a blackened shell. On the western interior wall, above where the high altar had stood, the words "The Lord Seeth" were still visible.

Within three months, a temporary Chapel of Our Lady of Consolation was erected on the site. The Augustinian order brought suit against the city, claiming it had failed to protect the church's property. After a long court case, the Augustinians were awarded damages of $47,434, roughly one-half of their total losses. Despite this setback, the case confirmed the rights of Roman Catholics to religious freedom under the U.S. Constitution.

With their award in hand, the Augustinians began to build a new church on the foundations of the original structure in 1847. To represent the phoenixlike resurrection of their church, the salvaged fragments of the Sister Bell were recast and sent to newly founded Villanova College as its college bell (today, the Sister Bell is on display in Villanova University's Falvey Memorial Library).

Designed in the Italian Revival style by Napoleon LeBrun (with a steeple by Edwin F. Durang added in 1867), the current St. Augustine's Church was completed in 1848. Unlike the original building, with its spacious windows and multiple doors, the façade of the new church presented a forbidding, fortified appearance, with no front windows and a single entrance.

St. Augustine's in flames, from an 1844 pamphlet describing the recent anti-Catholic riots. (The Library Company of Philadelphia.)

Bank of Pennsylvania

Location: 134–136 South Second Street (west side, between Lodge Street and Gold Street)
Completed: 1801
Demolished: 1867
Architect/Builder: Benjamin Henry Latrobe

As the financial center of the country until the 1830s, Philadelphia was home to the First and Second Banks of the United States, forerunners of the Federal Reserve Bank; the U.S. Mint; and the nation's first stock exchange, founded in 1790. Under the leadership of financial innovators like Robert Morris, Stephen Girard, and Clement Biddle, Philadelphia was also home to numerous private banks with semi-governmental functions. Realizing that appearance was all-important, each bank strove for a distinctive architectural style that would make it appear substantial yet progressive.

One of these institutions was the Bank of Pennsylvania, founded in 1793, which acted as the central reserve bank for the state. In April 1798, a recent arrival from England, architect Benjamin Henry Latrobe,

met with bank president Samuel M. Fox, who told Latrobe that his fast-growing bank would soon need a new building. Latrobe made a quick sketch of a domed structure in the "stripped classic" manner, reminiscent of John Soane's recently completed Bank of England. By November, the bank had accepted Latrobe's proposal, and the new building was soon under construction. The Bank of Pennsylvania was Latrobe's first commission in Philadelphia and his second, after the Virginia State Penitentiary in Richmond, in the United States.

The Bank of Pennsylvania has been called the first major neoclassical or Greek Revival structure in the United States, with elements drawn from such ancient structures as the Erectheum at Athens and the Temple of the Muses on the Illyssus River. Dignified and elegant despite its small size and cramped location, the

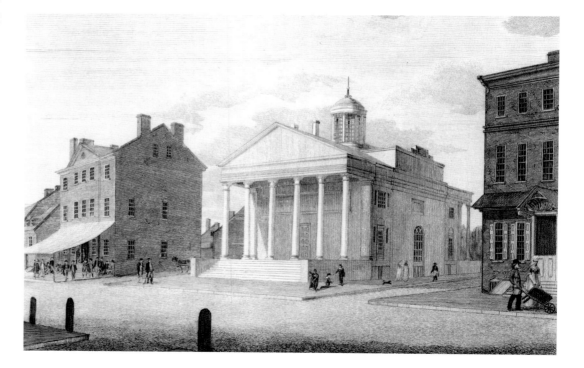

This William Birch print shows the recently completed Bank of Pennsylvania, with a huge cupola illuminating the main banking room. To the left stands the City Tavern, built in 1773, demolished in 1854–55, and rebuilt by the National Park Service for the nation's bicentennial. Partly visible at right is the former mansion of merchant David Franks. (The Philadelphia Print Shop.)

Bank of Pennsylvania firmly established the Greek temple as the appropriate architectural model for U.S. financial institutions.

The rectangular structure, roughly 50 by 120 feet, had porticoes on either end, each with six Ionic columns. The eastern portico faced Second Street and served as the public entrance, while the western one opened onto a small private park for bank officers. A large glass cupola in the low domed roof illuminated the 45-foot rotunda below that served as the main banking room, augmented by arched windows on the northern and southern walls. The bank's broad dome, sophisticated vaulting, and fireproof construction reflected Latrobe's training as an engineer and his familiarity with techniques still new to the United States.

The pale, cool gray of the exterior marble gave way to a rich, Adamesque color scheme inside the bank. The walls of the banking room were "warm oker," with white paneling and a white-and-russet frieze along the top, while the dome was in alternating shades of blue and white.[20] Smaller rooms were in more dramatic colors: the entrance vestibule walls were brown with a ceiling of white, pale blue and red. The directors' and president's rooms had gray walls with pale blue ceilings and ornamented bands of red and yellow.

The Bank of Pennsylvania occupied Latrobe's structure until 1857, when the bank failed during a financial panic. The building stood empty until the Civil War, when it was used as a federal prison. By this time, the building was considered too small and antiquated, and the neighborhood too unfashionable, for a modern bank. Latrobe's masterpiece was demolished in 1867, the same year the Slate Roof House came down directly across Second Street. In its place rose commercial buildings, including the Philadelphia Chamber of Commerce. One of its Ionic columns was salvaged and given to G.A.R. Post No. 8 to be used as a memorial for Civil War dead at Glenwood Cemetery. Others were incorporated into the 1871 Soldiers' and Sailors' Monument in Wilmington, Delaware. Since 1933, the Ritter & Shay–designed U.S. Custom House has occupied the site.

This 1867 John Moran photograph shows the Bank of Pennsylvania during demolition, soon to be replaced by modern commercial buildings similar to Napoleon LeBrun's 1855 Lennig building (to the left, with the statue). In the foreground, construction equipment sits among the ruins of the Slate Roof House, also demolished in 1867. (The Library Company of Philadelphia.)

Water Works Engine House

Location: Centre Square (later Penn Square, site of
Philadelphia City Hall)
Completed: 1801
Demolished: 1828
Architect/Builder: Benjamin Henry Latrobe

Before his death in 1790, the prescient Benjamin Franklin had
bequeathed his fast-growing city £100,000 to develop a supply
of water to "insure the health, comfort and preservation of its citizens," noting that "in Philadelphia everyone has a cistern and a well,
and the two are becoming indistinguishable."[21] During the following decade, Philadelphia's dreams of becoming the permanent capital were dashed, in part, by a string of devastating epidemics. Demand grew even stronger for a source of wholesome water, as much
to wash the town's filthy streets as to maintain its citizens' health.

The Delaware and Schuylkill Canal Navigation Company proposed a scheme to bring Schuylkill River water to Philadelphia
through a canal to the river's northern reaches. In 1798, architect-engineer Benjamin Henry Latrobe recommended instead that the
Schuylkill be tapped at the city itself, and that its water of "uncommon purity" be distributed via aqueducts and steam engines.[22]

According to Latrobe's plan, water would flow from a settling
basin along the riverbank at Chestnut Street through a tunnel to a
well in Centre Square on the city's western edge. There, it would
be pumped by steam power to a second aqueduct, from which
another steam pump would raise it to a tank high enough to let gravity distribute it throughout the city by wooden pipes. While water
would be free to the poor at street hydrants, businesses and homes
would pay to receive water directly.

Impressed by Latrobe's report, the city Watering Committee
accepted his plan and appointed him chief engineer. After numerous setbacks, equipment failures, cost overruns, and critical attacks,
the Philadelphia Water Works began operation on January 27, 1801.

By the end of the year, Schuylkill water was flowing from Centre
Square to sixty-three houses, thirty-seven public hydrants, four
breweries, and one sugar refinery.

The heart of Latrobe's system was the Centre Square Engine
House, a sixty-foot-tall brick structure sheathed in white marble.
An elevated water-storage tank and smokestack, hidden by a domed
cylindrical tower, emerged from a square base that housed the coal-burning pumping engines. Smoke from the engines was vented
through an oculus in the top of the dome. Greek Revival details,
including twin Doric porticoes and recessed arched windows, provided minimal decoration to the functional design. This unique
structure combined modern technology with classical architecture
that was, thanks to its unorthodox combination of geometric shapes,
equally cutting-edge.

To showcase one of Philadelphia's most important public buildings, its grounds were landscaped with walkways lined with Lombardy poplars. In 1809, the first public fountain in Philadelphia,
William Rush's *Water Nymph and Bittern*, was placed atop a base
of native rocks before the building's east entrance. Even Thomas
Cope, one of Latrobe's most persistent critics, had to admit by 1804
that "many also objected to the circular form given to the Centre
Square & to the erection of the House in the middle of it who are
now highly pleased with both. The shady walks already afford a
refreshing retreat."[23] Soon, the Centre Square Water Works
became the favored site for public parades and festivals, including
the Fourth of July celebrations memorialized in paintings by John
Lewis Kimmel and Paul Svinin.

Within its chaste casket, unfortunately, Latrobe's system malfunctioned on a regular basis. The inadequate steam engines and
boilers frequently broke down, caught fire, or exploded. Wooden
conduits rotted and had to be replaced with iron pipes. Deficits
mounted as the anticipated subscriptions to cover construction
and maintenance costs never materialized; after a decade of operation, only 2,127 Philadelphians out of 53,722 paid for their
water. While the Water Works made Latrobe's reputation as an

architect and engineer, it almost ruined him financially because of his investments in it.

In 1811, Water Works superintendent Frederick Graff recommended a pumping station and reservoir at Morris Hill, later called Fairmount. The new works were constructed between 1812 and 1822. By 1815, they were serving the city so well that the Centre Square Engine House was retired.

In 1827–28, Latrobe's structure was demolished so that Market and Broad streets could be run through the recently renamed Penn Square, which remained empty until construction began on City Hall in 1871. The Engine House's Doric columns were recycled into the portico of William Strickland's Congregational Unitarian Church at Tenth and Locust streets, where William Henry Furness was minister. Rush's statue of *Water Nymph and Bittern* was moved to the site of the new Water Works. In 1854, after the wood had begun to rot, it was cast in bronze. Rush's statue remained on the banks of the Schuylkill until 1940, when it was moved to the Philadelphia Museum of Art.

The east façade of the Centre Square Water Works ca. 1810, with William Rush's fountain installed. This Cornelius Tiebout engraving was issued ca. 1845, nearly two decades after the Water Works had been demolished. (The Philadelphia Print Shop.)

Sedgeley

Location: Sedgley Drive below Girard Avenue (east bank of the Schuylkill River, north of Lemon Hill, in Fairmount Park)
Completed: 1803
Demolished: 1857
Architect/Builder: Benjamin Henry Latrobe

After introducing the neoclassical style to Philadelphia, Latrobe helped launch the Gothic Revival with Sedgeley, a country estate built between 1799 and 1803 for merchant William Cramond. Originally, Sedgeley was part of the Robert Morris estate, the Hills, where the bankrupt Morris hid from his creditors. After his arrest, the Hills was divided up and sold at sheriff's sale in 1799.

The southern section became Lemon Hill, the Henry Pratt estate, and Cramond purchased the northern twenty-eight acres.

Latrobe designed a Gothic villa to stand on a promontory eighty feet above the Schuylkill River that commanded wonderful views of the surrounding countryside. The two-and-a-half-story rectangular, five-bay house with a red hipped roof featured a one-story porch on all four sides and corner pavilions marked by tall arches. Other Gothic detailing appeared in the cornices, window moldings, and porch posts. With its colonnaded porticoes and open arches, Sedgeley was designed to expose its owners to the beauties of nature in the best Romantic manner. Contemporary portraits show the house in a naturalistic, parklike setting, indicating the adaptation of the latest trends in English landscape design to the American countryside.

The front façade of Sedgeley, engraved in 1828 by C. G. Childs for his *Views of Philadelphia*. Childs' engraving emphasizes the picturesque setting of the mansion, with stylized trees lining the path to the front door. (The Philadelphia Print Shop.)

While some architectural historians consider Sedgeley the earliest Gothic Revival country residence in the United States, others view it as an essentially Federal building overlaid with Gothic details. Latrobe himself was unhappy with the final product, claiming that it had been butchered and its details blown out of proportion by contractors from the Carpenters' Company. Despite the architect's dissatisfaction, Sedgeley became one of the city's showpieces, appearing on a polychromatic amphora produced by the Tucker Porcelain Factory. The home also kicked off a craze for Gothic buildings in Philadelphia; by 1808, the Bank of Philadelphia, also designed by Latrobe, would grace the corner of Fourth and Chestnut streets with its pointed arches and rose window.

William Cramond was able to enjoy Sedgeley for only a few years before his business failed, and the property was sold at sheriff's sale in 1806. Next owned by the Mifflin and Fisher families, Sedgeley was acquired in 1836 by Isaac Lloyd, a real estate speculator, who chopped down many of its trees and laid out streets and building lots. When Lloyd's venture failed, a consortium of private citizens bought the property in 1857 and presented it to the city. Sedgeley was reunited with the former Lemon Hill estate to the south, which had been dedicated as a public common in September 1855. Together with the Fairmount Water Works, these two properties formed the nucleus of Fairmount Park in 1858.

Latrobe's mansion was demolished shortly after the city acquired the property. According to historian Thompson Westcott: "By this time the Sedgeley Mansion was much decayed, and no effort was made to save it from destruction; so that when the Park authorities directed that it should be taken down there was little difficulty in carrying out their command, for the work was already half accomplished."[24]

The surviving porter's lodge, on Sedgely Drive (at some point one of the E's disappeared) below Girard Avenue, was used as the headquarters of the Fairmount Park Guards until 1972. Built in a style similar to the adjoining mansion's but later Victorianized, the lodge was recently restored to its original appearance.

Permanent Bridge

Location: Schuylkill River at Market Street
Completed: 1805
Demolished: 1875
Architect/Builder: Timothy Palmer and William Weston (engineers); Adam Traquair, John Dorsey, and Owen Biddle (bridge cover)

Until 1805, the only way to cross the Schuylkill River was by ferry or the flimsy pontoon bridges at the Upper Ferry (Spring Garden Street), Middle Ferry (Market Street), or Lower Ferry (Grays Ferry Road). From 1750 on, Benjamin Franklin, Robert Smith, Thomas Paine, and other visionaries advanced schemes for a permanent bridge. In the first years of the nineteenth century, their vision was realized with the Market Street Permanent Bridge, one of the engineering marvels of the age. The completion of the bridge marked Philadelphia's turn westward, toward both the interior of Pennsylvania and new technology, and away from the Delaware and its traditional reliance on maritime commerce.

The repeated destruction of the temporary bridges by spring floods made a permanent bridge necessary. In 1798, the Pennsylvania Legislature created the Schuylkill Permanent Bridge Company, headed by Judge Richard Peters. After considering a stone bridge, Peters decided on a three-span structure of pine timber resting atop two masonry piers. An English engineer, William Weston, designed the caissons, while Timothy Palmer of Massachusetts designed the wooden superstructure. The cornerstone for the bridge was laid on the eastern bank at Market Street on October 18, 1800. Work on the two stone piers and their wing walls and abutments alone took two years. Caisson work on the piers reached bedrock forty-two feet below the river level, a record for the time.

The bridge opened to traffic on January 1, 1805, after five years and $300,000 in expenses. It was considered the largest wooden bridge in the world, reaching 550 feet from shore to shore, with an additional 750 feet of abutments and wing walls. Its forty-foot width permitted two lanes for vehicular traffic flowing east and west, with separate pedestrian walkways. At a tollbooth in the center of the bridge, a collector accepted tolls from both directions, although the bridge company did not show a profit for many years.

By the end of 1805, a decorated cover was added to the bridge to preserve it from the elements. Although Judge Peters took credit for the general concept and design of the cover, he acknowledged the assistance of draftsman Adam Traquair and architects John Dorsey and Owen Biddle. The cover, lit by elliptical windows, was painted to resemble cut stone topped by paneled sections with blind doorways.

In 1812, William Rush carved two recumbent figures for the pediments at both ends of the bridge, representing Commerce (over the Philadelphia entrance) and Agriculture (over the West Philadelphia entrance). During the same period, a stone obelisk inscribed with the bridge's history and key statistics was erected near the western approach. Some time after 1840, the obelisk was moved to the northeast corner of Twenty-third and Market streets, where it stood until the 1930s.

The Permanent Bridge enabled heavy traffic to cross the river in all weather and spurred the development of West Philadelphia and Blockley Township. Soon a cluster of inns and taverns stood at the western end of the bridge, surrounded by country estates. By 1840, the district of West Philadelphia consisted of roughly 150 buildings, including numerous furnaces and manufactories.

That year, the city acquired the permanent bridge for $110,000, ending tolls and making it a free passage. Ten years later, the city rebuilt the bridge to accommodate the tracks of the Columbia and Pennsylvania Railroads. The Market Street Railroad Bridge lasted until November 20, 1875, when a fire caused by a leaky gas main destroyed it in half an hour. Two other spans—a temporary wooden bridge built in twenty-one days, and an iron cantilever bridge completed in 1888—took its place before the current Market Street Bridge was erected in 1932.

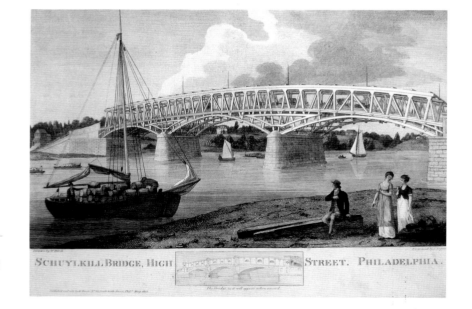

A steady flow of traffic crosses the uncovered Permanent Bridge in this William Birch engraving. An inset at the bottom shows the bridge as it would appear with the protective cover that was being installed at the time of the print's publication in May 1805. (The Philadelphia Print Shop.)

SCHUYLKILL BRIDGE, HIGH STREET, PHILADELPHIA.

Pennsylvania Academy of the Fine Arts

Location: North side of Chestnut Street, between Tenth and
  Eleventh streets
Completed: 1807
Demolished: 1845
Architect/Builder: John Dorsey (rebuilt by Richard A. Gilpin, 1845)

Home to such artists and architects as Thomas and William Birch, Gilbert Stuart, Benjamin Henry Latrobe, William Rush, Thomas Sully, and the Peale family, Federal Philadelphia warranted its title as the "Athens of America." In August 1805, three of these artists—Charles Willson Peale, his son Rembrandt Peale, and William Rush—met with a group of art-loving lawyers and businessmen to draw up plans for a society "to promote the cultivation of the Fine Arts in the United States of America.[25] This society was incorporated in March 1806 as the Pennsylvania Academy of the Fine Arts.

To house the Academy, its members selected the design of one of their own founders, the merchant John Dorsey. An amateur architect who contributed to the design of the Permanent Bridge cover, Dorsey was a thorn in the side of Philadelphia's professional architects. After Dorsey's design was selected, a despondent Benjamin Latrobe wrote:

John Dorsey has now no less than 15 plans now in progress of execution, because he charges nothing for them. The public affront put upon me as a professional man, in the erection of the Academy of Art from the design of John Dorsey, —by a vote of all the men who pretend to patronize the arts in this city, — would have driven any Artist from it.[26]

The original Academy was a simple, square building with neo-classical elements, including a round dome with an oculus and two Ionic columns framing a recessed entrance. An American eagle clutching an artist's palette and brushes, possibly carved by Academy member William Rush, glared down from above the entrance. Two sphinxes stood guard on the piers flanking the front steps. The Academy, which stood one hundred feet back from Chestnut Street, was the first art museum in the nation.

The Academy's principal room was a circular chamber forty-six feet in diameter lit by a skylight, where plaster casts of classical statues were displayed. The nude casts were removed on Mondays, which were set aside for female visitors exclusively. Through bequests and direct purchases, the Academy began to assemble a notable collection of paintings, including Gilbert Stuart's "Lansdowne" portrait of George Washington (donated by William Bingham) and Benjamin West's *King Lear and Cordelia*. By 1810, the Academy had proven so popular that a north gallery was added to the rear of the original building. In 1820, a sculpture gallery was constructed on the east side of the building, followed by a director's room and a library in 1823. During this time, the sphinxes and their piers were removed from the front.

In 1845, a catastrophic fire set by a deranged "incendiary" destroyed most of the building except for the central rotunda.[27] Benjamin West's *Death on a Pale Horse*, which the Academy had purchased for $7,000 in 1836 after mortgaging its building, was cut from its frame and saved, as was the "Lansdowne" Washington. Many other paintings were lost, as were the sixty statues in the sculpture gallery and the contents of the library.

Despite the submission of designs from John Haviland and John Notman, the commission to rebuild went to Richard Gilpin, whose brother Henry served on the Academy's Building Committee. Gilpin reconstructed Dorsey's rotunda, adding a larger entrance with Ionic columns supporting a classical pediment. Long picture galleries with skylights framed the central pavilion. The new building opened to the public in May 1847, and gradually, the Academy rebuilt its collections, ordering new plaster casts and acquiring paintings from Joseph Bonaparte and other private collectors.

During the 1840s and 1850s, the Academy went through a period of rapid growth in both membership and visitors. By 1860, it was apparent that the aging facility was unable to handle the Academy's larger collections and increased attendance. In 1865, a special committee reported to the board that the Chestnut Street building "in its present condition, not only impedes the operation of the Academy, but is rapidly hastening to distruction [sic] the works of art contained in it."[28] The Academy's Chestnut Street frontage had been sold off, and now a jumble of stores and signs nearly hid the building from view. In 1870, the Academy sold its original site for $135,000 and purchased its current site at Broad and Cherry streets. Furness & Hewitt's polychromatic masterpiece would open its doors at that location in 1876.

In 1871, shortly after Furness & Hewitt were awarded the commission for the new Academy, Fox's American Theater replaced the Chestnut Street building. Today, the original Dorsey building and its 1845 replacement survive only in the John Sartain engravings that grace Academy stockholders' certificates.

Masonic Hall

Location: North side of Chestnut Street, between Seventh and Eighth streets
Completed: 1811
Demolished: 1855
Architect/Builder: William Strickland

Philadelphia played a critical role in the history of the fraternal organization of the Masons. The first Masonic Hall in America was constructed in 1755 on Norris Alley near Second Street, although reports of lodge meetings in Philadelphia date back to 1715. Many of Philadelphia's leading citizens were Masons, including Benjamin Franklin, Philip Syng, Joseph Shippen, and George Washington.

Given this rich heritage, it's not surprising that Philadelphia has a tradition of elaborate Masonic Halls, starting with William Strickland's structure of 1809–11. The building was Strickland's first commission, awarded before his twenty-first birthday. Begun shortly after Latrobe's Philadelphia Bank was completed, Masonic Hall was another early example of the Gothic Revival style. Like Sedgeley and the Philadelphia Bank, however, Masonic Hall appeared to be a symmetrical Federal building with Gothic details applied.* The Hall, which took two years to complete, not only testified to the financial clout of Philadelphia's Masons, but also illustrated the former builders' guild's awareness of the latest architectural style.

Masonic Hall, 82 feet long by 169 feet deep, was a two-story brick structure encrusted with marble pilasters, surrounds, and

* Latrobe himself was not a fan of Strickland's creation. Writing to David Hare on May 30, 1813, he sneered: "The Free Masons' Hall, which is anything but Gothic, has made me repent a thousand times that I ventured to exhibit a specimen of that architecture. My mouldings & window heads appear in horrid disguise from New York to Richmond." (Quoted in Hamlin, *Benjamin Henry Latrobe*, 248.)

moldings. Pointed tracery windows, pinnacles, statues in niches, and a battlement gave it a suitably Romantic appearance. A multitiered tower, also decorated with Gothic arches and topped by a large weathervane, rose 180 feet from the center of the roof.

Inside, a grand saloon or ballroom featured an ornamental plaster ceiling and a music gallery. Statues of Faith, Hope, and Charity, carved in wood by William Rush and painted to look like bronze, decorated the room. A "geometrical" staircase of mahogany and curly maple led to private lodge and banquet rooms on the second floor.[29] The Masons opened the Hall on St. John the Baptist's Day, June 24, 1811, with a church service and parade of lodge members, followed by a grand ball and banquet.

In March 1819, a fire caused by a faulty flue destroyed the Hall's tower and interior. Strickland rebuilt the Hall in a simpler style, but the massive tower was never replaced. The repaired Hall was one of the first buildings in Philadelphia to be lit by gaslight and was the scene of a

A dramatic depiction of the conflagration of William Strickland's Masonic Hall, published three months after it occurred. The engraving's publishers "respectfully dedicated" it to "the active and much esteemed fire engine and hose companies" that saved the Hall from total destruction. (The Philadelphia Print Shop.)

reception and dinner for the Marquis de Lafayette (himself a Mason) in September 1824.

During the 1820s and 1830s, the grand saloon hosted numerous exhibitions, lectures, and concerts. Visitors could see Sinclair's celebrated grand peristrephic (moving panorama) of the Battle of Waterloo, study Daguerre's magical pictures, hear African American trumpeter Frank Johnson, or meet six Indian chiefs from the Rocky Mountains.

Despite this activity, the Grand Lodge of Pennsylvania was in serious financial trouble. In addition to the heavy debt incurred in restoring the Hall, membership was dropping due to a wave of anti-Masonic sentiment. Sometime after the Hall's restoration, the Masons sold its Chestnut Street frontage, and one-story shops then obscured most of the building's ground floor. In 1835, the Grand Lodge was forced to sell the Hall, which was bought by the Franklin Institute, and moved to Washington Hall on Third Street.

When the Franklin Institute defaulted on its mortgage in 1852, the Grand Lodge repossessed the building. In 1855, the Masons replaced Strickland's structure with a new Masonic Hall, a Gothic brownstone building designed by Samuel Sloan and John Stewart. The Masons occupied the Sloan & Stewart structure until 1873, when they took possession of their current Hall on North Broad Street.

CHAPTER 3

City in Transition

(1821 to 1860)

On May 14, 1831, the Philadelphia *Album* published an editorial extolling the city's phenomenal growth and prosperity. Noting that an estimated 1,600 new buildings would rise over the next few months, the *Album* rhapsodized:

> Philadelphia is truly the Athens of America: in its public institutions, in its benevolent and charitable societies, in its literary reputation—in its site, the beautiful regularity of its streets—its buildings both public and private—in every particular, except for the dust and dirt, the noise and bustle, which attends an extensive shipping, we are superior, without a doubt to every other City in the Union.[1]

The *Album* was not just spouting Chamber of Commerce hype. Despite the loss of the federal and state governments and a growing rivalry with upstart New York City, Philadelphia had flourished over the last three decades. The presence of the Second Bank of the United States and the plans for a grand new Merchants' Exchange confirmed its status as the financial heart of the country. Philadelphia remained a mercantile and industrial leader, ready to defend its prominence by building a breakwater in Delaware Bay to protect merchant vessels.

Although the American Athens continued to attract the finest talent in all cultural arenas, including literature, publishing, theater, art, and architecture, the city kept glancing over its shoulder to see how close New York was on its heels. In 1828, when William Strickland rebuilt the tower of the State House as it appeared before its removal in 1781, the City Councils told him to make his tower forty feet higher than the original, "to contribute greatly to the ornament of our city, which is so deficient in embellishments, which in other cities are considered as indispensable"[2] The unnamed indispensable embellishment was the soaring cupola of New York's City Hall, opened in 1812.

Aside from some riots between Irish immigrants and native-born Americans in far-off Kensington, few clouds hovered on

Facing page: **W**illiam Strickland's classical Chestnut Street Theatre, completed in 1822 to replace the one that had burned in 1820, reflected Philadelphia's ongoing status as the theatrical capital of the nation. By this time, however, New York and Boston were usurping Philadelphia's title as the Athens of America. (The Philadelphia Print Shop.)

Philadelphia's bright horizon in 1830. Who could foresee that the next two decades would bring financial depression, political instability, and mob violence?

President Andrew Jackson, suspicious of the financial power exerted by the Second Bank of the United States, refused to renew its charter in 1836. Although bank president Nicholas Biddle obtained a state charter, the withdrawal of federal support led to a financial panic, the eventual failure of "Biddle's Bank," and a decade-long depression in Philadelphia. During this period, New York City emerged as the financial and mercantile leader of the nation. In 1837, one merchant noted: "There is by no means the bustle and quantity of business down here that there is in New York. I think that as much is done in the latter city in one week as in a month here."[3]

The resulting unemployment and struggle for jobs heightened tensions in Philadelphia among native-born white Americans, African Americans, and Irish Catholics. Between 1820 and 1850, the population of the city nearly doubled, due in large part to immigration from Ireland and Germany. Native-born Americans, feeling threatened and disenfranchised, formed political groups like the Know-Nothings that fomented anti-Catholic, anti-immigrant, and anti-black violence. During the 1830s and 1840s, a series of bloody riots among the factions shattered Philadelphia's peace, culminating in the destruction of St. Augustine Roman Catholic Church in 1844.

Philadelphia confronted other challenges as rapid growth shredded its social fabric. Besides mob violence, gangs of hoodlums with names like the Blood-Tubs, Killers, Rats, and Bouncers terrorized the city. Since most gangs were based outside the city, they could wreak havoc and then return to Kensington or Moyamensing, leaving Philadelphia's marshals powerless to pursue them beyond Vine or South Street. The overcrowding of the poor in river-ward slums spurred epidemics of cholera, yellow fever, and other communicable diseases. Fires swept through the city regularly, while competing volunteer companies battled each other and let the flames spread.

Philadelphia responded to this social disintegration with the Consolidation Act of 1854, which unified the city and its surrounding county into one metropolis. Gradually, the new municipal government implemented coordinated systems for the provision of police and fire protection, water, sewage and gas services, health, education, and social welfare. To protect the city's drinking supply, the Councils acquired country estates on both banks of the Schuylkill River to create Fairmount Park. By 1860, the expanded city held 565,529 inhabitants, compared to 80,458 thirty years earlier.

Even during the worst of the preconsolidation chaos, Philadelphia was developing into the foremost industrial city in the United States. Its growth was fueled by both external factors (the development of the steam engine and railroad locomotive) and native advantages (location, ample land and water, a large base of workers, scientific tradition, and available wealth for capital investment). Anthracite coal from the Schuylkill Valley, delivered by canal and then by train, fired the engines of the city's factories, locomotives, and steamboats. Soon, the municipality was a leading manufacturer of textiles, carpets, locomotives, carriages, iron, chemicals, and furniture. By 1860, Philadelphia's industrial might had merged with its newfound political stability to forge a fresh phenomenon, the modern U.S. metropolis.

The new metropolis was a segmented one, with distinct districts for its industrial, financial, mercantile, and retail sectors, as well as for the residential areas of different social and economic classes. Thanks to the railroad, the affluent could commute downtown from rural suburbs such as Germantown or Chestnut Hill. Within Philadelphia proper, the upper classes moved westward from the impoverished, overcrowded older city along the Delaware, making Rittenhouse Square their urban enclave for the next century.

Thanks to its industrial wealth and technological innovation, Philadelphia remained the architectural center of the country for much of the period. Its leading architects—John Haviland, William Strickland, Thomas Ustick Walter, and John Notman—were recognized as the finest in the United States. These men experimented not only with new styles of architecture, such as Egyptian, Gothic, Italianate, and Eclectic, but with new techniques and materials, such as cast iron. Many of Philadelphia's most notable landmarks date from this period: the Second Bank of the United States (1824), Merchants' Exchange (1833), Eastern State Penitentiary (1836), Laurel Hill Cemetery (1836), Girard College (1847), the Athenaeum (1845), the Academy of Music (1857), and the Cathedral of SS. Peter and Paul (1864).

Philadelphia was also the center of efforts to organize and teach architecture as a profession. *The Builder's Assistant* by John Haviland, the first U.S. book to contain the Greek orders, was published in three volumes between 1818 and 1821, with plates by Hugh Bridport. During the 1830s, William Strickland delivered a series of lectures on architecture at the Franklin Institute; in 1841, Thomas U. Walter began a lecture series on architectural history and theory. In 1836, Strickland and Walter, along with Alexander Jackson Davis, founded the American Institution of Architects, the first professional organization of its kind in the country. Although the organization did not last, it provided the basis for the American Institute of Architects, founded in 1857 (in New York).

Sadly, the inertia spawned by the depression of the 1830s and 1840s ended Philadelphia's primacy in architecture. With the exception of a few notable buildings, mostly in the fields of health and social welfare, the city's architecture grew conservative, homogenous, and monotonous. To survive, its leading designers had to search elsewhere for commissions. Thomas U. Walter traveled as far as China and Venezuela before being engaged as the architect of the U.S. Capitol. John Haviland capitalized on his success with the Eastern State Penitentiary by designing prisons around the country. William Strickland spent his final days in Nashville and now spends eternity immured within the Tennessee State Capitol after dying in 1854 during its construction.

By the middle of the nineteenth century, the one-time Potters' Field known as the North-West Square had been transformed into a lush park named after James Logan, lined with elegant town houses and the unfinished Roman Catholic cathedral. (Courtesy of Robert M. Skaler.)

Mikveh Israel Synagogue

Location: North side of Cherry Street between Third and Orianna streets
Completed: 1825
Demolished: 1860
Architect/Builder: William Strickland

Federal Street Cemetery Gatehouse

Location: 1114 Federal Street
Completed: 1847
Demolished: 1963
Architect/Builder: Napoleon LeBrun

Although Philadelphia's Jews had gathered for religious services as early as 1745, it was not until the 1770s that Mikveh Israel was formally organized as the city's first Jewish congregation. Before the Revolution, Mikveh Israel met in a small house on Sterling Alley (now Orianna Street) between Cherry and Race, moving to a three-story brick house on the south side of Cherry Street opposite Sterling Alley in 1776. In 1782, the congregation acquired a lot on the north side of Cherry east of Sterling Alley. There, Philadelphia's first structure built specifically as a synagogue took shape between 1782 and 1784, a square, one-story brick building that seated 200.

By 1822, the congregation had outgrown its building and commissioned William Strickland to design a new synagogue on the same site. The old temple was demolished in September 1822, and the cornerstone for the new synagogue was laid before the end of the month. To raise construction funds, various parts of the building, including the four cornerstones and two doorposts, were auctioned off in exchange for congregational prayers and honors.

Strickland created the first Egyptian Revival building in Philadelphia for Mikveh Israel, introducing a style inspired by the redis-

covery of the ancient culture following Napoleon's Egyptian expedition of 1798. In the absence of a specifically Jewish architecture, Egyptian Revival was considered appropriate for synagogues because of its "Eastern" origins. Strickland's design, recalling the Jews' historic captivity in ancient Egypt while reflecting the latest architectural style, symbolized the growing social and economic status of Philadelphia's Jewish community at the same time it alluded to its biblical heritage.

The two-story building, constructed of stone quarried at the Falls of Schuylkill, stood forty feet long by seventy feet deep. The façade featured inclined jambs on the doorway and flanking windows and a winged-sun disk (the Egyptian symbol for immortality) on the cavetto (deeply concave with a heavy overhang) cornice. The Egyptian motif continued inside, where columns copied from a temple at Tentyra supported semi-circular balconies and rose to a skylit dome. On the eastern side, the ark containing the Torah was framed

The second synagogue of Mikveh Israel, designed by William Strickland and dedicated in 1825, from a contemporary woodcut. (The Library Company of Philadelphia)

by pilasters supporting another cavetto cornice, decorated with the marble tablets of the Ten Commandments and a winged sun.

Strickland's synagogue was finished in autumn 1824 at a cost of $13,000. Jewish leaders from New York, Baltimore, and New Orleans attended the dedication on January 21, 1825, as did Pennsylvania Supreme Court chief justice William Tilghman, Episcopal bishop William White, and other lay and religious dignitaries.

Soon members of Philadelphia's second congregation, Rodeph Shalom, began defecting to Mikveh Israel, attracted by its prestigious new synagogue. By the 1850s, however, the Strickland synagogue was inadequate for the growing congregation, and its declining neighborhood was no longer desirable or convenient for its congregants. In 1860, Mikveh Israel dedicated a new synagogue at Seventh and Arch streets designed by John McArthur Jr., future architect of City Hall. The Strickland building was demolished the same year.

Besides synagogues, the Egyptian Revival style was considered suitable for cemeteries because of ancient Egypt's funerary associations. Both the Grove Street Cemetery in New Haven, Connecticut (founded 1797), and Mount Auburn Cemetery in Cambridge, Massachusetts (founded 1831), boasted Egyptian Revival gatehouses. It was doubly appropriate that Mikveh Israel should erect an Egyptian gatehouse for its second cemetery on Federal Street between Eleventh and Twelfth streets, acquired in 1841 when its historic Spruce Street burial ground grew overcrowded.

Napoleon LeBrun, future designer of the Academy of Music and Cathedral of SS. Peter and Paul, created a building that served as both gatehouse and *metaher*, the house of purification where the dead were prepared for burial according to Jewish law. LeBrun's façade mimicked Strickland's synagogue, with inclined jambs framing the doorway, recessed blind windows on either side of the entrance, and a winged-sun disk on the cavetto cornice. Finished in 1847, the stuccoed brick gatehouse guarded the cemetery until the decrepit structure was demolished in 1963. During the cemetery's refurbishment in the late 1980s, a modern metal gate and fence were erected on Federal Street.

Napoleon LeBrun's Federal Street gatehouse for Mikveh Israel's second cemetery paid homage to William Strickland's synagogue with its inclined doorjambs, recessed windows, and winged-sun disk above the central doorway. (The Library Company of Philadelphia.)

Marble Arcade

Location: 615–19 Chestnut Street (north side, between Sixth and Seventh streets)
Completed: 1826
Demolished: 1860
Architect/Builder: John Haviland

By the 1820s, fine shops and boutiques were displacing residences on lower Chestnut Street as the street became Philadelphia's prime retail corridor. In 1826, a brick mansion once occupied by John Dickinson and Chief Justice William Tilghman was demolished for the Marble (or Philadelphia) Arcade, the first shopping arcade in the United States.

In 1826, lawyer and entrepreneur Peter A. Browne organized a joint stock company to replicate the Burlington Arcade in London. Designed by Samuel Ware in 1819 for Lord George Cavendish, the Burlington Arcade allowed affluent Londoners to shop for "jewellery and fancy articles of fashionable demand" at seventy-two fine establishments.[4] Protected from bad weather by its glazed roof and from the hoi polloi by its force of beadles, Regency society made the Burlington Arcade a favorite meeting place.

For the Philadelphia Arcade, British émigré John Haviland, who had created the Eastern State Penitentiary and Walnut Street Theater, designed a neoclassical three-story structure with a hundred-foot façade fronted by four Roman arches. Niches at either end of the marble façade were meant to hold iron statues of Commerce and Navigation, although these were never installed. Above the niches were bas-relief carvings of the coats of arms of the City of Philadelphia and the State of Pennsylvania.

The first two levels provided space for eighty-eight shops, arrayed on both sides of two skylit avenues that ran 150 feet from the Arcade's Chestnut Street façade to Carpenter Street. The third floor was designated for offices, while four cellars provided additional commercial and storage space. Haviland's innovative design

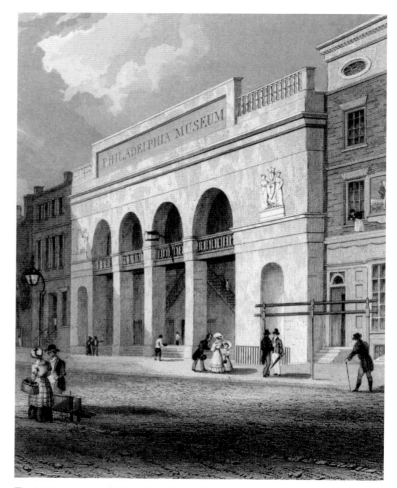

The Marble Arcade in 1831 at the height of its popularity, showing the sign for Peale's Philadelphia Museum and the coats of arms of Philadelphia and Pennsylvania. (The Philadelphia Print Shop.)

made heavy use of iron and stone to reduce the threat of fire and allowed retail spaces to be combined for larger stores.

Shortly after its completion, the Arcade gained a star tenant when the sons of the late Charles Willson Peale moved his museum from the State House to the third floor, filling it with Peale's portraits of national heroes, collections of stuffed birds and animals, Indian artifacts, and a mastodon skeleton. For a brief time, the Arcade attracted high society. Its prime location, on the same block as the new Chestnut Street Theatre and one block west of the State House, seemed to guarantee future success.

By the early 1830s, however, the Arcade was losing its luster, as "the great current of business swept by on Chestnut Street without eddying into this bay," in the words of Scharf and Westcott.[5] When Peale's Museum moved to its own building in 1836, the Arcade became known as "Browne's Marble Failure," where, according to one wit, "the tenants looked as poverty stricken as Romeo's apothecary."[6] The third floor became a music saloon, featuring Hungarian minstrels and polyphonist (ventriloquist) Dr. Love. On the lower floors, more mundane establishments, such as Thomas E. J. Kerrison's Arcade-Baths, replaced the fine boutiques.

By the early 1850s, the dainty shops of lower Chestnut Street were giving way to office buildings and business hotels. Patent-medicine tycoon Dr. David Jayne purchased the Arcade and turned its upper stories into the Arcade Hotel, competing with the neighboring Columbia House and Bolivar House. In 1860, Strickland's Arcade was demolished and replaced with Jayne's Marble Building, a large commercial structure designed by John McArthur Jr. that remained a Chestnut Street landmark until its demolition in 1959.

Pagoda and Labyrinthine Garden

Location: South side of Fairmount Avenue, between Twenty-fourth and Twenty-fifth streets
Completed: 1828
Demolished: ca. 1834–35
Architect/Builder: John Haviland

As Philadelphia grew more congested and dirty, entrepreneurs established pleasure gardens on its rural outskirts. For the price of a carriage ride and the entrance fee, frazzled urbanites could escape to these oases for refreshments, rest, and romance. Among the earliest public gardens in Philadelphia were Gray's Garden at Gray's Ferry, Harrogate in the Northern Liberties, and the Wigwam Baths at Race Street on the Schuylkill River, all founded before 1800.

The growing prosperity of the nineteenth century encouraged pleasure gardens to proliferate. Soon, Philadelphians flocked to the Sans Souci at Twentieth and Race streets, McAran's at Arch and Seventeenth, and Vauxhall Garden on South Broad, named after the London resort founded in 1661. Many of these establishments began as simple arboreta. As competition intensified and Philadelphians' tastes in entertainment grew worldlier, the gardens added concerts, vaudeville, dancing, fireworks, and novelties such as ice cream to attract customers.

To enhance the gardens' fairyland atmosphere, architects employed the most exotic and unusual styles, such as those of the Chinese bridges and summerhouse at Gray's Garden. Chinese styles enjoyed a fresh burst of popularity after British architect John Nash remodeled the Prince Regent's Brighton Pavilion as an Oriental pleasure dome between 1815 and 1823. Although the pavilion resembled a maharajah's palace outside, its Chinese interiors featured gilt dragons, faux bamboo staircases, and cast-iron palm-tree columns.

With the Philadelphia Arcade an apparent success, Peter A. Browne again in 1828 engaged John Haviland, who had apprenticed with John Nash. Their new project was a pleasure garden outside town, northeast of the new Water Works on the south side of Coates Street (Fairmount Avenue). For its centerpiece, Haviland built a 110-foot-tall Chinese pagoda of colored bricks, wood, and iron, and surrounded it with a "labyrinthine pleasure garden," a maze composed of boxwood hedges.[7] In front of the pagoda stood a two-story pavilion, also in the Oriental style, which contained ballrooms and a concert hall.

Although said to resemble a tower on the banks of China's Ta-ho River, Haviland's structure was based on a plate in Sir William Chambers' *Designs of Chinese Buildings*, published in London in 1757. Chambers, who had explored the Middle Kingdom in the 1740s, built a Chinese pagoda in London's Kew Gardens in 1763. Just as Browne and Haviland had attempted to recreate the Burlington Arcade in Chestnut Street, they were now transplanting a London park to Fairmount.

When the pagoda opened in July 1828, visitors could escape Philadelphia's summer heat by climbing a seven-story staircase. At the top, they could enjoy the view through a telescope while listening to the Oriental wind chimes that hung from the projecting beams of each story. But given its remote location and numerous competitors, Browne's pleasure garden failed to attract customers. It closed in the early 1830s, and Haviland's structures were dismantled shortly thereafter. The depot of the Green and Coates Street Passenger Railway Company soon occupied the site, and today the Philadelphian Apartment House stands there.

The back-to-back failures of the pagoda and the Marble Arcade nearly destroyed their creators. Haviland, who had invested heavily in both projects, illegally borrowed from funds meant for the construction of the U.S. Naval Hospital at Norfolk, Virginia, to cover his debts. Although Haviland's career almost ended when the scandal was exposed, he went on to design other notable structures, such as the Pennsylvania Fire Insurance Company on Independence Square and prisons in Trenton, Pittsburgh, and New York. Sadly, his bankrupt patron would be stuck with the mocking moniker Pagoda Arcade Browne, commemorating his two great failures.

John Haviland's pagoda and labyrinthine garden in a contemporary engraving. Unfortunately, the customers arriving by foot, by horse, and by carriage in the print failed to materialize in real life. (The Library Company of Philadelphia.)

Second U.S. Mint

Location: 1331–37 Chestnut Street (northwest corner of Chestnut and Juniper streets)
Completed: 1833
Demolished: 1902
Architect/Builder: William Strickland

By the 1820s, the expanding monetary needs of the United States had outstripped the limited capabilities of the original Mint at Seventh and Filbert streets. In early 1829, the U.S. government approved the purchase of a lot on the west side of Juniper Street, stretching from Chestnut Street to Penn Square. The new Mint's cornerstone was laid on July 4, 1829. Its location reflected the westward shift of the city, as well as the need for greater space for its expanded operations.

William Strickland, whose Second Bank of the United States had introduced monumental Greek Revival architecture to Phila-delphia, created a massive marble structure, 123 feet wide by 139 feet deep, with a copper roof. The Mint's classical design, modeled after a Greek temple on the Ilyssus River, exemplified the accepted ideal of a government building. Two-story porticoes with six Ionic columns supported pediment roofs at the Mint's north and south façades.

A central courtyard provided light and allowed access through cast-iron stairways and piazzas. Assaying, melting, and refining took place in the basement and coining and printing on the main floor, which also held the officers' rooms; the attic housed the standards of weights and measures. Strickland, conscious of the flammable nature of the Mint's operations, ensured that both the basement and main floor were arched and fireproofed.

The Mint was furnished with the latest manufacturing equipment from Europe, along with American machinery designed by chief coiner Franklin Peale, one of Charles Willson Peale's sons. In 1836, this equipment was used to strike the first U.S. silver dollars issued in more than thirty years, known as Gobrecht dollars because

The Second U.S. Mint still appeared pristinely classical in this 1840 engraving by J. T. Bowen, based on an earlier print by J. C. Wild. (The Philadelphia Print Shop.)

they were engraved by Christian Gobrecht. The obverse shows a seated figure of Liberty designed by Thomas Sully; on the reverse, an American eagle modeled by Franklin's brother Titian Peale soars through a field of stars.

Despite its magnificent structure and modern equipment, the second Mint still had trouble producing sufficient coinage for the growing nation. When congressional efforts to remove the Mint from Philadelphia failed, branches were established in several other cities, including Charlotte and New Orleans (both designed by William Strickland). By the Civil War, outbuildings and stacks of metal ingots crowded the Mint's courtyard, and a 130-foot-high brick chimney polluted the building's pure classicism. Finally, in 1873, the Bureau of the Mint was established in Washington, D.C., and the directorship moved there. The Philadelphia Mint became just another branch, governed by a lowly superintendent.

By the turn of the twentieth century, the nation's currency needs and new technology had once again rendered the Mint obsolete. City Hall occupied Penn Square, and the surrounding congested business and retail district did not welcome the Mint's smells and noise. A third Mint was constructed on Spring Garden Avenue between Sixteenth and Seventeenth streets in 1901. Today, it is the Philadelphia Community College, while the Philadelphia Mint has been located at Fifth and Arch streets since 1969.

Strickland's building was demolished in 1902. The four-story Mint Arcade building occupied the site for a decade before Horace Trumbauer's Widener Building replaced it in 1914. The second Mint's Ionic columns were salvaged and donated to the Jewish Hospital, later the Albert Einstein Medical Center, on the Old York Road. They stood in front of the Center's main building until 2001, when they were removed and placed in storage.

By the early 1870s, a brick smokestack spoiled the Mint's classical lines. Meanwhile, the tower of the new Masonic Hall (in the right background) testified to the development of Penn Square and the arrival of new architectural styles. (Courtesy of James Hill Jr.)

Blockley Almshouse

Location: Area bordered by South Street, Spruce Street, University Avenue, and the Schuylkill River, West Philadelphia
Completed: 1835
Demolished: 1920s–1959
Architect/Builder: William Strickland

In 1830, the City of Philadelphia purchased 187 acres of land in Blockley Township from the Hamilton estate for a new almshouse to replace the overcrowded facility at Tenth and Spruce streets. The move across the Schuylkill allowed the city to create a modern and spacious asylum in a rural setting, where the destitute could be removed from the evils of society and rehabilitated through meaningful labor.

Designed by William Strickland, the Blockley Almshouse consisted of four three-story buildings, each 500 feet long, arranged around a central courtyard. The roughcast brick structures, built to accommodate 4,000 inmates, were simple and utilitarian. On the main building, an imposing marble portico with eight Doric columns overlooked the swampy land that sloped toward the riverbank. As the surrounding area developed, a high board fence was erected around the grounds to hide the inmates from their neighbors.

For the rest of the nineteenth century, Blockley served not only as the city's poorhouse, but also as its hospital, orphanage, and insane asylum. Its name became a synonym for sordidness and suffering. While the number of inmates grew to nearly 5,000, the size of the property shrank steadily. In 1868, the city sold the northeast section to the University of Pennsylvania for its West Philadelphia campus. The land closer to the river was crowded with railroad tracks and factories; part of it later became the site of the Commercial Museum and Civic Center. As Blockley's original 187 acres dwindled to less than 20, new structures crowded its courtyard.

For most of the nineteenth century, Blockley was the last resort for poor, chronically ill, alcoholic, or incurably insane patients rejected elsewhere. Thanks to the wide range of patients and ailments encountered there, the Blockley hospital (named Philadelphia Hospital in 1835) became one of the city's great teaching and research centers. Under the leadership of William

The façade of the main building of Blockley Almshouse (Philadelphia General Hospital) at the start of the twentieth century, with a street gaslight directly in front of it. (Collection of the author.)

Osler and Alice Fisher, it was a nationally recognized leader in the fields of pathology and nursing. By 1900, its complex included medical pavilions, a maternity pavilion, apartments for nurses, laboratories, a children's hospital, buildings for insane and tubercular patients, an isolation unit for contagious patients, an electrical plant, and a pathology museum. In 1902, the hospital was officially renamed Philadelphia General Hospital.

In the 1920s, part of Strickland's original complex was demolished when a new campus was constructed for the hospital. According to one observer, Wing No. 1 of the old almshouse, demolished in 1927 "at the end of ninety-seven years, was found to be staunch and strong, its walls as perfect as the day upon which its cornerstone was laid."[8] Philadelphia General would remain one of the city's largest hospitals until 1977, when Mayor Frank Rizzo closed the then antiquated and financially troubled institution.

While the hospital grew, the original almshouse withered. In 1919, after the newly organized Department of Welfare wrested control of the almshouse from its corrupt board of managers, inmates were transferred to newer facilities around the city, such as the Home for the Indigent in Holmesburg and the Hospital for Mental Diseases at Byberry. Some of the original Strickland structures survived, ghostly reminders of a grimmer era; the last was demolished in 1959.

Today, academic and medical facilities cover the former Blockley Almshouse site, among them the University of Pennsylvania School of Nursing and the Children's Hospital of Philadelphia Wood Center. Although long vanished, Blockley made its presence felt again in 2001, when part of its burial ground was unearthed during the construction of a new cancer hospital on the site of the old Convention Center.

Philadelphia County (Moyamensing) Prison

Location: Square bounded by Reed Street, Passyunk Avenue, Dickinson Street, and Gerritt Street, South Philadelphia
Completed: 1835 (main prison); 1836 (debtor's wing)
Demolished: 1967
Architect/Builder: Thomas U. Walter

By the late 1820s, the City of Philadelphia and the State of Pennsylvania were taking steps to replace the overcrowded and obsolete Walnut Street Prison with modern facilities. In 1829, the Eastern State Penitentiary, designed by John Haviland, opened in a former orchard north of the city to handle prisoners from eastern Pennsylvania. During the same period, the Western State Penitentiary opened outside Pittsburgh.

To accommodate local prisoners, work began in 1832 on the Philadelphia County Prison, more than one mile south of the city in rural Moyamensing. The prison was the first major commission of Thomas Ustick Walter, a student of John Haviland, who would later design Girard College and the current dome of the U.S. Capitol.

Like Eastern State, Philadelphia County Prison (known as Moyamensing Prison or Old Moko) had a forbidding Gothic façade in the castellated mode. The pale granite façade featured crenellated battlements, slit windows, projecting turrets, portcullises, and a castellated central tower. The prison's resemblance to a medieval fortress was meant to impress onlookers with its impregnability and dissuade them from a life of crime. Conversely, the pastoral rural setting—at least what prisoners could glimpse of it through the slit windows—was meant to rehabilitate miscreants.

With a site too small for the radial design popularized by Eastern State, the Moyamensing complex consisted of the main block, two flanking wings, two rear prison cellblocks, and a separate rear structure. Moyamensing was built to house 400 prisoners in two cellblocks, each three stories tall. Despite its medieval appearance,

the prison was a technological wonder, boasting primitive systems for central heat and air conditioning, and individual hydrants and toilets in each nine- by thirteen-foot cell.

While prisoners at Eastern State Penitentiary were separated at all times according to the Pennsylvania system, Moyamensing operated on the Auburn system, which allowed prisoners to work together (albeit in complete silence), then return to their solitary cells at night. As at Eastern State, prisoners were put to work weav-ing, spinning, and making shoes and were paid for their work upon completion of their term.

In 1835, Walter designed an adjoining debtors' wing for the prison in the Egyptian Revival style, another mode considered suit-able for prisons after John Haviland used it for the Tombs prison in New York. Modeled on the Temple of the Sun on the Island of Ele-phantine in the Nile, the debtor's wing has been called "the first archaeologically based Egyptian Revival building in America."[9] Its red sandstone façade featured lotus-bud columns framing the doorway, which was flanked by windows with inclined jambs. Winged-sun disks, symbolizing immortality, decorated its cavetto cornices. The debtor's wing was finished in 1836, the same year that state laws requiring imprisonment for debt were repealed. It was used until 1868 for the confinement of witnesses and prisoners held for proceedings, and then as a women's prison.

Over time, the massive prison grew as overcrowded and obsolete as its predecessors. By the end of the nineteenth century, its rural isolation had given way to a bustling South Philadelphia neighborhood. After Holmesburg Prison opened in 1896, Moyamensing was used primarily to detain prisoners awaiting trial or sentencing, or serving short terms. During the twentieth century, escapes from the antiquated facility became common. The prison was finally vacated in 1963, after the Torresdale detention center opened.

While preservationists acknowledged that saving the entire complex was infeasible, many hoped to preserve the debtor's wing, one of the finest examples of Egyptian Revival architecture in Philadelphia. But both the prison and debtor's wing were torn down in November 1967, except for part of the prison power plant, which now serves as a storage facility for an adjacent police station. At the demolition ceremony, Mayor James Tate, up for reelection, implied that Moyamensing had imprisoned all of South Philadelphia: "The important thing is that this old building can come down so that this fine old neighborhood can get ahead, so that this neighborhood can breathe again in freedom. We are looking ahead, we are going to do great things because this is the end of despair and oblivion. We're finally going to take Old Moko down."[10]

Although a South Philadelphia Regional Playground was proposed for the prison site, an Acme supermarket and shopping strip soon replaced Old Moko.

The portico of the Moyamensing Prison debtor's wing has been preserved at the Smithsonian Institution, while the cast-iron winged orb over its doorway is now at Independence National Historical Park.

Pennsylvania Hospital for the Insane

Location: 4401 Market Street, West Philadelphia
Completed: 1841
Demolished: 1959 (portico left standing)
Architect/Builder: Isaac Holden, Samuel Sloan, Thomas Kirkbride

By the early 1800s, the Pennsylvania Hospital, which had treated "lunaticks or Persons distemper'd in Mind" since its founding in 1751, found that its mentally ill patients outnumbered its physically ill patients two to one.[11] Most of the insane were crowded together in unheated cells in the hospital basement, sedated or restrained to prevent them from disturbing the patients and doctors upstairs. In 1832, the hospital passed a resolution that "a separate Asylum be provided for our insane patients with ample space for their proper seclusion, classification and employment."[12]

In 1836, the hospital managers purchased a 101-acre farm in Blockley Township between the Westchester and Haverford roads. Isaac Holden, a British immigrant, won the competition for designing the new facility with an innovative echelon plan in which overlapping wings extended outward from a central pavilion to house various wards. The main building was a two-story granite ashlar structure in the Greek Revival style with a Doric portico, gable roofs, and a central dome; the wings were constructed of stuccoed rubble in a simpler style. In 1838, with the hospital under construction, Holden returned to England because of failing health. His foreman, Samuel Sloan, finished the hospital with the cooperation of the hospital superintendent, Dr. Thomas Kirkbride.

Kirkbride, a Quaker physician, who believed in treating the insane in an environment that was restful and domestic yet controlled, worked closely with Sloan to create a hospital that embodied his philosophy. To fireproof the building, iron was used for columns, stairs, doorframes, and window sashes. The latest advances in heating, ventilation, and sanitation made patients as comfortable as possible. The echelon plan not only allowed maximum sunlight

A ca. 1860 engraving of the Pennsylvania Hospital for the Insane, showing the beautifully landscaped grounds meant to assist in the rehabilitation of patients. (The Library Company of Philadelphia.)

and fresh air in each ward, but also enabled Kirkbride to segregate patients according to illness. Each ward had a wide central corridor opening onto comfortable parlors and single-patient bedrooms.

The hospital was dedicated on January 1, 1841, and all patients were transferred from Pine Street by June. Kirkbride replaced such traditional treatments as mercury, bleeding, and purges with books, lectures, billiards, dances, and Bible readings. Outside, patients could ride a small circular railroad through landscaped pleasure grounds and flower gardens. Within a year, however, the hospital had to erect two detached buildings to isolate violent patients unresponsive to gentler therapy.

Thanks to Kirkbride's innovations, Philadelphia regained its leadership in the field of mental health. In October 1844, Kirkbride was one of thirteen physicians who met in Philadelphia to found the Association of Medical Superintendents of American Institutions for the Insane, the forerunner of the American Psychiatric Association. During his forty-three-year tenure at the hospital, which came to be known as Kirkbride's, the physician wrote extensively on the architecture of insane asylums, establishing standards for their design and construction.

Samuel Sloan also became a renowned expert in the field of hospital design as the leading practitioner of the Linear Kirkbride Plan, or the Pennsylvania School of Hospital Design. Over his career, Sloan designed more than thirty hospitals around the country, many of which were variations on Isaac Holden's original echelon plan. In 1856, Sloan created a near-replica of Holden's design for the hospital as a separate Department for Males. The new facility stood five blocks west of the original hospital, which became the Department for Females.

In 1918, the hospital's name was changed to the Department for Mental and Nervous Diseases, reflecting changing views on the treatment of the mentally ill. In the 1950s, after the Market Street elevated subway ran a loop through the hospital grounds, the original hospital was closed. All patients were consolidated at the former Department for Males, which became the Institute of Pennsylvania Hospital.

The Philadelphia Housing Authority acquired Holden's building and planned to build Westpark Apartments on the site. Although the newly founded Historical Commission lobbied to save the hospital, the Authority demolished it in April 1959, except for its eastern portico. In exchange, the Authority agreed to spare the nearby Busti mansion, now the Lee Cultural Center. Today, a crumbling set of steps and four graffiti-covered Doric columns serve as "West Philadelphia's doorway to nowhere," in the words of a 1998 *Inquirer* article.[13]

The Samuel Sloan Department for Males, which served as the Institute of Pennsylvania Hospital until it was sold in 1997, still stands at 111 North Forty-ninth Street. It was designated a National Historic Landmark in 1965.

Monument Cemetery

Location: 1900 North Broad Street (at Berks Street)
Completed: 1837
Demolished: 1956
Architect/Builder: Philip Price, John Sartain

With the founding of Laurel Hill Cemetery in 1836, Philadelphia became the second U.S. city with a private rural cemetery modeled after Père Lachaise in Paris (the first was Cambridge, Massachusetts, home to Mount Auburn, established in 1831). Set on more than thirty handsomely landscaped acres, Laurel Hill provided Philadelphians with an attractive alternative to overcrowded and unsightly churchyards and generated a handsome profit for its owners. Soon other entrepreneurs were purchasing land on the city's outskirts (including the Woodlands, the Hamilton estate in Blockley), hoping to cash in on the rural cemetery craze.

In 1837, Laurel Hill's first competitor opened on North Broad Street, a narrow rural lane two miles north of the city. Dr. John Elkinton converted his country estate, Sydney Place, at Broad Street and Turner's Lane into a private cemetery. Engineer Philip Price laid out the grounds in a design reminiscent of L'Enfant's original plan for the District of Columbia, with horizontal and vertical avenues named after Revolutionary heroes within a diamond-shaped parcel.

Originally, Elkinton called his new venture Père Lachaise after the Parisian cemetery. When local newspapers criticized his foreign pretension, he changed the name to Monument, after a proposed memorial to Washington and Lafayette. Due to financial difficulties, the monument, a massive obelisk designed by artist and engraver John Sartain, was not erected until 1869. Sartain also designed the cemetery's gatehouse and chapel, a Gothic brownstone structure with a soaring spire, erected on Broad Street in 1840.

Monument never became a carriage-trade cemetery like Laurel Hill or the Woodlands but catered to the respectable middle

Design for an Entrance to Monument Cemetery, on Broad Street.

J. D. Jones, Archt.   R. S. Gilbert, Eng.

Ground Plot of MONUMENT CEMETERY.

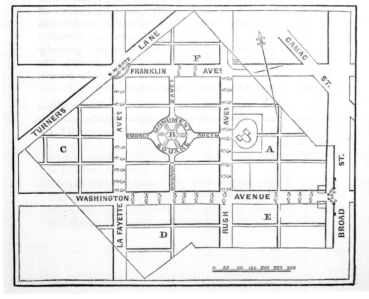

An 1839 map of Monument shows its Broad Street entrance, central monument, and principal avenues named for Washington, Lafayette, Franklin, and Rush. The proposed entrance shown at top was never built. (The Library Company of Philadelphia.)

The Gothic gatehouse and chapel for Monument Cemetery, engraved by its architect, John Sartain, stood on North Broad Street from 1840 until 1903, when it was demolished to make way for Berks Street. (Collection of the author.)

class. Among those buried there were John Sartain and his family; Dr. Russell Conwell, founder of neighboring Temple College, and his wife; and Anna M. Ross, a principal of the Hospital Annex at the Cooper Shop Volunteer Saloon. Many mutual aid societies and charitable institutions held cemetery lots, including the Association for the Relief of Disabled Firemen, Typographical Society, Widows' Asylum, and Artists' Fund Society.

After the Civil War, North Broad Street became a desirable residential neighborhood. As North Philadelphia blossomed, Monument Cemetery withered away. In 1872, the Pennsylvania legislature fought the cemetery's owners all the way to the U.S. Supreme Court to force the opening of Fifteenth, Sixteenth, and Norris streets through the site. In 1903, when Berks Street was opened through the cemetery, the Sartain gatehouse had to make way for it. By this time, Monument had been nearly halved in size, from its original twenty acres to eleven.

After a long, slow decline, Monument suffered a fatal collision with Temple University's expansion plans in the early 1950s. Temple needed land for parking lots and playing fields, and Monument was the only available open space. The university persuaded community and religious leaders to testify that Monument was a magnet for crime and vandalism. After years of public hearings and legal action, Temple acquired Monument in 1956. It moved the bodies of Dr. Conwell and his wife to a memorial garden on the Temple campus. The other 20,000 bodies were removed to Lawnview Cemetery in Montgomery County during a stifling summer, when, in the words of one observer, "The odors in the air were well-nigh intolerable."[14]

Most of the monuments, including Sartain's obelisk, ended up in the Delaware River as part of the foundation of the Betsy Ross Bridge, then under construction. Today, one can spot dozens of submerged tombstones in the Delaware near Castor Avenue. The names of many Monument interments have been recorded from these stones, including Elkinton and Sartain. Most of what was once Monument Cemetery is today Parking Lot No. 1 on the Temple University campus.

Municipal Gas Works

Location: Area bordered by J.F.K. Boulevard, Twenty-second Street, Market Street, and the Schuylkill River
Completed: 1836
Demolished: Late nineteenth century–1926
Architect/Builder: Samuel V. Merrick

In the early nineteenth century, the introduction of manufactured gas for lighting had the same impact that the invention of the incandescent bulb would have at the century's end. Philadelphia was a gaslight pioneer: As early as 1796, coal gas lit elaborate chandeliers for a theatrical spectacle. In 1816, the Chestnut Street Theatre was the first playhouse in the country to use gas illumination; that same year, Charles Willson Peale advertised "gas-lights—lamps burning without wick or oil" at his State House museum.

The Philadelphia Gas Works in 1852, looking northeast from the High Street Bridge. In the foreground stands the purifying house, with the coke sheds behind it running east toward the gasholders. The retort houses with their Doric smokestacks stand in the left and central background. (The Library Company of Philadelphia.)

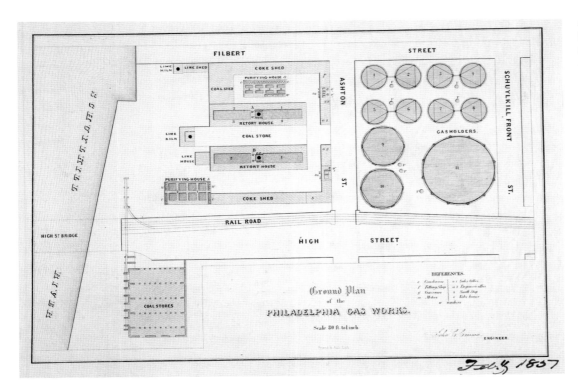

An 1857 ground plan of the High Street Gas Works, drawn by engineer John C. Cresson, designer of the Point Breeze Gas Works. (The Library Company of Philadelphia.)

In terms of establishing a municipal gas system, however, Philadelphia lagged behind Boston, New York, and Baltimore (where Philadelphian Rembrandt Peale founded the Gas Light Company of Baltimore in 1817). As late as 1831, the City Councils voted against a gas works, warning that its vapors would cause ill health, explosions, and odors.

Finally, engineer and gas advocate Samuel V. Merrick arranged to be elected to the Councils and promptly went abroad to study European gas production. When Merrick returned in 1834, he issued a comprehensive report that persuaded the Councils to pass an ordinance "for the construction and management of the Philadelphia Gas-Works" following Merrick's design, with Merrick himself as superintendent.[15] The Gas Works was a semiprivate corporation, with an initial capitalization of $100,000 raised through public subscription.

The Gas Works plant was erected on the land bordered by High Street, Schuylkill Front (Twenty-second Street), Filbert Street (J.F.K. Boulevard), and the Schuylkill River. This sparsely populated area was an industrial district, home to manufactories that, like the Gas Works, produced noxious smoke and smells. The massive complex consisted of a retort house, where gas was drawn off from burning coal; a purifying house, where the gas was condensed and purified; a meter room, where the gas volume was measured and recorded; two gasholders or storage tanks; and a labyrinth of pipes and guide conduits for the gas. Gas was pumped through a main that ran east under Filbert Street, branching off at cross streets.

Built at the height of the Greek Revival style's popularity, the retort house had smokestacks in the form of gigantic Doric columns. The largest storage tank used twelve sets of cast-iron classical columns, four tiers high, as conduits. Columns for the first tier were Tuscan; for the second, Doric; for the third, Ionic; and for the top tier, Corinthian.

The plant went into operation on February 8, 1836, and was expanded within a year to meet increased demand. The introduction of gaslight to Philadelphia revolutionized labor patterns, allowing longer workdays and fueling the city's rising industrial power. Gaslight also created a boon for other industrialists such as the city's nascent iron manufacturers, who grew rich providing wrought-iron pipes, retorts, and gasholders.

In 1841, the city government bought out private shareholders in the Philadelphia Gas Works and converted it to a public utility. By 1852, the Gas Works maintained ninety miles of street mains that lit 1,718 lamps in streets, squares, and private houses. As demand continued to rise, the Market Street plant was expanded again to include four retort buildings, eleven gas containers, two purifying houses, and two meter rooms. But the original plant's maximum capacity of 1.68 million cubic feet was inadequate for the city's growing needs. In 1854, a larger facility opened at Point Breeze, near Passyunk and Schuylkill Avenues below Gray's Ferry, followed by facilities in Northern Liberties, Manayunk, and Frankford. Designed by John C. Cresson, the Point Breeze Gas Works featured buildings in the Gothic style.

Most of the buildings of the Market Street plant were demolished in the late nineteenth and early twentieth centuries as commercial development spread westward. A few of the original gasholders remained at the northwest corner of Twenty-third and Market streets until 1926, when they were torn down during the city's beautification program for the nation's sesquicentennial. Today, the Philadelphia Electric Company tower at 2301 Market Street occupies part of the Gas Works site.

Baldwin Locomotive Works

Location: South side of Spring Garden Street between North Broad and North Eighteenth streets; other shops located between Twenty-sixth and Twenty-eighth streets near Pennsylvania Avenue
Completed: 1836
Demolished: 1937
Architect/Builder: Various

From its founding in 1835 until its dissolution in 1950, the Baldwin Locomotive Works was the leading U.S. manufacturer of locomotives, building more than 100,000 engines for use around the world. Over 60,000 were manufactured in a multisite complex that sprawled across North Philadelphia from Broad to Twenty-eighth Street.

In the 1820s, Matthias Baldwin, a manufacturer of bookbinders' tools, developed an efficient upright steam engine that became his primary product. In 1831, he incorporated this engine into a small locomotive capable of drawing two cars with four people. Seeing this miniature iron horse on display at Peale's Museum, officers of the Philadelphia, Germantown & Norristown Railway Company placed an order for a working locomotive. Baldwin's first steam locomotive, Old Ironsides, made its initial run between Philadelphia and Germantown on November 23, 1832. The first U.S.-built locomotive to run in this country, it reached an amazing twenty-eight miles an hour. Baldwin locomotives replaced horses on the State Road to Columbia, the first leg of the Main Line to Pittsburgh.

Baldwin's firm was soon producing almost half of all U.S. locomotives. In 1835, Baldwin acquired a large tract of land at the southwest corner of North Broad and Spring Garden streets, where he built a three-story brick factory for his 300 workers. Gradually, the factory expanded into a series of semi-independent shops in various locations that manufactured individual parts (boilers, tenders,

axles, bolts, etc.), which were assembled in the erecting shop at Broad and Spring Garden.

Over the course of the century, the Civil War and the nation's westward expansion ensured the company's uninterrupted growth. By the time of Baldwin's death in 1866, the Works constructed more than a hundred locomotives each year. When the original factory burned in 1884, it was rebuilt within a year to accommodate more than 3,000 employees. One of Philadelphia's first factory neighborhoods grew up around the plant, filled with workers who walked to their jobs every day.

By the time of its incorporation in 1907, Baldwin was the largest employer in the Philadelphia region and a symbol of the city's manufacturing might. At this point, the Works' thirty-nine buildings covered seventeen acres and housed 15,500 workers in twenty departments who produced more than 2,000 locomotives a year. While the main complex stretched from Broad Street to Eighteenth Street (interrupted by the U.S. Mint between Sixteenth and Seventeenth), other shops were located as far west as Twenty-eighth Street and Pennsylvania Avenue.

In the early 1920s, shortly after the 50,000th Baldwin locomotive came off the line, the company began to transfer most of its operations to a new plant at a 616-acre site in Eddystone, Delaware County. Gradually, Baldwin closed its vast urban facility, which could not accommodate the huge cranes and assembly lines needed to produce modern locomotives. Some of the smaller, westernmost shops were demolished for construction of the Philadelphia Museum of Art and the Fairmount Parkway. After city production ended in 1928, Baldwin's vacant buildings were used by the city to shelter the homeless during the Depression. The central complex between Broad and Sixteenth streets remained standing until 1937, when the city condemned the site.

Ironically, Baldwin's suburban plant began operations just as the market for steam locomotives started to diminish. The firm declared bankruptcy and reorganized on a much smaller scale during the Depression, firing more than 85 percent of its workers. While World War II revived Baldwin briefly, a misguided postwar decision not to manufacture diesel locomotives hindered its long-term recovery. Baldwin merged with the Lima-Hamilton Corporation in 1950; by 1972, the Eddystone complex had shut down permanently.

Central High School

Location: South Juniper Street, facing Penn Square
Completed: 1838
Demolished: 1853
Architect/Builder: Unknown

Free public education came to Pennsylvania on April 1, 1834, when the state legislature passed "An Act to Establish a General System of Education by Common Schools," also known as the Free School Law. Until then, a variety of private, religious, and charitable or "pauper" schools had provided a limited and uneven education to select groups of children. Philadelphia's initial attempt at a public school system in 1819 had resulted in ten overcrowded, disorganized schools, with ten teachers supervising an average of 285 students apiece.

In 1836, the Central High School of Philadelphia, considered by some the first public high school in the country, received its charter as a result of the Free School Law. A three-story Greek Revival building with an Ionic portico and a cupola was erected on Juniper Street east of Penn Square. The school opened on October 26, 1838, with four instructors teaching eighty-nine boys, most from working-class homes. The curriculum included English, history, Latin, Greek, foreign languages, ethics, mental science, mathematics, science, and astronomy. Central High's rigorous standards earned it the name Poor Man's College. Wary of competition, the University of Pennsylvania attempted to reduce the school's state appropriations. Despite this politicking, the state legislature decreed that qualified high school graduates were eligible to receive a bachelor of arts degree in 1849.

Shortly after the school's construction, an observatory was installed in its cupola, and many considered its telescopes, sidereal

The Juniper Street façade of the Central High School for Boys, photographed by Frederick DeBourg Richards in 1853 shortly before its demolition. (The Library Company of Philadelphia.)

clock, comet searcher, sextant, and other instruments superior to those at Harvard University and the U.S. Naval Observatory. The high school achieved scientific immortality when a young mechanic, Joseph Paxton, leaned out a window at the U.S. Mint in October 1839 to take a daguerreotype of the school with a camera he had built after reading an article in the *United States* Gazette. The resulting blurry image is the earliest surviving U.S. photograph.[16]

By 1842, enrollment had grown to 383. Many of Central High's early graduates would become the city's leaders, including ship-builder William Cramp, Governor Robert E. Pattison, traction magnate Peter A. B. Widener, Mayor George H. Boker, journalist George Alfred Townsend, and lawyer–art collector John G. Johnson. In 1848, a similar institution for females, the Girls' Normal School (today the Philadelphia High School for Girls), opened as the first secondary public school for girls in Pennsylvania.

Within a decade of its founding, Central High School had outgrown its original building, and its managers wished to escape the noise and crowds of busy Penn Square. In January 1853, the Pennsylvania Railroad purchased the site for $45,000 and replaced the high school with a freight depot. The following year, the school moved to a new structure at Broad and Green streets, then outside the city limits.

Today, the Central High School of Philadelphia is located at Ogontz and Olney avenues. The former John Wanamaker department store, now Macy's, occupies its original site on Penn Square.

Pennsylvania Fire Insurance Company

Location: 508–10 Walnut Street
Completed: 1838
Demolished: 1971 (façade preserved)
Architect/Builder: John Haviland (addition by Theophilus P. Chandler)

Philadelphia was an early center of the insurance industry, thanks in part to Benjamin Franklin, who in 1736 helped found the first volunteer fire force and then formed a fire insurance company for its volunteers. Franklin was also a founder in 1752 of the Philadelphia Contributionship for the Insurance of Houses from Loss by Fire, the first property-insurance company in North America. By the end of the eighteenth century, four other Philadelphia insurance companies had been established, including the first U.S. stock-insurance company, the Insurance Company of North America (today part of CIGNA).

By the 1820s, Philadelphia was home to more than a dozen new insurance companies, among them the Pennsylvania Fire Insurance Company, incorporated in 1825 with a capital stock of $200,000. At first, the fledgling company met in the house of Jonathan Smith, one of its incorporators and founders, at 134 Walnut Street (today 510 Walnut), opposite the State House Yard.

By 1838, the firm had prospered enough to buy Smith's property and hire John Haviland to design an office building. Haviland, who designed New York's Tombs prison in the Egyptian Revival style, found the style equally suitable for a Philadelphia insurance company. He crafted a four-story brick building twenty-two feet wide by fifty feet deep with a marble façade. Its papyrus-leaf columns and winged orbs lent an air of permanence to the enterprise, reassuring clients that in an age when fires could demolish landmarks overnight, the Pennsylvania would ensure the existence of their concerns in perpetuity.

By 1902, the Pennsylvania Fire Insurance Company was one of the bastions of Insurance Row, as Walnut Street below Sixth Street

Above: **T**he original Pennsylvania Fire Insurance Company at 510 Walnut Street as it appeared between 1838 and 1902, when Theophilus P. Chandler expanded the structure. (Collection of the author.)

Right: **T**he 1971 destruction of the expanded Pennsylvania Fire Insurance Company building by its new owner, the Penn Mutual Insurance Company. Mitchell/Giurgola Associates dismantled the Haviland/Chandler façade, razed the rest of the structure, and reassembled the façade in front of the completed Penn Mutual Tower. (Temple University Libraries, Urban Archives, Philadelphia.)

was known. The growing company acquired 508 Walnut and hired Theophilus P. Chandler to expand its office. Chandler doubled the existing building, creating a 45-by-138 foot structure with a six-bay front, and duplicating the cavetto cornices, winged-sun disks, and papyrus-leaf columns on the new portion of the façade. At the top of the building, a marble winged-sun disk crowned the company name and united the old and new sections.

By 1971, the Penn Mutual Insurance Company, whose office buildings occupied the rest of the block, had acquired the Pennsylvania Fire Insurance Company building. Penn Mutual hired Mitchell/Giurgola Associates to replace the older building with a modern, twenty-one-story, 375-foot tower to handle its expanded operations. Rather than destroy the historic structure completely, Mitchell/Giurgola dismantled its Egyptian façade stone by stone, then rebuilt it as a courtyard screen to the Penn Mutual Tower. According to the architects, the preserved façade maintained a human scale for pedestrians and served as "a four-story freestanding sculpture defining the new building's entrance plaza."[17]

This may have been the first recycling of a historic façade for a modern building in Philadelphia, a practice that has grown more common in recent years. Today, architects, critics, and preservationists argue fiercely over whether such "façadectomies" are a justifiable compromise between saving the most visible parts of historic structures and allowing new development to flourish.

Pennsylvania Hall

Location: West side of Sixth Street between Race and Cherry
Completed: 1838
Demolished: 1838
Architect/Builder: Unknown

The 1830s saw an increase in racism against African Americans, as native-born Americans and European immigrants competed with them for jobs in a depressed labor market, and as Southern states stiffened their resistance to the abolition of slavery. Their worsening status was vividly illustrated by the passage of a new Pennsylvania state constitution in 1837 disenfranchising blacks, who would not regain the vote until 1870. Gone was the hopeful atmosphere in which blacks and whites served each other dinner at the 1793 roof raising for the African Church, except for the efforts of a small but determined abolitionist movement.

In 1837, abolitionists formed a joint stock company called the Pennsylvania Hall Association to erect a building dedicated "to Liberty and the Rights of Man."[18] Pennsylvania Hall not only would serve as a meeting place, publishing office, and bookstore, but also would symbolize the growing abolitionist movement in Philadelphia. Besides abolitionism, the hall would serve as a center for such allied causes as temperance, women's rights, Indian rights, and free education. More than 2,000 people bought shares, raising $40,000 dollars to build Pennsylvania Hall.

Completed in spring 1838, the three-story building stood on the southwest corner of Sixth and Haines streets, between Race and Cherry. The Greek Revival structure measured sixty feet wide by one hundred feet deep. The ground floor was divided into four storefronts along Sixth Street, offices, and a lecture room. The second floor held a large auditorium, or saloon, with a capacity of 3,000, with galleries on three sides. At the western end, a speaker's podium stood under a large archway that displayed the Pennsylvania state motto, "Virtue, Liberty, and Independence," in gold letters.

At the dedication of Pennsylvania Hall on May 14, 1838, a letter was read from former President John Quincy Adams, who expressed his satisfaction that Philadelphians had a place "wherein liberty and equality of civil rights can be freely discussed, and the evils of slavery fearlessly portrayed."[19]

Immediately after the dedication, the second annual conference of the Anti-Slavery Convention of American Women opened in the Hall. Several thousand men and women of both races attended the conference, including noted abolitionists Lucretia Mott, William Lloyd Garrison, and Angelina Grimké Weld. The first two days of the conference passed without serious disturbance. On the evening of Tuesday, May 15, however, ominous placards appeared throughout the city claiming: "A convention to effect the immediate emancipation of the slaves throughout the country is in session in this city, and it is the duty of citizens who entertain a proper respect for the Constitution of the Union and the right of property to interfere."[20]

On Wednesday, May 16, and Thursday, May 17, hostile crowds gathered outside Pennsylvania Hall, growing more violent as the convention progressed. On Thursday afternoon, Angelina Grimké Weld's speech was interrupted when the mob began throwing stones, breaking many windows. When the managers requested protection from Mayor John Swift, he refused to intercede on the convention's behalf. The managers cancelled the evening's lectures, closed the hall, and turned its keys over to the mayor in the presence of the crowd outside the building. Swift accepted the keys, arrested one troublemaker, asked the mob to behave, and went home.

The destruction of Pennsylvania Hall on May 17, 1838, drawn and engraved by eyewitness John Sartain. In the foreground, a vast crowd watches as firemen train their hoses on adjacent houses and let the Hall burn. (The Library Company of Philadelphia.)

Shortly after Swift left, the mob battered down the doors, wrecked the hall, turned on the gas, and set a fire. According to newspaper reports, a crowd of nearly 15,000 watched the destruction, yet police made no effort to protect the building or arrest the arsonists. Volunteer firemen hosed down surrounding buildings but did not attempt to extinguish the blaze. The destruction of Pennsylvania Hall unleashed a wave of violence against the city's black community; mobs attacked the Shelter for Colored Orphans and the Bethel Church on Friday night.

When Pennsylvania Hall's managers sued the city to recover damages, the city argued that "promiscuous intermingling indoors and out of blacks and whites" had provoked the riot.[21] Eventually, the city would reimburse the managers for one-third of their loss of $100,000. The blackened shell of Pennsylvania Hall stood on the site until the Odd Fellows bought the land in 1845. The fraternal organization incorporated much of the remaining structure into their temple, which was demolished in 1907. Today, the WHYY Technology Center occupies the site.

Wire Suspension Bridge

Location: Schuylkill River at Callowhill Street
Completed: 1842
Demolished: 1875
Architect/Builder: Charles Ellet Jr.

As Philadelphia grew westward, so did the need to expand the city across the Schuylkill River. In 1812, Louis Wernwag's Fairmount Bridge (the Colossus) at Upper Ferry joined the Permanent Bridge at Market Street. The longest single-arch bridge in the world, with a span of 340 feet, Wernwag's wood and iron bridge boasted a decorative cover designed by Robert Mills. Together with the nearby Fairmount Water Works, the Colossus represented the supremacy of Philadelphia engineers and mechanics in Federal America. When the Colossus burned in 1838, however, the city needed a new bridge to handle traffic between Spring Garden, north of the city, and West Philadelphia.

Charles Ellet Jr., an engineer who had studied at l'École des Ponts et Chaussées in Paris, proposed a wire-suspension bridge using the latest French technology. Unlike earlier bridges that were held aloft by iron chains, Ellet's featured galvanized wires spun together into large cables. These cables had excellent tensile strength and were less prone to cracking or corrosion than were chains or untreated wire. While a primitive wire-suspension footbridge spanned the Schuylkill for less than a year in 1816, Ellet's was the first permanent suspension bridge designed for heavy traffic.

On January 2, 1842, the Wire Suspension Bridge opened at Callowhill Street. The bridge, 343 feet long between abutments and 27 feet wide, was held aloft by ten cables strung between two sets of thirty-two-foot granite pylons. To convince cautious Philadelphians of its durability, Ellet crowded the bridge with 200 pedestrians and thirty-nine horse-drawn carts carrying two tons of stone. The twenty-nine-year-old engineer calculated that the bridge could carry five times this load, for a maximum of 2,100 tons.

Streetcars and carriages cross the Wire Suspension Bridge in this view looking southeast from West Philadelphia toward Fairmount ca. 1870. (Courtesy of James Hill Jr.)

Ellet's demonstration paid off, and soon carriages, wagons, and foot traffic crowded the bridge. Mantua and Powelton Village in West Philadelphia grew into popular suburbs. Beer gardens lined the bridge approaches on both sides of the Schuylkill, attracting visitors who came to see the bridge and Fairmount Water Works, and to enjoy such entertainments as tightrope walkers crossing the river below the bridge.

Ellet's bridge continued in service until 1875, when new technology and increasingly heavy traffic rendered it obsolete. A single-span, double-deck bridge replaced it, the lower level connecting Callowhill Street with Thirtieth Street on the west, and the upper level carrying Spring Garden Street across the river. Thanks to the success of Ellet's bridge, the wire-suspension bridge remained a favorite design for nineteenth-century spans, including the Brooklyn Bridge, completed in 1883.

Phil-Ellena

Location: 6800 Germantown Avenue at Carpenter Street
Completed: 1844
Demolished: 1898
Architect/Builder: William L. Johnston (architect),
   Nathan Smedley (builder)

On November 23, 1832, the Philadelphia, Germantown & Norristown Railway Company inaugurated service between Philadelphia and Germantown. Within a few years, the railroad transformed Germantown from a semirural village into a wealthy commuter suburb of elegant villas.

One of the most impressive residences was that of patent medicine tycoon George Washington Carpenter, whose Medicine Chest Dispensatory, a combination first-aid manual and kit, accompanied thousands of pioneers west. Phil-Ellena (meaning "for love of Ellen," Carpenter's wife's name) was a Greek Revival mansion with a two-story Ionic portico, set 200 feet back from Main Street south of Carpenter Lane. An oversized observatory from which one could view ships sailing on the Delaware eight miles away surmounted the house. Although Carpenter claimed that "no architect was employed about the buildings—the plan being that of the proprietor,"[22] the sprawling mansion was an early commission of carpenter-architect William T. Johnston, who would later design the Jayne Building.

Phil-Ellena stood within a 500-acre estate that extended from Main Street to Wissahickon Avenue, and from Carpenter Lane to Upsal Street. A thirty-six-acre central plot, surrounded by a stone wall topped by a red cedar fence, contained the mansion and its outbuildings. These included an Italianate clock tower with works by Isaiah Lukens, an octagonal summer house with a weathervane in the form of Mercury, a 6,000-square-foot hothouse warmed by six furnaces, and a museum for Carpenter's collections of minerals and rare coins. Nearly seventy statues of classical gods carved "by Rush" (whether William or his lesser-known son John is unspecified) decorated the grounds and buildings.[23]

Carpenter was so proud of his estate that he published *A Brief Description of Phil-Ellena*, a detailed catalogue of the mansion's treasures and the artisans who created them: eighteen-branch chandeliers from Cornelius & Company, copies of Raphael's frescoes by Monachesi, silver-plated locks and hinges by Mr. Rogers of Seventh Street, French pane mirrors with gilded frames by Robinson of Chestnut Street, and Gothic Revival rosewood furniture from Crawford Riddell's Journeyman Cabinetmaker's Furniture Warehouse. A gallery displayed paintings by "eminent artists of Europe and America," most of whom are little known today: Rochen, Pages, Midi, and Jacquand.[24]

Carpenter was able to enjoy his pleasure palace for sixteen years, until his death in 1860 at age fifty-eight. By the time Ellen Carpenter died more than thirty years later, Germantown had become a bustling city within a city. The Pennsylvania Railroad had opened a line through the west side of Germantown, where Phil-Ellena lay; the resulting rise in land values made such a large estate unaffordable. In 1893, Carpenter's children sold the bulk of the land to Anthony J. Drexel and Edward T. Stotesbury.

Phil-Ellena was demolished in 1898 and replaced by Pelham, a stylish suburb designed by Herman Wendell and Willard Bassett Smith, who also created the planned communities of Wayne and Overbrook Farms. Most of Carpenter's collections were sold at auction; his minerals were donated to the Academy of Natural Sciences. The Italianate clock tower survived until 1902, when it was sold for junk.

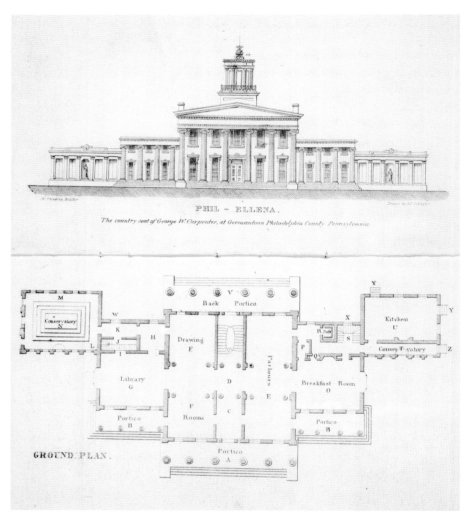

PHIL - ELLENA.

The country seat of George W. Carpenter, at Germantown Philadelphia County Pennsylvania.

GROUND PLAN.

The front elevation of Phil-Ellena and the ground-floor plan, from George W. Carpenter's book describing the glories of his country seat. (The Library Company of Philadelphia.)

United States Hose Company #14

Location: 423 Buttonwood Street
Completed: 1843
Demolished: 1953
Architect/Builder: William L. Grubb (carpenter),
     Charles Twadell (bricklayer)

By the 1850s, nearly a hundred volunteer fire companies, comprising 4,000 active firefighters, served Philadelphia and surrounding districts. Many became important social and political organizations for both Irish immigrants and the nativists who resented them. Ethnically divided, protective of their turf, and awash in testosterone, volunteer companies battled each other as often as they fought fires. Some were even suspected of setting fires to create opportunities for showing off their prowess.

The United States Hose Company was established on July 4, 1826, in Northern Liberties, one of the battlegrounds between nativists and immigrants. An earlier, unrelated company of the same name founded in 1807 lasted less than a year, while a predecessor, the United States Bucket Company, was organized around 1820. As the Fairmount Water Works' network of water conduits and street hydrants spread through the city and adjacent districts, hose companies like the United States replaced the earlier bucket brigades.

In 1843, the United States Hose Company erected its first permanent station house on Tammany Street (later 423 Buttonwood Street). The Blue Dick, as it was nicknamed, was an example of the volunteer firehouses that dotted the city, with ornamentation that advertised their firefighters' avocation and patriotism. The stuccoed brick Greek Revival firehouse, twenty feet wide by fifty feet deep, featured a second-story verandah with Doric columns and an iron railing with the words "United States." A sculpture of a water pump stood in the third-story niche.

Double doors on the ground floor accessed the chamber that housed the company's high-wheeled carriage with its ornate bells

This ca. 1855 lithograph shows the United States Hose Company pulling their hose carriage onto York Avenue from their Tammany Street firehouse, past the Tamany Hall oyster house. A watchman shouts directions from the top of the firehouse tower. Another hose carriage stands in front of a dry-goods store at right, allowing viewers to admire its elegant details. (The Library Company of Philadelphia.)

and hose reel. An observation tower in the rear of the building allowed watchers to spot smoke and shout directions to firefighters pulling the hose carriage on the street below. Inside, the tower provided space for the company to hang and dry their long fabric or leather hoses. The firehouse also featured quarters for bunkers—usually bachelors who lived there full time—as well as facilities for company dinners and drinking parties.

The volunteer fire companies, with their camaraderie, fierce rivalries, and political clout, persisted for sixteen years after the city's consolidation in 1854. During the 1860s, horse-drawn, steam-powered engines rendered hose carriages and hand-powered pumps obsolete. This costly new technology, which few volunteer companies could afford, helped the city gain control over the independent units. Massive brawls between companies at the scenes of fires—including an 1865 riot where firemen fought each other while a hundred buildings burned and nine people died—turned public opinion against the volunteers.

When the city eliminated the volunteer companies in December 1870 to create the Philadelphia Fire Department, widespread rioting erupted and the mayor was burned in effigy. The United States Hose Company celebrated its dissolution by battling the nearby America Hose Company on January 2, 1871. Police stormed the United States house and took thirteen prisoners, three of whom belonged to the company. On March 15, 1871, the municipal fire department went into operation and spent its first hours putting out fires started by former volunteers.

While the city fire department took over some volunteer firehouses, the United States Hose Company was too small to accommodate the new steam engines and the horses needed to pull them. After the company disbanded in 1871, its firehouse was converted to commercial use, and the tower and water-pump sculpture were removed. The Blue Dick survived until 1953, when it was demolished during the development of the Callowhill Industrial District.

Floating Church of the Redeemer

Location: Delaware River at Dock Street (anchorage)
Completed: 1848
Demolished: 1868
Architect/Builder: Clement L. Dennington

Beginning in the 1820s, the religious revival known as the Second Great Awakening renewed American Protestantism with a fresh evangelical fervor directed toward the fast-growing ranks of the urban lower classes. One striking example of this zeal was the Floating Church of the Redeemer, built for the Churchmen's Missionary Association for Seamen of the Port of Philadelphia in 1848. The waterborne church, built on the hulls of two flat boats, ministered to the sailors and other denizens of Philadelphia's swarming and often sinful waterfront.

Designed by New York architect Clement L. Dennington in the Carpenter Gothic style, the Floating Church of the Redeemer was built in a Bordentown, New Jersey, shipyard in 1848. The frame church, ninety feet long and thirty feet wide with a seventy-four-foot steeple, seated between 500 and 600 worshippers. Its interior, painted to resemble brownstone, featured frescoes by H. & O. Filolet of New York.

On December 22, 1848, "one of the most beautiful Floating Churches in the world," in the words of the *Public Ledger*, was towed from Bordentown by the steamboats *Fashion* and *Washington* and delivered to the board of managers of the Churchmen's Missionary Association.[25] Dedicated on January 11, 1849, the church sailed the Delaware River when it was not anchored at the foot of Dock Street and usually flew a large flag reading "Bethel" atop its steeple, which served as inspiration for a hymn, "Fling Out the Banner." Word of the floating church's fame spread to London, where a model of it was exhibited in the American Section of the Great Exhibition in 1851.

Even the most zealous missionary, however, had to concede the logistical difficulties of a floating church. The church sank once and on another occasion was tipped over by high winds. During choppy weather, seasick worshippers often left services early, and even the pastor had trouble staying upright during communion. Sailors on shore leave who wanted to hear the word of the Lord usually preferred to attend one of the city's many landlocked churches rather than board another ship.

After its dock space was leased for commercial purposes in 1851, the Missionary Association finally admitted defeat and sold the Church of the Redeemer to a parish in Camden, New Jersey, where it was reconsecrated as the Church of St. John's in 1853. The former floating church was set on a brick foundation on Lower Broadway in Camden, where it remained until fire destroyed it on Christmas morning, 1868. Today, the Seaman's Church Institute, successor to the Churchmen's Missionary Association, maintains offices at 475 North Fifth Street, well inland.

Jayne Building

Location: 242–44 Chestnut Street
Completed: 1850
Demolished: 1957
Architect/Builder: William Johnston, Thomas U. Walter

During the dark ages of U.S. medicine, as the first half of the nineteenth century has been called, poorly trained physicians still prescribed bleeding as a general curative. Not surprisingly, many Philadelphians tried to doctor themselves with patent medicines like those of William Swaim, Thomas Dyott, and Dr. David Jayne. From Jayne's drugstore at 20 South Third Street poured forth a cataract of cure-alls, including Carminative Balsam, Tonic Vermifuge, Life Preservative, and his popular Indian Expectorant.

By 1849, Jayne had sold enough vermifuge and expectorant to erect the most elaborate and innovative office building in the country. William Johnston, the architect of Phil-Ellena, drew up plans for an eight-story tower to overshadow its neighbors on crowded Chestnut Street. His Venetian Gothic design featured clustered columns soaring to form pointed arches at the seventh floor, topped by quatrefoil windows at the eighth floor. The building was designed to advertise both its patron and his products, with Jayne's name engraved in the entablature and a large mortar and pestle on each of the front corners of the roof parapet. Johnston died in 1849, when only the cellars had been dug for the building. Thomas U. Walter, his replacement, added a castellated, two-story tower to the design.

As completed, the Jayne Building measured 42 feet wide by 133 deep, with a seven-bay façade of Quincy granite. At 129 feet, it was the tallest structure in Philadelphia. It incorporated the latest technology, with cast-iron columns and a spring-seat water closet on each floor. Gothic turrets on the roof concealed machinery for hoisting goods to the various floors. An underground tunnel connected the building with the Dock Street post office (another Jayne-built building), facilitating delivery of its medicines throughout the country. Costing more than half a million dollars, the Jayne Building was called "the most extensive as well as expensive" building in the United States by the *Public Ledger* in 1850.[26] After its completion, other commercial structures began to adapt Gothic and Renaissance styles.

As Jayne's patent-medicine empire grew, he poured his profits into real estate, erecting the post office on Dock Street and commercial buildings on Chestnut Street. He also commissioned John McArthur Jr. to build a four-story mansion for the Jayne family at 1826 Chestnut Street. After a fire gutted the Jayne Building in 1872, the structure was rebuilt except for the castellated tower. In 1907, Frank Furness added a southern entrance to the building for Dr. Horace Jayne, an in-law for whom Furness had designed a town house at 320 South Nineteenth Street in 1895.

As U.S. health care improved and as large drug conglomerates took over the home-medication market, demand dwindled for Jayne's patent remedies. After the Depression, the firm became largely inactive and vacated its showcase structure. In the 1950s, the U.S. government acquired the Jayne Building as part of its Independence National Historical Park.

A battle broke out among the leaders of the park project over both the future of the Jayne Building and the purpose of the park. Charles E. Peterson, historical architect of the National Park Service, advocated preserving the building, which he considered a proto-skyscraper. He noted that as a young man, Louis Sullivan had apprenticed at the offices of Furness & Hewitt, directly across from the Jayne Building. Peterson argued not only that the building was worth preserving in its own right, but also that its verticality might have inspired Sullivan to develop the modern skyscraper after his move to Chicago in 1873.

Judge Edwin O. Lewis, head of the park campaign, and City Planning Commission executive director Edmund N. Bacon dismissed the Jayne Building as a Victorian intrusion and insisted on its removal. Melford O. Anderson, superintendent of park devel-

opment, pointed out that there were other early skyscrapers in Philadelphia and said that the building's "fundamental interest is architectural and has no basic relationship to the park story—America's political development between 1774 and 1800." Despite the pleas of Peterson, Henry-Russell Hitchcock, Philip Johnson, and others, the anti-Jayneites won the battle, and the Jayne Building was demolished in 1957. Under "Justification," the demolition permit noted that "this building is not of historic interest or practical use."

This ca. 1855 lithographic advertisement for Dr. D. Jayne's Family Medicines shows the groundbreaking building topped by Thomas U. Walter's two-story castellated tower. The fanciful mortars and pestles at the parapet corners were never constructed. (The Library Company of Philadelphia.)

Joseph Harrison Jr. Residence and Harrison Row

Location:
- Harrison Residence: 221–25 South Eighteenth Street at the northeast corner of Eighteenth and Locust streets
- Harrison Row: Locust Street between Seventeenth and Eighteenth streets

Completed: 1857
Demolished: 1925–28
Architect/Builder: Samuel Sloan

By the 1850s, Philadelphia's industries, especially its railroads, had produced a class of successful proprietors, managers, engineers, and inventors. The wealthier members of this new technocracy built homes on a scale not seen since the Bingham mansion. Among them was Joseph Harrison Jr., partner in Eastwick & Harrison, one of the few steam-locomotive manufacturers able to compete with Matthias Baldwin.

Harrison, a mechanical genius, developed the powerful Gowan & Marx engine and patented several improvements to the steam locomotive. In the 1840s, he made a fortune directing the construction of a railroad line from St. Petersburg to Moscow for Czar Nicholas I. When Harrison returned to Philadelphia in 1855, he purchased a lot on South Eighteenth Street facing Rittenhouse Square, a

transitional area where handsome town houses alternated with brickyards and workers' shacks. The marshy lot, which flooded frequently, was used as a skating pond during the winter.

For his architect, Harrison chose Samuel Sloan, who had recently completed Bartram Hall, country estate of Harrison's partner, Andrew M. Eastwick. Sloan designed an Italianate mansion based on a Russian palace Harrison admired. The symmetrical three-story mansion, framed by side portals and two-story dependencies, set a new standard for luxury and established Rittenhouse Square as the city's finest neighborhood. Sloan's design featured an octagonal greenhouse, a fifty-foot dining room, and a billiard salon with a ten-pin bowling alley. A new safety steam boiler designed by Harrison himself heated the house.

A domed picture gallery held Harrison's art collection, which included Gilbert Stuart's 1795 portrait of George Washington, Benjamin West's *William Penn's Treaty with the Indians*, and Charles

The Joseph Harrison mansion in 1859. Its neighbors included the mansions of hotel entrepreneur George W. Edwards at 1724 Walnut and gentleman William H. Harrison (no relation) at 227–29 South Eighteenth Street. (The Library Company of Philadelphia.)

Willson Peale's *The Artist in His Museum*. The newly rich Harrison used art to break into Philadelphia's upper crust, serving on the boards of the Philadelphia School of Design for Women, the Pennsylvania Museum and School of Industrial Art (precursor of the Museum of Art), and the Pennsylvania Academy of Fine Arts. After Harrison's death in 1874, the Academy received the bulk of his collection.

While his mansion was under construction, Harrison commissioned Sloan to create a row of town houses adjoining it along the north side of Locust Street to Seventeenth Street. Harrison Row was an early experiment in community planning, a speculative venture designed to attract affluent neighbors to the mixed-income area. The high-stooped houses, each twenty-five by sixty feet, were built in a simplified Renaissance style that complemented Harri-

son's mansion. Amenities included central heating and rear conservatories that opened onto an extensive garden shared with the Harrison residence.

In 1912, banker Edward T. Stotesbury acquired the Harrison mansion, still considered the most luxurious in the city, from Harrison's son, using it primarily for volunteer activities. A decade later, the original residences on Rittenhouse Square were giving way to high-rise apartments. In 1925, the Harrison Mansion was replaced by the Penn Athletic Club (converted to the Parc Rittenhouse Condominiums and Club in 2006), and the eastern end of Harrison Row was demolished for the Warwick Hotel. When the hotel was extended an additional hundred feet in 1928, the rest of the row was destroyed.

Continental Hotel

Location: 824–38 Chestnut Street (southeast corner of
Ninth and Chestnut streets)
Completed: 1860
Demolished: 1924
Architect/Builder: John McArthur Jr.

Philadelphia, the "city of homes," was slow to adopt the concept of a luxury hotel designed to accommodate hundreds of temporary residents daily. While Boston's Tremont House and New York's Astor House date to the 1830s, most Philadelphia hotels remained small enterprises, housed in former residences like the Bingham and Morris mansions. Even the United States Hotel, Philadelphia's premier hotel for a quarter century after its 1826 opening, was converted from two houses.

By the 1850s, the volume of visitors to the city had increased to the point that even conservative Philadelphia acknowledged the need for a grand hotel. In 1852, the Girard House opened at the northeast corner of Chestnut and Ninth streets, followed by the La Pierre Hotel on South Broad Street in 1853. John McArthur Jr. designed both.

In 1854, a fire consumed the Chinese Museum and Burton's National Theatre at Chestnut and Ninth streets, creating a prime parcel of open land on Philadelphia's main retail and commercial corridor. A group of investors commissioned McArthur to design his grandest hotel, the Continental, which opened across from the Girard in February 1860. The massive structure, six stories high on Chestnut Street and eight on Sansom, measured 170 feet on Chestnut by 235 feet on Ninth Street. It was designed as an Italian palazzo, with a sandstone façade, a massive stone portico with eight columns, and a heavy

The Chestnut Street façade of the Continental Hotel ca. 1865. President-elect Abraham Lincoln addressed a crowd of Philadelphians from the lower balcony in February 1861 en route to his inauguration in Washington, D.C. The white building to the left, also designed by John McArthur Jr., once housed the J. E. Caldwell & Co. jewelry store. (Courtesy of James Hill Jr.)

cast-iron cornice. An elegant colonnade of cast-iron piers framed the luxury shops that lined the hotel's street frontage.

Like most hotels of the time, the Continental was designed primarily for male business travelers. The ground floor held the Gentlemen's Reading and Writing Room, Gentleman's Parlor, Bar and Smoking Saloon, Billiard Room, and Business Exchange, where businessmen could conduct meetings, send telegrams, and receive the latest financial news. Meanwhile, a separate ladies' entrance on Ninth Street allowed female guests to bypass the lobby and ascend to the second floor while their escorts dealt with the sordid business of registering.

From the lobby, guests could take a "self-sustaining" (free-standing) staircase to the second floor's grand promenade, 165 feet long, which led to an exterior balcony overlooking Chestnut Street. The second floor was more feminine than the first, with the Grand Dining Room, Tea Room, Ladies' Parlor, dressing rooms, and private parlors and dining rooms. An early elevator known variously as a "vertical railway," "hoisting machine," or "steam elevating car," carried the hotel's 1,200 guests to the 700 rooms on the upper four floors.

By the outbreak of the Civil War, the Continental was the most elegant hotel in Philadelphia. President-elect Abraham Lincoln stayed there in February 1861 en route to Washington for his inauguration, the first in a string of presidential lodgers that continued uninterrupted until William McKinley. Other guests included Nathaniel Hawthorne, Charles Dickens, the Prince of Wales (later Edward VII), Nellie Melba, Lillian Russell, and the Brazilian emperor Dom Pedro. For the remainder of the nineteenth century, the hotel was the scene of innumerable banquets, celebrations, and balls, where Philadelphians could even dance the Continental schottische.

According to architectural experts, the average hotel reaches obsolescence in thirty years. The Continental struggled to stay modern, having Frank Furness remodel the Chestnut Street entrance for the nation's centennial, and making further alterations in 1903 and 1911. By this time, however, the Bellevue-Stratford and Ritz-Carlton on South Broad Street had set higher standards for luxury. Even with retrofitting, the aging Continental could not compete against these newcomers, built with electricity, central heating, and individual bathrooms in place. It closed its doors on September 9, 1923, some sixty years after its opening. After a public auction of its contents, the Continental was demolished in 1923–24 and replaced by the 1,200-room Benjamin Franklin Hotel.

CHAPTER 4

Workshop of the World

(1861 to 1900)

The Civil War pushed Philadelphia to the forefront of the country's industrial revolution. As a central railroad hub, major supplier of military goods, site of the U.S. Navy Yard and the Frankford Arsenal, and the first large city north of the Mason-Dixon Line, Philadelphia was poised to become a transportation and manufacturing leader.

More troops passed through Philadelphia, the gateway to the South, than through any other Union city during the Civil War. Vast temporary compounds sprang up to handle the influx of soldiers: military bases like Camp William Penn and Camp Philadelphia, army hospitals like Mower and Satterlee, and volunteer saloons like Union Volunteer and Cooper Shop. These buildings, along with other war-related structures like the Great Central Fair, taught Philadelphia architects and artisans to build quickly, cheaply, and on a massive scale.

Philadelphia industry, nourished by military contracts during the Civil War, flourished with Reconstruction and postwar expansion. By 1870, Philadelphia had the most factories of any U.S. city and led the nation in the production of steam engines, locomotives, textiles, and steel ships. It was also a major manufacturer of rugs, hats, sugar, cigars, and beer. By the century's end, it was home to some of the country's largest corporations, including the Pennsylvania Railroad, Baldwin Locomotives, Midvale Steel, and Cramp's Shipbuilding.

The rapid expansion of industry and business smashed the familiar patterns of the 200-year-old colonial city beyond recognition. Philadelphia's political center shifted from Fifth and Chestnut streets to Penn Square when construction began on John McArthur's Public Buildings (City Hall) in 1871. Commercial and financial firms moved westward as well, eddying around Penn Square and then flowing up and down Broad Street to form an urban core that would later be called Center City. When the railroad tracks were removed from Market Street, it once again became the premier retail corridor, filled with large new emporia called department stores. Center City took on the appearance of a modern

In the aftermath of the Civil War, Philadelphia cleared the grounds of Penn Square to erect the largest, costliest, and most ornate Public Buildings in the United States. No one could foresee that construction would last thirty years, or that the Philadelphia City Hall would be derided as obsolete almost as soon as it was completed. (Collection of the author.)

vertical metropolis, thanks to the development of steel-frame construction and reliable electric elevators. The city's growth was so rapid that by the time structures like the Drexel Building and Broad Street Station were finished, they had to be expanded almost immediately.

Between 1870 and 1900, Philadelphia's population jumped from 675,000 to more than 1.3 million; to handle this increase, developers constructed more than 100,000 houses. Philadelphia had given birth to the nation's first building-and-loan association in 1831. By 1876, nearly 500 such groups helped Philadelphians of moderate means afford houses, turning it into the "city of homes"

(a phrase coined by building-and-loan officer Addison Burk in 1881). In 1900, Philadelphia's urbanized area extended north to Erie Avenue, west to Forty-ninth Street, and south to Snyder Avenue, spurred by the introduction of electric streetcars in 1892. Yet the city still had 83,000 acres of open land on which to build, compared to New York's 25,000.

As the city spread, it became even more rigidly stratified by class, race, and income. Rows of small houses sprouted across North Philadelphia's industrial neighborhoods for the workers at nearby factories; more spacious residences welcomed the growing middle class to West Philadelphia. While North Broad Street gleamed with the mansions of the newly rich, the old-line gentry made the Rittenhouse Square district their enclave, except for a few brave souls who began to live year-round in Chestnut Hill or on the Main Line. Meanwhile, the old district near the river degenerated into slums for poor newcomers, including Southern blacks, Italians, Russians, and Eastern Europeans.

Sadly, Philadelphia's dynamic physical growth contrasted with a corresponding ossification in civic affairs. As municipal government became the exclusive property of political bosses and party hacks, corruption and mismanagement grew endemic. On the verge of financial collapse, by the 1870s Philadelphia was declared "the worst paved and the worst cleaned city in the civilized world."[1] Despite having fewer slum dwellings than other major U.S. cities, Philadelphia had a higher mortality rate from communicable diseases like typhoid and tuberculosis.

This municipal torpor was symbolized by the incredibly slow progress of City Hall, its cornerstone laid on July 4, 1874, in the hope that it would be completed for the nation's centennial. Instead, construction dragged on until 1901, well after the death of its original architect, John McArthur Jr. Its final cost had mushroomed to two and a half times its original $10 million budget, while rumors of graft and kickbacks abounded. Meanwhile, thanks to the managerial expertise of Philadelphia's private sector, the 1876 Centennial Exposition trumpeted the country's accomplishments to the world while actually turning a profit.

Although no longer the national capital of architecture, Philadelphia was home to Frank Furness, Theophilus P. Chandler, G. W. & W. D. Hewitt, the Wilson Brothers, James Windrim, Addison Hutton, Wilson Eyre Jr., and Cope & Stewardson. Led by Furness, many of these architects championed combining histori-

cal styles into an amalgamation known as picturesque eclecticism. To these men, only a judicious blending of all that was best from the past would befit the nation's limitless wealth, power, and modernity.

A stroll down Chestnut or Market streets in Center City took one past Gothic, Moorish, Tudor, and Romanesque designs, often side by side—and sometimes in one structure. Oddly, this remembrance of architecture past was combined with Philadelphia's trademark technological prowess. The exposed steel girders in many of these structures curved upward in a graceful Gothic arch.

Gradually, the restrained classicism of the Beaux-Arts and American Renaissance schools won out over picturesque eclecticism. Leadership in architecture passed to New York and to Chicago after the 1893 Columbian Exposition that established Beaux-Arts as the latest style. Thanks to the influence of Furness and imitators like Willis Hale and Otto Wolf, however, the eclectic and Victorian Gothic styles lasted longer in Philadelphia than in other U.S. cities. This conservatism made Philadelphia's architecture a laughingstock among modernists, such as the writer for the *Architectural Record* who in 1892 pronounced the city "undoubtedly the most backward and provincial of American cities" in terms of its commercial architecture.[2]

Philadelphia's most monumental buildings from this period—including Broad Street Station and City Hall—looked out-of-date as soon as they were erected. Only a decade after City Hall's completion, one architectural critic called it "ungainly in mass and poor in detail; a distorted reminiscence of the stately pavilions of the Louvre," while another described it as "begun a generation too soon, at a most unfortunate period, and under most unfavorable conditions."[3]

Union Volunteer Refreshment Saloon

Location: Southwest corner of Swanson Street and
Washington Avenue
Completed: 1861
Demolished: ca. 1866
Architect/Builder: Unknown

Cooper Shop Volunteer
Refreshment Saloon

Location: 1009 Otsego Street, south of Washington Avenue
Completed: 1861
Demolished: ca. 1866
Architect/Builder: Unknown

During the Civil War, more troops passed through Philadelphia than through any other Northern city. Starting in the spring of 1861, regiments from New England, New York, New Jersey, and the Midwest crossed the Delaware by boat, landed at the Navy Yard near the foot of Washington Avenue, and then marched to the Philadelphia, Wilmington & Baltimore Railroad terminal at Broad Street for the trip south.

Almost immediately after the outbreak of war, Philadelphians banded together to provide facilities where soldiers could wash and eat a hot meal before proceeding to the front. Although such arrangements were at first informal, two organizations—the Union Volunteer Refreshment Saloon and the Cooper Shop Volunteer Refreshment Saloon—soon emerged, maintaining a friendly rivalry throughout the Civil War. Founded within one day of each other, the two saloons existed only a few blocks apart, and each insisted it was the "first institution of its kind" in the United States. Unlike more elite volunteer organizations, the two saloons were highly democratic, with merchants, machinists, housewives, bricklayers, and clerks supporting the Union cause.

In early 1861, B. S. Brown, a grocer, leased a small, two-story brick boat shop at the southwest corner of Swanson Street and Washington Avenue as a free refreshment saloon for soldiers. At first called Brown's, the enterprise was organized as the Union Volunteer Refreshment Saloon on May 27, 1861, under the direction of a fifty-six-member committee. At 3:00 the next morning, it fed the 800 men of the Eighth New York Volunteer Infantry. Gradually, the main saloon covered a lot 95 by 150 feet, augmented by large sheds where 1,200 men could be served at one time. On January 1, 1863, a gilded eagle fourteen feet wide by six feet high, carved by workers at the Navy Yard, was mounted over the main entrance.

In September 1861, the Union's managers founded a small volunteer hospital—the first military hospital in Philadelphia—next to the saloon. As the number of patients grew, it moved into a 400-bed facility on the west side of Swanson Street and was renamed the Citizens' Volunteer Hospital. A nearby plot of land was turned into a graveyard for soldiers who died at the hospital.

The Union's competitor, the Cooper Shop Volunteer Refreshment Saloon, was established on May 26, 1861, on nearby Otsego Street south of Washington Avenue. (While the Cooper Shop was formally organized one day before the Union, the Union based its claim to primacy on its early operations under Brown.) The saloon derived its name from the two-story cooperage (barrel-maker's shop) on Otsego Street where it was based. Although smaller than the Union at first, the Cooper Shop expanded to the point where it could feed a thousand soldiers in an hour.

Although the two saloons refused to combine operations, they coordinated their activities to handle alternate troop arrivals. When a troop train left Jersey City, a telegram was dispatched to both saloons. A small cannon in front of a flagpole on Washington Avenue was fired, alerting volunteers to hurry to their saloon regardless of the hour. Meals were hearty and simple, consisting of beef, ham,

As the first saloon to begin operations (if not to organize formally), the Union was originally called the Volunteer Refreshment Saloon. In the upper panel of this 1861 lithograph, soldiers embark and detrain from rail cars on Washington Avenue while onlookers cheer. The original boat shop stands at the far left, surrounded by auxiliary structures. The lower panels show the saloon's washroom, main dining tent, and kitchen facilities. (The Library Company of Philadelphia.)

EXTERIOR VIEW

The Cooper Shop Volunteer Refreshment Saloon advertised itself as "the first opened for Union volunteers in the United States" in this 1862 lithograph. The upper panel shows the Otsego Street complex, with the original cooperage at far right. The lower panel shows the Cooper Saloon's managers in the dining hall; note the separate table for officers to the right. (The Philadelphia Print Shop.)

bread and butter, potatoes, pickles, pie, cake, tea, and coffee. On an average day, a single saloon might serve seven barrels of coffee and 15,000 cooked rations. Both saloons also had facilities for soldiers to bathe, sleep, and write letters home, which were mailed free of charge.

Like the Union, the Cooper Shop Volunteer Refreshment Saloon organized a hospital; it also purchased a burial lot at Mt. Moriah Cemetery for its unclaimed dead. In December 1863, the Cooper Shop opened a retreat for destitute and invalid servicemen at Race and Crown streets, the Cooper Shop Soldiers Home. In 1864, this organization merged with the Union Soldiers Home, moving to a new facility at the southeast corner of Filbert and Sixteenth streets. Even after the combined Soldiers Home closed in 1872, its managers took care of the orphaned sons and daughters of Union casualties until 1886.

Both the Union and Cooper Shop Saloons ceased operations on August 28, 1865, with official ceremonies at the Academy of Music. Shortly after, they reopened to feed 30,000 returning soldiers, finally closing their doors on December 1, 1865. During the four years of their existence, the Union served roughly 900,000 men at a cost of $100,000, while the Cooper Shop fed about 400,000 men at a cost of $70,000. Together, the two hospitals cared for roughly 20,000 soldiers. All operations for both saloons were financed by private contributions and run by volunteers, with no federal, state, or city aid.

As Washington Avenue and its surrounding streets became an industrial district after the war, factories and warehouses gradually replaced the Cooper Shop and Union buildings. The gratitude and fond memories of countless soldiers for the city that truly loved them back lasted for decades after the Cooper Shop and Union had disappeared.

Mower U.S. Army General Hospital

Location: Area bounded by Abington Avenue, Springfield Avenue, Stenton Avenue, and the R7 SEPTA line
Completed: 1863
Demolished: 1866
Architect/Builder: John McArthur Jr.

To handle thousands of battlefront casualties during the Civil War, twenty-four military hospitals were built in and around Philadelphia, usually near railroad depots to receive wounded personnel directly from the trains. Volunteers organized many of the first hospitals, reflecting the U.S. government's woeful lack of planning and inability to deal with the unanticipated flood of wounded and sick.

Starting in 1862, the U.S. Surgeon General's Office mobilized a campaign to erect government hospitals on the outskirts of cities for the growing number of patients requiring convalescent care and long-term treatment. John McArthur Jr. turned from creating luxury hotels to designing twenty-five of these hospitals. The largest was the Mower U.S. Army General Hospital, covering twenty-seven acres in Chestnut Hill in the northwest corner of the city. Mower stood on the highest piece of level ground within the city limits, between County Line Road (Stenton Avenue) and the Edgewood

Station of the Philadelphia, Germantown & Chestnut Hill Railroad (today the Wyndmoor station on the SEPTA R7 line).

The hospital opened on January 17, 1863, roughly four months after construction began. McArthur created a vast frame pavilion with fifty 175-foot long wards radiating from an inner rectangular corridor. Due to the small number of patients in each ward, this hub-and-spoke design allowed Mower to accommodate thousands of patients while minimizing the spread of infection.

Mower's design incorporated the latest engineering and organizational principles, enabling its managers to track each of the hospital's 3,600 patients from arrival to discharge. Casualties were unloaded from the train station directly outside the entrance and processed in the central ward, which contained the Medical Department. From the inner corridor, doctors and nurses could supervise an entire ward, checking on activity and attending to problems. Tramways extended through the corridor and along each ward to speed the flow of food and supplies. Fresh water was

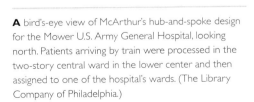

A bird's-eye view of McArthur's hub-and-spoke design for the Mower U.S. Army General Hospital, looking north. Patients arriving by train were processed in the two-story central ward in the lower center and then assigned to one of the hospital's wards. (The Library Company of Philadelphia.)

pumped from the nearby reservoir of the Chestnut Hill Water Company into four 18,000-gallon tanks; water outflow was used to flush waste.

The main administration building and facilities for the kitchens, operating rooms, power plant, dining rooms, chapel, and library stood in the central courtyard, where a large bandstand sheltered a military band that entertained patients every day and a large grove of chestnut trees served as a recreation area. Thanks to its wholesome atmosphere and good hygiene, Mower's mortality rate was low even for a convalescent facility. Of the 20,595 patients treated by Mower between its opening on January 17, 1863, and the end of 1865, only 257 patients, or 1.2 percent, died.

Like other military hospitals, Mower was meant to be a temporary facility. The vast complex was razed in early 1866. Some of its wood was recycled for nearby houses, and its chapel bell was moved to the Christ Ascension Lutheran Church at Southampton and Germantown avenues. After the Civil War, its land became part of the Randal Morgan estate, Wyndmoor, which lent its name to the Montgomery County suburb bordering Chestnut Hill on Stenton Avenue. Today, the Chestnut Hill Village apartment complex and the Market Square shopping center occupy the Mower site. In September 2000, the Pennsylvania Historical and Museum Commission erected a marker near the Wyndmoor train station of the SEPTA R7 line to commemorate the vanished hospital.

Great Central Fair

Location: Logan Square
Completed: 1864
Demolished: 1864
Architect/Builder: Strickland Kneass, B.H. Shedaker,
    Henry E. Wrigley

The U.S. Sanitary Commission, a volunteer organization founded in 1861, worked with the government to collect money, medical supplies, and clothing for sick and wounded Union combatants. In 1864, the commission organized a series of thirty sanitary fairs around the country, raising millions of dollars for its operations. Philadelphia's contribution, the Great Central Fair, opened June 7, 1864, at Logan Square, a tree-shaded plaza lined with residences and dominated by the newly finished Roman Catholic cathedral of SS. Peter and Paul on its eastern end.

More than 3,000 volunteers, including leaders from Philadelphia society, industry, and finance, served on a hundred committees to organize the fair. Thousands more businesses and individuals donated a day's receipts or wages to finance the erection of a complex of temporary structures on Logan Square. Philadelphia's carpenters and bricklayers contributed the labor, using 1.5 million feet of lumber to construct 6,500 feet of buildings in only forty days. A lofty vaulted gallery designed by Strickland Kneass, Union Avenue, bisected the square from east to west, stretching 540 feet from Eighteenth to Twentieth Street. Inside, exposed steel girders stretched fifty feet high to form a Gothic arch, and skylights illuminated the vast array of donated exhibits.

Halfway down Union Avenue, two domed rotundas formed a north-south axis, housing a restaurant and a horticultural exhibit. Enclosed galleries around the perimeter of the square held commercial and historical exhibits, a Pennsylvania Dutch kitchen, a Turkish divan, a skating pond, and a parlor containing mementos of William Penn. Along the north side of Logan Square stood a 500-

The Great Central Fair on Logan Square, looking southeast from the corner of Vine and Twentieth streets. Union Avenue, in the arched vault, bisected the square from Eighteenth to Twentieth streets, and secondary galleries ran around and through the square. The large cylindrical structures on either side of Union Avenue housed a restaurant and horticultural displays. (The Philadelphia Print Shop.)

foot gallery organized by connoisseur Joseph Harrison. The skylit structure contained more than 1,500 works of art, the largest art exhibition ever held in the United States.

Besides paying between twenty-five cents and one dollar for admission, visitors to the fair could purchase nearly all the goods on display. One of the prize items was a poets' album with original contributions by Emerson, Longfellow, Whittier, Holmes, Bryant, and Lowell that sold for $500, more than the average worker's annual salary. Visitors could also pay two dollars to vote for which general would receive a $2,500 sword (Philadelphia's own George Gordon Meade, hero of Gettysburg, was the winner).

Between June 7 and June 28, the Great Central Fair received more than 250,000 visitors and raised nearly $4.5 million for the U.S. Sanitary Commission. When Abraham Lincoln visited the fair on June 16, the crowds were so thick that he could barely reach the entrance. Diarist Sidney George Fisher, a frequent visitor, called the fair and the Sanitary Commission "miracles of American spirit, energy & beauty."[4]

Once the fair ended on June 28, demolition began almost immediately. The art gallery survived into July while the remaining artworks were auctioned off there. Within only a few weeks, Logan Square had regained its pristine, parklike appearance.

Despite its brief existence, the Great Central Fair had a strong impact on the city. The historical artifacts on display, ranging from William Penn's clock to the chair used by Thomas Jefferson as he drafted the Declaration of Independence, gave Philadelphians a deeper appreciation of their disappearing heritage—although not sufficiently deep to prevent both the Slate Roof House and the Graff House from being demolished within a few years.

The fair itself served as a dress rehearsal for the 1876 Centennial Exposition, proving that Philadelphia could mount a successful world's fair. John Welsh, who chaired the executive committee of the Great Central Fair, led the 1876 Exposition to success as president of the Centennial Board of Finance, and many of his committee members who had worked on the fair also played important roles in the later celebration.

Rittenhouse Square Townhouses

Location: Rittenhouse Square
Completed: ca. 1860–1900
Demolished: 1913–72
Architect/Builder: Various

Although wealthy Philadelphians had begun to live on and around Rittenhouse Square as early as the 1840s, it did not become an elite enclave until the Civil War. Even then, the cows and pigs of nearby residents still grazed there. By 1870, Rittenhouse Square was lined with town houses interspersed with an occasional school or church. John Notman's Romanesque Church of the Holy Trinity (1856–59) dominated the northwest corner, setting the height standard for surrounding buildings. In 1878, the Social Art Club moved to 1811 Walnut Street and renamed itself the Rittenhouse Club.

During the late nineteenth century, noted architects replaced or rebuilt many earlier, nondescript residences speculators had erected. The newer structures, with steam heat, gas and electric lighting, speaking tubes, and electric bells, reflected the increasing luxury of the Gilded Age, although their facades remained subdued and circumspect. Newcomers like the Wideners and Elkinses built their ostentatious mansions on North Broad Street; the subtle elegance of Rittenhouse Square reflected old Philadelphia's understated wealth.

By the early twentieth century, Rittenhouse Square had become a victim of its own success. Rising land values and the desirability of a Rittenhouse Square address dictated that concentrated development would replace its uninterrupted façade of town houses. In 1913, the year Paul Philippe Cret laid out the square in the Beaux-Arts style, Samuel P. Wetherill erected its first apartment building, a fifteen-story luxury structure with sixty-six suites, a palm garden, and a tearoom. As Rittenhouse Square residents abandoned their town houses for more spacious living in

The Rogers-Cassatt house ca. 1900, later the Episcopal Diocese Church House. Part of John Notman's Church of the Holy Trinity appears on the right. (Collection of the author.)

Chestnut Hill or on the Main Line, development accelerated. During the 1920s, nearly a dozen high-rise buildings were built on and around the square.

After World War II, groups like the Center City Residents' Association, Historic Rittenhouse, Inc., and the Friends of Rittenhouse Square blocked plans to put a parking garage under Rittenhouse Square and to demolish the Church of the Holy Trinity. They were less successful at saving the remaining town houses, most of which were replaced by high-rises; in 1950, seven vacant houses on the south side of the square were demolished for the Rittenhouse Savoy. Nearly all the survivors of the square's golden years today house nonprofit institutions, such as the Art Alliance (the Samuel Wetherill House), the Philopatrian Society (the McKean-Stotesbury House), and the Curtis Institute of Music (the George W. Childs Drexel House).

The structures gone from Rittenhouse Square include:

- The Rogers-Cassatt House at 202 South Nineteenth Street. The four-story brick mansion with brownstone and copper trim and a mansard roof was built in 1856, just south of the

Church of the Holy Trinity. In 1872, Furness & Hewitt heavily redesigned it and added an art gallery for the collection of owner Fairman Rogers, patron of Thomas Eakins. In 1888, Furness, Evans & Co. remodeled it again for its new owner, Alexander J. Cassatt, president of the Pennsylvania Railroad and brother of painter Mary Cassatt. From 1921 until 1972, it served as the Church House for the Episcopal Diocese of Pennsylvania. When the diocese announced plans to sell the Church of the Holy Trinity and the Church House to developers in 1970, community activists and preservationists were able to preserve Notman's masterpiece but lost the battle to save the Church House, which was demolished for the Rittenhouse Towers.

- The William Weightman mansion at 1724 Walnut Street, a two-story Italianate residence with a high, elaborate cornice and a pedimented entrance, was built by Napoleon LeBrun in 1849 for hotelier George W. Edwards. In 1898, the house was acquired by William Weightman, partner in the chemical firm of Powers & Weightman and the largest individual owner of Philadelphia real estate. Weightman had the house rebuilt as a four-story Beaux-Arts mansion with a porticoed entrance and walled garden. Although no architect is credited with the remodeling, it was probably the work of Willis G. Hale, who designed most of Weightman's rental housing, as well as his country estate, Ravenhill. After Weightman's death, the house passed to his daughter, Anne Weightman Walker Penfield. Mrs. Penfield lived in New York, and the Weightman mansion was sold and demolished in 1929. The site was used as a parking lot until 1951, when the twenty-five-story Rittenhouse Claridge was built there.

The William Weightman residence at the southeast corner of Walnut and Eighteenth streets, with a walled private garden and stable. (Collection of the author.)

The Thomas Alexander Scott mansion at the corner of South Rittenhouse Square and Nineteenth Street, its two-story ballroom in the foreground. (Collection of the author.)

The Thomas Alexander Scott residence at 1832–34 South Rittenhouse Square was built in the early 1870s by Furness & Hewitt for Cassatt's predecessor as president of the Pennsylvania Railroad, who had purchased the lot in 1867. The brick and brownstone residence contained fifty-two rooms on four floors connected by a grand staircase of black walnut. An adjoining two-story ballroom decorated in the Egyptian style later replaced a stable at the corner of Nineteenth Street. When Scott's son moved to a Trumbauer-designed residence in the suburbs, the Scott mansion became the first on the square to be torn down. In its place rose the Wetherill apartment building, designed by Frederick Webber. On February 24, 1913, the *Philadelphia Telegraph* described the destruction of the Scott mansion: "The pick-axes ate into the $20,000 mahogany ceiling and paneled walls of the library. . . . Just inside the massive door was a lofty open hall, with a ten-foot high fireplace and mantel of red sandstone. It cost $1,200 and anyone who wants it can now have it for $30."[5]

Forgotten Philadelphia

136

Rodeph Shalom Synagogue

Location: 609–17 North Broad Street at Mt. Vernon Street
Completed: 1869
Demolished: 1926
Architect/Builder: Fraser, Furness & Hewitt

After the Civil War, North Broad Street became Philadelphia's Champs-Élysées, a wide boulevard lined with fine public buildings and ostentatious mansions. The area bordered by North Broad, Spring Garden, Seventeenth, and Diamond streets also became home to the city's prosperous German Jews, many of whom were members of Rodeph Shalom, the oldest Ashkenazic congregation in the United States.

In 1866, the congregation appointed a new rabbi, Marcus Jastrow, a German immigrant. Religiously conservative but organizationally innovative, Jastrow helped create the Young Men's Hebrew Association, Maimonides College (Philadelphia's first rabbinical seminary), and the United Hebrew Charities, predecessor of the current-day United Jewish Federation. Under Jastrow's leadership, the congregation decided to move uptown from their synagogue, a former church on Juliana (Randolph) Street between Fifth and Sixth. In 1868, they purchased a double lot at the corner of North Broad and Mount Vernon streets for $41,113 and solicited designs for a new synagogue.

The winner was the firm of Fraser, Furness & Hewitt. While the senior partner, John Fraser, was past his prime, the middle partner, Frank Furness, was a dynamic Civil War veteran who vowed to wage architecture as he had waged war. The firm's first major commission, Rodeph Shalom, was partly the result of clever poli-

ticking by Furness's scholarly brother Horace, a good friend of Rabbi Jastrow.

Frank Furness and George Hewitt created a synagogue in the Moorish or Saracenic style. Since many of the details were copied from Owen Jones's drawings of the Alhambra in Spain, some critics described the building as "Alambraic."[6] As with the Egyptian Revival style fifty years earlier, this style was considered appropriate for synagogues because of its "Eastern" associations. Moorish

Rodeph Shalom synagogue, ca. 1870, one of the first major commissions of architect and Medal of Honor winner Frank Furness. Its polychromatic exterior and historical elements represented the latest trends in post–Civil War architecture. (Historical Society of Pennsylvania.)

designs had been used already for such fashionable Reform synagogues as the Oranienburgerstrasse Synagogue in Berlin and the Temple Emanu-El in New York City.

Rodeph Shalom's colorful façade featured horseshoe arches of alternating yellow and red sandstone topping polished red granite columns and decorated with Furness's trademark floral designs. An octagonal corner tower rose 125 feet from a square base and ended in a bulbous onion dome. With little of the exterior's exoticism, the interior resembled a Christian church, despite its unusual trilobed dome. Its subdued design, along with its organ and its pews for men and women on the same level (although separated by an aisle), reflected the assimilationist tendencies of the Reform congregation.

Dedicated on June 21, 1871, Rodeph Shalom was an artistic success, ensuring the future of Furness & Hewitt (the firm soon dropped Fraser), and leading to commissions such as one for the Pennsylvania Academy of Fine Arts. Furness would go on to become the favored architect of the German Jewish community, designing the Jewish Hospital, Jewish Orphanage, Mt. Sinai Cemetery chapel, and homes for many of the synagogue directors.

Fifty years later, however, the Rodeph Shalom congregation found their synagogue's idiosyncratic Moorish design hopelessly old-fashioned, the religious equivalent of a Turkish smoking divan. Their new rabbi, Louis Wolsey, wished to consolidate Rodeph Shalom's religious school at Broad and Jefferson into the synagogue, which would require a larger structure. When the construction of the Broad Street subway in 1926 called for the demolition of the Furness & Hewitt synagogue, the congregation willingly sacrificed it.

In its place rose a fortresslike Byzantine structure by Simon & Simon, with decorations and stained glass by D'Ascenzo Studios. The congregation retained the Furness-designed sculptures, lighting fixtures, and furniture, which still grace the synagogue's chapel. Recently, Rodeph Shalom completed a $5.5 million restoration and modernization of the North Broad Street structure, its sole home since the sale of its Suburban Center in 2004.

John B. Stetson Hat Company

Location: Area roughly bounded by Cecil B. Moore Avenue, Germantown Avenue, North Fifth Street, Berks Avenue, North Third Street, and North Orianna Street, Kensington
Constructed: 1874–1930
Demolished: 1977–80
Architect/Builder: George T. Pearson, J. Oliver Potts, and others

In the days when every gentleman wore a hat outdoors, one of the largest hat manufacturers in the country was the John B. Stetson Hat Company. Best known for his ten-gallon cowboy hat, Stetson was also responsible for many of the fedoras, homburgs, opera hats, and straw boaters that graced Easterners' heads for nearly a century. During that time, the Stetson complex in Kensington became a Philadelphia landmark.

After a stay in Colorado to cure his tuberculosis, John B. Stetson, son of a bankrupt hatmaker, founded his own hat manufacturing business at Seventh and Callowhill streets in 1865. To differentiate himself from Philadelphia's other hatters, he focused on the western markets, where he knew his customers and where he faced significantly less competition. Stetson's first ten-gallon hat, a modified sombrero called the Boss of the Plains, was an immediate success, even at prices ranging from ten to twenty dollars.

By the early 1870s, Stetson was successful enough to purchase land for a new factory at 1740–44 North Fourth Street in Kensington. The outlying district offered room for expansion, as well as access to the Reading Railroad's American Street line. Stetson was one of the first hat manufacturers to combine all processes in one centralized location, from cleaning animal skins to finishing and packing hats, allowing for better economies of scale and quality control. Stetson's success enabled him not only to use the finest materials but also to package his products in handsome hatboxes.

By 1882 Stetson was Philadelphia's largest hatmaker, with more than 700 workers. By the time of his death in 1906, his factory com-

The Stetson factory ca. 1900, when it covered ten acres of floor space, housed 2,000 workers, and produced more than a million hats a year. The copper-clad clock tower rises at the right. (Collection of the author.)

plex consisted of twenty brick and steel-frame buildings, with thirty-two acres of floor space. While George T. Pearson designed many of the later structures, the Stetson Company also employed other architects, among them J. Oliver Potts. Given the flammable nature of his business, Stetson made sure that his factory buildings incorporated sprinkler systems, fire extinguishers, and other safety features unusual for the period. He even advised the builders of his workers' row houses on ways to maximize light and air circulation.

Some of the factory buildings reflected Stetson's paternal attitude toward his workers. A longstanding Kensington landmark was Pearson's six-story triangular structure at the junction of Fourth and Cadwallader streets, fronted by an eight-story copper-clad clock tower with an elaborate Gothic Revival clock. This structure, built in 1892, served as the employees' social center, with a library, reading room, dispensary, and gymnasium. Nearby, a low Gothic build-

ing housed the Union Mission Sunday School. Stetson also constructed a 5,500-seat auditorium, savings bank and home loan association, hospital and dental clinic, cooperative store, and school. He and his successors hoped that these benefits would protect their company's status as one of the nation's largest nonunion manufacturers.

The Stetson Company reached its peak during World War I when, thanks in part to military contracts, it became the largest hat factory in the world. Its 5,000 employees made more than three million hats a year, using sixteen million animal pelts. The surrounding neighborhood of Lower Kensington was a virtual factory town. Within a decade, however, the Stetson Company had begun to decline. The Depression forced the company to mechanize production and to slash both staff and benefits, prompting strikes and unionization by its remaining workers. During World War II, the

Workshop of the World | 139

The Stetson factory in March 1979, with demolition under way on most of the remaining structures. The landmark clock tower at Fourth and Cadwallader streets appears at the far right. (Temple University Libraries, Urban Archives, Philadelphia.)

company demolished nine of its buildings, including its Sunday school, supposedly to provide 4,000 tons of scrap metal for the war effort. Stetson was actually consolidating its operations to compete with smaller, more profitable hatmakers.

The company continued to shrink in the postwar era, as fewer men wore hats. President John F. Kennedy, who went bareheaded to his own inauguration in 1961, is credited with putting the final nail in the hatmakers' coffin. Production hobbled along until 1971, when the company closed the Kensington plant, dismissed the remaining 300 employees, and moved its activity to other states.

In May 1977, the John B. Stetson Company donated the remaining 8.95-acre site and its buildings to the City of Philadelphia, which demolished most of the buildings two years later in hopes of turning the factory site into an industrial park. Arsonists took care of the three remaining structures on September 4, 1980, including the landmark clock-tower building at Fourth and Cadwallader.

Horticultural Hall

Location: North Horticultural Drive and Belmont Mansion Drive,
West Fairmount Park
Completed: 1874
Demolished: 1955
Architect/Builder: Hermann J. Schwartzmann

In 1876, Philadelphia threw a one-hundredth-birthday party for the United States that became the standard for every successive World's Fair. The International Exhibition of Arts, Manufactures, and Products of the Soil and Mine celebrated not only a century of independence, but also the country's recovery from the Civil War. Ten years in the planning and at a cost of more than $11 million, the Centennial Exhibition also showcased Philadelphia's cultural, industrial, and organizational resources.

More than ten million visitors—roughly one of every five Americans—attended the exhibition between May and November 1876. Spread out over 450 acres in West Fairmount Park, it featured 30,000 exhibitors in five major buildings and dozens of smaller ones. The three largest structures—the Main Building, Agricultural Hall, and Machinery Hall—were meant to be temporary. The two smaller buildings—Memorial Hall and Horticultural Hall—were designed to be permanent. Today, only Memorial Hall survives.

The smallest of the Centennial's five major buildings, Horticultural Hall was created as a dazzling centerpiece for one of the largest urban parks in the world. The iron and glass structure, 383 feet long by 193 feet wide, was the largest conservatory built up to that time. Designed in the Moorish style, Horticultural Hall consisted of a tall rectangular structure topped by a lantern skylight and surrounded by curving glass greenhouses. Entrances at the front, back, and sides glittered with polychromatic Saracenic ornamentation in red, green, and yellow. Spires, onion domes, and cast-iron finials decorated the upper stories.

Visitors approached Horticultural Hall through thirty-five acres of beautifully landscaped grounds filled with statuary, sunken parterres, and a reflecting pool. Ascending long flights of blue marble steps, they passed under horseshoe arches of black, cream, and red brick into a soaring interior illuminated by hundreds of colored windows by day and dozens of chandeliers by night. A large marble

Horticultural Hall rises from the grounds of the Centennial Exhibition like an Oriental jewel box. (The Philadelphia Print Shop.)

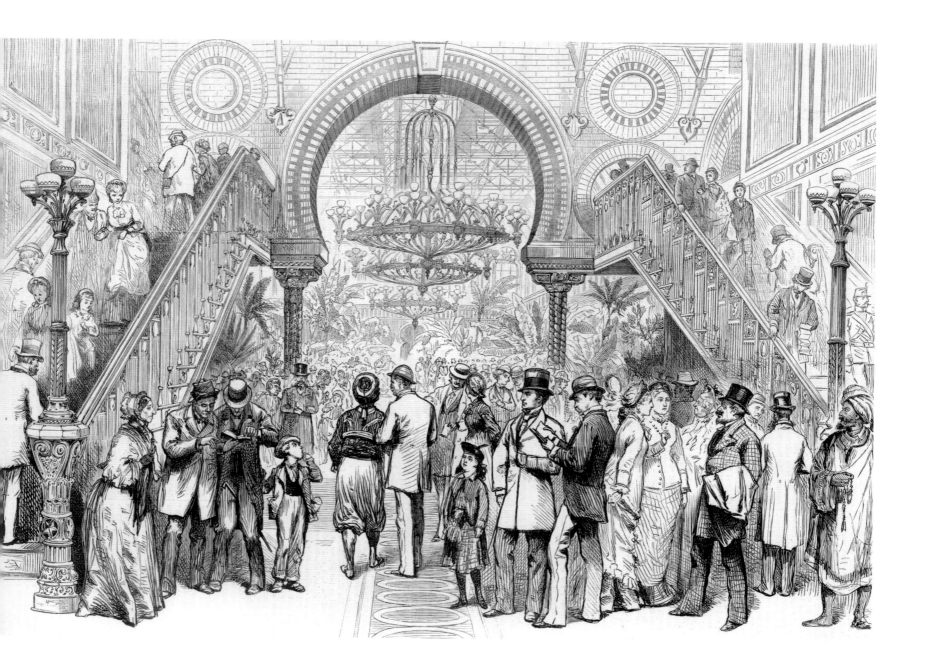

fountain by U.S. sculptor Margaret Foley stood in the center of the pavilion amidst a jungle of tropical plants. Cast-iron ornamental staircases led to upper galleries and outside balconies, where visitors could enjoy a bird's-eye view of both the vast interior and the surrounding exposition.

Over the years, Horticultural Hall attracted fewer and fewer visitors, as its bright hues dulled, its ironwork rusted away, and clear glass or wood replaced its colored panes. Despite decades of deferred maintenance by the Fairmount Park Commission and a severe fire in 1931, Horticultural Hall stood intact until October 1954, when it was slightly damaged by Hurricane Hazel. Even though the amount of storm damage for all of Fairmount Park was estimated to be less than $100,000, the Fairmount Park Commission seized on the cost of repairs as an excuse to demolish the coal-heated, high-maintenance structure.

Starting in late 1954, Horticultural Hall's rare collection of tropical plants was dispersed: Larger specimens went to the New York Botanical Garden, the Bronx Zoo, and other institutions, while smaller ones were sold at public auction. Once the statuary was put in storage, "the greatest Victorian building of its kind" was razed in the spring of 1955.[7] In 1958, the Fairmount Park Commission considered demolishing Memorial Hall, the other "permanent" building from the exhibition, whose leaking dome was topped by a crumbling statue of Columbia. Luckily, the commission was able to raise the $200,000 needed to stabilize the building, and Memorial Hall escaped its sister structure's fate.

In 1979, an architecturally insignificant Horticultural Center was erected on the site of the original Horticultural Hall.

Facing page: **C**entennial visitors from all nations throng the Grand Entrance of Horticultural Hall, with its keyhole archways and elaborate brickwork, before entering the tropical forest beyond, in this May 1876 *Harper's Weekly* illustration. (The Philadelphia Print Shop.)

Guarantee Trust and Safe Deposit Company

Location: 316–20 Chestnut Street
Completed: 1875
Demolished: 1956
Architect/Builder: Furness & Hewitt

After their success with the Rodeph Shalom synagogue, Frank Furness and George Hewitt embarked on a series of innovative buildings. Among them were two stylistic twins: the Pennsylvania Academy of the Fine Arts on North Broad and Cherry streets (completed 1876), and the Guarantee Trust and Safe Deposit Company on lower Chestnut Street, then the heart of the financial district.

Despite their different uses, each building featured a paired entrance, extensive ironwork decoration, and a polychromatic façade composed of brick, sandstone, and marble. Each combined elements of the late Gothic Revival with French Renaissance features like mansard roofs. While the Academy boasted a projecting central pavilion flanked by two lower wings, the recessed central section of the Guarantee Trust withdrew behind two towers, like sentinels guarding the fortunes stored within.

The segmented interior of the Guarantee Trust reflected its dual functions as bank and safe-deposit company. Customers passed through a narrow entrance hall to the Money and Trust Department, a high-ceilinged space lined on both sides by tellers' cages. Through another narrow passage, visitors entered the Safe Deposit Department, a second lofty chamber with rows of screened desks where box holders could inspect their valuables. Both rooms had a churchlike atmosphere, with vaulted ceilings, Gothic-arched windows topped by a clerestory, and a central aisle lined with chambers that resembled confessionals. In the rear of the building, the medieval church effect gave way to that of an ancient

The Guarantee Trust and Safe Deposit Company in the 1890s. (Courtesy of James Hill Jr.)

catacomb: Ornamental iron stairs led to a three-story stone mono-lith that contained the Guarantee Trust's "unpregnable and exten-sive system of burglar proof vaults," protected by "six Hall Double Chronometer Time Locks."[8]

The building's historical guise cloaked a state-of-the-art infra-structure, with steel vaults and an electric burglar alarm and com-munication system. Modern technology joined with innovative architecture to forge a corporate identity for the young company, which had been organized in 1872 and barely survived the financial panic of 1873. The Guarantee Trust building was both a critical and a popular success; one critic called it "a handsome building that attracts unusual attention from the unique appearance and bold departure from the prevailing architecture of our public buildings."[9] Its popularity helped Furness win commissions for a dozen more financial institutions, including the Provident Life & Trust Com-pany, the Penn National Bank, and the extant Centennial National Bank (now the Paul Peck Alumni Center at Drexel University).

By the 1950s, the idiosyncratic designs of Furness & Hewitt appeared tired and fussy. Philadelphia's bankers preferred either the neocolonialism of Society Hill (traditional, all-American values) or the modernism of Penn Center (savvy, forward thinking). The former Guarantee Trust, by then home to the Tradesmens National Bank & Trust Company, looked drab and forlorn, its ironwork stripped away and its colors dimmed by time and pollution.

The building's nineteenth-century appearance also clashed with the eighteenth-century atmosphere of the proposed Independence National Historical Park. Citing the need to reduce the risk of fire to nearby Carpenters' Hall, the National Park Service had the build-ing demolished in 1956. In the 1960s, a reconstruction of the 1775 Joseph Pemberton House was erected on the site; today it houses the Army-Navy Museum.

Ridge Avenue Farmers' Market

Location: 1810 Ridge Avenue (between Ginnodo Street and
  West Girard Avenue)
Completed: 1875
Demolished: 1997
Architect/Builder: Davis E. Supplee

The demolition of the High Street market sheds in 1859 sparked the establishment of indoor markets throughout the city, where farmers could sell their goods to urban residents. As the city expanded, new market buildings sprang up in outlying districts.

Among them was the Ridge Avenue Farmers' Market, a Gothic structure built in 1875 in the Francisville section of North Philadelphia. The one-story building, with its red and black bricks, sandstone trim, and cast-iron piers, was distinguished by its jerkin-head roof and segmental, pointed-arch windows. Inside, elaborate wooden trusses supported balconies and created a large, soaring space illuminated by skylights. Its 40,000 square feet provided 125 stalls for farmers from Montgomery, Chester, and Lancaster Counties, who could stay overnight at an adjacent hotel.

Starting in the 1960s, the decline in North Philadelphia's population, coupled with an increase in crime, prompted many merchants to leave the Ridge Avenue Farmers' Market for other venues. In 1967, the market was sold for $100,000 to two Philadelphia businessmen, David Rosen and Ronald Raiton. After a series of riots swept through North Philadelphia, the market closed permanently in 1971.

In 1983, developer and entrepreneur Raymond Wood bought the market, restored the exterior, and announced plans to reopen as the International Farmers Market, providing 250 jobs and a job-training program for the surrounding community. Despite the support of political and community leaders, Wood's efforts failed. In August 1988, four years after the market was designated a National Historic Landmark, the *Inquirer* described it as "a vast, empty, rot-

The interior of the market in 1968, with its wooden trusses and carved stalls. (Temple University Libraries, Urban Archives, Philadelphia.)

The exterior of the Ridge Avenue Farmers' Market during renovations in 1968. (Temple University Libraries, Urban Archives, Philadelphia.)

ting shell, filled with the sound and the mess of pigeons and vermin. Its once grand windows have long since been shattered and covered. Its ceiling has rotted, its bricks have cracked. Much of it has fallen apart."[10]

In March 1997, part of the market's rear wall collapsed. The Department of Licenses and Inspections demolished the crumbling structure within days, removing one of Philadelphia's few remaining examples of a nineteenth-century farmers' market.

Wanamaker's Grand Depot

Location: 1313 Chestnut Street (block bounded by Chestnut, Juniper, Market, and Thirteenth streets)
Completed: 1876
Demolished: 1910
Architect/Builder: Unknown (1888 addition by Theophilus P. Chandler)

By the Civil War, Philadelphia's industrial revolution had created a middle class with unprecedented disposable income. Thousands of Philadelphians enjoyed the luxuries of indoor plumbing, coal furnaces, wool carpeting, and wallpaper in the new row houses spreading across the city. As their pay increased, so did their desire to acquire the latest fashions in clothing, furniture, and decorations. To meet the needs of the nation's first wave of mass consumerism, retail outlets developed on a larger scale than ever before.

In April 1861, only ninety-four hours before the outbreak of the Civil War, John Wanamaker and Nathan Brown opened the Oak Hall Clothing Bazaar at Market and Sixth streets. Wanamaker's flair for promotion and advertising, as well as some fortuitous contracts to equip soldiers, helped the business prosper. By 1875, Wanamaker (the sole proprietor after Brown's death in 1868) was ready to move westward when he was unable to expand his Oak Hall store.

For $505,000, he purchased the cavernous Pennsylvania Railroad freight sheds on Market Street between Thirteenth and Juniper, abandoned when the construction of City Hall forced the removal of railroad tracks from Broad and Market streets. Built in 1853, the depot consisted of a vast shed with a pitched roof fronting on Market Street, next to a four-story brick office building and three truss-roof additions along Thirteenth Street. Wanamaker, a devout Presbyterian, rented the depot for three months (at a dollar a month) to the evangelical preachers Moody and Sankey, who attracted nearly one million Philadelphians to their revival meetings during the winter of 1875–76.

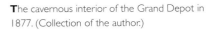
The cavernous interior of the Grand Depot in 1877. (Collection of the author.)

included women's clothing and dry goods. Within a year, an elegantly decorated tent dominated the center of the store; there, women could view fabrics under gaslight to see how they would appear when transformed into ball gowns for evening parties.

In an era when even the largest outlets specialized in a single line of goods, Wanamaker created what he advertised as a "New Kind of Store" where an upwardly mobile housewife could outfit both family and home, from her personal stationery to her bedroom suite. Wanamaker's emporium, with its forty departments, became one of the first true department stores in the country. Even its illumination was novel: On December 26, 1878, the Grand Depot became the first U.S. store lit by electricity.

By 1885, the huge success of the Grand Depot enabled Wanamaker to acquire the entire block bordered by Juniper, Chestnut, Market, and Thirteenth streets. Soon his store was a sprawling collection of new and existing buildings two to eight stories in height. A group of Federal buildings on Chestnut Street was transformed into an arcade, with iron awnings and a Moorish arch topped by a statue of Atlas holding up the world. In 1888, Theophilus P. Chandler added a six-story building along Thirteenth Street and a clock tower at the corner of Thirteenth and Market.

Less than four months after the last hallelujah had died away, Wanamaker had transformed the empty sheds into his Grand Depot, "the largest space in the world devoted to retail selling on a single floor."[11] Perhaps influenced by the Moorish splendor of Horticultural Hall, Wanamaker had the exterior of the building refitted as an Oriental palace, with corner and midblock towers, minarets, filigree decorations, and arched windows. Inside the hangarlike space, stained-glass skylights and gasoliers illuminated 129 sales counters and 1,400 stools, arranged in a series of concentric circles.

The Grand Depot opened on May 6, 1876, just in time to attract the throngs descending on Philadelphia for the Centennial Exposition. Originally limited to clothes for men and boys, the store soon

Gradually, the Grand Depot became known as Wanamaker's. By the turn of the century, it was the largest department store in the world, with nearly 10,000 employees, a New York store in addition to the one in Philadelphia, and offices in London and Paris. John Wanamaker decided the time had come to erect a modern, architecturally unified structure to house his vast enterprise. Ground was broken on February 22, 1902, for a ten-story, granite and limestone palace designed by D. B. Burnham in the American Renaissance style.

Wanamaker insisted that the new building be on the same site as the old, but he wanted the existing store to remain open during construction. The new store went up in three sections over nearly a decade, proceeding from Market Street to Chestnut as the former Grand Depot and its dependencies disappeared. Eight years after the groundbreaking, John Wanamaker set the capstone on his new store on Completion Day, June 11, 1910. By this time, his store's presence had established East Market Street as Philadelphia's retail hub, home to Strawbridge & Clothier, Lit Brothers, Gimbels, Snellenberg's, and other department stores.

Wanamaker's would reign as Philadelphia's premier department store for nearly eighty years, until changing markets, shaky leadership, and industry consolidation brought it down. Today, another store inhabits the first three floors of the building, while the remaining seven floors house corporate offices.

Broad Street Theater/Kiralfy's Alhambra Palace

Location: 237 South Broad Street (east side, between Locust and Spruce streets)
Completed: 1876
Demolished: 1937
Architect/Builder: Frank H. Loenholdt

In 1876, Bolossy and Imre Kiralfy, two Hungarian impresarios, arrived in Philadelphia to cash in on the crowds of centennial visitors hungry for entertainment. They purchased a former coal yard on South Broad Street, Philadelphia's Gay White Way, directly across from the Academy of Music and near other playhouses, including the Empire Theatre.

Their architect, Frank H. Loenholdt, concocted a Moorish confection, Kiralfy's Alhambra Palace. The theater's outstanding features were two large polychromatic domes set above the thrust

sections, echoed by two smaller domes at the ends of the building. Large, stained-glass fanlights topped the fourteen arched doors and windows on the symmetrical façade. A second-floor balcony offered fresh air to theatergoers during intermission. Gilded and polychromed wood and plaster, intricately carved surfaces, and elaborate gas fixtures encrusted the theater's interior. The ticket booth looked like a genie's bottle, with a golden dome, stained-glass windows, and fringe-shaded lightbulbs.

The Alhambra's large stage was the setting for extravaganzas such as *Uncle Tom's Cabin, The Black Crook,* and *Around the World in Eighty Days,* complete with dancing girls, large choruses, "original Parisian scenery, gorgeous costumes, armors, jewels, and paraphernalia!"[12] Ignoring the traditional advice to actors never to share the stage with children or animals, the Kiralfys introduced menageries into their productions, with herds of fawns, packs of hunting dogs, and even an elephant. After the show, patrons could visit the beer garden north of the theater and stroll among stone grottoes, marble statues, and fountains.

Unfortunately, the pricy paraphernalia of the Kiralfy brothers' spectacles always outstripped their ticket sales. In 1888, the theater was sold at auction to J. M. Fox, who hired John D. Allen to tone down Loenholdt's original design and opened the venue the following year as the Broad Street Theater. In its subdued reincarnation, the Broad Street became the preferred playhouse for genteel society, the "premier house of our temples of drama, where you took your mother or your best girl" to see Sarah Bernhardt, Mrs. Fiske, or John Drew.[13] In 1904, a second redesign by Rush Plowman removed the building's trademark domes. Later, writer and critic Alexander Woollcott remembered the Broad Street Theater as the place "where I kept the red plush of the gallery rail moist with my tears over the nightly death of Nat Goodwin as Nathan Hale."[14]

The Broad Street Theater ca. 1890, after its Moorish exoticism had been slightly restrained. (Athenaeum of Philadelphia.)

Broad Street (Pennsylvania Railroad) Station

Location: Block bounded by Market, North Broad, Filbert, and North Eighteenth streets
Completed: 1882 (expanded 1894)
Demolished: 1952
Architect/Builder: Wilson Brothers & Co./Furness, Evans & Co.

By the 1870s, a railroad war raged in Philadelphia between the venerable Reading and the upstart Pennsylvania, with the Baltimore & Ohio running a distant third. The Pennsylvania Railroad, already one of the world's largest corporations with nearly 60,000 employees, upped the stakes by building a Center City station at the southwest corner of Merrick (Broad) and Filbert streets. The location, directly across from City Hall, then under construction, reflected the influence of the politically powerful railroad over the municipal government.

John and Joseph Wilson, graduates of the Pennsylvania's engineering department, designed a five-and-a-half-story brick and granite Gothic castle with terra-cotta trim and an eight-story clock tower. To bring trains into Center City from its West Philadelphia depot at Market Street and Lancaster Avenue, the Pennsylvania erected a retaining wall that stretched more than 2,000 feet, from the Schuylkill River to Sixteenth Street. This became the Chinese Wall, which bisected the city, covered eighteen acres of valuable real estate, and obstructed traffic for generations.

Shortly after Broad Street Station's completion in 1882, it became clear that the structure was too small for the Pennsylvania's operations. At the same time, the rival Reading announced plans to construct an elegant American Renaissance headhouse at Twelfth and Market, backed by the world's largest train shed.

In response, the Pennsylvania bought the land south of its original station, along Market Street between Fifteenth and Sixteenth.

By the 1930s, the combined impact of talking pictures and the Depression had devastated Philadelphia's live theaters. Between 1936 and 1940, five houses shut their doors: the Adelphi, the Broad Street, the Chestnut Street Opera House, the Garrick, and the Lyric. The final curtain fell on the Broad Street's last show, *Fresh Fields*, on May 9, 1936. The theater was demolished in August 1937, and its site was used as a parking lot for many years. Today, the Doubletree Hotel stands on the site.

After a fifty-year decline, South Broad Street has been reborn as Philadelphia's theatrical center under the name Avenue of the Arts. Since 1993, the Kimmel Center for the Performing Arts, Philadelphia Clef Club, Wilma Theater, Philadelphia Arts Bank, and other venues have joined the Academy of Music and the Merriam Theater (formerly the Shubert), the two survivors of South Broad's theatrical heyday.

Karl Bitter decorated the enlarged structure with an allegorical series of terra-cotta sculptures and bas-reliefs, mirroring Alexander Milne Calder's statuary on City Hall. Above the main entrance at the corner of Broad and Market, a clock surrounded by the figures of Time, Mortality, and Fate urged tardy commuters on their way. The world's largest terra-cotta sculpture, fifty feet long, stood over the Market Street entrance and depicted Humankind, represented by Man, yoking Fire and Water to a chariot. Inside the station, a huge bas-relief, "The Spirit of Transportation," showed humanity's progress from chariots and covered wagons to locomotives and airplanes. (In 1933 this bas-relief was moved to the newly completed Thirtieth Street Station, where it remains today.)

At its completion in 1894, the expanded Broad Street Station was the largest passenger railroad terminal in the world, with more than 450 trains

Furness, Evans & Co. doubled the station's size with a ten-story office building to house the Pennsylvania's executive offices. The addition, capped by an ornate tower at Broad and Market, dwarfed the original station. Furness, Evans also created a new layout for the combined structure, turning the entire ground floor into an entrance hall and ticket office, with a grand staircase leading to the waiting rooms and restaurant on the second level. Wilson Brothers replaced the four original train sheds with the largest shed in the world, a glass and steel arch measuring 591 by 306 feet and rising a hundred feet above the tracks.

arriving and departing daily. But the station's glory days were already passing. As with City Hall, the station's Victorian architecture had fallen out of fashion, while Beaux-Arts and American Renaissance styles were in the ascendancy. In 1908, critic Huger Elliot condemned the station's "pseudo-Gothic towers and pinnacles" and found Bitter's sculpture "of a kind to make the judicious weep."[15] Although Broad Street was the Pennsylvania's most heavily used passenger terminal, it was overshadowed by McKim, Mead & White's classical Pennsylvania Station in New York, completed in 1910. Finally, Broad Street Station's inefficient stub design meant

The Furness, Evans & Co. addition to Broad Street Station at the intersection of Broad and Market streets, ca. 1925, from City Hall Plaza. A pedestrian bridge connecting the station with the Commercial Trust Building on the south side of Market Street is visible at left. (The Library Company of Philadelphia.)

Broad Street Station, the Depression and World War II extended the older terminal's life for another two decades.

On April 27, 1952, the last train pulled out of Broad Street Station, carrying Eugene Ormandy and the Philadelphia Orchestra. Demolition on the station began less than twelve hours after the last strains of "Auld Lang Syne" had faded away. Some of Broad Street Station's statuary and fittings were salvaged, including a number of doorknobs that were mounted on marble and presented by the Pennsylvania Railroad to its directors as relics of what it had once called "America's Grandest Railway Terminal." Much of the rubble from the station was hauled to South Philadelphia, where it was used as fill for the Greenwich ore pier.

Over the next two decades, the Penn Center office complex took shape on the site of the former Chinese Wall. Much of the footprint of the station itself was covered by the northern end of the Philadelphia Redevelopment Authority's Plaza Project (now Dilworth Plaza), built between 1966 and 1977 to create a pedestrian terrace symbolically linking City Hall with J.F.K. Plaza and the parkway beyond.

that trains had to leave in reverse and turn around at Thirtieth Street, adding to travel time.

After World War I, the city government and Pennsylvania Railroad developed plans to replace Broad Street Station with modern stations for electrified trains and subways that would arrive via tunnel, allowing the Chinese Wall to be demolished and its land to be developed. A massive fire that destroyed Broad Street Station's train shed in 1923 increased public pressure to remove the station and tracks from Center City. Although Suburban Station and Thirtieth Street Station were constructed between 1927 and 1933 to replace

Drexel Building

Location: Southeast corner of Fifth and Chestnut streets
Completed: 1885 (expanded 1889)
Demolished: 1955
Architect/Builder: Wilson Brothers & Co.

While much of Philadelphia commerce and society moved west in the nineteenth century, the conservative financial sector remained on Third Street near Chestnut. One of the fixtures of Bankers' Row was the firm of Drexel & Co. at 34 South Third Street. Its founder, Francis Martin Drexel, was an Austrian immigrant and painter who had traveled to South America to make a killing with his portraits of the late liberator Simon Bolivar. While

there, Drexel picked up the more lucrative art of currency exchange and arbitrage; returning to Philadelphia in 1837, he established an investment banking firm. When Biddle's Bank collapsed in 1841, Drexel & Co. emerged as the leading private bank in Philadelphia, financing railroads and bankrolling the Union during the Civil War.

Well before Francis Drexel's death in 1863, control of the firm had shifted to his son, Anthony J. Drexel, who established offices in London, Paris, Chicago, and San Francisco and engineered a profitable partnership with a young New York banker, J. P. Morgan. With George W. Childs, Drexel co-owned the *Public Ledger* and developed the railroad suburbs of Pelham, Wayne, and Overbrook Farms. He also founded the Drexel Institute, today Drexel University.

In 1885, Anthony Drexel moved the firm two blocks west from Chestnut and Third streets to the southeast corner of Chestnut and Fifth. The Wilson Brothers demolished Library Hall for a marble building with massive columns framing tall, Roman-arched windows. Inside, the main banking room rose four stories to a height of fifty feet, with no interior supports.

By 1887, the expansion-minded Drexel had acquired all the property on the block south to Chancellor Street and east to the Custom House, with the exception of the 27-by-105 foot Independence National Bank on Chestnut Street. That year, the Wilson Brothers redesigned the Drexel Building as a modern, eleven-story, H-shaped office building that incorporated the original bank as the lower half of the west wing. The H-shape was built to accommodate the Independence National Bank, which found itself walled in on three sides after refusing to sell out.

To support the weight of the new floors atop the original bank, the Wilson Brothers developed an innovative structural technique,

The original House of Drexel at the southeast corner of Fifth and Chestnut streets shortly after its completion in 1885. (Collection of the author.)

an A-frame of diagonal braces reinforced by tie-rods and struts. Four electric fans on the roof provided an early form of air conditioning. The Drexel Building was decorated with 71,000 square feet of marble inside, and 11,000 square feet of white enameled brick outside.

When the 135-foot-tall structure was finished in 1889, the Drexel Building was one of the city's first skyscrapers, its rooftop viewing pavilion a popular tourist attraction. In 1901, Drexel's estate acquired the Independence National Bank Building and replaced it with a starkly simple, neoclassical central entrance.

For more than thirty years, the Drexel Building was the center of Philadelphia's financial life. Besides Drexel & Co., it housed the Philadelphia Stock Exchange from 1888 to 1902 and from 1912 until 1934. After the stock exchange moved, the library of the American Philosophical Society occupied those quarters.

In the 1920s, Drexel & Co., then under the leadership of Edward T. Stotesbury, joined the westward trek to City Hall, constructing a new headquarters in 1927 at the northeast corner of Fifteenth and Walnut streets. The company used the Chestnut Street building for backroom operations or rented it out to smaller businesses. When Independence National Historical Park was laid out in the 1950s, the Drexel Building's proximity to Independence Hall was its ticket to extinction; it was demolished in 1955. Its former tenant, the American Philosophical Society, constructed a replica of Library Hall on its site in 1959.

The original home of Drexel & Co. at 34 South Third Street survived until 1975, when it too was demolished. After several mergers, the company ended its days as part of Drexel Burnham Lambert, dissolved in 1990 after a federal investigation into the illegal activities of its junk-bond king, Michael Milken. In January 2004, however, an advertisement in the *Wall Street Journal* announced the rebirth of Drexel, Morgan & Co., an investment advisory firm for financial consultants.

In contrast to its classical exterior, the interior of the original Drexel Building featured cerulean blue glazed bricks and ornamented iron crossbeams trimmed in yellow, red, green, and gold. (Collection of the author.)

Peter A. B. Widener Residence

Location: 1200 North Broad Street
Completed: 1887
Demolished: 1980
Architect/Builder: Willis G. Hale

After the Civil War, the self-made men who dominated Philadelphia business, politics, and industry were politely but firmly excluded from the old-line society that clustered around Rittenhouse Square. In response, some of these men built large mansions on North Broad Street, just as they would later establish palatial estates further north along Old York Road in Cheltenham Township when old Philadelphia moved south and west to the Main Line and Chestnut Hill.

Foremost among Philadelphia's new men was Peter Arrell Brown Widener, a butcher who parlayed profitable Civil War contracts to supply meat to the Union Army into his first fortune. After the war, as city treasurer, he used his political connections and insider knowledge to gain a monopoly of Philadelphia's trolley lines and became one of the city's traction kings, along with his old friend William Elkins. By the 1880s, P.A.B. Widener had become one of the wealthiest and most powerful businessmen in the country, owning traction lines in Philadelphia, Chicago and New York, and with major interests in steel, oil, railroads, utilities, tobacco, real estate, and steamships.

To proclaim his status, Widener acquired a large lot at the northwest corner of Broad Street and Girard Avenue in 1886. For his architect, he selected Willis G. Hale, who had designed speculative row-house developments for Widener near the traction king's North

Facing page: The P.A.B. Widener mansion ca. 1940, when it was being used as a branch of the Free Library. The two-and-a-half-story structure behind the mansion once housed Widener's art collection. (Temple University Libraries, Urban Archives, Philadelphia.)

In 1979, one year before the house was destroyed by fire, the entrance hall looked much as it had during the Wideners' ownership. (Temple University Libraries, Urban Archives, Philadelphia.)

Philadelphia trolley lines. Noted for his buildings' flamboyant eclecticism, Hale drew up plans for an North German Renaissance palace that was, in the words of one newspaper, "all that an ex-City Treasurer and Traction Railway magnate could desire and it is safe to say that no English earl will be able to boast a handsomer house in London."[16]

The 53-by-144 foot mansion rose four-and-a-half stories from a raised basement, its sensuous curves and rounded walls leading the eye skyward to its pointed roofs and gables. A curving double staircase flowed up to a large arched entrance flanked by arched windows and topped by a four-arched balcony. On both ends of the façade, circular towers with large bay windows rose to conical roofs that framed an oversized Flemish gable. Along the sides of the house, tall chimneys topped with onion domes flanked other Flemish gables. The brownstone and brick walls were decorated with carving, pilasters, belt courses, and terra-cotta garlands and bouquets.

The high level of detail continued in the mansion's interior, designed by noted decorative artist George Herzog. The entrance hall was graced by a coffered wood ceiling inlaid in bronze and tile, its elaborate designs mirroring those on the mosaic floor. The stairs to the second floor featured a balustrade and support pillars with alabaster columns and bronze bases and capitals. The two-story dining room walls, decorated with heavily carved wooden paneling and pilasters, encompassed a musician's gallery and a gigantic fireplace and inglenook. At the room's second-floor level, Herzog filled spaces between the pilasters with murals of the Widener children in antique dress, wandering through a fantasy landscape of sunlit gardens and Baroque villages.

On the second floor, a grand ballroom ran the depth of the house and opened onto the four-arched balcony, affording guests the chance to promenade or rendezvous between dances. The mansion was furnished with the latest conveniences, including an elevator, dynamos to provide electric light, electric bells in every room to summon servants, and even a new type of inner window blind patented especially for the house. Widener had a glass conservatory at the rear of the house replaced in 1892 by a two-and-a-half-story picture gallery for his growing art collection.

On the land north of his mansion, Widener built a twin house for his son George (who perished on the *Titanic* in 1912); George's wife, Eleanore (William Elkins' daughter); and her brother George. William Elkins completed the family compound by building a mansion opposite the Widener residence at the northeast corner of Broad and Girard.

Within a decade, Widener was ready to move north to Cheltenham Township, tired of being snubbed by society and needing more space for his collections of art, antiques, and tapestries. He might also have been ashamed of his *schloss*, which appeared outdated as Beaux-Arts architecture became the rage after the 1893 Columbian Exposition. For his country estate, Widener passed over Hale and selected the rising star Horace Trumbauer, who had designed the handsome Georgian structures for Widener's Willow Grove Amusement Park. In 1897, Trumbauer began designing Lynnewood Hall in Elkins Park, a 110-room neoclassical mansion that sits abandoned and crumbling today.

In 1897, Widener announced plans to donate his city mansion to the Free Library in memory of his late wife. Renovated by Trumbauer, the H. Josephine Widener Memorial Free Library opened in May 1900 and occupied the mansion until 1946. After that, a number of institutions occupied the Widener mansion, including the Conwell Theological Seminary and the Institute for Black Ministries. The house remained intact until July 1980, when a three-alarm fire damaged it beyond repair, forcing its demolition. Today, fast-food restaurants occupy the corner of Broad and Girard; all that remains of the Widener residence is the one-story shell of the stable and carriage house on Carlisle Street.

William Penn Charter School

Location: 12 South Twelfth Street (southwest corner of Twelfth and Market streets)
Completed: 1888
Demolished: 1929
Architect/Builder: Cope & Stewardson

Education was always a high priority for the Quakers. William Penn's Frame of Government for Pennsylvania, published in 1682, directed that "the Governor and Provincial Council shall erect and order all public schools, and encourage and reward the authors of useful sciences and laudable inventions."[17]

In 1689, the Monthly Meeting of Friends founded a public grammar school "to encourage relations and well disposed persons to become tutors of the youth in useful and necessary instruction; also, that the children of the poor might have the benefit of proper learning."[18] Penn granted the school a charter in 1708, along with a seal combining his family coat of arms with biblical quotations from Proverbs ("Good instruction is better than riches") and Romans ("Love one another"). In 1744, a two-story, four-classroom brick schoolhouse was built on Fourth Street between Chestnut and Walnut.

In the 1870s, the school's overseers consolidated it with several other Friends' schools and renamed the combined entity the William Penn Charter School. To accommodate the new school, its overseers acquired the brick residence of the Pennock family at the southwest corner of Twelfth and Market streets. The William Penn Charter School opened there on February 2, 1875, with seventeen scholars, who could walk across the school's courtyard to the Twelfth Street Meeting House.

Within five years, the school, with 117 students, had outgrown its home. In 1888, its managers commissioned the firm of Cope & Stewardson (whose principals were members of old Quaker families) to design a new school building on Twelfth Street in front of

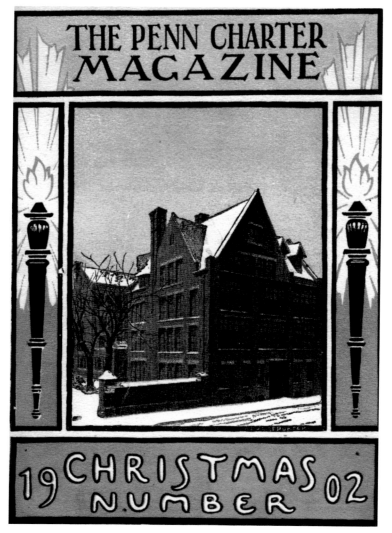

THE PENN CHARTER MAGAZINE

19 CHRISTMAS 02 NUMBER

The William Penn Charter School was featured on the Christmas 1902 issue of the student literary magazine. (Collection of the author.)

the Pennock residence. The four-and-a-half-story structure, of red brick with marble trim, featured tall chimneys and a cross-gabled roof. While the Elizabethan Tudor design evoked the architecture of Philadelphia's earliest days, the modern, oversized windows filled the classrooms with sunlight.

The first three floors held classrooms, while the lunchroom, selling such delicacies as ten-cent jelly sandwiches and Pennsylvania Dutch pretzels, was on the fourth floor. The two-story basement held the gymnasium until a separate athletic facility, designed by Walter Smedley, was built in 1892.

Within fifteen years, the school's Center City location was destined for obsolescence. In 1903, the school was willed 22.5 acres on rural Queen Lane, between Germantown and East Falls. Its managers initiated plans to relocate the school at once, although the move to the new campus (designed by Zantzinger Borie & Medary) would not occur until 1922. In the meantime, the Queen Lane location was used for William Penn's athletic fields, to which students took the Pennsylvania Railroad's Chestnut Hill Local from Broad Street Station.

In 1925, the Philadelphia Savings Fund Society purchased the school's 58-by-132-foot property for $1.6 million, demolishing the building in 1929 for its new office building. Ironically, a small PSFS branch designed by George Howe stood across the street from Penn Charter, its Elizabethan design mirroring that of the school. Within a few years, the redbrick gables and chimneys of Cope & Stewardson's structure had given way to Howe and Lescaze's iconoclastic International Style skyscraper.

Compton

Location: Meadowbrook Avenue (Morris Arboretum), Chestnut Hill
Completed: 1888
Demolished: 1968
Architect/Builder: Theophilus P. Chandler, Jr.

After the Civil War, improved railroad service made regular travel between a suburban home and Center City a reality. Rural Chestnut Hill, in the northwestern corner of the city, had been a summer retreat for wealthy Philadelphians since the 1830s; now many began to live there for most or all of the year. Their expansive estates, some of them working farms covering hundreds of acres, usually centered on a massive house resembling a medieval fortress. Architects like Theophilus P. Chandler Jr. developed a style

cynically referred to as "Corporate Feudal" or "Robber Baronial"for these houses, with irregular floor plans, cross-gabled roofs, rusticated granite, crenellated towers, and large balconies and piazzas.[19]

One of Chandler's most notable commissions was Compton, the country estate of John and Lydia Morris. The brother and sister were both unmarried, descendants of a notable Quaker family, and heirs to an ironworks fortune. By the 1880s, industrial development surrounded Cedar Grove, the Morrises' 1749 family home in Frankford. (Lydia Morris later donated it to the city and had it moved to its present location in Fairmount Park.)

In 1887, the Morrises purchased a twenty-six-acre farm on the outskirts of Chestnut Hill and named it Compton, after their family's ancestral village in England. Between 1887 and 1915, they expanded their holdings to 165 acres in both Chestnut Hill and neighboring Montgomery County. They created a magnificent garden estate, with an English park, Japanese gardens, Grecian temple, fountains, oak allée, swan pond, sunken grotto, and ornate fernery (a conservatory devoted to ferns, a Victorian favorite). Exotic plants collected on their world travels graced the estate, including katsuras, Asian maples, Engler beeches, and Scotch elms.

Sitting on the estate's highest point was Chandler's mansion, a two-and-a-half-story, roughhewn-granite structure based on John Morris's floor plan. The asymmetrical house featured hipped and gabled roofs with Flemish cross gables, elaborate stone carvings, and a pyramidical roof emerging from the crenellated top of a square tower. At the northern end of the house, a rounded conservatory with a semicircular balcony offered views of Bloomfield Farm, the

An unidentified man and woman enjoy the summer breeze on the wraparound porch at Compton ca. 1890, in this view looking northwest from near the site of the current Marion W. Rivinus Rose Garden. (Courtesy of the Morris Arboretum of the University of Pennsylvania.)

Compton's main tower falls to the wrecking ball in September 1968. (Courtesy of the Morris Arboretum of the University of Pennsylvania.)

Morrises' adjoining farm in Montgomery County, and the White-marsh Valley beyond. On the southern end, a wraparound porch overlooked the estate's gardens and swan pond. The house's interior featured heavy oak doors, elaborately carved staircases and fire-places, beamed ceilings, stained-glass windows, and paneling.

The Morrises used Compton primarily as a summer home, maintaining their city residence at 826 Pine Street. Both John and Lydia planned for their country showplace to be used as a botani-

cal garden, horticultural school, and museum after their deaths. After John died in 1915, Lydia lived at Compton year-round until her own death in 1932. Following the instructions of the Morrises' wills, their house and estate became the Morris Arboretum of the University of Pennsylvania. For many years, the Chandler mansion housed the offices and laboratories of the university's Botany Department.

In the 1940s, the university acquired Overlea, a nearby Wilson Eyre mansion, renamed it Gates Hall, and transferred most of the arboretum's administrative and laboratory activities there. By the 1960s, the Morris mansion was used only by local teenagers for late-night frolics. A 1967 *Bulletin* article noted that the University of Pennsylvania, unwilling to restore or maintain the vandalized, high-maintenance house, planned to replace it with a new educational and research facility.

Ignoring community opposition, the university razed the man-sion in September 1968 after removing some of its ironwork, light-ing fixtures, and fireplaces. Arboretum representatives were instructed to answer all questions with the statement: "Demolition of the Mansion was ordered by the Board of Managers of the Mor-ris Foundation in accord with Miss Morris' expressed wishes." This justification was based on a sentence in Lydia Morris's will stating: "All things considered, I feel the only thing to do with our home is to take it down, if it cannot be kept up in the way it has been and nothing else would satisfy us."[20]

The controversy over Compton's demolition helped unify local support for the Morris Arboretum, ensuring its continued existence at a time when the University of Pennsylvania was questioning its feasibility, and initiating a period of growth that continues today. Today, the arboretum's operations are divided among Gates Hall, the George D. Widener Education Center (located in the former carriage house), and a grounds and nursery center on Bloomfield Farm that is soon to be rebuilt. The mansion site remained empty until 1993, when the arboretum erected on it an aluminum kinetic sculpture by George Rickey, *Two Lines Variable—Thirty Feet*.

Philadelphia Art Club

Location: 220 South Broad Street (at southwest corner of Chancellor)
Completed: 1890
Demolished: 1976
Architect/Builder: Frank Miles Day

After the Civil War, the former Athens of America became an artistic backwater. The Pennsylvania Academy of the Fine Arts focused on providing classical training for artists, firing Thomas Eakins when his study of the human nude became too uncomfortably direct. The closest thing Philadelphia had to a municipal art museum was Memorial Hall in Fairmount Park, where leftover relics from the Centennial Exposition moldered. To remedy this stagnation, wealthy citizens joined forces with local artists and architects to create a number of associations, including the Philadelphia Society of Artists, the Plastic Club, and the T-Square Club.

In 1887, a group of civic leaders and artists, including Pennsylvania Railroad executive Alexander J. Cassatt and painter Thomas Hovenden, founded the Philadelphia Art Club to "advance the knowledge and love of the Fine Arts, through the exhibition of works of art, the acquisition of books and papers for the purpose of founding an art library."[21] The Art Club's original home was Mrs. Griffith's boardinghouse at 220 South Broad Street, where charter members George Henry Boker and Charles Godfrey Leland lodged. In 1888, the club acquired the boardinghouse and held an architectural competition for a building on the site, drawing submissions from many of the city's rising architects, including Cope & Stewardson, Edwin F. Durang, Wilson Eyre, Willis G. Hale, and Hazlehurst & Huckel.

The winner, Frank Miles Day, created a Northern Italian Gothic palazzo of buff brick with limestone trim, with low-hipped tile roofs and a third-story balcony on its northeast corner. The four-story club was highly decorated with terra-cotta ornaments over its

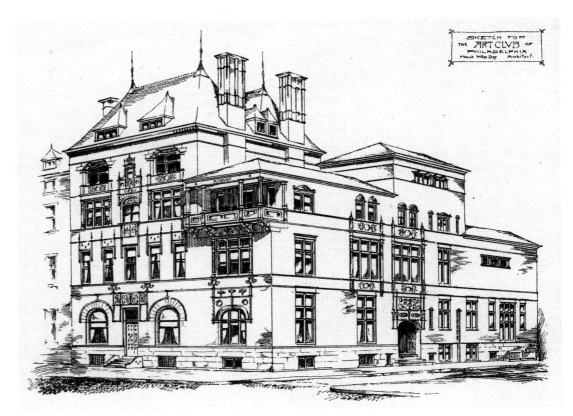

Frank Miles Day's winning design in the 1888 architectural competition for the Philadelphia Art Club. (© The Architectural Archives of the University of Pennsylvania.)

The Art Club shortly after its completion in 1890. The shaded windows and roof tents indicate that this photograph was taken during the summer. The third-story balcony overlooking South Broad Street testifies to the low volume of traffic at the time, confirmed by a 1905 photograph that shows sheep being herded down the boulevard. (© The Architectural Archives of the University of Pennsylvania.)

front entrance and upper-story windows, stained-glass windows on the ground floor, and tall chimneys. The historical accuracy of Day's design, drawn from his own European travels, represented a major shift from the eclecticism favored by post–Civil War architects like Frank Furness. The club's moderate size (64 by 116 feet) suited a Broad Street that was still in transition from a fashionable residential boulevard to a busy thoroughfare filled with hotels and theaters.

The palazzo's interior layout reflected the club's social proclivities, with much more space dedicated to restaurants, private dining rooms, billiard rooms, and wine cellars than to art galleries. For forty years, Philadelphia's political, financial, and industrial leaders rubbed shoulders with its artistic and architectural elite at the men-only club. Members included Mayor Edwin Fitler, Cyrus H. K. Curtis, and John Wanamaker, as well as Alexander Stirling Calder, Theophilus P. Chandler, and Leopold Stokowski. Club dinner parties, held in rooms with frescoed ceilings and paneled walls imported from Italy, featured such guests as Sarah Bernhardt and Walt Whitman.

The club's wealthy patrons financed numerous alterations to the building, including a seven-story rear addition and roof garden designed by Newman and Harris in 1907. The additional gallery space provided by this addition allowed the club to hold annual competitions that helped launch the careers of Childe Hassam, Cecilia Beaux, and Maxfield Parrish. In 1917, an exhibition of works by women artists led to the creation of the Women's Art Alliance, also known as the Philadelphia Ten.

By the 1920s, the Art Club began to lose steam, especially after the opening of the Philadelphia Museum of Art and the Art Alliance. Bankrupted by the Depression, the moribund club disbanded on November 9, 1940. After sitting empty for several years, its building housed the Keystone Automobile Club from 1946 to 1968, then served as headquarters for several losing causes, including Thatcher Longstreth's 1971 mayoral campaign and George McGovern's 1972 presidential campaign.

In 1975, Bankers Securities Corporation, owner of the Art Club and the adjacent Bellevue-Stratford Hotel, announced plans to demolish the vacant building for a parking lot. Local preservationists, led by architect Harry V. Bonner Jr., promoted the Art Club as a Bicentennial visitors' center, while the Philadelphia Historical Commission forced the club's owners to delay demolition for six months. Despite these efforts, and despite the club's inclusion on the Pennsylvania Register of Historic Places, it was demolished in early 1976. Today, its site is occupied by a parking garage and the Michael Graves–designed athletic club of the Park Hyatt at the Bellevue.

Betz Building/Lincoln Building

Location: One South Broad Street (at South Penn Square)
Completed: 1892
Demolished: 1929
Architect/Builder: William H. Decker

The Betz Building, a ponderous, Romanesque structure that once stood at the southeast corner of Broad Street and South Penn Square, was the embodiment of a rags-to-riches—or at least a beer-to-boodle—success story. John F. Betz (1831–1908) was one of the great beer barons of nineteenth-century Philadelphia. An apprentice in 1844, Betz owned his own brewery in New York by 1855. In 1867, he moved to Philadelphia and purchased the brewery that had once belonged to Robert Hare, maker of the first porter in America.

By 1889, Betz's combined New York and Philadelphia operations produced more than 300,000 barrels of beer, ale, and porter a year, at a value of over $3 million. The Betz Brewery occupied a six-story structure with a castellated clock tower on the block bordered by Callowhill, Crown, Willow and Fifth streets. Betz established beer gardens on Petty's Island and at the mouth of the Wissahickon Creek and earned the nickname Commodore for his fleet of steamboats that ferried customers to these retreats. (When he died in 1908, one obituary writer sniffed that Betz "owned more corner properties in this city than any other individual, most of which were saloons.")[22]

In 1891, Betz commissioned a corner property that was definitely not a saloon: a 212-foot-high, $1.5-million office tower at Broad Street and South Penn Square, the former site of Napoleon LeBrun's Tabernacle Presbyterian Church. Rising thirteen stories above ground, the building included two full stories below ground in addition to a cellar and a subcellar. William H. Decker's design featured massive Richardsonian Romanesque arches above the main entrances and five wells of projecting bay windows in the

The Betz Building in 1894, when it towered over other buildings on South Broad Street, looking southeast from City Hall Plaza. (The Library Company of Philadelphia.)

building's middle section, also topped by arches. In a second-floor recess, Betz placed bronze statues of William Penn, the goddess Germania, and Mrs. Betz. Bronze heads of the U.S. presidents from George Washington to Benjamin Henry Harrison adorned the building's granite front.

Thanks to its location across from the unfinished City Hall, the Betz Building became the political rialto of the city, where the

Vares, McNichols, and other Republican bosses maintained their offices. The building's Rathskeller, run by bartender Charlie Soulas, was one of the largest beer halls in the city and a popular hangout for politicians, lawyers, lobbyists, and other City Hall denizens.

Some architectural historians consider the Betz Building to be Philadelphia's first commercial skyscraper. Before its erection, the only office building on South Broad Street was Addison Hutton's eight-story Girard Trust Building at Broad and Chestnut. When the Betz Building began to rise next door, its greater height provoked Girard Trust into adding another six stories to its building, which in turn spurred Betz to increase his building's height with an elaborate cornice. Soon afterward, the Land Title, Real Estate Trust, North American, and other commercial buildings crowded each other on South Broad Street. Not everyone was a fan of the Betz Building; in 1908, *Architectural Record* critic Huger Elliot wrote that the building was "of a bastard Richardsonian type; it needs no other comment."[23]

Within two years of Betz's death, his landmark was renamed the Lincoln Building. Shortly after the stock market crashed, demolition began on the Lincoln Building and its neighbor, the Liberty Building (formerly the Girard Trust Building). In their place rose the twenty-seven-story Lincoln-Liberty Building. This sleek, Art Moderne structure, which opened in 1932, was the home of the John Wanamaker's Men's Store until 1952, when it became the Philadelphia National Bank (PNB) Building. Today it houses the offices of Wachovia Bank, which recently caused an uproar by removing the trademark PNB sign from the building's bell tower.

Hohenadel Brewery

Location: 3500–3506 Indian Queen Lane (at Conrad Street),
East Falls
Completed: 1894
Demolished: 1999
Architect/Builder: A. Wagner

As any visitor to an Eagles, Flyers, or Phillies game knows, Philadelphia loves its beer. The city's German population, its pure water, and its proximity to farms that produce fine hops and wheat made it a beer lover's paradise from its earliest days. William Frampton was brewing beer on Dock Creek before William Penn landed in 1682. A century later, Philadelphian Robert Hare made some of the first porter in America for George Washington, who had it shipped to Mount Vernon.

The wave of German immigration in the nineteenth century enhanced Philadelphia's status as a beer bastion. John Wagner, a Bavarian émigré, brewed the nation's first lager at Third and Poplar streets in 1840. Soon, the district bounded by Thirtieth Street, Oxford Street, Thirty-third Street and Girard Avenue was called Brewerytown. A dozen breweries operated within the seven-block area, drawn by its artesian wells and German popula-

tion. By 1880, Philadelphia had more than a hundred breweries and malt houses, many with Teutonic names. While a few brands like Schmidt's and Ortlieb's achieved national prominence, most were consumed within the city or even within a single neighborhood. Among these were the products of small and medium-sized breweries, including Joseph Kohnle, Liebert & Obert, and John Hohenadel.

The Hohenadel family had been brewing beer for nearly a century by 1894, when John Hohenadel erected a new brewery at the southwest corner of Conrad Street and Indian Queen Lane, north of the Reading Railroad tracks. The triangular brick structure stood seven stories high and measured 50,000 square feet. There, Falls Brewery workers created Indian Queen Ale and other brands for

The Hohenadel saloon ca. 1900. In the left background stands John Hohenadel's Falls Brewery at Conrad Street and Indian Queen Lane. (The Library Company of Philadelphia.)

the local market. At one end of the building, a two-story saloon served Hohenadel beer to local tipplers. John Hohenadel's brewery brought him success and respectability; before his death at eighty-nine, he had become president of the East Falls Bank and Trust Company, a member of the Germantown Cricket Club, and a resident of posh Oak Road.

In 1920, Prohibition turned Brewerytown into a ghost town, throwing thousands of workers into unemployment. Hohenadel's Falls Brewery managed to stay open by manufacturing "near beer," which contained only 0.5 percent alcohol (and which could be turned into the real thing by adding yeast). Unlike many Philadelphia breweries, the Hohenadel plant resumed full operations after Prohibition was repealed in 1933. Renamed John Hohenadel Brewery Inc., it continued to produce beer for another twenty years.

After World War II, U.S. beer production consolidated under national giants like Anheuser-Busch. By 1950, Hohenadel's was one of only six brewers left in Philadelphia. In December 1952, the Hohenadel plant closed suddenly, idling its seventy-five employees and moving the copy editor of the Philadelphia *Bulletin* to compose an elegy:

> Hohenadel, she hits der spot;
> But business lately, it ain't so hot;
> Send the empties to Adam Scheidt;
> We're shutten down the old plant tonight.[24]

Between 1952 and 1959, the former brewery housed Bev-Rich Products, a soft-drink manufacturer, then stood vacant for forty years. In the early 1990s, it was the gallery and studio of alternative artist Todd Gilens, who filled its nineteen rooms with fantastic murals of birds and flowers. By 1997, bricks and masonry from the crumbling structure were crashing down on sidewalks and parked cars. The City of Philadelphia, responding to numerous community complaints, demolished the derelict brewery in 1999. Since then, its site has been used for the Brewery Garden Project, a community garden for residents of East Falls.

Hotel Metropole/Hotel Walton/ John Bartram Hotel

Location: 233–47 South Broad Street (between Locust and Spruce streets)
Completed: Southern section (Hotel Metropole), 1892; northern section (Hotel Walton), 1895
Demolished: 1967
Architect/Builder: Angus S. Wade

Thanks to its proximity to Broad Street Station and City Hall, South Broad Street became a favorite site for hotels catering to business travelers in the late nineteenth century. Among them was the Hotel Metropole, which opened at Broad and Locust streets in 1892, replacing the Coliseum Theater and Thron's Broadway Garden. Its architect, Angus S. Wade, was known as "Anxious" Wade for his fussy, over-the-top designs for the Hotel Rittenhouse and Hotel Hanover. The Hotel Metropole was no exception: The nine-story brick and brownstone structure featured four Moorish arches on the ground floor, asymmetrically placed oriels, and an oversized central gable framed by two corner towers.

In 1896, Robert Goelet purchased the Metropole and the adjoining Empire Theatre. Goelet demolished the Empire and incorporated the Metropole into the new Hotel Walton (named after his son), also designed by Wade in what one newspaper described as "Americanized Moorish."[25] The first two stories were rusticated brownstone, while the remaining nine were brick. A corner turret topped by a conical, witch's-hat roof looked north up Broad Street, balanced by smaller towers at the building's ends. Moorish arches on either side of the turret mirrored those on the earlier Metropole. From the hotel's high-pitched Flemish gables terra-cotta grotesques leered down.

Guests passed under a large porte-cochere into an ornate lobby with an arched, paneled ceiling, murals, and walls lined with marble

pilasters and onyx panels. A grand staircase led to lavish public rooms on the second floor, including the Ladies' Restaurant (cream and gold décor, with a frescoed ceiling, floral carpet, and copies of paintings by Watteau and Boucher), the Palm Café (Venetian Gothic, with oak paneling and red and gold brocade drapes), and the Turkish Room (Oriental, with red lights and luxurious divans). In addition to its lush furnishings, the Walton boasted cast-iron tube radiators, fireproof Pompeian brick, electricity, telephones, and separate baths for half its 400 rooms. Besides businessmen, the Walton attracted Philadelphia's more raffish high society, such as big-game huntress and *Titanic* survivor Charlotte Drake Cardeza, who stayed there between world voyages.

Like Broad Street Station, the Hotel Walton's style had already begun to pass from public favor by the time of the building's grand opening on February 12, 1896. In 1910, William F. Gray, head of the Art Department at the Central High School, wrote: "If there is any more extraordinary creation than the Hotel Walton it is in some very remote town."[26] When the Bellevue-Stratford and Ritz-Carlton Hotels opened in the early twentieth century, their restrained elegance won the hearts of Philadelphia society, and the Walton was relegated to B-list status. During the 1920s, conventioneers and traveling salesmen enjoyed bootleg booze and curvy chorines at Jack Lynch's Walton Roof Garden.

As the twentieth century progressed, the Walton's appearance grew even more outdated, despite modernizations in 1925 and 1948 that stripped its interiors of their Victorian splendor and covered its ground floor with stainless-steel facades. After the 1948 renovation, the Walton was renamed the John Bartram Hotel. By the early 1960s, the area around Spruce and Locust had become a red-light district, home to the Bag of Nails, Copa Club, and other strip joints and sleazy bars. The Bartram's claim to fame during this period was comedian Lenny Bruce's arrest there on September 29, 1961, on a trumped-up narcotics charge (later dismissed).

Shortly afterward, the hotel closed its doors and was slated for demolition. Even the architectural historian documenting the hotel for the Historical American Buildings Survey had trouble working up enthusiasm for the doomed structure, calling it "a strained asymmetrical attempt at picturesque splendor."[27] In 1967, the building was demolished for a proposed apartment complex. That deal fell through, and the site was used as a parking lot until 1983, when the glass-fronted Hershey Hotel (today the Doubletree) was built there.

Woodside Amusement Park

Location: South side of Ford Road, east of its intersection with Monument and Conshohocken roads (Five Points), Wynnefield Heights
Completed: 1897
Demolished: 1955
Architect/Builder: Various

By the 1890s, trolley tracks transected Philadelphia streets, carrying passengers throughout the city and into the surrounding countryside. To increase ridership during their down time on weekends and evenings, traction companies constructed amusement parks at the ends of their lines. For a nickel, urban residents could escape the crowded city and flee, via an open-air trolley, to a rural fairyland like Willow Grove Park or the White City outside Chestnut Hill.

Woodside Park, founded in 1897 by the Fairmount Park Transportation Company, was the only amusement park within the city limits. It was located southeast of the intersection of Monument Avenue, Ford Road, and Conshohocken Avenue in the Wynnefield Heights section on a former estate called Woodside. The Fairmount Park Trolley, a nine-mile trolley line, stopped at Woodside Park, conveniently located near its storage facility for spare cars. Although outside the western borders of Fairmount Park, the tree-shaded playground appeared to be within the park.

Visitors to Woodside enjoyed swimming in the Crystal Pool, bicycle races on a circular track, swan boats on Chamounix Lake,

Facing page: **A**n aerial view of Woodside Park ca. 1925, looking west up Ford Road (in the center of the photograph) toward Monument Avenue. The Crystal Pool lies to the right of Ford Road in the foreground, with the Park Midway, featuring a roller coaster, skating rink, carousel pavilion, and other attractions, to the left. (Print and Picture Collection, Free Library of Philadelphia.)

picnics under the trees, and a small scenic railway. Woodside also boasted more than forty rides, including carousels built by Gustav Dentzel and his son William, an early roller coaster called a mountain scenic railway, Bump the Bumps and Tickler slide rides, Laff Trail and Jollier funhouses, and more obscure attractions with names like Katzenjammer Castle and Human Laundry. In the park's early years, an orchestra played in an open-air shell designed by James Hamilton Windrim, architect of the Masonic Hall. (The bandleader, Fritz Scheel, became the first conductor of the Philadelphia Orchestra in 1901.)

Although smaller and simpler than Willow Grove Park, Woodside became a favorite destination for Philadelphians because of its proximity to the city. In 1902, Philadelphia film pioneer Siegmund Lubin released a five-minute short, *Woodside Park Trolley Panorama*. According to the Lubin catalog, the film took viewers on a trip during which "the trolley winds in and out of curves of trees where thousands of persons visit almost daily during the summer months, and many young persons congregate on pleasure bent."[28] When a fire swept Woodside in 1926, causing $50,000 in damage, the park was rebuilt with more modern attractions, including three roller coasters—the Tornado, the Hummer, and the Wildcat.

After World War II, many of Woodside's former visitors purchased cars and moved to the suburbs. Now, a Saturday trip demanded a more exotic destination than West Philadelphia—someplace like the Jersey Shore, Allentown's Dorney Park, or Hershey Park in Amish country. At the same time, prices for land on Philadelphia's outskirts rose as builders sought space for new housing. In 1946, the Fairmount Park trolley ceased operations, and carless visitors had to take the No. 85 bus to Woodside.

Woodside Park was sold in October 1955, dismantled, and its land turned over to residential and business development. Today, the only remaining trace is a paved walkway that once led from the trolley stop to the park entrance. Even Chamounix Lake is gone, drained and filled in during the construction of the Schuylkill Expressway.

Woodside Park's William Dentzel carousel, however, has returned to Philadelphia after extended stays at the Smithsonian Institution and the Pennsylvania Historical and Museum Commission. The Please Touch Museum has leased the 1924 carousel, with its fifty-four carved horses, rabbits, cats, pigs, goats, and chariots, and plans to restore it and operate it at its new facility in Fairmount Park's Memorial Hall.

CHAPTER 5

The Consumer City

(1901 to 1940)

Facing page: **C**enter City Philadelphia in the 1920s, looking west. Wanamaker's Department Store and City Hall are in the left and center foreground. Behind City Hall stand Broad Street Station and the Chinese Wall. Right of City Hall, the new Fairmount Parkway (renamed for Benjamin Franklin in 1937) extends northwest past Logan Circle to the unfinished Museum of Art. (Collection of the author.)

At the stroke of midnight on December 31, 1900, Philadelphia's City Hall (nearly complete after twenty-nine years of construction, and at 2.5 times the projected budget) exploded with light, outlined by 12,000 electric bulbs from William Penn's hat to the courtyard arches. Fireworks wired all over the structure burst into flowers of flame, turning the tallest masonry tower in the world into a gigantic Roman candle as thousands of Philadelphians roared their delight.

This blazing spire symbolized the prosperity and optimism with which the city greeted the twentieth century, fueled by the industrial expansion of the previous decades. Philadelphia was the country's third-largest metropolis, a major center of finance and manufacturing, and a technological innovator. The city government may have been remarkably corrupt, as journalist Lincoln Steffens claimed, but as long as there was enough wealth to line everyone's pockets, most Philadelphians were content.

But not all. Owen Wister, scion of an old Quaker family, created the modern Western with *The Virginian* in 1902 and began a second novel, *Romney*, in 1914. In a lightly disguised Philadelphia called Monopolis, *Romney*'s characters express the despair and impotence felt by Wister and many of his fellow citizens, disgusted by their town's pay-to-play paralysis: "The city is a shame. They're proud of it, yet take no care of it. They don't seem to feel that it's their business. The bad gas, the bad water, the nasty street-cars that tinkle torpidly through streets paved with big cobble-stones all seem to them quite right. It surprises them if you mention it. . . . But isn't it strange that such nice people should tolerate such a nasty state of things?"[1]

By the time Wister wrote those words, fewer Philadelphians were willing to put up with the status quo. In 1909, the opening of the Torresdale filtration plant guaranteed safe drinking water for the entire city and reduced its scandalously high level of typhoid deaths. The organization of the Philadelphia Electric Company and the Philadelphia Rapid Transit Company, along with attempts to reform the United Gas Improvement Company during the century's first decade, may have enriched political insiders but also provided the city with reliable services and utilities.

Between 1900 and 1930, a combination of public and private transportation initiatives, collectively known as the Improvements, reshaped the face and the flow of Philadelphia. The Improvements included transit systems like the Frankford Elevated, Broad Street Subway, and Market Street Subway-Elevated Lines; major roadways like the Fairmount (later Benjamin Franklin) Parkway, Schuylkill River Drive, and Roosevelt Boulevard; the Delaware River (later Benjamin Franklin) Bridge; and the Thirtieth Street and Suburban stations of the Pennsylvania Railroad. These projects encouraged the movement of middle- and upper-class Philadelphians from Center City to its outskirts. Meanwhile, older sections of the city were surrendered to Italians, Eastern European Jews, and Southern blacks, who helped swell the city's population to 1,684,000 by 1915.

Philadelphia expanded both outward and upward. To the north and northwest, thousands of row houses were built for Philadelphia's new commuter class, as developers turned farmland into the communities of Olney, Logan, Mt. Airy, East Oak Lane, Mayfair, and Oxford Circle. By 1912, the city had more owner-occupied houses than any other large U.S. city could claim, and 9,000 new dwellings were going up each year. Blithely ignoring the squalid river wards, the *Public Ledger* in 1922 called Philadelphia the "City without a Slum," using some dubious math to calculate that "virtually every family in Philadelphia lives in its own individual home."[2]

Downtown Philadelphia—now known as Center City—became a cluster of skyscrapers, their steel frames swathed in the Beaux-Arts or American Renaissance styles popularized by the 1893 World's Columbian Exposition. Most of the major buildings erected through 1930—the Bulletin Building, Bellevue-Stratford Hotel, Shibe Park, Wanamaker's Department Store, Girard Trust Building, Philadelphia Museum of Art, and Free Library—evoked the splendor of other lands and ages.

Meanwhile, as Owen Wister noted gloomily, the glories of Philadelphia's own past continued to be obliterated in the name of progress: "The beautiful old colonial house torn down to make way for three dozen or four dozen or five dozen up-to-the-minute American 'homes'? No Declaration of Independence signed in any of 'em—but they've got a bathroom on every floor!"[3] In response, concerned citizens began to develop a modern historic preservation movement. Frances A. Wister founded the Philadelphia Society for the Preservation of Landmarks in 1931, which rescued the Samuel Powel House, Hill-Physick-Keith House, and other historic residences from destruction. In northwest Philadelphia, the Germantown Historical Society helped preserve the Concord School House, Johnson House, and Vernon Mansion.

Fueled by Philadelphia's seemingly endless prosperity, a new consumer culture arose. By 1930, the City of Homes was also a city of theaters, department stores, sports stadiums, swimming pools, and speakeasies where its two million inhabitants could spend their time and cash. Toward the end of the decade, Philadelphia's architecture began to assume a more modern and sophisticated appearance, with Art Deco structures like the WCAU Building, N. W. Ayer headquarters, Drake Hotel, and One East Penn Square Building. The decade culminated with George Howe's and William Lescaze's modernist masterpiece, the Philadelphia Savings Fund Society (PSFS) Building, on the site of Penn Charter's red-brick school.

Both the city's wealth and its building boom dissipated with the 1929 stock market crash and the ensuing Depression. Per capita income shrank to half its pre-1929 level, as thousands of financial institutions failed and mortgage foreclosures soared. Once the spate of buildings initiated before the crash was finished, the city saw little new construction for the rest of the decade, except the Hoovervilles that sprouted on the former Sesqui-Centennial grounds and near the new Museum of Art. When the PSFS Building was completed in 1932, local citizens joked bitterly that the

glowing red letters atop the structure stood for "Philadelphia Slowly Faces Starvation."

Government money financed many buildings completed in the mid to late 1930s, such as the Federal Reserve Bank, the U.S. Naval Hospital, and housing projects sponsored by the Public Works Administration and the Philadelphia Housing Authority. The period that began with the luxurious classicism of the Belle-vue-Stratford and John Wanamaker's Department Store ended with the stark utilitarianism of the Carl Mackley Houses and Tasker Homes.

Gimbel Brothers' Department Store

Location: South side of Market Street between Eighth and
   Ninth streets
Completed: 1896–1927
Demolished: 1979
Architect/Builder: Cope & Stewardson; Willis G. Hale; Angus S.
   Wade; Francis H. Kimball; Graham, Anderson, Probst & White

Although Milwaukee merchants Jacob and Isaac Gimbel opened their first Philadelphia store in 1894, the explosive expansion of Gimbel Brothers in the following years marked the emergence of twentieth-century mass consumer culture in the city. Located between Eighth and Ninth streets, Gimbels joined the string of department stores lining Market Street east of City Hall, which included John Wanamaker's, Lit Brothers, Strawbridge & Clothier, and Snellenburg's. Gimbels would prove to be as innovative in the twentieth century as Wanamaker's had been in the nineteenth.

Like most of its competitors, Gimbels occupied a hodgepodge of structures, erecting or purchasing buildings as it expanded. The original store, designed by Cope & Stewardson and finished in 1896, was a seven-story brick and terra-cotta structure with a curving arcade of Roman arches across the first two floors. Gradually, Gimbels expanded east along Market to Eighth

Street. By the time Gimbels opened a $10 million, fifteen-story addition along Chestnut Street in 1927, it occupied nearly the entire block bounded by Eighth, Ninth, Market, and Chestnut streets and boasted that it was the largest department store in the world.

Gimbels never aspired to the swank of Wanamaker's or the restraint of Strawbridge & Clothier. Instead, it offered a vast array of goods at bargain prices, like Schiaparelli sweater knockoffs for $7.99 in the 1920s. It also made shopping exciting through its use of the latest technology. In 1901, Gimbels introduced the first store escalators in the country, followed by an underground "subway store" accessible from the Market Street Subway in 1912. In 1922, it inaugurated the city's first radio station, WIP (Wireless in Philadelphia). In 1932, Gimbels even demonstrated a primitive form of mechanical television, featuring an appearance by John Barrymore.

Gimbel Brothers' Department Store at the southeast corner of Market and Ninth streets, ca. 1900. Cope & Stewardson built the section of the store closest to the foreground in 1896. (Courtesy of James Hill Jr.)

After World War II, the store advertised its wares via in-house television and became the first single sponsor of an entire television program. In 1945, Gimbels demonstrated the first Slinky, invented by an engineer at Cramp's Shipyard, and sold out its stock of 400 in ninety minutes. Gimbels ended the decade by offering its customers a "charge-a-plate," asking the enticing question, "Would you like to shop without cash?"

Gimbels' most enduring innovation was the Thanksgiving Day parade, first held in Philadelphia in 1920. Originally called the Gimbel Brothers Toyland Parade, it consisted of fifty costumed employees in fifteen autos, followed by a fire truck that hoisted Santa Claus to the Gimbels roof on its ladder. For nearly sixty Thanksgivings, thousands of Philadelphians packed Market Street to watch Santa Claus (always played by a local fireman) ascend a fire ladder with his bag of toys to an upper-story window at the store. Gimbels' parade was quickly appropriated by its rivals, including Macy's New York in 1924. (Boscov's now sponsors the nation's oldest Thanksgiving Day parade, and today Santa ascends the steps of the Museum of Art à la Rocky.)

From the 1920s onward, store presidents Charles and Ellis Gimbel assumed the mantle of civic responsibility once worn by John Wanamaker. Starting in 1932, the Gimbel Awards recognized women who provided humanitarian service on the local, national, or international level; recipients included Eleanor Roosevelt, Amelia Earhart, and Marian Anderson. In 1940, Gimbels established the Young Artists Show, annually exhibiting works by local high school students. In 1947, more than 400,000 Philadelphians visited the Better Philadelphia Exhibition at Gimbels to inspect a fresh vision of their city, engineered by Ed Bacon and Oskar Stonorov.

Between 1954 and 1974, the Market Street store grew shabby as Gimbels opened ten suburban stores to reach its retreating customer base. In 1977, Gimbels (then owned by Brown & Williamson Tobacco) moved across the street to anchor the new Gallery urban mall, a keystone of the Market Street East renovation envisioned in the Better Philadelphia Exhibition. By that time, changing markets,

Gimbels' main entrance at Market and Ninth streets in 1978, a year before the store's demolition. The illuminated slogan, "Save Time and Money—You Will Find It At Gimbels," was a Market Street landmark for many years. (Temple University Libraries, Urban Archives, Philadelphia.)

new competitors, and corporate retrenchment had slashed the chain's profitability. Two years later, Gimbels closed its doors in Philadelphia, and the original store was demolished except for the 1927 office building at Ninth and Chestnut. Gradually, all of Gimbels' other stores closed, including its flagship store in New York's Herald Square in 1987.

For more than twenty-five years, the two-acre Gimbels site in Philadelphia has remained a parking lot on a rejuvenated Market Street East, while various developers have tried and failed to erect a bank corporate headquarters, a Sears store, and a DisneyQuest complex. In January 2004, the latest development plan was announced: a retail and entertainment complex featuring a Target store.

Arcade Building/Commercial Trust Building

Location: 1428–34 Market Street (block bordered by Market Street,
South Broad Street, South Penn Square, and Fifteenth Street)
Completed: 1902
Demolished: 1969
Architect/Builder: Furness, Evans & Company

In 1900, Alexander J. Cassatt, controlling partner of the six-year-old Commercial Trust Company, asked his favorite architect, Frank Furness, to help him solve a logistical problem. Cassatt, who was also president of the Pennsylvania Railroad, wanted to build a headquarters for the Commercial Trust on the south side of Market Street across from his Broad Street Station. He owned only limited space on the eastern and southern sides of the block, however; the owners of the remaining parcels, knowing they had Cassatt over a barrel, refused to sell.

The solution proposed by Furness, Evans & Company was a slim, steel-frame arcade building modeled on the Galleria Vittorio Emanuele in Milan. The new L-shaped structure was thirteen stories tall and 230 feet long, but only 50 feet wide except at its South Penn Square end, where it widened to 120 feet. Elevator banks were installed at both ends, leaving the length of the building along Fifteenth Street available for offices. Covered pedestrian arcades supported by massive stone columns ran around the building. Thanks to Cassatt's political influence, the architects extended these arcades out to the street, maximizing the building's interior space.

Originally, Frank Furness had wanted to create a Victorian Gothic twin to his Broad Street Station. Cassatt, realizing how tastes had changed, convinced him to create instead a subdued palazzo

The Arcade Building before its 1904–6 expansion, looking south along Fifteenth Street. At lower left, a pedestrian bridge connects the Arcade Building with Broad Street Station on the north side of Market Street. (Courtesy of James Hill Jr.)

with coursed ashlar and terra-cotta walls, balconies at the sixth and ninth floors, and simple pediments at the corners and far ends. Despite its difference in style, the Arcade Building complemented Broad Street Station in scale. Together, the two buildings created a monumental portal, commemorating Cassatt's power and prestige at the heart of the city.

The gateway metaphor became even more pronounced when Furness, Evans added a pedestrian bridge over Market Street that connected the Arcade Building with Broad Street Station. Now visitors could proceed directly from their train to the Commercial Trust offices without descending into the hurly-burly of Market Street. Some postcards even referred to the Arcade Building as the "Broad Street Station Annex."

After the building's completion, the owners of the adjacent properties admitted defeat and sold out to Cassatt. Between 1904 and 1906, Furness, Evans expanded the Arcade Building to South Penn Square, doubling its size and changing the design from an L-shape to a U-shape. In 1913, Furness, Evans added a twenty-one-story tower with a central dome to the northern end of the building. The original Arcade Building, completed a decade earlier, turned out to be Frank Furness's last major commission; he died in 1912.

By the 1960s, the Commercial Trust Company had gone through a series of mergers to become part of the First Pennsylvania Bank (now part of Wachovia). Meanwhile, the Arcade Building had grown tired and shabby, especially compared to the gleaming towers of nearby Penn Center. The building was demolished in 1969 for the Philadelphia Redevelopment Authority's Plaza Project, renamed Dilworth Plaza upon its completion in 1974.

Bulletin Building/Penn Square Building

Location: 1315–25 Filbert Street (at Juniper Street)
Completed: 1908 (remodeled 1937)
Demolished: 1985
Architect/Builder: Edgar V. Seeler (remodeled by George Howe)

In 1847, Alexander Cummings founded the *Cummings Telegraphic Evening Bulletin*. Despite its grandiose name, the underachieving *Bulletin* barely limped along through the nineteenth century. When William McLean purchased it in 1895, it was the smallest of the city's thirteen dailies, with a staff of six and a circulation of 6,300. With a drive worthy of Charles Foster Kane, McLean transformed the *Bulletin* within a decade into the city's largest newspaper, with a circulation over 200,000.

Despite its dynamic growth, the *Bulletin*'s outlook, like its readership, was cautious, conservative, and Republican. When the N. W. Ayer ad agency created a new slogan in 1905—"In Philadelphia, Everybody Reads the *Bulletin*"—the meticulous McLean changed it to "In Philadelphia, Nearly Everybody Reads the *Bulletin*." The slogan would be used for the next sixty years, even working its way into the 1955 Alfred Hitchcock thriller, *To Catch a Thief.*

To mark the phenomenal growth of his newspaper, McLean moved the *Bulletin* offices from 607 Chestnut Street to the northeast corner of Juniper and Filbert streets in 1906. Although sandwiched between Masonic Hall and the Hotel Vendig, the new location was adjacent to City Hall, Broad Street Station, and the city's commercial and entertainment districts. Edgar V. Seeler, later architect of the Curtis Building on Independence Square, designed a ten-story Beaux-Arts structure with a ground floor of Indiana limestone and upper floors of brick faced with terra-cotta. The rounded bay of the northeast corner—the only part of the façade with an unobstructed view—was topped by a tower with a glittering green-and-white enamel and terra-cotta dome.

The elegant main entrance featured three large Roman arches topped by gently curving iron and glass canopies lined with light bulbs. Above the central arch, an elaborate carving depicted the head of Mercury supporting the globe, flanked by printing presses and topped by a massive pair of wings and a scroll with quill pens. Despite its elegant exterior, the Filbert Street offices held the most modern newspaper printing plant of the period.

Soon the Bulletin Building was known as the "Gray Old Lady of Filbert Street," referring to its conservative outlook as well as its soot-stained façade. As the paper grew, Seeler designed a ten-story addition at 1315–17 Filbert Street in 1916, followed by a seven-story annex at Juniper and Arch streets in 1922.

By the late 1930s, the *Bulletin*'s circulation was nearly 700,000, making it the largest evening paper in North America. The McLean family hired George Howe, codesigner of the PSFS Building, to modernize the building. Howe removed the cornice and stripped away much of the ground-floor decoration, adding a glass-block front and other Art Moderne elements for a streamlined look similar to Hood and Howells' 1930 Daily News Building in New York.

By the end of World War II, the *Bulletin* had outgrown its quarters opposite City Hall. In 1955, it moved to a new building at 3100 Market Street, opposite Thirtieth Street Station. The modern structure, designed by George Howe and Robert Montgomery Brown, provided the paper's 2,500 employees with 562,000 square feet of floor space on a six-acre plot. The *Bulletin* was published at 3100 Market until 1982, when increased costs, declining ad revenues, and competition from television, radio, and the *Inquirer* forced it to close. After nearly 135 years of reporting the news to Philadelphians, the *Bulletin* published its last edition on January 29, 1982.

The 3100 Market Street building is now part of the Drexel University campus.

The Bulletin Building (renamed the Penn Square Building after the paper's move in 1955) survived its former occupant by three years. In December 1984, Mayor Wilson Goode announced plans to replace the building with a new justice center, despite its inclusion in the National Register of Historic Places. The city ignored the pleas of preservationists to incorporate the building into the new center, or at least to preserve its unique façade and dome. In June 1985, a wrecking ball smashed into the building's walls. Today, the Philadelphia Criminal Justice Center occupies the sites of the Bulletin Building and the adjacent Essex Hotel.

Shibe Park/Connie Mack Stadium

Location: 2701 North Twenty-first Street (block bounded by Lehigh Avenue and Somerset, Twentieth, and Twenty-first streets)
Completed: 1909
Demolished: 1976
Architect/Builder: Benjamin F. Shibe, William Steele & Sons

At the turn of the twentieth century, Philadelphia was considered one of the nation's best baseball cities, home to the American League Athletics and the National League Phillies. While the Phillies' performance was erratic at best (*plus ça change . . .*), the Athletics were a powerhouse under the management of Cornelius McGillicuddy (aka Connie Mack), winning the league pennant in 1902 and 1905.

Athletics owners Mack and Ben Shibe wanted a top-of-the-line facility for their championship team, even better than Philadelphia Park (later known as Baker Bowl), the Phillies' modern ballpark. The men drew up plans to replace 9,500-seat Columbia Park at Twenty-ninth and Columbia streets with the first reinforced-concrete-and-steel baseball sta-

dium in the major leagues. This innovative construction would prevent the fires and collapses that plagued wooden sports facilities. The chosen site, in a marshy North Philadelphia neighborhood called Swampoodle, was still open land, permitting the construction of an extremely large ballpark (originally 378′ left, 340′ right, and 502′ center). Despite its remote location, the site was near major trolley and railroad lines.

Masking Shibe Park's utilitarian skeleton was an elegant French Renaissance façade of brick with terra-cotta trim, featuring mansard roofs with green slate shingles, bas-reliefs with baseball motifs, a second-story Ionic arcade, and a four-story domed corner tower. Terra-cotta busts of Shibe and Mack gazed down from cartouches over the two main entrances. Constructed at a cost of $300,000 and

The main entrance of the recently renamed Connie Mack Stadium at Lehigh Avenue and Twenty-first Street in April 1954. The utilitarian press box and second decks added in the 1920s rise above the original elegant 1909 façade. (Temple University Libraries, Urban Archives, Philadelphia.)

capable of holding 40,000, Shibe Park was described by the *Bulletin* as "the baseball showplace of the country."

Shibe Park opened on April 12, 1909, with the Athletics winning 8–1 over the Boston Red Sox. The Athletics' new home continued to bring them luck: Between 1910 and 1915, they won the American League pennant four times and the World Series three times, thanks to a "$100,000 Infield" consisting of Stuffy McInnis, Eddie Collins, Jack Barry and Frank "Home Run" Baker.[4]

Over the next fifty years, numerous additions and renovations were made to the park, including a left-field grandstand (1913); second decks on the left- and right-field stands (1925); a press box and 3,500 additional seats (1929); electric lights for the first night baseball games in the American League (1939); and an electric scoreboard atop the right-field wall (1956). Less popular was Mack's 1935 decision to raise the east wall along right field from ten to fifty feet, blocking the view of the diamond from Twentieth Street. Until then, row-house owners along the street sold seats on their roofs and balconies for half the price of a ballpark ticket, a cottage industry ended by the "spite fence."[5]

Shibe Park was home to the Philadelphia Athletics from 1909 to 1954, when they moved to Kansas City. Between 1938 and 1954 the Athletics shared the park with the Phillies, who bought the stadium for $2 million when their hometown rivals left. During the joint occupancy, baseball fans could go to a game every day from April to September, since one team was always at home. In 1940, the Philadelphia Eagles also moved to Shibe Park; on December 19, 1948, the park was the site of the first NFL championship game in Philadelphia, which the Eagles won 7–0 over the Chicago Cardinals in a blinding snowstorm. Off-season, Shibe Park witnessed boxing and wrestling matches, circuses, jazz concerts, religious revivals, and campaign rallies for Franklin D. Roosevelt and Richard M. Nixon.

In 1953, a year before the Athletics moved, Shibe Park was renamed Connie Mack Stadium, after the man who had managed the A's for more than fifty years (Mack had refused an effort to change the name in 1941). By this period, the ballpark's poor condition, the lack of parking, and concerns over neighborhood safety prompted plans for a replacement. In 1964, voters approved a bond

The abandoned, burned-out stadium in October 1973, looking west toward Twenty-first Street. (Temple University Libraries, Urban Archives, Philadelphia.)

Nixon Theatre

Location: 24–28 South Fifty-second Street (at Ludlow Street),
    West Philadelphia
Completed: 1910
Demolished: 1984
Architect/Builder: John D. Allen

The early twentieth century was the golden age of live Philadelphia theater. On North Eighth Street between Vine and Race streets alone, more than twenty theaters vied for attention. Although some were equipped to show motion pictures (including Keith's Bijou, where Philadelphians saw their first projected film on Christmas Day, 1895), vaudeville's parade of ethnic comedians, performing dogs, and Oriental acrobats held sway at most houses.

While Philadelphia's largest and grandest theaters were clustered downtown, each self-respecting neighborhood boasted its own odeum. The opening of the Market Street Elevated Passenger Railway between Fifteenth and Sixty-ninth streets in 1907 encouraged the rapid development of West Philadelphia. To entertain the area's growing population, the 1,870-seat Nixon Theatre opened on November 21, 1910 at Fifty-second and Ludlow streets. The theater, just a few steps from the Fifty-second Street Elevated station, replaced a tent that had offered customers five vaudeville acts for a dime.

The French Renaissance structure, built of concrete, sandstone, and white pressed brick, sported a façade with two arched entryways supported by Ionic columns, a large second-story bay window above the main entrance, and a broken pediment. A hanging sign spelled out "Nixon Vaudeville" in dazzling electric lights. The theater, 115 feet wide by 200 feet deep, had a seating capacity of over 2,000. Mindful of recent fires, such as the one that killed 602 at Chicago's Iroquois Theatre in 1903, the Nixon boasted numerous safety features: fireproof concrete construction, multiple exits, an automatic fire-protection system, and asbestos stage curtains.

to build a new multipurpose stadium for the Phillies and Eagles. In 1971, both teams moved to Veterans Stadium in South Philadelphia, taking with them the Harry Rosin statue of Connie Mack installed at the old ballpark in 1957.

Philadelphia's baseball showplace suffered an inglorious death. Shortly after the final game against the Montreal Expos began on October 1, 1970, attendees began to scavenge anything they could tear loose. A riot broke out the second the game ended, with "fans" ripping out turnstiles, toilets, and entire rows of the stadium's bright red seats. A postgame ceremony to officially close the stadium was quickly canceled. The following year, the looted ballpark was badly damaged by an arson fire and then used as a junkyard. During an all-star game at Veterans Stadium in June 1976, what remained of Connie Mack Stadium was demolished. Since 1990, the 5,100-seat Deliverance Evangelical Church has stood on the site.

Although located in West Philadelphia, the Nixon offered the amenities of a Center City theater: twelve private boxes, ladies' parlors and retiring rooms, gentlemen's smoking rooms, and even a ballroom. Patrons who paid a whopping twenty cents to sit in the balcony could enter via a separate side-street box office, avoiding the hoi polloi who paid a measly dime to sit in the ground floor or gallery. Inside, all theatergoers could enjoy an unobstructed view of the stage, with its marble columns and gaily painted curtain, and be soothed by strains from a nine-rank Moeller organ.

According to the November 14, 1910, edition of the *Public Ledger*, the opening of the Nixon Theatre was "an epoch-marking event in the history of West Philadelphia" that doubled nearby property values. Soon, Fifty-second Street was West Philadelphia's Broadway, boasting three other theaters besides the Nixon.

Although the Nixon began to show movies shortly after its opening, it remained a vaudeville house for many years. One of its most memorable performers was soprano Rosa Ponzillo, who sang oper-

atic selections with her sisters. As Rosa Ponselle, she later became the toast of the Metropolitan Opera. A then-fourteen-year-old West Philadelphian named Jeanette McDonald would later recall that her dreams of being a great singer came from listening to Rosa Ponzillo at the Nixon in 1917.

After World War II, the surrounding neighborhood became largely African American. The Nixon adapted to its new audience, showcasing black films and performers. Instead of Rosa Ponselle, soul and R&B groups like the Ambassadors appeared on its stage. In a March 15, 2004, *Daily News* interview, author Leslie Esdaile-Banks recalled her childhood experiences at the Nixon:

As kids, we'd walk from my grandmother's house with cousins, and we'd sit there all afternoon and watch every "black film" (now called blaxpoitation flicks). But who could resist Pam Grier or Calvin Lockhart? Maybe that's what made me go to school to be a filmmaker, go figure. Fifty cents for a ticket; a bag of popcorn and an orange soda, not much more. . . . And no "predators" to worry about on the way home. That's what I miss most, the "old" West Philly.[6]

Between 1941 and 1992, the number of single-screen theaters in Philadelphia dwindled from 380 to 5. Smaller movie theaters like the Nixon found it extremely hard to survive, especially when their neighborhoods began to deteriorate. In 1984, the Nixon Theatre was demolished and replaced by a retail business.

Lubinville/Lubin Manufacturing Company Studios

Location: 1920 West Indiana Avenue (block bordered by Twentieth, Indiana, Nineteenth, and Cambria streets)
Completed: 1910
Demolished: 1995
Architect/Builder: Unknown

Today, Philadelphia is a popular setting for Hollywood movies as diverse as *The Sixth Sense* and *Rocky Balboa*. But in the early 1900s, Philadelphia was Hollywood, with its local version of MGM at Twentieth Street and Indiana Avenue.

Siegmund Lubin (born Lubszynski) emigrated from Prussia in 1876, opening an optical shop in Philadelphia in 1883. Fascinated by early experiments in what were then called life motion pictures, he purchased a camera in 1895 and filmed his horse eating hay. By 1897, he was selling his projector, the Lubin Cineograph, while his optical shop at 21 South Eighth Street became the office of "S. Lubin, World's Largest Manufacturer of Life Movies." In 1899, Lubin built an ornate theatre—possibly the first in the world designed specifically to show motion pictures—on the site of the future Civic Center.

Among Lubin's early offerings was a shot-for-shot remake of Thomas Edison's *The Great Bank Robbery* titled *The Bold Bank Robbery*. Lubin seemed genuinely surprised when Edison sued him for copyright infringement. Edison also sued Lubin for patent violation, creating a legal entanglement that was not resolved until 1907 with the creation of a cartel, the Motion Picture Patents Company.

Despite his legal disputes, Lubin became one of the leaders of the infant film industry, with a national chain of more than 100 movie theaters. He was the first vertically integrated movie magnate, controlling the production and distribution not only of his films but also of his movie equipment through the Lubin Manufacturing Company. He shot films throughout the city, recreating the Spanish-American War in Fairmount Park and the Garden of Eden (starring burlesque queen Mademoiselle Fifi from the nearby Trocadero as Eve) on the roof of his first studio at 912 Arch Street.

In 1909, Lubin sold his theaters and used the proceeds to build Lubinville, a state-of-the-art studio complex in North Philadelphia. The main studio was a hangar-like steel and glass structure with a powerful indoor-lighting system where five movies could be filmed

The interior of Lubinville's glass-walled studio. (Theater Collection, Free Library of Philadelphia.)

The Lubin Manufacturing Company (Lubinville) ca. 1910, showing the exterior of the glass-walled studio. (Theater Collection, Free Library of Philadelphia.)

at once, rain or shine. Three of its four walls were made of a special prismatic glass Lubin invented, which diffused natural light throughout a space larger than a basketball court. An open tank under the floor enabled Lubin to shoot floods or other watery scenes.

Covering the rest of the block were brick buildings that housed offices, editing and screening rooms, laboratories, machine shops to manufacture cameras and projectors, and construction shops for sets, costumes, and props. Lubinville was the largest film studio in the United States until the completion of the Vitagraph facility in Brooklyn in 1911.

Hundreds of films were produced at Lubinville, including an account of the San Francisco earthquake, *When the Earth Trembled,* that may have been the first U.S. disaster film. Between 500 and 700 people worked there in its heyday, among them such silent-screen luminaries as Pearl White (later of *Perils of Pauline* fame), Florence Lawrence, and Marie Dressler.

With the Lubin Manufacturing Company worth over $11 million, Lubin in 1912 purchased Betzwood, the Valley Forge estate of the late beer baron John F. Betz. He spent more than $2 million to transform Betzwood into another cutting-edge studio, with air-conditioned, automated film labs. The mansion and its surrounding 350 acres offered the perfect settings for any film, from Westerns to society sagas.

Unfortunately, a string of disasters struck Lubin when he was financially overextended. On June 13, 1914, an explosion and fire shook Lubinville, destroying the master negatives for all Lubin's films along with sixteen row houses on nearby Garnet Street. That same year, World War I cut U.S. film distributors off from lucrative European markets. In 1915, a federal judge ordered the dissolution of the Motion Picture Patents Company. When Drexel & Company called in a $500,000 loan in 1916, Lubin was forced to surrender both Lubinville and Betzwood to his creditors. Despite repeated attempts at a comeback, Lubin died in 1923 at age seventy-two without making another movie.

After the film studio left in 1916, Lubinville housed a ball-bearing factory and other industries. When the Merit Products paint factory vacated the space in 1990, Lubinville stood vacant but intact until 1995, the earliest surviving film studio in the country. According to Lubin biographer Joseph P. Eckhardt, many of its original features were still in place, including its pressed-metal ceilings. On April 26, 1995, a four-alarm fire set by arsonists ravaged the complex, only hours before a wrecking crew was to demolish it to expand a neighboring industrial site.

After housing an industrial park for many years, the former Betzwood estate is now being restored as a residential, retail, and office development called Riverview at Valley Forge, with many of its original studio buildings still standing. In 1994, a Pennsylvania Historical and Museum Commission marker was placed at the site of Lubin's Eighth Street optical shop. Of the more than 5,000 films Lubin created between 1897 and 1916, fewer than 300 are known to survive.

Reyburn Plaza and City Hall Bandstand

Location: Block bordered by North Broad Street, John F. Kennedy Boulevard, North Fifteenth Street, and Arch Street
Completed: ca. 1915 (bandstand completed 1928)
Demolished: 1961
Architect/Builder: Jacques Gréber, Paul Philippe Cret

In the early twentieth century, Philadelphia's politicians, business leaders, and designers combined forces to remodel their grimy industrial town along the lines of the City Beautiful movement. Among their outstanding achievements was the Fairmount Parkway (renamed the Benjamin Franklin Parkway in 1937), modeled after the Champs-Élysées. This grand diagonal boulevard slashed across William Penn's original grid, connecting sooty Center City with the open green space of Fairmount Park. Ironically, this massive improvement was championed by the corrupt and contented Republican administration and opposed by many reform-minded Democrats, who were shocked by the lucrative contracts awarded to the administration's cronies.

To anchor the parkway's southeastern end, and to illustrate its purpose—bringing the park to the city—the municipal government acquired the block north of City Hall for a great urban forum. Between 1910 and 1915, buildings on the square were cleared for City Hall Plaza. Jacques Gréber, landscape architect for the parkway, designed the plaza as a small park with tree-lined allées and borders. In 1915, it was renamed Reyburn Plaza after the late John E. Reyburn, who had championed the parkway as mayor from 1907 to 1911. An adjacent park between Fifteenth and Sixteenth streets, bisected by the parkway, was known as Reyburn Plaza West.

Beginning in 1925, Paul Philippe Cret instituted a beautification project for the still-rustic space. He designed a public band shell in a simplified Grecian style on the north side of the Plaza, completed in 1928 at a cost of $67,000. The rectangular limestone structure with square buttresses stood forty by sixty feet. On its left

stood a statue of Major General Peter Muhlenberg sculpted by J. Otto Schweizer in 1910, moved from the South Plaza of City Hall to Reyburn Plaza in 1920. On its right stood a statue of Stephen Girard created by J. Massey Rhind in 1897.

Philadelphia Orchestra director Leopold Stokowski was an acoustic adviser for the shell, which was conceived in part as a venue for public concerts by the orchestra. At Stokowski's suggestion, an angled wooden ceiling, painted with bright frescoes, replaced Cret's original flat plaster ceiling to ensure better tone production.

Reyburn Plaza became Philadelphia's answer to Hyde Park, especially when the Depression heightened civil protest. Crowds trampled much of Gréber's landscaping, and the grassy park became a gravel-covered common. In August 1932, the Battle of

Reyburn Plaza broke out when Mayor J. Hampton Moore ordered police to disperse a crowd of 1,500 unemployed Philadelphians demanding public relief. That same year, Leopold Stokowski conducted a band of unemployed musicians in the band shell to bring attention to their plight.

Throughout the 1930s, the local branch of the Communist party battled police at Reyburn Plaza during its May Day celebrations. The pro-Nazi German-American Bund rallied there, waving American and swastika flags; so did 20,000 Philadelphians protesting Hitler's anti-Semitic edicts. When the United States entered World War II, Reyburn Plaza was the site of war-bond rallies, recruitment centers, scrap-metal drives, U.S.O. dances, and African American civil rights protests. In the 1950s and 1960s, Harry S. Truman, Richard Nixon, and John F. Kennedy addressed political rallies there. During its fifty-year existence, Reyburn Plaza also served as a skating rink, playground, Christmas display, outdoor festival site, parking lot, and Salvation Army booth.

As early as the 1920s, the city government planned to locate a municipal office building on Reyburn Plaza. Paul Philippe Cret envisioned demolishing City Hall (except for its tower) and relocating all the city's workers to a U-shaped structure built on the plaza. Along with most of Philadelphia's redevelopment, these plans were put on hold during the Depression and World War II.

By the 1950s, the heavily used plaza had become a "deliberately cultivated eye-sore," in the eyes of the *Evening Bulletin* editorial page, which described it as: "2.17 acres of gravel and cement, with a little grass around the edges. It contains a bandstand which is used almost solely as a perching place for pigeons, and other loungers. The replacement of this structure would offend no disciple of the fine arts, living or dead. . . . A few benches are at hand for citizens who devote them to dormitory use between visits to their parole officers."[7]

The creation of Penn Center and the need for more municipal office space brought an end to Philadelphia's great urban forum. In 1961, Cret's band shell was demolished, and the statues of Girard

and Muhlenberg were moved to the terraces behind the Art Museum, joining the statues of other foreign-born patriots. Between 1962 and 1965, Vincent J. Kling's Municipal Services Building went up on the site. To replace the lost public space, the Fairmount Parkway was terminated at Sixteenth Street and the halves of the bisected block known as Reyburn Plaza West were reunited as John F. Kennedy Plaza (today Love Park).

Since its dedication on July 19, 1977, Dilworth Plaza, west of City Hall, has replaced Reyburn Plaza as the stage for many of Philadelphia's public demonstrations.

Sears Distribution Center and Warehouse

Location: 4640 East Roosevelt Boulevard (at Adams Avenue),
    Northeast Philadelphia
Completed: 1920
Demolished: 1994
Architect/Builder: Nimmons, Carr & Wright

By 1900, the Sears, Roebuck mail-order catalog was a household fixture across the country, and the company delivered everything from pickle jars to prefabricated houses to its customers' doorsteps. In 1919, Sears president Julius Rosenwald dispatched his son Lessing to Philadelphia to open a regional distribution center that would expedite delivery of goods to East Coast customers. Philadelphia's central location, its status as a major transportation hub, and its proximity to many of Sears' providers made it the natural choice.

Lessing Rosenwald oversaw the construction of a seven-building complex on forty acres at Roosevelt Boulevard and Adams Avenue in Crescentville, a rural community in Northeast Philadelphia. At its heart stood a nine-story Industrial Gothic merchandise building dominated by a fourteen-story clock tower. This central building, covered in brick with terra-cotta trim, was the largest concrete-reinforced structure in the country at the time. The clock tower served as a central elevator bank, and its top concealed the sprinkler tanks for the entire complex.

Sears was so anxious to commence operations in Philadelphia that the center opened unfinished on October 18, 1920. Employees worked in their coats and gloves in offices whose windows still lacked glass. Soon, the Roosevelt Boulevard center was a regional headquarters, handling all distribution for the northeastern United States from Maine to North Carolina and stocking 200,000 products.

Within a few years, the open fields around the Sears complex gave way to row houses, whose residents viewed the clock tower as a neighborhood landmark. Roosevelt Boulevard became such a busy thoroughfare that a tunneled walkway was constructed underneath it, allowing workers to travel safely to and from the bus stop on the opposite side of the street.

Even during the Depression, the Sears center's constant activity made it a capitalist showcase. The 1937 *WPA Guide to Philadelphia* described "girls dashing about on roller skates and collecting

The central building of the Sears Distribution Center ca. 1925. (The Library Company of Philadelphia.)

goods from a giant conglomeration of bins; merchandise whizzing through chutes; thousands of workers performing, in carefully allotted time, the minutely specialized tasks involved in filling mail orders."[8] During their lunch hour, Sears workers could enjoy the athletic fields, tennis courts, and gardens that covered much of the campus, dance to the music of an employee band in a second-floor auditorium, or shop at the employee discount store, or "junkie."

Over the years, the Sears campus expanded from 40 to more than 120 acres, becoming the company's second largest center. In August 1955, the Sears retail store moved from the ground floor of the merchandise building to a modern facility at Adams Avenue and Whitaker Street. By 1966, Philadelphia was second only to Sears' Chicago headquarters in sales, with more than 6,000 employees filling upward of 7,000 orders every fourteen minutes. The catalog division was known as the Frankford High School Continuation School for the ready employment it offered local grads.

During the 1970s and 1980s, Sears' hold on the U.S. consumer began to loosen. Following the recessionary seventies, a nationwide proliferation of malls and discount outlets reduced the company's catalog sales. Its efforts to diversify backfired (including a campaign to become a "financial supermarket" offering brokerage services), hurting its retail stores' profitability. In 1990, Sears closed the Adams Avenue store. In 1993—the last year the Sears catalog was published—the distribution center and warehouse closed, sending the surrounding community into a financial and emotional depression.

The Rubin Organization bought 48 acres of the 120-acre property and announced plans to erect a shopping mall on the site. Demolition on the smaller buildings began in mid-1994. At 9:00 AM on October 30, 1994, more than 50,000 onlookers watched the landmark clock tower crash to the ground when the merchandise building was demolished in the largest implosion ever undertaken at the time. More than 12,000 pounds of dynamite reduced the structure's 2.6 million square feet to rubble in only 7.5 seconds. Within a year, the Northeast Tower Shopping Center stood on the site.

Philco Corporation Radio and Television Plant

Location: Block bordered by Tioga, C, Ontario, and Rosehill streets, North Philadelphia
Completed: ca. 1920
Demolished: ca. 2000
Architect/Builder: Various

In the early 1920s, radio was the scientific wonder of the age, and the Philadelphia region was the Silicon Valley of this new technology. The RCA Victor Company dominated downtown Camden. In Philadelphia the Atwater Kent Radio plant sprawled over fifteen acres at Abbotsford Road and Wissahickon Avenue, while the industry leader, Philco Radio, stood on C Street in an industrial North Philadelphia neighborhood.

Philco began life in 1906, when a failing carbon-arc lamp company was reorganized as the Philadelphia Storage Battery Company at Emerald and Tioga streets. In 1909, the company, which produced batteries for electric cars, trucks, and mine locomotives, moved to nearby Ontario and C streets. By 1920, the company (renamed Philco) had annual revenues of more than $4 million from its Diamond Grid batteries. After a 1920 fire, the company built a new plant, a six-story brick and concrete structure with a ten-story tower.

When the radio craze hit in the early 1920s, Philco began to produce radio batteries and battery eliminators. The invention of AC tubes in 1927 meant an end to Philco's primary product line, triggering a switch to manufacturing radio sets. Philco's best-selling Model 20 cathedral radio, introduced shortly afterward, soon established it as the leading radio maker in the country.

In 1929, Philco built a corporate headquarters at the southwest corner of Tioga and C streets, across from its plant. The six-story concrete and brick structure with large studio windows was similar

in design to the production facilities. It housed the company's engineering, product design, and development departments, responsible for such innovations as automatic tuning and volume controls, high fidelity, and wireless remote control.

Philco's mastery of modern business techniques, including an efficient assembly line, enabled it to mass-produce inexpensive radios and survive the Depression, despite a four-month shutdown in 1937–38. In 1941, Philco manufactured roughly one-third of all radios sold in the United States, earning revenues of $77 million. By comparison, its major competitor, Atwater Kent, which had produced large, expensive radio sets, closed its doors in 1936.

In 1932, Philco also began to manufacture experimental television sets. It established Philadelphia's first television station, W3XE (later WPTZ), at its C and Tioga streets headquarters, broadcasting to the homes of 100 employees. During this time, a wooden tower was constructed on the headquarters roof, later replaced by a taller metal tower with green neon tubes spelling "PHILCO." By 1941, more than 800 local households received Philco broadcasts of Penn football games, the Mummers' Parade, and the Republican National Convention.

During World War II, Philco pioneered in the field of electronics, developing the radar bombsite and manufacturing radio and electronic equipment for planes, tanks, and ships. While ENIAC, the Electronic Numerical Integrator and Computer, was still under wraps at the University of Pennsylvania, Philco developed a primitive 126-vacuum tube computer called a Master Mind, capable of recording dial readings faster than any human could.

Philco made the mistake of concentrating on radio and appliance production after World War II, while RCA and other companies took the lead in television. In June 1953, Philco sold WPTZ-TV to Westinghouse Radio Stations, Inc. (later Group W), which renamed the station KYW-TV. After a burst of postwar profitability, Philco began a descent that culminated in its sale to Ford Motor Company in 1961.

In the mid-1970s, the company was split up, with its television division sold to GTE-Sylvania and its international sales and marketing divisions sold to White Consolidated. During this period, its Philadelphia facilities were gradually downsized, then phased out completely in 1974. In 1988, the last Philco local office in suburban Blue Bell closed its doors and moved to White Consolidated's Pittsburgh office. Today, Philco is a subsidiary of Nordyne Corporation, manufacturing low-cost home appliances for the overseas market.

The North Philadelphia production plant and corporate headquarters were both demolished between 1998 and 2000. On the adjacent block (bounded by C, Tioga, Arbor, and Ontario streets), several Philco structures from the 1930s and 1950s still stand.

The Arena

Location: 4530 Market Street, West Philadelphia
Completed: 1920
Demolished: 1983
Architect/Builder: George W. Pawling

Early twentieth-century Philadelphians were obsessed with indoor sporting events, from boxing to bicycle races. On Valentine's Day 1920, the Philadelphia Auditorium and Ice Palace (soon renamed the Arena) opened at 4530 Market Street in West Philadelphia with a Yale-Princeton hockey game. For nearly sixty years, the Arena, the city's first major indoor sports complex, served as Philadelphia's answer to Madison Square Garden. Besides hosting countless sports events, the building was also large enough for roller derbies, rodeos, rock concerts, religious revivals, and rocking-chair marathons.

The Arena was a sprawling, hangar-like brick structure with a peaked roof that resembled a train station or warehouse. Only the white-tiled entrance hall on Market Street, with its marquee and billboards promoting events, made a stab at respectability.

The cavernous, 9,000-seat auditorium hosted the National Basketball Association Warriors, as well as the Quakers and

Ramblers ice hockey teams. Other sports events held at the Arena included tennis matches, swimming meets, six-day bicycle races, and even a bloodless bullfight. The Arena's greatest claims to fame involved boxing and wrestling. Sugar Ray Robinson, Lew Tendler, Gene Tunney, and Joe Frazier all boxed there. Long before the Rock became a media darling, the World Wide Wrestling Federation made the Arena its home from 1965 to 1975, hosting such matches as Stan Stasiak's 1973 win over Pedro Morales.

Besides sporting events, the Arena hosted skating spectaculars starring Sonja Henie, as well as rodeos featuring Gene Autry and Roy Rogers. In 1946, a funeral was held there for a cowgirl who

The Arena in June 1977, shortly after it was sold at auction for $165,000. (Temple University Libraries, Urban Archives, Philadelphia.)

died riding a bucking bronco during Roy Rogers' rodeo; Rogers and the Sons of the Pioneers sang "Roundup in the Sky" before everyone rode out to the cemetery. The Arena also hosted many rock stars, including Elvis Presley, Chuck Berry, Jimi Hendrix, Frank Zappa, and Jim Morrison.

In the late 1940s, Walter Annenberg, head of Triangle Publications, acquired the Arena. Between 1948 and 1952, he erected one of the first structures built specifically for television broadcasting next to the Arena, at 4548 Market Street. The WFIL Studios (later home to *American Bandstand*) shared a party wall with the Arena, and television equipment was installed in the stadium to allow live coverage of professional sports.

After 1967, many of the events that would once have been held at the Arena moved to the new Spectrum in South Philadelphia (although the Arena won back some business when large chunks of the Spectrum roof blew off in a 1968 windstorm). In 1977, the auditorium was renamed the Martin Luther King Arena in honor of the visionary who had addressed a civil rights rally there in October 1966. Attempts to revive the moribund facility ended when an arson fire destroyed the building's roof in October 1981. In August 1983, a second fire destroyed the boarded-up structure, except for its marquee and entrance hall.

More than twenty years after the Arena's demise, sports fans still mourn its special charm, completely absent from its successor, the antiseptically modern Wachovia Complex. Bob Vetrone, writer for the *Bulletin* and *Daily News*, offered this elegy for the Arena: "It was down and dirty. People today wouldn't believe what it was like. It was just indescribable. It was the last of the smoke-filled arenas. It was fun. There will probably never be another like it, and maybe that's fortunate."[9]

Mayfair House

Location: 401 West Johnson Street, West Mt. Airy
Completed: 1926
Demolished: 2001
Architect/Builder: Sugarman & Berger

While apartment living had been a feature of city life for decades, the 1920s saw it spread to less-developed areas like Germantown and Mt. Airy. Apartment houses not only reflected rising land values in these neighborhoods, but also signaled both the emergence of an automotive culture among affluent Philadelphians and the difficulty of maintaining large houses when servants grew scarce after World War I.

Areas overlooking the Wissahickon section of Fairmount Park, which runs through northwest Philadelphia, were especially popular for upscale apartment houses. Starting in 1925, the Justus Strawbridge estate on Wissahickon Avenue in Germantown was developed into Alden Park, a complex of three Jacobean Revival apartment towers. Still in business today, Alden Park was the first apartment complex in the United States surrounded by a park and formal gardens. Among its amenities were a central garage, a nine-hole golf course, and a year-round swimming pool with a retractable roof.

That same year, Mayfair House (also known as Mayfair Court) was erected at the southwest corner of Johnson Street and Lincoln Drive. Conveniently located along the main automobile artery between Center City and Chestnut Hill, Mayfair House served as the symbolic entrance to the fast-growing neighborhood of West Mt. Airy. Designed in the Colonial Revival style, Mayfair House was constructed of brick with terra-cotta trim. The fourteen-story, 244-unit apartment house was built in an L-shape, with a two-story central belvedere overlooking the Wissahickon woods. Its rooftop restaurant offered views of the new skyscrapers of Center City.

The interior design of Mayfair House was also Colonial Revival, with murals painted on the walls of the public rooms. An elegant ballroom on the first floor featured large arched windows, a bandstand in the form of an ornamental plaster shell, and a white and blue Wedgwood color scheme. Despite its size, the Mayfair seemed to complement, rather than overwhelm, the neighboring houses.

Unlike Alden Park, Mayfair House suffered financial problems soon after its opening. In 1928, three years after it was built for $2.5 million, it was sold at sheriff's sale. The building changed owners four times in its first five years and several times later in its history, at least twice at auction.

In the 1960s and 1970s, the affluent clientele sought by the Mayfair moved either back into Center City or farther out to the suburbs. The apartment house gradually deteriorated, until the city, in response to community complaints, closed the building in 1989. The ninety remaining tenants were relocated, and the building was effectively abandoned by its owners. Over the next decade, Mayfair House became a public nuisance, home to drug dealers, prostitutes, and scavengers who threw air conditioners and refrigerators out the windows to cart away. In 1992, the *Inquirer* described Mayfair House as "a grotesque, vandalized building with broken window panes, rotten doors, rusty steel railings and a ripped front-entrance awning."[10]

When several attempts to rehabilitate the structure proved unsuccessful, the surrounding neighborhood petitioned the city to demolish Mayfair House. Although the building had been added to the National Register of Historic Places in 1982, the city paid the Preservation Alliance $25,000 to surrender the property easement. After Mayfair House was dismantled in 2001, its former site was deeded to the Fairmount Park Commission, which worked with local residents to turn the land into a small park.

Sesqui-Centennial Exposition Entrance

Location: Marconi Plaza (South Broad Street between Oregon
Avenue and Bigler Street), South Philadelphia
Completed: 1926
Demolished: 1927
Architect/Builder: Westinghouse Electric and Manufacturing
Company

In 1926, Philadelphia hoped to repeat the dazzling success of the 1876 Centennial with a Sesqui-Centennial International Exposition. Besides celebrating 150 years of independence, the Sesqui-Centennial would herald the nation's emergence as the world's technological and industrial leader, showcasing such developments as airplanes, automobiles, radio, motion pictures, electric locomotives, and dial telephones. A giant Liberty Bell at the entrance, ablaze with light, would beckon guests from around the globe to the southernmost tip of Philadelphia. Sadly, a combination of graft, poor planning, insufficient funds, and a prolonged rainy spell kept visitors away.

Political boss William S. Vare arranged for the Sesqui-Centennial to be held, not in Fairmount Park, but on 450 acres of marshland he owned on League Island. Vare-controlled contractors erected the Rainbow City, so-called because most of the buildings were stucco tinted in pastel hues and lit with colored lights at night. Congress kicked in only $1 million to finance the fair, while the State of Pennsylvania contributed nothing, leaving the city and private investors to finance most of the fair themselves. As a result, many of the elegant buildings depicted in the advance publicity were never built. In an ironic touch, the Liberty Bell—its large crack prominently displayed—was chosen as the Sesqui-Centennial symbol.

Mayor W. Freeland Kendrick, an Imperial Potentate of the Order of the Mystic Shrine, insisted that the exposition's grand opening coincide with his fellow Shriners' annual convention in Philadelphia. Most of the buildings and exhibits were unfinished when the fair opened on May 31, 1926, including its grand entrance, a gigantic replica of the Liberty Bell located at Marconi Plaza, a new park honoring the developer of radio.

The giant Liberty Bell at the entrance to the Sesqui-Centennial, looking north up Broad Street. City Hall Tower appears in the distance, directly under the bell's clapper. (The Library Company of Philadelphia.)

The eighty-foot, forty-two-ton Liberty Bell was designed and constructed by engineers of the Westinghouse Electric and Manufacturing Company. The bell's metal skin was studded with 26,000 fifteen-watt lightbulbs; its underskirt presented a blue, starry dome, illuminated by more bulbs in its enormous clapper. The rim of the bell stood twenty feet above Broad Street, allowing cars and people to pass underneath. Two seventy-foot support towers decorated with carved garlands and topped by stone eagles supported the bell. In early June, when a grand parade of 100 bands and 135 floats passed beneath the giant clapper, scaffolding still girded the towers. At night, when the scaffolds were invisible, the illuminated bell became a more presentable beacon, visible as far north as City Hall.

Reports of the Sesqui-Centennial's unfinished status, coupled with rain on 107 of its 184 days, dampened enthusiasm. Fewer than seven million of the anticipated forty million visitors actually showed up, compared to more than ten million guests at the Centennial fifty years earlier. When the fair closed in November 1926, the city was left with a $5 million deficit to pay from the public coffers. The Sesqui-Centennial Exhibition Association in charge of the ill-fated fair declared bankruptcy a few months later.

In July and August 1927, Philadelphia auctioneer George C. Freeman held a series of sales on the Sesqui-Centennial grounds to satisfy the fair's numerous creditors. The Palace of Education, built for $1 million, brought only $10,750; the Tower of Light, on which the city had lavished $300,000 before deciding it was too expensive to finish, sold for $1,000. The massive Liberty Bell, complete with its 26,000 bulbs and 30,000 feet of wire, fetched only $60. Within a decade, the Rainbow City site was covered with car graveyards and the tar-paper shacks of Philadelphians ruined by the Depression.

Today, Marconi Plaza is a nineteen-acre public park, home to bocce courts, Mummers concerts, and an annual Columbus Day festival.

Municipal Stadium/John F. Kennedy Stadium

Location: 3601 South Broad Street
Completed: 1926
Demolished: 1992
Architect/Builder: Simon & Simon

Only two permanent structures remained from the ill-fated Sesqui-Centennial: the John Hanson–John Morton Memorial Building (today the American Swedish Historical Museum) and the Philadelphia Sesqui-Centennial International Exposition Stadium.

Construction began in April 1925 on the horseshoe-shaped stadium, budgeted at $2 million and made of concrete with an exterior of buff brick and gray limestone. Seventy-seven tiers of seats accommodated 105,000 spectators for football games and 126,000 for boxing matches, although the gradual slope meant poor visibility for those sitting in the top rows. In April 1926, a *Bulletin* exposé of cracks and flaws in the new stadium led to demands for an inquiry into its contractors. Despite the scandal, the stadium opened on May 15, 1926, one of the few attractions actually completed before the official Sesqui-Centennial opening.

During the fair, the stadium was used for athletic meets, rodeos, and pageants, including the spectacle "Freedom," with 2,000 actors, 200 horses, a herd of camels, and a troop of elephants. The first major sporting event at the stadium was a boxing match between Gene Tunney and Jack Dempsey on September 23, 1926. A drenching rain did not deter 120,757 fans from watching the underdog, Tunney, a young ex-Marine, win the heavyweight title from Dempsey.

Facing page: **T**he Sesqui-Centennial International Exhibition Stadium under construction in late 1925, with Broad Street at upper left. (Collection of the author.)

After the Sesqui-Centennial ended in a sea of red ink, members of City Council called for an inquiry into the stadium's construction costs, which had mushroomed to $3.6 million. Renamed Philadelphia Stadium and then Municipal Stadium, the facility became a white elephant during the Depression, earning less than $100 during 1933. For a few years, Municipal Stadium housed the freshly renamed Philadelphia Eagles (formerly the Frankford Yellow-jackets) until they moved to Shibe Park.

Plans were afoot to sell the stadium when the U.S. Military and Naval Academies agreed in 1936 to move their annual football game there from the University of Pennsylvania's Franklin Field. The Army-Navy game would remain the arena's primary tenant until 1980, when it moved to nearby Veterans Stadium. At halftime ceremonies for the 1964 game, Mayor James Tate renamed the facility John F. Kennedy Stadium after the president who had flipped the coin at midfield two years earlier.

Aside from Army-Navy games, the stadium saw little regular use after World War II. Professional sports teams preferred other venues, especially after Veterans Stadium and the Spectrum opened in the 1970s. Occasionally, the stadium was used for a boxing event, such as the September 1952 heavyweight title bout between Rocky Marciano and Joe Walcott, but even this event drew only 40,000 fans.

Instead, the stadium became the place where teams commemorated sports victories achieved elsewhere: The Flyers celebrated their second Stanley Cup there in 1975, and the Phillies celebrated their World Series victory five years later. JFK Stadium also hosted concerts by the Beatles, the Rolling Stones, Bob Dylan, and Pink Floyd. In July 1985, JFK Stadium was the site of the U.S. section of the Live Aid Concert, in conjunction with Wembley, England; three years later, it was one of only two U.S. stops for the star-studded Amnesty International concert.

In 1987, private developers floated a plan to transform JFK Stadium into an outdoor winter wonderland, with ski slopes, a skating rink, and a bobsled course. By then, years of deferred maintenance by a cash-strapped city government had rendered the stadium structurally unsound. After a Grateful Dead concert on July 13, 1989, it was officially closed, remaining vacant until its demolition in April 1992. Parts of the stadium, including its flagpoles, metal gates, decorative eagles, and the limestone entrance for VIPs, were salvaged and placed in storage for a future Philadelphia Sports Hall of Fame.

A decade later, a $100 million, 21,000-seat arena called Spectrum II (today the Wachovia Center) opened on the site as the new home of the Flyers and 76ers.

Mastbaum Theater

Location: Northwest corner of Twentieth and Market streets
Completed: 1929
Demolished: 1958
Architect/Builder: Hoffman-Heron Co.

By the 1920s, Philadelphia's entertainment district had shifted from South Broad Street to Market Street. Movie houses lined Market Street, including the Palace (built in 1908 for film pioneer Siegmund Lubin), Earle, Erlanger, Fox, Stanton, and Victoria. As movies became more elaborate and opulent, so did the buildings in which they played. While all these theaters were designed for movies, most included orchestra pits and full proscenium stages for live performances.

The largest and grandest movie theater in Philadelphia (and the eighth largest in the United States) was the Mastbaum. Brothers Jules and Stanley Mastbaum owned the Stanley Company, which had grown from a single nickelodeon into Philadelphia's largest theater chain in only twenty years. Stanley Mastbaum already had a theater named after him, the Stanley, at Nineteenth and Market streets. The new theater at Twentieth and Market was going to be named the Jules, until Jules died suddenly in 1926. His brother and Warner Brothers, which had acquired the Stanley Company, instead named it the Mastbaum Memorial Theater. Built at a cost of more than $5 million, the "Taj Mahal of Philadelphia theaters" opened on February 27, 1929, with a preview of *Sonny Boy* starring Davey Lee.[11]

The Mastbaum's exterior, 220 by 180 feet, was a classical palace. Above the marquee, four pairs of Ionic columns supported a projecting cornice with a scalloped edge. The columns framed three large stained-glass windows, backlit and framed by elaborate cast-iron scrollwork. At night, floodlights bathed the theater's shining marble façade. Atop the building, a triptych electric sign flashed the Mastbaum name.

An artist's sketch of the Mastbaum Theatre, from the December 29, 1928, issue of *Motion Picture News*. (Athenaeum of Philadelphia.)

The American Theatre Historical Society would later describe the Mastbaum's interior décor as "French Renaissance with a vengeance."[12] The theater had five lobbies and eight levels. In the main lobby, reached through three sets of bronze doors, a tile and marble fountain stood before a grand staircase with railings of Breches Pavazzano, a richly colored purple and white Tuscan marble. Huge hand-painted murals, many acquired from the Metropolitan Museum of Art, covered the walls.

The 4,738-seat theater itself dripped with gold-coated plaster ornamentation, brocade curtains, and filigree screens. Hidden lighting cast a dusklike pink and amber hue over the rich interior, while elaborate ceiling fixtures disguised the loudspeakers. A 200-piece orchestra accompanied the silent pictures, ascending to the orchestra pit via three stage elevators. An innovative signal system told ushers which seats were occupied before they escorted patrons into the darkened theater.

Despite such luxuries and the lure of a forty-eight-girl chorus line called the Roxyettes, the huge theater was forced to close in the Depression year of 1932, throwing 400 employees out of work. Except for a few special events, it remained dark until September 4, 1942, when it reopened with the film *Tales of Manhattan.* That year, it also hosted the live stage show *This Is the Army*, in which Irving Berlin sang, "Oh, How I Hate to Get Up in the Morning." The Mastbaum remained popular through the 1940s and early 1950s, not only for movies but also for live appearances by such stars as Judy Garland, Danny Kaye, Dean Martin, and Jerry Lewis.

By the late 1950s, however, both movies and Market Street had changed. After a federal law decreed that movie studios had to divest themselves of their theater chains, the Stanley Warner Theater Company found itself saddled with a white elephant. Even

though the Mastbaum was one of the first theaters equipped for CinemaScope and 3-D movies, its audiences continued to dwindle as television took hold of the nation. Meanwhile, Center City redevelopment plans called for lining both Market Street and Pennsylvania Avenue with office towers.

The Mastbaum closed on April 16, 1958. Although a Stanley Warner spokesperson stated that "this should not be regarded as

the death knell of the theater," demolition began almost immediately. The theater's elaborate fittings and furnishings were auctioned off. Its Wurlitzer organ, the largest in the city, was moved to Cincinnati's Springdale Music Palace, where it was badly damaged in a 1992 fire; one of the Mastbaum's huge chandeliers now graces a Spaghetti Warehouse in Atlanta, Georgia.

After serving as a parking lot for many years, the Mastbaum site is occupied today by an office building. Meanwhile, the Rodin Museum on the Benjamin Franklin Parkway, established by Jules Mastbaum shortly before his death and dedicated on November 29, 1929, survives as a memorial to the theater mogul.

Boulevard Pools

Location: Block bordered by Roosevelt Boulevard, Princeton Avenue, Brous Street, and Tyson Avenue, Northeast Philadelphia
Completed: ca. 1929
Demolished: 1980
Architect/Builder: Unknown

The Northeast became Philadelphia's fastest-growing residential community in the 1920s, thanks to the Broad Street Subway, the Frankford Elevated, and Roosevelt Boulevard. As car ownership grew, so did neighborhoods like Oxford Circle and Mayfair, their freshly paved streets lined with middle-class row houses. The Northeast's booming population required recreational facilities on a large scale.

Boulevard Pools was established in the late 1920s on Roosevelt Boulevard on the outskirts of Mayfair. The ten-acre spread contained one of the city's largest outdoor pools, the hub of an entertainment complex that eventually included an amusement park and dance hall. Its clubhouse stood at the corner of Brous Street and Princeton Avenue. The large, Mediterranean-style stucco building, flanked by two low wings, had tall, Roman-arched windows and red tile porches and roofs.

After paying fifty cents inside the grand entrance hall, with its vaulted ceiling and classical pillars, men turned left and women turned right to their respective changing rooms.

Besides the large main pool, swimmers could select a lap pool, a diving pool with three springboards, or a smaller children's pool. Sand-covered "beaches" that surrounded the pools covered an ice-skating rink used during the winter season. Between swims, visitors could enjoy homemade picnics or refreshment-stand snacks under covered pavilions. Boulevard Pools was hugely popular, especially during the Depression when a day trip to the Jersey Shore was beyond many people's means. On some hot days, more than 8,000

Crowds frolic in the main pool at Boulevard Pools ca. 1930, in front of the clubhouse. A smaller diving pool lies behind the crowds to the right. (The Historical Society of Pennsylvania.)

visitors sought relief at the pools, forcing the owners to shut the doors shortly after their 10:00 AM opening because of the crowds.

In the 1940s, a small amusement park, Playland, opened next to Boulevard Pools. The park's attractions, which included a miniature-golf course, roller coaster, merry-go-round, boat pond, Ferris wheel, and bumper cars, allowed Northeast families to enjoy an entire day of leisure without leaving their neighborhood. During the same period, Boulevard Pools opened the Boulevard Ballroom on the second floor of its main building, offering weekend dancing and the prospect of romance to local teenagers.

After World War II, the pace of growth in Northeast Philadelphia accelerated; between 1950 and 1960, its population increased from 200,000 to 300,000. While the farmland above Pennypack Park filled with suburban development, older neighborhoods like Mayfair and Oxford Circle became as densely packed as Center City. The intersection of Roosevelt Boulevard and Cottman Avenue, just north of Boulevard Pools, was the region's shopping district, with hundreds of stores clustered around Roosevelt Mall. Roosevelt Boulevard itself became part of Route 1, a multilane highway lined with strip malls and office buildings.

Boulevard Pools closed forever after Labor Day 1976, the victim of free city pools, mounting maintenance costs, and rising land values. Demolition started in 1978, with the erection of stores on Tyson Avenue and duplex houses on Brighton Street. An arsonist set fire to the main building during its demolition in March 1980, hastening its destruction. The neighboring Playland survived until 1982, when it was replaced by a K-Mart.

Palumbo's

Location: 824–30 Catharine Street (block bounded by Eighth, Ninth, Darien, and Catharine streets), South Philadelphia
Completed: ca. 1930
Demolished: 1994
Architect/Builder: Unknown

In 1884, Francesco Palumbo, an Italian immigrant from Abruzzo, opened a boardinghouse on Catharine Street in South Philadelphia. Palumbo's boardinghouse was a mecca for other young immigrants from Abruzzo, many arriving with a piece of paper pinned to their clothes that read "Palumbo." For ninety cents a week, the new arrivals got bed and board. Palumbo helped many of his boarders find jobs by allying himself with the Vare political machine. Over the years, he expanded his operation, purchasing adjacent row houses.

Around 1930, Palumbo's son Frank opened a restaurant on Catharine Street. Frank continued his father's habit of acquiring adjoining properties, creating a mazelike entertainment complex that covered a city block. Housed in twenty brick row houses were Palumbo's Restaurant at Darien and Catharine streets (with a main dining room seating 800), the Nostalgia Room (located in a former funeral parlor on Ninth Street), and the private CR Club on Christian Street, as well as two showrooms, four banquet rooms, three kitchens, and a number of apartments and offices.

Palumbo's was the heart of South Philadelphia, where weddings, christenings, graduations, and other major events were celebrated. With an eye for publicity, Frank Palumbo became the city's best-known host, throwing wedding parties for World War II brides separated from their servicemen husbands, serving free cake to war-bond buyers, and treating neighborhood children to junkets at Woodside Park, the zoo, and Shibe Park.

A savvy networker, Palumbo befriended politicians of all stripes. Bill Meade, a Republican ward leader, and Bill Barrett, Democra-

tic congressman from South Philadelphia, both held their fundraisers at Palumbo's. So did Frank Rizzo, a staunch friend and ally whom Palumbo had cultivated when the future mayor was a young police lieutenant. In 1975, Palumbo's friends on City Council renamed the stretch of Darien Street by his complex Palumbo Plaza.

Inside Palumbo's warren of row houses was some of the hottest entertainment in Philadelphia, with a dance orchestra and chorus line performing elaborate production numbers. Frank Sinatra ate there whenever he was in town, usually on the house. One night, after Sinatra treated his fellow diners to a medley to thank Palumbo for his hospitality, his host repaid the favor by presenting Ol' Blue Eyes with a new Lincoln Continental. On other nights, guests might hear Jimmy Durante sing "Inka Dinka Doo," Bobby Darin perform "Mack the Knife," or Sergio Franchi croon "Come Back to Sorrento."

Palumbo's began its downward slide in 1978, when its headliners decamped to the new casinos in Atlantic City. Five years later, Frank Palumbo died at the age of seventy-two. While Palumbo's continued to operate for another decade, the glamour and excitement that had marked its heyday evaporated. The twenty-nine-member band shrank to six musicians, who performed on weekends instead of seven nights a week. In 1993, Frank Palumbo Jr., a lawyer

with aspirations to a judgeship, began to sell off parts of the business. A May 12, 1994, *Inquirer* article reported rumors that Palumbo's might close, the property having been used as collateral to take out more than $1 million in lines of credit from the Philadelphia Police and Fire Federal Credit Union. The same article noted that there were no bookings listed after June 12.[13]

On June 20, 1994, a four-alarm fire gutted most of the Palumbo complex. Two months later, on August 25, a second fire destroyed the CR Club, the only part of Palumbo's that had survived the earlier blaze. A third fire swept the site in September; eventually, all three fires would be declared arson. Within a year, a 9,000-square-foot Rite Aid drugstore stood on the site.

Convention Hall/Municipal Auditorium/ Civic Center Auditorium

Location: South Thirty-fourth Street and Civic Center Boulevard, West Philadelphia
Completed: 1931
Demolished: 2005
Architect/Builder: Philip H. Johnson

In the boom year of 1929, many of Philadelphia's Improvements were in place, including the Benjamin Franklin Parkway, Roosevelt Boulevard, and the Delaware River Bridge. Work was under way on other important structures, including Suburban and Thirti-eth Street stations, the Franklin Institute, Philadelphia Savings Fund Society, and Convention Hall. The completion of these projects during the early 1930s conveyed the illusion that Philadelphia was still growing, despite the deepening Depression.

Convention Hall opened on September 17, 1931, on the west bank of the Schuylkill, next to the aging Philadelphia Commercial Museum. Covering more than 96,000 square feet, the marble, limestone, and steel structure in the Italian Renaissance style was designed to provide an elegant yet modern forum for public gatherings. A rectangular entrance hall with bas-relief carvings on the friezes and window lintels stood on Vintage Avenue (renamed Convention Avenue and later Civic Center Boulevard), lending a human scale to the building's façade. It opened onto a vast main hall, 300 feet long by 226 feet wide. The arched roof, rising 88 feet from the floor, was supported by twelve giant trusses so that no pillars would block the view. The main hall seated 13,500 spectators, while its stage could hold another 1,500 people. Convention Hall also contained a second floor ballroom, twenty-three meeting rooms, and a restaurant.

As the auditorium's construction costs mounted to over $5 million, an insolvent city government attempted to cut corners. Instead of modern air-conditioning, roof fans blew across huge blocks of ice, a primitive cooling system. Once finished, the hall became notorious for its poor management, sloppy maintenance, and no-show staff. Despite these shortcomings, the new facility helped win the city the 1936 Democratic National Convention, where Franklin D.

Conventioneers congregate on and around the steps of the Municipal Auditorium for the 1940 Republican National Convention. To the left, a Public Telephones trailer provides additional phone access for reporters covering the convention; to the right, a "Convention Hall–Center City" bus prepares to depart. (The Library Company of Philadelphia.)

Roosevelt was nominated to a second term. Four years later, the Republicans nominated Wendell Willkie for president in the hall.

During the summer of 1948, Convention Hall hosted three national presidential conventions—Democratic, Republican, and the splinter Progressive party. This allowed the nascent television networks to broadcast proceedings for all three conventions to roughly ten million viewers on the eastern seaboard. Unfortunately, glaring TV lights combined with a heat wave to overwhelm the Hall's ineffective ice-and-fan system. At the Democratic Convention in mid-July, more than 100 delegates and guests were treated for heat prostration.

After the politicians dispersed, Convention Hall hosted a papal visit, a Beatles concert, Atlantic Ten basketball games, the Philadelphia Flower Show, and countless other sports events, trade shows, college graduations, concerts, and folk pageants. By the late 1950s, thanks to years of deferred maintenance, Convention Hall was crumbling, and Philadelphia was losing business to newer facilities like the New York Coliseum. The city finally air-conditioned Convention Hall and constructed a $15 million, 180,000-square-foot Exhibition Hall to create the Philadelphia Civic Center. Despite a brief burst of activity, the consensus was that Philadelphia needed a newer, larger, centrally located facility to win convention business.

After many years of planning, negotiation, and construction, the Pennsylvania Convention Center opened in Center City in 1993. In 1996, the Philadelphia Flower Show moved to the new facility, leaving the Civic Center complex largely unused. In 2001, the University of Pennsylvania Health Systems purchased the Civic Center from the city to construct a research and treatment center on eleven acres of the nineteen-acre site.

Prior to its demolition in 2005, Convention Hall was stripped of many architectural features, including leaded-glass windows, chandeliers, fluted marble columns, and brass radiator covers. In early 2006, the University of Pennsylvania unveiled its designs for the Perelman Center for Advanced Medicine, designed by Kimmel Center architect Rafael Viñoly, which will stand on the Convention Hall site.

U.S. (Philadelphia) Naval Hospital

Location: 1400–1989 Pattison Avenue (area bordered by South Broad Street, Pattison Avenue, Twentieth Street, and Hartranft Street), South Philadelphia
Completed: 1935
Demolished: 2001
Architect/Builder: Walter Karcher, Livingston Smith

The Depression ended nearly all new construction in Philadelphia. Many of the larger projects realized during the decade were financed by government money, including the Federal Reserve Bank and the U.S. Naval Hospital on Pattison Avenue. Commissioned by an act of Congress to replace the century-old hospital at the U.S. Naval Home, the Naval Hospital was acclaimed as one of the finest Art Deco buildings in the city.

Construction began in February 1933 on land that had once held the Sesqui-Centennial Gladway but that had given way to a city dump and squatters' shacks. The site was near the Philadelphia Navy Yard at the foot of Broad Street, a requirement imposed by the secretary of the navy.

Unlike earlier naval facilities, which usually consisted of a campus of smaller structures, the new structure concentrated most of its activities in one thirteen-story tower, making it the first high-rise naval hospital. The main section of the hospital consisted of a light-colored central wing framed by two taller wings in darker tones. The two pylons at either end, along with recessed windows and rising piers that broke the roofline, made the hospital seem grander than it was, especially in the flat landscape of South Philadelphia. Symmetrical five-story wings extended from the central section to the sides, front, and back, while covered walkways led to other structures. Contrasting materials—brown terra-cotta, limestone, and aluminum trim against yellow brick—gave the relatively simple design a rich appearance.

The U.S. Naval Hospital complex in the final stages of construction in 1934. (Collection of the author.)

Built for an economical $3.2 million, the Naval Hospital opened on April 12, 1935, with 650 beds for U.S. servicemen. With an eye to the hospital's convalescent function, the building was angled to provide maximum light to the building's wards, solariums, and roof gardens. Gradually, the rat-infested dump around the hospital was transformed into twenty-two landscaped acres for patients' exercise and recreation. Trees from each of the forty-eight states were planted on the grounds. Over time, more buildings were added, and the hospital became the central structure on a forty-eight-acre campus.

During the next fifty years, the Naval Hospital treated U.S. soldiers wounded in World War II, Korea, and Vietnam. Special emphasis was placed on the rehabilitation of blinded and permanently disabled patients, and the hospital became nationally known for its work with prosthetics. During World War II, it served as the main recovery facility for navy amputees east of the Rocky Mountains. Budget cuts and a reduced patient base meant the end for the hospital, which was decommissioned in 1991 and vacated in 1993 under the Base Realignment and Closure Act.

In 2000, the U.S. Navy conveyed the Naval Hospital campus and buildings to the Philadelphia Authority for Industrial Development (PAID). In doing so, they ignored the Advisory Council on Historic Preservation, which recommended that historic preservation of the older structures be a condition of the property transfer. That year, one Art Deco structure was demolished for a training facility for the Philadelphia Eagles. In June 2001, PAID had the Naval Hospital imploded for a 1,500-car parking lot for the new sports complex, despite its designation as a National Historic Landmark.

Tasker Homes

Location: Area bounded by Tasker Street, Twenty-ninth Street, New Hope Street, and Vare Avenue, South Philadelphia
Completed: 1940
Demolished: 2001
Architect/Builder: Various

One of the goals of the New Deal was to provide decent, affordable housing for the "one-third of a nation ill-housed, ill-clad, and ill-nourished," in the words of Franklin D. Roosevelt's second inaugural address. Philadelphia, with an estimated 80,000 substandard dwellings, desperately needed improved housing. In 1933, the local chapter of the Hosiery Workers Union began to build cooperative housing for its members. The Carl Mackley Houses at M and Bristol streets, designed by Oskar Stonorov and Alfred Kastner, became the first New Deal housing project in Philadelphia.

Later in the decade, the Federal Housing Administration and the Public Works Administration cooperated with the newly founded Philadelphia Housing Authority to construct government-financed public housing. In 1936, ground was broken for the Hill Creek Homes, the first federally funded housing project in the city. In 1939, the Philadelphia Housing Authority began two new projects, the Richard Allen Homes at Ninth and Poplar, and the Tasker Homes in South Philadelphia.

The Tasker Homes were established on a forty-acre former dump in a neighborhood that would later be called Grays Ferry. The International Style project, designed by a committee of architects headed by Walter Karcher and Carl Ziegler and built at a cost of $5.3 million, consisted of 1,100 units in 125 two- and three-story brick buildings. To create a sense of intimacy and community, buildings were placed in groups of four around central courtyards. Rents for the three- to six-room apartments ranged from $14 to $25.75 a month. On December 14, 1940, Marine Corps private Thomas Hunt and his family became the first residents of the Tasker Homes when they moved into 1602 South Thirtieth Street.

The development was spartan and treeless, with views of the nearby oil refineries at Point Breeze. The dwellings, however, were

An artist's sketch of the proposed Tasker Homes complex ca. 1939, looking north from Mifflin Street with Thirty-first Street leading to the community center in the middle of the development. At the upper left of the complex stands Audenried Junior High School; at the upper right is the Lanier Park playground. (Print and Picture Collection, Free Library of Philadelphia.).

new, clean, sanitary, and up to code. The units featured gas ranges, electric refrigerators, and access to modern community laundries, amenities that many Depression-era Philadelphians lacked. To acclimate new residents to middle-class responsibilities, consultants educated them on nutrition, hygiene, and home decoration. The Junior League offered advice on repairing and refinishing cheap furniture from the Salvation Army.

During World War II, defense workers and their families filled the Tasker Homes. To accommodate the influx of new residents, seventy-seven units in ten buildings were added on an adjoining four-acre site in 1942–43. Residents worked hard to make the development homelike, planting victory gardens and organizing a football team, the Tasker Tigers. The Tasker Homes—also known as "the projects" or "PJs"—were seen as a stepping stone, an affordable enclave for young families saving to buy their first house.

After World War II, the Tasker Homes, along with other Philadelphia housing projects, entered a period of neglect and deterioration. Starting in the 1950s, the Schuylkill Expressway hemmed in the Homes on the western side. When black tenants first arrived in large numbers in the 1960s, frequent confrontations occurred between them and the predominantly white community around the Homes. During the fiscal crisis of the 1970s, the poorly maintained units began to fall apart. Crime and drugs became part of daily life. In 1979, followers of Representative Milton Street occupied vacant units, highlighting the Philadelphia Housing Authority's failure to maintain the project.

In the 1990s, the Philadelphia Housing Authority began to rebuild or remodel many of its earlier projects, acknowledging that the original designs no longer functioned as safe or decent housing. The Tasker Homes were demolished in 2001. In 2003–4, a mixed-income community, Greater Grays Ferry Estates, rose on the site. The new development features 554 single-family dwellings on the same forty acres that once held the 1,081 units of the Tasker Homes.

CHAPTER 6

Renaissance and Retrenchment

(1940 to the present)

During September 1947, nearly 400,000 Philadelphians crowded into Gimbels Department Store, not for a back-to-school sale, but to see what their city would look like in 1980. The Better Philadelphia Exhibition, designed by architect Oskar Stonorov and city planner Edmund N. Bacon, gave Philadelphians a glimpse of tomorrow worthy of the General Motors Futurama at the 1939–40 New York World's Fair. Colorful exhibits illustrated the city's past, projected its future growth (by 2000, its population was expected to approach three million), explained the role of the City Planning Commission, and stressed the need for controlled development, urban renewal, and community activism. A sign above the exhibition's exit asked, "What kind of Philadelphia are you going to give your children?"

The most popular exhibit was a room-sized scale model of Center City as it appeared in 1947. With the press of a button, entire sections of the city disappeared, while a vision of the future (ironically, incorporating many ideas proposed in the 1920s but abandoned during the Depression) rose from the depths. Models of Broad Street Station and the Chinese Wall, as dark as the soot-covered originals, gave way to an avenue of gleaming white skyscrapers. The crowded business section around Independence Hall dissolved into a broad expanse of park. Along the Delaware River, dilapidated piers became an elegant embarcadero. Expressways routed cars around Center City and into the suburbs, relieving traffic jams. Even the tattered food-distribution district on Dock Street vanished, revealing the neoclassical splendor of William Strickland's Merchants' Exchange.

Public fascination with the Better Philadelphia Exhibition reflected the city's postwar optimism. Philadelphia was coasting on a wave of prosperity, its factories and businesses temporarily revived by wartime production. While some businesses retrenched after V-J Day (Baldwin Locomotives and Midvale Steel laid off thousands of workers, and Cramp's Shipyard closed), firms like Philco expanded to meet the demand for consumer goods. The adoption of a new city charter, along with the election of a reform Democratic admin-

The Independence Hall group ca. 1940, with soda fountains and parking lots upstaging the most historic buildings in the nation. This urban blight inspired the creation of Independence Mall and Independence National Historical Park to provide a proper setting for Philadelphia's crown jewels. (Collection of the author.)

istration in 1952 (the first since Rudolph Blankenburg's forty years earlier) exemplified the city's heady, anything-is-possible attitude.

Most civic leaders, Democratic or Republican, agreed that the physical redevelopment of their city, neglected after years of depression and war, was a priority. Philadelphia was the birthplace of America, as well as of such modern wonders as electronic television and the computer. Yet much of the city, including its most historic district, was jammed with shabby Victorian buildings. An estimated 30,000 properties stood vacant, while over half the city's industrial facilities were obsolete.

Starting in 1948, hundreds of nineteenth-century buildings— including such historic structures as the 1850 Jayne Building, 1851

Penn Mutual Building, 1875 Guarantee Trust Company, and 1885 Drexel Building—were demolished to clear space for Independence National Historical Park and Independence Mall. Meanwhile, a 1953 show on nineteenth-century buildings at the Art Alliance (which would later result in Theodore B. White's influential *Philadelphia Architecture in the Nineteenth Century*) marked the dawn of a new appreciation of Frank Furness and other Victorian designers that would not gain momentum until most of their oeuvre had been eradicated. While some Philadelphians mourned the widespread destruction of the Victorian city, many more preferred to look back to its Federal glory, or ahead to a gleaming glass and steel future.

In 1949, Edmund N. Bacon was appointed executive director of the Philadelphia City Planning Commission, a post he would hold for the next twenty-one years. As the city's development czar, Bacon saw his mission as liberating Philadelphia from its crowded, unhygienic, soot-covered Victorian prison and forcing it into a dazzling twentieth-century world of modernist skyscrapers, multilane expressways, and spacious plazas.

While disdaining the city's immediate past, Bacon glorified its colonial and Federal heritage: His work with Society Hill saw the salvation and restoration of what is now considered the largest collection of eighteenth-century buildings in the country. The Society Hill development also helped bring affluent white residents back into the city (while banishing many of the area's African American residents to outlying districts, in what critics labeled "Negro removal").

With the blessings of successive Democratic administrations, Bacon and the City Planning Commission recreated Philadelphia with Independence Mall, Penn Center, Penn's Landing, the Packer Avenue Food Distribution Center, the Commuter Rail Tunnel, JFK Plaza, Market Street East, and the Gallery. By 1980, Center City bore a remarkable resemblance to the model exhibited at Gimbels in 1947.

Led by the visionary Louis I. Kahn, a group of architects—the Philadelphia School, including Oskar Stonorov, Ehrmann Mitchell,

Romaldo Giurgola, Robert Venturi, and Denise Scott Brown—reestablished the city as a center of architectural innovation. Many of the major buildings erected during this time, however, were standard if stylish modernist boxes manufactured by such firms as Vincent G. Kling & Associates, Carroll Grisdale & Van Alen, and Kohn Pederson & Fox.

Sadly, Philadelphia's physical rejuvenation, funded in large part by federal dollars, contrasted with the steady erosion of its population, jobs, and revenue. While Society Hill brought some suburbanites back into Center City, it could not stanch the flight of residents and employers from the city as a whole. Between 1950 and 2000, the city's population decreased by 27 percent, from 2.1 million to 1.5 million. As of 2006, what was the third-largest U.S. city in 1950 was slugging it out with Phoenix for fifth place. Between 1955 and 1975, the peak period of its redevelopment, Philadelphia lost 75 percent of its manufacturing jobs and more than 30 percent of its Center City retail stores. Meanwhile, the reform-minded dynamism of the 1950s gave way in succeeding decades to Philadelphia politics as usual, with its cronyism, corruption, petty tyranny, and fiscal irresponsibility.

As factories closed their doors, many industrial neighborhoods deteriorated into slums. Some of Philadelphia's best architects, including Kahn and Stonorov, cut their teeth designing postwar public housing projects. Meant to resemble the luxury apartment towers or colonial row houses in more affluent districts, many projects degenerated into hotbeds of violence and crime. Since 1996, the Philadelphia Housing Authority has demolished several, replacing them with low-rise, mixed-income housing.

Over the past fifty years, the city's economic health has veered from stable to perilous, flirting with bankruptcy in the 1980s, enjoying a precarious prosperity in the 1990s, and facing a hopeful yet unsure future in the new millennium. The past decade has seen a flood of important new buildings in Philadelphia, most designed to nourish the local service economy with tourist dollars: the Kimmel Center for the Performing Arts, National Constitution Center, Liberty Bell Center, Independence Visitors Center, Lincoln Financial Field, Citizens Bank Field, and Wachovia Center.

On the private front, the national real estate boom has been further stimulated on the local level by an influx of residents to Center City, tax abatements to spur residential construction and redevelopment, and the legalization of casino gambling. Thanks to these factors, the centralized planning of the Bacon years has given way to a building frenzy unmatched since the 1920s. According to the Design Advocacy Group, Center City boasted ninety-seven current and proposed residential construction projects as of December 2005, involving twelve million square feet of space, mostly condominiums.

In early 2006, seven luxury condominium/casino projects were in the planning or construction stages along the Delaware River between the Ben Franklin Bridge and Penn Treaty Park, although some were in jeopardy as signs of a real estate slowdown grew stronger. Even blighted North Philadelphia neighborhoods have seen prices for some houses soar nearly 1,000 percent in recent years. Some planners predict that by 2010, Center City will be redefined to include Girard Avenue to the north, Washington Avenue to the south, and University City to the west.

Meanwhile, Philadelphia continues to debate which elements of its rich architectural past to salvage and which to jettison. In early 2005, its last remaining Art Deco theater, the Boyd, was saved from destruction by the intervention of dedicated volunteers and corporate sponsors. The long-neglected Victory Building at Tenth and Chestnut streets has been restored to its Second Empire glory. At the same time, conflicted preservationists argue over whether the late Mayor Richardson Dilworth's house on Washington Square—a 1950s Colonial Revival dwelling for which two stately Federal buildings were demolished—should be replaced or overshadowed by a condominium designed by Robert Venturi.

On a broader scale, the entire preservation movement in Philadelphia may be at risk, due to the changing makeup of the Philadelphia Historical Commission (founded in 1955 as the first agency with comprehensive preservation jurisdiction over an entire city), and recent efforts by City Council members to control the historic designation process. While Philadelphia has entered the twenty-first century with a better balance between old and new than most U.S. cities, its future is far from certain.

Philadelphia Municipal Airport Terminal

Location: Area bounded by Fort Mifflin, Island Avenue, Penrose
   Avenue, and Tinicum Island Road, South Philadelphia
Completed: 1941
Demolished: 1977
Architect/Builder: Horace Caster

Philadelphia International Airport Main Terminal

Location: Area bounded by Fort Mifflin, Island Avenue, Penrose
   Avenue, and Tinicum Island Road, South Philadelphia
Completed: 1953 (expanded 1968)
Demolished: 1977
Architect/Builder: Carroll, Grisdale & Van Alen; Vincent G. Kling
   & Associates

The terminal and control tower at Philadelphia Municipal Tower, June 1951. (Temple University Libraries, Urban Archives, Philadelphia.)

After World War I proved the capabilities of flying machines, many U.S. cities built airports. In 1925, Philadelphia spent $15,000 to construct a 123-acre airfield with a grass landing strip along Island Avenue in the southernmost part of the city. On October 22, 1927, Charles A. Lindbergh landed his *Spirit of St. Louis* on the site and raised an American flag to dedicate Philadelphia Municipal Airport. Shortly afterward, the first mail plane to land at the airport was destroyed when it hit a mud hole and flipped over.

In 1931, the city paid $3 million for the 1,369 acres of the adjoining Hog Island tract, site of World War I shipbuilding yards. Although this purchase increased the airport's size to nearly 1,500 acres, nearby Camden Central Airport in Pennsauken Township, New Jersey, was seen as far superior. In the early 1930s, Camden Central was the busiest airport in the United States, handling more than 9,000 passengers a year (about one-third of all domestic air travel).

In 1940, Philadelphia sought to regain its edge by building a real airport. It extended the main runway to 5,000 feet, making it one of the longest in the nation. Horace Caster designed the airport's first terminal, a square two-story building on Island Avenue flanked by low wings and topped by the airport's control tower. Shortly after the terminal's opening, the Department of Public Works constructed a utilitarian restaurant and lavatory building nearby. The four airlines serving Camden Central (American, Eastern, TWA, and United) moved to Philadelphia.

During its first year of operation, roughly 40,000 passengers passed through the new terminal. In December 1943, military security forced the closing of Philadelphia Municipal Airport, leaving the city without commercial service until the end of World

By 1953, Carroll, Grisdale & Van Alen's sleek international terminal had replaced Horace Caster's humble building. (Athenaeum of Philadelphia.)

War II. The airport reopened for business in June 1945 and officially became Philadelphia International Airport when American Overseas Airlines inaugurated transatlantic service.

In 1950, construction began on a $15 million terminal building on Industrial Highway. The International Style structure by Carroll, Grisdale & Van Alen demonstrated how far air travel had come in the previous decade. Passengers arriving by car disembarked under a curved, winglike canopy and entered a glass-walled, multistory main hall. After checking in, they walked to either end of the long, rectangular, multilevel terminal, where elevated, covered walkways led to their airplanes. The gleaming new airport fascinated Philadelphians; 400,000 people attended its dedication in December 1953, creating one of the worst traffic jams in the city's history. Visitors waited in line for a chance to tour the latest airplanes, including Pan Am's Strato Clipper and United's Mainliner. The new terminal became a favorite weekend destination for families, who watched planes taking off and landing. Instead of a small diner, visitors enjoyed the Skyview Restaurant, an elegant upper-level dining room offering views of the airfield and Delaware River.

By 1970, the rising volume of air travel had overwhelmed the terminal's capabilities, despite a 1968 expansion by Vincent G. Kling & Associates and the extension of the main runway to 9,500 feet to accommodate jets. In 1973, the airport attempted to reduce its congestion by moving international flights to the overseas terminal, a

former aircraft hanger located 1.5 miles from the main terminal. Four years later, a $300 million modernization and reconstruction of the main terminal replaced the central structure with four unit concourses and two multilevel parking garages. During this development, the 1940 and 1953 terminals were both demolished.

A six-year, $500 million capital-expansion campaign at the airport in the 1980s and 1990s saw the construction of a new international terminal in the long-unfinished A concourse. More recent capital improvement programs have given the airport its current appearance, with a second international terminal, a new commuter-airline terminal, and the renovation of all existing terminals. A Philadelphia MarketPlace with dozens of shops and restaurants occupies much of the site of the 1953 terminal. From 40,000 passengers in 1940, Philadelphia International Airport served 31.5 million passengers in 2005, making it the twenty-fifth-busiest airport in the world.

Budd Company Red Lion Plant

Location: Area bordered by Red Lion Road, Verree Road,
 Tomlinson Road, and Pine Road (Montgomery County),
 Northeast Philadelphia
Completed: 1942
Demolished: 1999
Architect/Builder: Ballinger Company

The industrial buildup before and during World War II reinvigorated many moribund Philadelphia factories. Companies like Cramp's Shipbuilding and Baldwin Locomotives, shuttered during the Depression, reopened their doors and hired thousands of workers. Founded in 1912, the Edward G. Budd Manufacturing Company had survived the 1930s by churning out automobile parts and railroad cars at its factory at Hunting Park Avenue and Twenty-fourth Street. In 1942, the U.S. government spent $20.6 million to build an aircraft-manufacturing plant on 572 acres of farmland at Red Lion Road west of Bustleton Avenue in Northeast Philadelphia, then turned it over to the Budd Company to operate.

The hastily constructed plant was built of reinforced concrete to conserve the use of steel and to withstand possible attack by enemy bombers. The curved metal roofs were the barrel-shell or Z-D type developed by the engineering firm of Roberts and Schaefer, with a sectional design suited to the speed and economy of wartime construction. A nearby brick and concrete building housed administrative offices.

Within the plant, the main assembly area consisted of two adjacent one-story hangars with arched roofs, 1800 feet long and 600 feet wide. Each hangar held a high-bay assembly line five stories high and as long as four football fields. On the plant's south side stood a secondary structure composed of six narrower sections, also 1800 feet long. The entire complex covered more than one million square feet of floor space.

The Red Lion plant was set up to manufacture a prototype twin-engine cargo plane, the RB-1 Conestoga, nicknamed the "Flying Boxcar." The Conestoga was the first factory-produced aircraft constructed of stainless steel, introducing features that became standard in military cargo aircraft, such as a high wing and a rear ramp to facilitate loading. It was flight-tested on two runways in an open field north of the plant in 1943–44.

Soon after testing began, the RB-1 acquired a new nickname—Patches—because of the constant patching needed to repair the

The Budd Company Red Lion plant in October 1956, with Red Lion Road in the foreground. (Temple University Libraries, Urban Archives, Philadelphia.)

Railroad passenger cars on the Red Lion plant high-bay assembly lines in January 1950. (Temple University Libraries, Urban Archives, Philadelphia.)

cracks in its thin aluminum skin. The government cancelled its order for 800 planes, leaving only twenty prototypes to show for its $98 million investment. When the RB-1 project was terminated, the Red Lion plant was retooled to produce artillery shells for the U.S. Army.

After World War II, the Budd Company paid the federal government $5.25 million for the plant. It immediately retooled the facility for nonmilitary purposes and moved its railcar-manufacturing division from Hunting Park to the newer plant. On October 15, 1945, the first stainless-steel railroad car manufactured by Budd since 1942 rolled off the assembly line and was shipped to the Atchison, Topeka & Santa Fe Railway Company.

For the next thirty years, the plant's 2,500 workers produced thousands of cars for railroads, subways, and surface rail lines, including the original Metroliner cars for Amtrak, passenger cars for the Pennsylvania Railroad (many of which later ran on SEPTA regional rail lines), and steel cars for the PATCO high-speed line. In addition to its mass-produced railcars, Budd created specialty cars for VIPs like the king of Morocco, whose private railway carriage featured gold-plated bathroom fixtures and steel machine-gun emplacements. Budd also produced automotive parts, including 4,000 chassis frames a day for General Motors.

In 1978, a German firm, Thyssen A.G., acquired Budd and established a separate subsidiary for the rail and automotive parts business called Transit America. After years of declining orders, Transit America closed the Red Lion plant in 1987 and consolidated its operations in Detroit. The complex stood empty for a decade, becoming a preserve for hundreds of white-tailed deer.

In the early 1990s, Transit America and the Pennsylvania Department of Environmental Protection began a $31 million environmental cleanup of the highly polluted site as part of the state's land-recycling ("brown fields") program. The two organizations removed 1,640 cubic yards of soil contaminated with PCBs, asbestos, solvents, and volatile organic compounds. As part of the decontamination project, the plant complex was demolished around 1999.

In 2001, the Island Green Golf Course opened on 214 reclaimed acres of the former Red Lion campus. Much of the concrete from the plant was recycled and crushed into a layer separating the underlying soil from the sand and artificial turf surface of the golf course. Today, a sixty-four-station, 400-yard-long driving range stands on the site of the main assembly building.

Chestnut Hill Gulf Express-Stop Station

Location: Germantown Avenue and Bethlehem Pike, Chestnut Hill
Completed: 1947
Demolished: 1966
Architect/Builder: Unknown

The end of World War II released Americans' long-delayed desire for new automobiles. Car manufacturers that had spent the war producing tanks, jeeps, and dive-bombers couldn't retool quickly enough to meet demand. Between 1945 and 1950, the number of registered cars in Pennsylvania jumped 51 percent, from 1.68 million to 2.54 million. The car was king, and in Chestnut Hill its palace was the Gulf Express-Stop Station at Germantown Avenue and Bethlehem Pike.

The intersection of these two roads had long been an important junction, connecting the northwest corner of Philadelphia with rural Pennsylvania. By the late 1940s, it was also the last major crossroads motorists passed as they left the city for the fast-growing suburbs of Montgomery County. In 1946, the Gulf Oil Corporation purchased the property at the northwestern corner of the two roads. It replaced a decrepit strip of stores with a showcase Streamline Moderne station designed to fit the triangular tract.

The Gulf Express-Stop was a chevron-shaped, two-floor structure covered with gleaming white porcelain tile, with symmetrical wings extending from either side of a central tower. The square tower had glass block inserts and "GULF" spelled out in orange neon letters on all four sides, broadcasting the station's presence down both highways.

On the ground floor, each wing held three service bays and was fronted by a two-pump island. Upstairs were an office, a customer waiting room, a service room, an employee-training room, and a salesroom for automotive parts and accessories. On both floors, streamlined ledges with aluminum trim topped large plate-glass windows. Orange and dark blue detailing reflected the colors of the

Gulf corporate logo. The Express-Stop officially opened on March 6, 1947, when Elsie Douglas stopped by around 9:00 AM to have her La Salle filled with Gulf No-Nox.

The Express-Stop represented both the increasing standardization of national gas station chains and their changing status within the community. Before Gulf opened the first off-street filling station in Pittsburgh in 1913, motorists could find gas pumps at any convenient roadside spot, including feedstores and lumberyards. By the 1920s, gas companies had discovered architecture, and their stations masqueraded as mosques, pagodas, or castles. Most stations, however, attempted to look like cottages to soften their intrusion into residential communities, with stucco walls, tile or shingle roofs, and shutters. A cottage-style Gulf Oil Station from the 1920s still stands on Twentieth Street between Arch and Cuthbert streets in Center City, having been placed on the Philadelphia Register of Historic Places in 1981.

The central tower of the Gulf Express-Stop Station ca. 1963, looking northeast from Germantown Avenue. (Chestnut Hill Historical Society.)

In the 1930s, oil companies sought to maximize their visibility with streamlined oblong stations covered in white tile, well marked with the corporate logo and brightly lit at night. This simplified "ice-box" design quickly became standard: not only did it reduce construction costs, but it created more space for car-repair bays and auxiliary product display. Unique signage helped gas stations differentiate themselves from their proliferating competitors (shortly after the inauguration of the Express-Stop, a Sunoco station opened directly across from it). In an affluent area like Chestnut Hill, where car ownership was higher than in most of Philadelphia, the Gulf station's high profile and central location gave it a major edge.

In the mid-1950s, Chestnut Hill's community leaders banded together to revitalize the Germantown Avenue retail corridor. Mirroring the redevelopment of Society Hill and the Independence Hall district, they sought to emphasize Chestnut Hill's colonial heritage, even though the neighborhood had been sparsely populated until the nineteenth century. The few Federal structures on Germantown Avenue were lovingly restored, while dozens of Victorian buildings were "colonialized" to look a century older.

At the top of the hill, the dazzling white Express-Stop looked increasingly out of place. Around 1966, Gulf tore down the streamlined structure and replaced it with a smaller, pseudocolonial station that didn't clash with neighboring structures. This station was, in turn, replaced by a Borders Book Store in 1990.

Independence Mall

Location: Area bordered by Fifth, Sixth, Chestnut, and Race streets
Completed: 1967
Redesigned: 1993–2003
Architect/Builder: Roy F. Larson; Harbeson Hough, Livingston & Larson

Between 1915 and 1940, at least twelve proposals were advanced to replace the congested business district north of Independence Hall with an open green space that would frame the historic building and protect it from fire. For the Sesqui-Centennial, Jacques Gréber proposed a mall stretching from Chestnut to Market Street. Gréber's National Memorial Court of Independence was a marble plaza lined with neo-Palladian buildings that surrounded the Liberty Bell, removed to a classical shrine in the court's center. In the 1930s, Paul Philippe Cret proposed a smaller, simpler park along Chestnut Street.

During World War II, public attention focused on "rescuing" Independence Hall from the increasingly shabby district around it. A group of civic leaders headed by Judge Edwin O. Lewis formed the Independence Hall Association, lobbying for the establishment of a park to be administered by the National Park Service. In 1948, the federal government established Independence National Historical Park, encompassing Independence Hall and the other buildings on Independence Square, as well as the three blocks east of the square.

In 1949, the Commonwealth of Pennsylvania and the City of Philadelphia established Independence Mall on the three blocks north of Independence Hall, from Chestnut Street to Race Street between Fifth and Sixth streets. The impetus for the mall owed as much to the pocketbook as to patriotism: three major companies, employing over 15,000 people, had threatened to leave the city unless the area was improved.

The original model for Independence Mall, prepared by the firm of Harbeson, Hough, Livingston & Larson (today H2L2) in 1952. (Athenaeum of Philadelphia.)

Roy F. Larson, a junior partner of Paul Philippe Cret, designed a central greensward, flanked by footpaths and allées of trees, that would connect with the Delaware River Bridge and proposed Vine Street Expressway to serve as a grand gateway into the city's historic district. The middle block, between Market and Arch streets, featured a reflecting pool along Market Street and rows of classical, porticoed pavilions, as well as the 1783 Free Quaker Meeting House in its northeast corner. A circular fountain graced the northernmost square, between Arch and Race streets.

With City Planning Commission czar Edmund Bacon championing the projected mall, the city began to acquire and demolish buildings in 1950. By the end of 1954, the block between Chestnut and Market was cleared of its "incongruous mixture of cheap buildings on the one hand, and heavy pseudo-Roman architecture on the other, all so strikingly out of accord with the beauty and simplicity of the colonial group of buildings across the street on Independence Square."[1]

Among the "pseudo-Roman" buildings demolished were the Trust Company of North America, the Pennsylvania Company for Insurances on Lives and Granting Annuities, and other nineteenth-century landmarks. Roughly 500 buildings were razed to clear all three blocks of the mall.

The block between Market and Arch was finished by 1957, and the block between Arch and Race by 1963. In 1967, the brick pavilions and sunken terrace of the Judge Edwin O. Lewis Quadrangle took shape on the middle block after underground parking garages were constructed. A fountain replaced the reflecting pool Larson had envisioned in the central block, but the mall reflected all the other components of his original design. In 1974, ownership was transferred to the National Park Service, and the mall became part of Independence National Historical Park. Two years later, the Liberty Bell was moved from Independence Hall to a new pavilion on the first square of the mall. By this time, the mall was lined with hulking, modern structures, including the Rohm & Haas headquarters, U.S. Mint, Federal Reserve Bank, Federal Office Building, and U.S. Court House.

Despite official pride in the city's fifteen-acre urban park, many architectural critics found little to love in the mall. In a 1956 *New Yorker* article, Lewis Mumford found its "great Baroque axial scheme" at war with the restrained Georgian buildings on Independence Square. In 1965, Ian Nairn echoed Mumford, criticizing the "vast formal axis galloping off to nowhere, focused on a building [Independence Hall] which is too small to stand up to it."[2]

By the 1970s, many Philadelphians had come to agree with Mumford and Nairn. Apart from festivals, concerts, and other large events, the mall north of Market Street became an urban wasteland, used by the homeless and destitute and avoided by everyone else. Tourism experts complained that after visitors saw Independence Hall and the Liberty Bell, they fled the sterile vacuum of the mall.

A new generation of city planners, schooled on William H. Whyte and Jane Jacobs, criticized the mall for blotting out the pattern of organic urban life and creating a barrier between Old City and the western sector. Shortly before his death, Louis I. Kahn made sketches for new Bicentennial structures on the mall, which were never realized.

Beginning in the early 1990s, the city, state, and federal governments joined forces to redesign Independence Mall, ignoring the highly vocal indignation of Edmund Bacon. In its revised incarnation, new buildings and landscaping reconnected the vast open space to the urban grid. A string of tourist attractions—the Liberty Bell Center, Independence Visitor Center, and National Constitution Center—went up along Sixth Street between 1999 and 2003. The Fifth Street side of the mall was redesigned with trees, cafes, benches, and other park-like amenities. The reduced lawn in the middle is crossed by east-west walkways aligned with the side streets obliterated in the 1950s.

While many critics have bemoaned the undistinguished architecture of these additions, Independence Mall is no longer the empty, unused space it was two decades ago. In the year after the opening of the Liberty Bell Center and Constitution Center, the number of visitors to Independence National Historical Park increased by more than 30 percent.

Facing page: Independence Mall in 1957, looking south toward Independence Hall. The first square of the mall, between Chestnut and Market streets, is complete, while the second square is under construction. In the foreground runs Filbert Street, later closed off to form the second square of the mall between Market and Arch streets. (Athenaeum of Philadelphia.)

Original Latin Casino

Location: 1309 Walnut Street
Completed: 1947
Demolished: 1964
Architect/Builder: Unknown

Despite the widespread belief that postwar Philadelphia was duller than wartime Berlin after dark, a small but lively nightclub district flourished in Center City. Popular spots in the 1940s and 1950s included Frank Palumbo's Click Club (with the "World's Longest Bar"—442 feet, with 400 barstools), the Latimer Club (with its Sinatra Room, a shrine to Ol' Blue Eyes), Lew Tendler's Restaurant (run by a retired boxer known as "the greatest southpaw in ring history"), and the Latin Casino. Located at 1309 Walnut Street between 1947 and 1960, the Latin Casino offered top-flight entertainers like Lena Horne, Pearl Bailey, Lionel Hampton, Tony Bennett, Mel Tormé, and Eddie Fisher.

The casino occupied the basement of an unprepossessing, one-story building with a black tile front on which large white letters spelled out headliners' names. During one appearance, native son Joey Bishop cracked, "It's so great to come back home and see my name out front in Bon Ami!"[3] Across Walnut Street was the Latin Casino's unofficial annex—a men's clothing store, Sidney Arnold Clothiers. Arnold became known as "Tailor to the Stars," thanks to his ability to provide crisply tailored suits for rumpled celebrities, often on credit and on very short notice, before they stepped onto the casino stage.

The casino itself was a subway nightclub, although owners Harry Steinman and Dallas Gerson preferred to call it a "theater-restaurant." Guests went downstairs to a room with a vaulted ceiling that held between 500 and 600 guests, depending on how many bribes the maitre d' had accepted that night. Across from a large oval bar, tiny tables and chairs crowded around a semicircular raised

The Latin Casino chorus line poses onstage on December 14, 1952. (Temple University Libraries, Urban Archives, Philadelphia.)

stage, where leggy showgirls kicked up their heels between sets by Buddy Greco and Patti Page.

According to legendary publicist Sam Bushman, the casino drew a motley, Runyonesque "money crowd—business people, swingers, gamblers, racket guys."[4] In 1948, the *Daily News* described it as "the rendezvous of the smart, the sophisticated, the playboys, and local café society as well as just ordinary Joes and their gals."[5]

In 1960, then-owners Gerson and Dave Dushoff left 1309 Walnut Street for Route 70 in Cherry Hill, New Jersey, across from the Garden State Race Track. Their new "Showplace of the Stars" was a spacious, circular structure designed by John Sabatino and Morton Fishman, seating 2,000 and built at a cost of $2.5 million. In addition to more space, the Cherry Hill locale offered the Latin Casino owners an escape from Philadelphia's restrictive blue laws, which had forced them to stop serving drinks at midnight on Saturdays.

The Latin Casino continued to attract top names, including Frank Sinatra and Johnny Mathis, as well as promising newcomers like George Carlin and Liza Minnelli. During this period, however, the new casinos in Atlantic City were siphoning off its pool of tal-

ent, and business was dwindling. The Latin Casino closed on June 28, 1978, with a performance by comedienne Totie Fields. After a short-lived stint as the Emerald City disco, the building closed as an entertainment venue in 1982. Shortly after, it was demolished and replaced by the national headquarters of Subaru of America.

The original Latin Casino on Walnut Street was demolished in 1964 for the 161-room Holiday Inn Midtown, the first Holiday Inn built in a downtown location. In 1993, the hotel became the chain's first limited-service hotel and was renamed the Holiday Inn Express Midtown.

Mill Creek Apartments

Location: Area bounded by Fairmount Avenue, Belmont Avenue, Brown Street, and North Forty-sixth Street, West Philadelphia
Completed: Phase 1, 1956; phase 2, 1963
Demolished: 2002
Architect/Builder: Louis Kahn & Associates

In the years after World War II, the Philadelphia Housing Authority (PHA) expanded the public housing program launched before the war with the Hill Creek Homes, Richard Allen Homes, and Tasker Homes. Between 1946 and 1970, the PHA built or acquired nearly 20,000 low-rent housing units. Most were in densely developed, industrial neighborhoods in North, West, and South Philadelphia. As factories closed and jobs dwindled, many of these communities became slums. Vast public housing projects were seen as a way to enact both urban renewal and social reform, clearing away dilapidated buildings while offering residents refuge from poverty and blight.

One of the earliest postwar public housing developments was the 441-unit Mill Creek Apartments, a multistage project first envisioned by Louis I. Kahn, Kenneth Day, Louis E. McAllister, and Anne Tyng in the late 1940s. The development was located in a predominantly African American section of West Philadelphia. Kahn's original plan introduced pedestrian greenways linking the new housing with the older neighborhood, similar to the greenways proposed by Edmund Bacon for connecting Society Hill with Independence National Historical Park.

After numerous changes to the original plans due to budget restrictions and bureaucratic tinkering, the first phase of the project was built between 1951 and 1956: three seventeen-story apartment towers adjacent to a block of two-story units, constructed of exposed reinforced concrete. Innovative landscaping by George E. Patton (who also landscaped the Vine Street Expressway and Locust Walk) softened the starkness of the buildings and created more intimate streetscapes. In phase 2, constructed between 1956 and 1963, Kahn and his associates added red-brick row and twin houses and a community center.

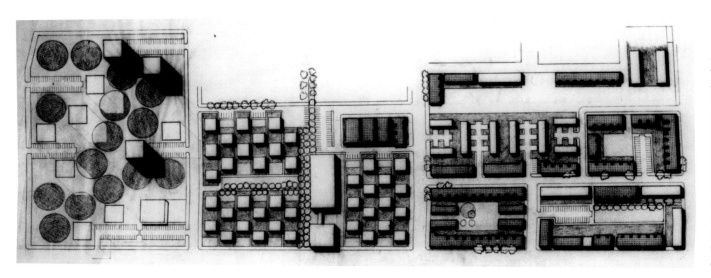

The original site plan for what was then called the Mill Creek Project, prepared by Louis I. Kahn ca. 1950. The tall apartment blocks at left were balanced by smaller-scale row houses, twin houses, and two-story apartment units, all connected by a series of greenways. (© 1977 Louis I. Kahn Collection, University of Pennsylvania and Pennsylvania Historical and Museum Commission.)

The completed phase 1 of the Mill Creek Apartments ca. 1960, with three apartment blocks and adjacent two-story units. (© 1977 Louis I. Kahn Collection, University of Pennsylvania and Pennsylvania Historical and Museum Commission.)

Unfortunately, the complex was built over an underground stream, causing the cheaply built foundations and walls to sag and crack within a few years of construction. Like many other housing projects, the Mill Creek Apartments became a center of crime and violence. Photos of the phase 2 housing in 1980 show graffiti-scrawled walls and trash-strewn streets bereft of the original land-scaping. Concrete canopies over the doors and windows of the row houses, added to break up the monotonous facades, instead give them an oppressive, prisonlike appearance.

On November 24, 2002, the Mill Creek Apartments, vacant since 1998, were imploded to the cheers of 300 onlookers. Among them was City Council member Lucien Blackwell, who said that the Mill Creek Apartments "should not have been built in the first place. The intentions were good, but it didn't work out."[6]

In 2003, construction began on a new development on the same site, the Lucien E. Blackwell Homes, named after the councilman, who had died shortly after witnessing Mill Creek's destruction. Reflecting changes in public housing policy, the Blackwell Homes are a low-rise, mixed-income development of 627 units, both rental and market value. Rather than isolating inhabitants in towers, the Blackwell Homes are fully integrated into the street grid. The redevelopment plans also include a 2.5-acre park and a community center offering programs for job training, small-business development, and drug-abuse counseling.

Schuylkill Falls Apartments

Location: Area bounded by Ridge Avenue and Calumet, Cresson, and Merrick streets, East Falls
Completed: 1955
Demolished: 1996
Architect/Builder: Oskar Stonorov

Although most Philadelphia Housing Authority projects were built in inner-city neighborhoods, an exception was the Schuylkill Falls Apartments at Ridge Avenue and Merrick Street in East Falls. Designed by German-born architect Oskar Stonorov, Schuylkill Falls was built on a twenty-two-acre parcel known as Laboratory Hill, once occupied by the Powers & Weightman Chemical Works (now part of Merck & Co.).

Stonorov, who had designed the Carl Mackley Houses in 1932, believed that slum clearance only worsened the existing housing shortage. He advocated building public housing on vacant land near the outskirts of cities and persuading slum dwellers to leave their tenements and join the middle classes. By locating Schuylkill Falls in a middle-class, predominantly Irish-Scottish-German community, Stonorov and the PHA created tensions between project residents and the surrounding area.

Stonorov's design reflected his training in modernist, International Style architecture. His plan consisted of two large, rectangular apartment buildings surrounded by a series of two-story row

houses. The apartment buildings featured long, common balconies on each floor, similar to Le Corbusier's "streets in the sky" design, which provided children with play space. Each building also had multiple elevators that offered access to a few apartments on each floor, eliminating the need for long, internal corridors. The sleek high-rises mirrored the luxury Presidential Apartments recently constructed near City Avenue across the Schuylkill River.

Shortly after the project opened, complaints began to surface about shoddy construction, leaking radiators, and broken elevators. Within a few years of the towers' completion, as conditions worsened and crime increased, families began to move out. In 1975, a child opened a seventh-floor eleva-

The Schuylkill Falls project under construction in 1954, looking northwest from the intersection of Ridge Avenue at left and Calumet Street at right. (Temple University Libraries, Urban Archives, Philadelphia.)

The southern Schuylkill Falls tower, 1979, viewed from a balcony on the northern tower, both abandoned in 1976. In the left background are the Presidential Apartments on the west bank of the Schuylkill River. (Temple University Libraries, Urban Archives, Philadelphia.)

tor door onto an empty shaft and fell to his death. That same year, Schuylkill Falls—nicknamed "Sin City" by its remaining residents—witnessed three murders, four rapes, and 159 robberies and assaults. Stonorov's design unintentionally exacerbated the situation, since PHA police could not monitor the multiple elevators and long, open balconies.

In 1976, the Schuylkill Falls towers were deemed unfit for habitation and vacated. For two decades they stood abandoned, their windows smashed and their walls covered by graffiti, because the city lacked the money to demolish them. Community pleas to have them destroyed went unanswered, even after the body of a murdered child was discovered on the site in 1980. Finally, on December 8, 1996, 350 pounds of dynamite brought the longest-standing vacant public housing high-rises in the country crashing to the ground. Three years later, most of the surrounding townhouses were also vacated and demolished.

Shortly after the implosion, Falls Ridge, a low-density, mixed-income housing development, began to take shape on Laboratory Hill. The long-standing tension between the housing project and the surrounding community continues to simmer, however. Bowing to a lawsuit brought by local residents, PHA sold half the property to a private developer for market-rate homes and built public housing on the other half. Development has been delayed, however, by conflict between PHA and the developer over the ratio of public to private units to be built on the site.

American Federation of Labor Medical Service Plan Building

Location: 1326–34 Vine Street (between Watts and Juniper streets)
Completed: 1957
Demolished: 1973
Architect/Builder: Louis I. Kahn

With the realization of his designs for the Mill Creek Apartments and the Yale University Art Gallery in the mid-1950s, Louis I. Kahn emerged as a major architect, as well as a leading theoretician and teacher. In 1954, he was commissioned to design a building for the American Federation of Labor Medical Service Plan at 1326–34 Vine Street, where 70,000 union members and their families would receive free medical care. Kahn, along with his former partner Oskar Stonorov, had been involved in a number of union-sponsored projects in Philadelphia, including a 1950–51 clinic renovation at St. Luke's Hospital for the American Federation of Labor.

Like the Yale Art Gallery, the AFL Medical Service Plan Building was a severely geometric structure, a four-story square topped by a central two-story penthouse that concealed elevator machinery and air-conditioning equipment. The lobby, offices, and indoor parking occupied the first two floors; the upper two floors housed medical offices, a clinic, laboratories, and meeting rooms. The simple, compact design reflected the AFL Medical Service Plan's modest budget and matched the scale of adjacent nineteenth-century buildings. Although Kahn's original design called for marble paving, slate, ceramic tile, and glazed brick, cost restraints resulted in the substitution of concrete and stainless steel for more expensive materials.

On the first two stories, plate glass wrapped around exposed steel columns permitted natural light to flood the spacious entrance and lobby areas, creating a "friendly and generous" entrance for union members, in Kahn's words.[7] On sunny days, the glass walls reflected the sky and the passing traffic. Alternating glass and concrete panels on the exterior of the top two stories, along with projecting cornices at each floor level, defined the structure's form and gave it a sense of mass.

Vierendeel trusses supporting the ceilings and walls created a recurring motif of horizontal hexagons throughout the building's interior. Stainless steel, which Kahn used in depth for the first time, represented a recurring theme in the doorknobs, hinges, and laboratory fixtures. Despite attempts to maintain a strict budget, construction costs for the Medical Service Plan Building, originally set at $550,000, swelled to $1.5 million by the building's completion in early 1957.

The Vine Street façade of the AFL Medical Service Plan Building, with its two-story lobby, Vierendeel trusses, and the penthouse that architect Louis Kahn called "that raw thing." (© 1977 Louis I. Kahn Collection, University of Pennsylvania and Pennsylvania Historical and Museum Commission.)

Many admirers of Kahn's architecture, including Vincent Scully Jr., viewed the Medical Service Plan Building as a transitional design, not fully reflecting the architect's mature vision. Even Kahn was unhappy with the protruding penthouse that detracted from the smooth design of the main structure, referring to it as "that raw thing up there, unfinished."[8] The Vine Street structure did enunciate many of the themes that would become Kahn's trademarks, including space suffused with natural light, the segregation of mechanical services in "servant spaces," and a reworking of the standard modernist glass box with fresh materials and patterns.

After the Medical Service Plan Building, Kahn went on to create two of his most ground-breaking works, the Alfred Newton Richards Medical Research Building at the University of Pennsylvania and the Jonas Salk Institute for Biological Studies in San Diego. Between 1967 and 1972, with his design for the Phillips Exeter Academy Library, he returned to the square box sheathing a dramatic interior space.

In the early 1970s, Kahn's Medical Service Plan Building was doomed by the rebirth of the Vine Street Expressway project, moribund for nearly twenty years. In the 1950s, the city had begun to widen Vine Street in expectation of building a sunken, multilane expressway (a stage of the project which did not reach completion until 1991). Construction of the twelve-lane surface street required the demolition of buildings along a nearly two-mile strip east of Broad Street.

The Medical Service Plan Building was demolished in July and August 1973, along with many of its neighboring structures. Although some thought was given to removing the building's aluminum fixtures and tinted glass, the demolition firm concluded that the building's complex and interlocking construction would make such salvaging prohibitively expensive. Kahn himself viewed the destruction of his only Center City building with stoic detachment: "There is a lesson in the building. The most valuable part of a man's work is that it doesn't belong to him. A man is better than his works."[9]

Sheraton Hotel/Philadelphia Centre Hotel

Location: JFK Boulevard between Seventeenth and Eighteenth streets
Completed: 1957
Demolished: 1987
Architect/Builder: Vincent G. Kling & Associates; Perry, Shaw, Hepburn & Dean

The Sheraton Hotel was a key element of the Penn Center development. As the first major hotel built in Center City in thirty years, the success of the Sheraton was seen as critical to the renaissance of downtown Philadelphia. Adjacent to both Suburban Station and the Transportation Building, and convenient to Thirtieth Street Station and the new Schuylkill Expressway, the hotel would shelter thousands of business travelers drawn to Philadelphia's new commercial hub. The Sheraton was not only the state's largest hotel, but also one of only eight downtown hotels built in the United States during the 1950s, the golden age of the motel.

The twenty-one-story rectangular building was constructed of concrete and steel, with a sleek, International Style profile meant to evoke both the Lever House and the UN Secretariat. Its status as a luxury hotel was announced by its nonmodernist ornamentation, such as aluminum paneling in a turquoise and chrome checkerboard pattern on the lower floors, and a bongo-shaped pylon topped by a glowing red ball on the roof. An arcade of upscale shops extended on either side of the main entrance, with its scalloped portico topped by the hotel's name in large neon letters.

The luxurious decoration continued inside with the lobby's terrazzo floor, marble walls, and Venetian glass mosaics. Each of the 950 rooms featured air-conditioning, television and radio, and a view from its wall-of-glass window; the wealthy could rent their own penthouse suites, complete with private terrace, on the exclusive twenty-second floor. The 7,774-square-foot Grand Ballroom could accommodate more than 1,100 guests, while the 6,300-square-foot

Pennsylvania Ballroom was available for more intimate affairs. To extend its appeal beyond the old world of assemblies and charity balls to the new world of business conventions and trade shows, the Sheraton also offered conference rooms with closed-circuit TV, a theater-sized stage, and an Auto Lift freight elevator.

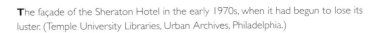

The façade of the Sheraton Hotel in the early 1970s, when it had begun to lose its luster. (Temple University Libraries, Urban Archives, Philadelphia.)

The Sheraton invited Philadelphians to take a sneak peek at their new treasure on January 27, 1957, when it hosted the Academy Ball, celebrating the centennial of the Academy of Music. Photographs of the event show men in white tie and women in ball gowns descending the curved staircase in the Grand Ballroom, framed by abstract gold trellises. Other photos—of the same elegant guests standing in long buffet lines or eating while crouched on the floor, as honorary hostess Perle Mesta snarled at waiters to fetch chairs and tablecloths—suggest that the Sheraton needed to fine-tune its event planning. Impromptu entertainment was provided outside the main entrance, when waiters began a fistfight with union pickets protesting Sheraton labor policies.

The Sheraton's official opening on March 3–5, 1957, went more smoothly. Dave Garroway hosted NBC-TV's *Today Show* from locations throughout the hotel. The Wharton School of Business sponsored a conference titled "Looking Ahead to the Year 2000." Ye Cheshire Cheese Chop House hosted a gentlemen's luncheon with "Quaint Olde English musick," while the Café Carême served up delicacies of the Napoleonic era. The opening was capped by the Navy League Ball in the Grand Ballroom, with the secretary of the navy in attendance.[10]

The Sheraton occupied the building until 1981, when the company shifted its focus to newer facilities in University City and Society Hill. The building's new owners renamed it the Philadelphia Centre Hotel and spent $10 million refurbishing the façade, lobby, and public rooms in a more subdued décor. Unfortunately, the hotel reopened just as Philadelphia entered one of its worst hotel slumps, experiencing the lowest average occupancy rates of any city in the Northeast. After struggling financially for several years, the Centre Hotel closed in 1986, the same year the Bellevue Stratford closed its doors.

The former Sheraton was demolished in 1987 and its vacant site used as a parking lot for more than a decade. In 2001, Liberty Property Trust announced plans to build One Pennsylvania Plaza, a 725-foot skyscraper designed by Robert A. M. Stern, on the site. In January 2005, Comcast Corporation signed a fifteen-year lease to occupy nearly one-half of the building's 1.2 million square feet of office space. With its star tenant in place, Liberty Property Trust renamed the structure Comcast Tower, increased its height to 975 feet (making it the tallest in the city), and revised the design from a golden Kasota stone façade to a glass curtain wall.

Aquarama

Location: 3300 South Broad Street (at Hartranft Street),
  South Philadelphia
Completed: 1962
Demolished: ca. 1969
Architect/Builder: Erling H. Pedersen

Two years after the Fairmount Water Works closed in 1909, the Philadelphia Aquarium was installed in the basement of the Engine House, built by Frederick Graff between 1812 and 1815. When the city cut back its financial support after World War II, the facility grew decrepit. The seals and sea lions sickened and died, while the few remaining fish were barely visible behind the algae that coated their giant indoor tanks. Plans announced in 1957 for a new municipal aquarium to be built on the Schuylkill north of the Water Works were dropped shortly afterward. In 1962, the city closed the Water Works aquarium, by then a public embarrassment.

To replace it, wealthy businessman Isaac "Ike" Levy, the Fairmount Park commissioner who had been in charge of the Water Works facility, decided to create a private commercial aquarium. Levy and a group of investors raised $3 million dollars to found "Aquarama—Theater of the Sea." The Aquarama complex stood north of the U.S. Naval Hospital, across Broad Street from the future site of Veterans Stadium.

Opened in December 1962, Aquarama was designed to be as modern and spacious as the Water Works facility had been old-fashioned and cramped. The sprawling concrete and steel structure with its slanted roof looked like a World's Fair pavilion, featuring a space-age design of angled exterior wall panels inset with multicolored, multitextured tiles. Wave-shaped canopies and porticoes shaded the doors and windows. In front of the main building, facing Broad Street, stood several abstract structures of fake stone that looked like sets for *The Flintstones*.

Aquarama attempted to balance serious marine display and research with crowd-pleasing attractions. In addition to standard aquarium exhibits, visitors enjoyed "living dioramas," where scuba divers interacted with sharks and other exotic fish. Pilot whales swam in an in-ground pool that held 50,000 gallons of salt water. The heart of the

Aquarama in September 1964, after Steel Pier owner George Hamid had taken over operations. (Temple University Libraries, Urban Archives, Philadelphia.)

complex was the Theater of the Sea, a 100-by-25-foot aboveground glass tank topped by plastic splash panels and surrounded by raked rows of seats. Here, pretty girls swam with the "world's greatest performing porpoises" to the recorded strains of "Tara's Theme" from *Gone with the Wind*.

Despite these attractions, Aquarama lost nearly $100,000 within its first two years because of its remote location and lack of municipal support. (Levy had offered the city a long-term lease on the facility but was turned down.) In 1964, George Hamid, owner of the Steel Pier in Atlantic City, replaced Levy. To bring in revenue, Hamid rented out Aquarama for parties, built a movie theater on the property, and even leased the porpoise tanks at night for testing space capsules' buoyancy.

Hamid turned to TV to promote his water circus, producing *Ed Hurst at Aquarama*, a music show for teens with guests like Diana Ross and the Supremes, the Four Tops, and Marvin Gaye. Airing on Saturday afternoons, the Aquarama show was similar to *American Bandstand*, but with cutaway shots of sharks and barracudas. Hamid also hired Gene Hart, a former schoolteacher, as an announcer. (After his stint at Aquarama, Hart was the voice of the Flyers hockey team for twenty-eight years.)

By 1969, Hamid had given up, and Aquarama closed, drowning in a sea of red ink. Its buildings were demolished shortly after its closing and replaced by a retail/office complex that now houses a CVS Pharmacy, Social Security Administration offices, a credit union, and the Wills Hospital Surgery Center.

Shortly before the water circus shut its doors, one local journalist tried to find a silver lining: "The fate of Aquarama is sad. But perhaps now, the city will get a genuine aquarium, one that seems to fit an inland eastern city, down on the riverfront at the new Penns Landing project."[11] Philadelphia would have to wait twenty-three years for a genuine aquarium, and when it arrived, it would be across the Delaware River from Penns Landing. In 1992, the $52 million Thomas H. Kean New Jersey State Aquarium opened on the Camden waterfront.

Liberty Bell Park

Location: Area bounded by Woodhaven Road, Knights Road, and Poquessing Creek, Northeast Philadelphia
Completed: 1963
Demolished: 1987
Architect/Builder: Alexander Ewing & Associates

Surrounded by rich farms and pastureland on all sides, Philadelphia became a center of horse racing early in its history. Sassafras Street gained its current name, Race, from the horse races held there in the eighteenth and early nineteenth centuries; during this period, both Centre Square and Hunting Park were also used as racetracks. Equines from the Philadelphia area have made their mark on racing history—from Messenger, one of the first thoroughbreds imported to America, who stood at stud here in 1788 before being sold to New York's Astors; to George Cadwalader and his trotter, Ned Forrest, the world's fastest in the nineteenth century; to Smarty Jones and the late Barbaro today.

Despite this rich heritage, Pennsylvania's restrictive blue laws made horse racing illegal from 1820 until the 1960s. Philadelphians who wished to watch (and, more importantly, bet on) horse races had to travel south to Delaware or west to New Jersey until 1963. That year, Liberty Bell Park opened as the first modern racetrack in the Philadelphia area, covering nearly 300 acres in the still-undeveloped northeastern corner of the city. A state-of-the-art lighting system and 110-foot light poles allowed the park to offer the novelty of nighttime racing.

At first, Liberty Bell Park offered only harness racing on a 5/8 (.625) mile track; when thoroughbred racing was legalized in Pennsylvania in 1968, a one-mile track was laid out, using the homestretch and front of the harness track. Liberty Bell's attractive, up-to-date grandstand offered a number of stylish amenities, including the all-weather Turfside Terrace, where well-heeled gamblers could dine on gourmet fare while they watched the races. In

the 1970s, a Bicentennial-era makeover clothed the grandstand in garish shades of red, white, and blue.

Throughout the 1960s and 1970s, Liberty Bell Park was a popular stop for racing aficionados along the East Coast, even after its thoroughbred racing moved to Bucks County's new Keystone Racetrack (now Philadelphia Park) in 1974. Starting in 1980, Liberty Bell went into the red, hurt by legalized gambling in the form of casinos and state lotteries, and relentless competition from the twenty-three other racetracks within a few hours' drive (including a rebuilt Garden State Park in Cherry Hill).

From hosting nightly crowds of more than 20,000 and handling bets of $1.6 million in the early 1970s, Liberty Bell declined in 1984 to an average attendance of fewer than 3,000 and an average handle of $340,000 per night. Struggling to survive, the park offered pen and watch giveaways, airline ticket drawings, and an annual family day with clowns and balloons. To compete with Delaware's Brandywine Park, Liberty Bell held more than 250 nights of harness racing a year, which caused attendance and revenues to drop even further. The park's owners were barely able to maintain the aging facility, let alone upgrade to such basics as air-conditioning and ceilings for the grandstand levels.

The racetrack shut down in August 1985 and never reopened. In May 1986, Liberty Bell Park's owners sold the 288-acre property, now surrounded by neighborhoods of tightly packed row houses, twins, and garden apartments, for $26 million. Its new owner, the Western Development Corporation, announced plans to build a large enclosed shopping mall to be called Liberty Mills on the site. In May 1987, the Liberty Bell Park grandstand was demolished and ground was broken for the 1.8 million-square-foot mall. Some parts of the racetrack were recycled, such as its light poles, which now illuminate Saint Joseph University's baseball field in Norristown's Elmwood Park.

In May 1989, the $300 million Franklin Mills (its name changed to honor Benjamin Franklin), then touted as the world's largest outlet mall, opened on the site of the old racetrack, along with the Philadelphia Home and Design Center and a French hypermarket called Carrefour (now closed).

Since Liberty Bell Park closed, the number of Philadelphia-area racetracks has dwindled as declining attendance and development pressures have taken their toll. Brandywine Raceway's grandstands were imploded in 1995 to make way for a shopping center, Brandywine Town Center. Garden State Park saw its last race on May 3, 2001, and was demolished for a retail and housing development in 2003. Locally, Philadelphia Park and Delaware Park continue the thoroughbred horse-racing tradition. The financial survival of the first, however, is secured by its phone betting service, while the latter relies on its 79,000-square-foot casino and thousands of slot machines.

Holiday Inn Motor Court/
Adam's Mark Hotel

Location: 4000 Monument Road (at City Avenue)
Completed: 1965
Demolished: 2006
Architect/Builder: Aaron Colish

Before World War II, City Avenue (originally City Line Avenue), which separated West Philadelphia from lower Montgomery County, was a bucolic boulevard lined with country estates, the Belmont Reservoir, and public institutions like the Presbyterian Home for the Aged, St. Joseph's College (today St. Joseph's University), and Episcopal Academy. In 1950, the Lower Merion Board of Commissioners rezoned a 600-foot strip along the eastern end of City Avenue in Bala Cynwyd for commercial use. Shortly thereafter, radio and television station WCAU commissioned George Howe and Robert Montgomery Brown to build a broadcast center at City Avenue and Monument Road.

Commercial development intensified when the Schuylkill Expressway opened its City Avenue exit on September 1, 1954. Soon, City Avenue between the Schuylkill River and St. Joseph's College was a glitzy commercial corridor known as the Golden Mile, home to WCAU-TV, WPVI-TV, Presidential Apartments, Philadelphia College of Osteopathic Medicine, Germantown Savings Bank, General Refractories, Esso, Lord & Taylor, and Saks Fifth Avenue. The stylish district attracted business travelers, shoppers, and celebrities, along with major hotel chains like Marriott.

In 1965, the 515-room Philadelphia Holiday Inn Motor Court opened on a fourteen-acre campus on East City Avenue, directly across from the deluxe Marriott. The Motor Court was part of a coordinated campaign by Holiday Inn to penetrate the lucrative Philadelphia market; its Midtown hotel had opened on Walnut Street the year before. The City Avenue Holiday Inn was designed by Aaron Colish, architect of numerous hotel and apartment complexes around the region, including the 2601 Parkway Apartments and the Atlantic City Holiday Inn.

Colish's main building, a twenty-three-story rectangle of blue wall-length windows set within patterned, buff-colored concrete, stood near Monument Avenue, separated from City Avenue by a vast parking lot. The tower flared outward at the top to accommodate the hotel's fifty-nine executive suites, offering spectacular views of Fairmount Park and the Philadelphia skyline. Next to the tower squatted the brick and glass annex that housed twenty-four meeting rooms and a 12,144-square-foot Grand Ballroom. To lure diners from the Marriott's exotic Kona Kai restaurant, the Holiday Inn offered the Top of the Line, a rotating gourmet restaurant perched above the roof.

In 1982, the Philadelphia Holiday Inn was sold to HBE Corporation, owner of the upscale Adam's Mark hotel chain. After a $32 million makeover, the hotel reopened as the Philadelphia Adam's Mark in April 1983, the sides of its concrete tower bearing the chain's red trademark. The Top of the Line was dismantled and replaced by the Marker, an elaborate gourmet restaurant on the ground floor.

Just as the revamped Adam's Mark was opening, the Golden Mile's glitter was fading. With the opening of the Pennsylvania Convention Center and new downtown hotels like the Marriott, Center City regained its supremacy as Philadelphia's lodging and entertainment nexus. Neighborhoods like Manayunk and Chestnut Hill emerged as hot spots for dining and shopping, and City Avenue became just another four-lane highway lined with gas stations and fast-food outlets.

By the 1990s, the Adam's Mark was scrambling for business, hosting Starving Artist art sales, sci-fi conventions, and Pickle Packers International meetings. Its parent company, HBE Corp., was

financially damaged by a racial discrimination suit brought by the NAACP in 1999 and settled out of court for $2 million. The travel slowdown after September 11, 2001, further hurt the struggling company. Starting in 2003, HBE sold seventeen of its twenty-three Adam's Mark hotels; the Philadelphia location was purchased by the Target Corporation in November 2004.

The City Avenue Adam's Mark—which the city's PR machine had once described as an example of "the spirit and drive of a city truly being reborn"—shut its doors on January 30, 2005.[12] In early February, the hotel's contents, ranging from 3,000 chairs to the imported crystal chandeliers from its Grand Ballroom, were sold at auction. Later that year, former Philadelphia 76ers president Pat Croce scuttled his tentative plans to build a casino at the location, shot down by community opposition and Target's refusal to sell the land. The fourteen-acre site was cleared of its buildings in 2006, with a new Target store scheduled to open in 2007.

Veterans Stadium

Location: South Broad Street north of Pattison Avenue
Completed: 1971
Demolished: 2004
Architect/Builder: Ewing, George & Co.; Hugh Stubbins &
  Associates; Stonorov & Haws

The completion of the Houston Astrodome in 1965 triggered a demand for multipurpose municipal sports stadiums that could be used for football and baseball, as well as for concerts and other civic gatherings. Soon other circular concrete arenas sprouted in St. Louis, Atlanta, Cincinnati, and Pittsburgh.

In the early 1950s, the City of Philadelphia began discussions with the Phillies and the Eagles about replacing both the aging Baker Bowl and Connie Mack Stadium with a new facility. After years of wrangling over location, design, and cost, Philadelphia held the ground-breaking ceremonies for its multipurpose sports stadium on October 2, 1967. The chosen site was on South Broad Street, north of Municipal Stadium and the newly completed Spectrum. Despite protests from the antiwar movement, the city named the unfinished facility Veterans Stadium in 1970.

At a cost of $52 million, Veterans Stadium, known as "the Vet," was one of the most expensive sports arenas in the country.

Seating 62,000, the Vet was also the largest stadium in the National League. Located on a seventy-four-acre tract, the stadium was built in the shape of an "octorad," a word invented by its architects to describe its rounded rectangular form, derived from eight points on a radius (Philadelphians nicknamed it "the big doughnut"). More than 100 massive concrete columns around its perimeter supported the building, roof, and rows of seats. Its telescoping stands could be moved to change the stadium configuration for baseball or football. Steel cables rather than columns supported the eight pedestrian access ramps, another stadium first.

On April 10, 1971, more than 55,000 spectators packed Veterans Stadium for the inaugural game against the Montreal Expos.

The unnamed octorad during construction in November 1969, its 100 concrete support columns in place around its perimeter. (Temple University Libraries, Urban Archives, Philadelphia.)

Super Bowl (which they lost to the Oakland Raiders, 27–10). The team that opened their Vet history with a loss closed it the same way, falling to the Tampa Bay Buccaneers at the NFC championship game on January 19, 2003. From 1980 on, the Vet was also the site of the Army-Navy football game.

Philadelphia's temperamental sports fans made the Vet their home away from home. According to one sports writer, the Vet had "the smallest hot dogs and the loudest boos in baseball."[12] In 1977, thousands of jeering fans unnerved a Dodgers pitcher, forcing him to leave the mound midgame. Two decades later, after an Eagles fan shot a flare gun into some empty seats and another fan wearing 49ers gear was attacked, the city set up an Eagles Court at the stadium to discipline drunken and rowdy fans on the spot.

By this time, the stadium was showing its age, partly as a result of deferred maintenance on the city's part. During the 1990s, the city and the Phillies spent more than $40 million to refurbish the Vet. They replaced the garish orange, yellow, brown, and red seats with more conservative blue ones, added a state-of-the-art Phanovision scoreboard, and exchanged the dangerously hard Astroturf for NeXturf. Despite these upgrades, the stadium's decrepitude was made painfully clear on December 5, 1998, when a railing collapsed during the ninety-ninth Army-Navy game, injuring ten West Point cadets.

The ceremonial first pitch was dropped from a helicopter to Phillies catcher Mike Ryan, starting a tradition of offbeat Opening Day baseball deliveries. After popular TV talk show host Mike Douglas sang the national anthem, the Phillies beat the Expos, 4–1.

Over the next thirty years, Veterans Stadium would host All-Star games in 1976 and 1996, and World Series appearances in 1980, 1983, and 1993. On October 21, 1980, Tug McGraw struck out Willie Wilson of the Kansas City Royals to win the Phillies' only World Series championship.

The Eagles went on to a more checkered career at the Vet, losing their first game against the Dallas Cowboys, 42–7, on September 26, 1971. In January 1981, the Eagles defeated the Dallas Cowboys 20–7 in the NFC championship, advancing to their only

By this time, plans had been drawn up for the Vet's replacements: Lincoln Financial Field for the Eagles (opening in 2003) and Citizens Bank Park for the Phillies (opening in 2004). The Vet closed in October 2003, shortly after the Atlanta Braves defeated the Phillies, 5–2, in the final game at the stadium. Before the Vet's demolition, more than 20,000 stadium seats were sold at $280 a pair. Other items, including the Vet's lights, artificial turf, outfield wall, and electronic scoreboard, were donated or sold to schools and Little League teams around the region. Still others were salvaged for future inclusion in the Philadelphia Sports Hall of Fame, including exit turnstiles, section signs, railings, lockers, and ticket-window grilles.

On Sunday, March 21, 2004, the thirty-three-year-old stadium was imploded. Former Phillies star Greg "the Bull" Luzinski pushed the ceremonial plunger at 7:00 AM, triggering sixty-two seconds of explosions that left only a crater ringed by twisted metal and crushed concrete. Despite the Vet's reputation as one of the worst stadiums in the major leagues, thousands of spectators showed up for its demolition, many with tears in their eyes. The next day, hundreds of the curious and nostalgic swarmed over the site, hoping to retrieve a lump of concrete as a souvenir. As ESPN writer Jeff Merron put it: "It was an eyesore, but it was Philadelphia's eyesore."[13]

On September 28, 2005, the second anniversary of the final Phillies game at the Vet, an official state historical marker was dedicated on the site, now a 5,500-car parking lot for Citizens Bank Park.

Fidelity Mutual Life Building/ One Meridian Plaza

Location: 1414 South Penn Square (between Fifteenth and Ranstead streets)
Completed: 1973
Demolished: 1998–99
Architect/Builder: Vincent G. Kling & Associates

One of the final steps in the redevelopment of the Center City business district was the construction of the Fidelity Mutual Life Building between 1968 and 1973. Designed by Vincent G. Kling, the thirty-eight-story structure stood across from City Hall. Erected to house the Fidelity Mutual Life Insurance Company and the Girard Trust Company, Kling's building was the tallest office tower in Philadelphia. Despite this, it was still lower than the statue of William Penn atop City Hall, reflecting the unwritten "gentleman's agreement" that would remain intact until the completion of One Liberty Place in 1987.

The building featured concrete and steel construction with granite wall panels, and solar bronze-glass windows in anodized aluminum frames. In the Sky Lounge on the top two floors, executives and their guests could enjoy panoramic views of the city through two-story projecting solar-glass bay windows, then depart via the rooftop heliport. An exterior stairwell on the building's east side connected it with the adjacent Girard Trust Tower, designed in 1930 by Furness, Evans & Co.

From the beginning, plans for the vast structure went awry. In August 1970, a steel cable holding a six-ton concrete slab snapped, sending two workers hurtling ten stories to their deaths and crushing the legs of a third worker. The building finally opened in 1973, nearly three years after its original estimated completion date. Kling's plans had called for a later extension of the building to Chestnut Street to accommodate its tenants' expected growth, but

The architect's conception of the Fidelity Mutual Life Building ca. 1968. Looking south down Fifteenth Street, Kling's high-rise is flanked by the Girard Trust Tower, with the PNB Building across Broad Street. Part of City Hall and Dilworth Plaza are visible in the lower left corner. (Temple University Libraries, Urban Archives, Philadelphia.)

when Mellon Bank acquired the venerable Girard Trust in 1983, the building was renamed 3 Mellon Center and plans for its expansion died. A few years later, Fidelity Mutual failed due to aggressive real estate speculation and was taken over by the Pennsylvania Insurance Department. In 1989, the former Fidelity Mutual Life Building became One Meridian Plaza in recognition of its new lead tenant, Meridian Bank, a Reading-based financial institution entering the Philadelphia market.

On the evening of February 23, 1991, a fire began in a pile of oily rags left by workers on the twenty-second floor. Since only the top eight floors of One Meridian Plaza were equipped with sprinklers, the fire spread upward quickly, burning out floors twenty-two through twenty-nine. More than 300 firefighters from seventy-seven companies responded to the twelve-alarm fire. Hampered by inadequate water pressure and the failure of the building's electrical system, they were unable to extinguish the blaze.

The fire burned for nineteen hours, until it reached the thirtieth floor, where the sprinkler system extinguished it. By then, the fire had killed three firefighters, injured twenty-four more, and caused more than $100 million in damage. Reaching temperatures of 2,000 degrees in some spots, it had come dangerously close to spreading to adjacent structures, creating an uncontrollable inferno. The Meridian fire led to a major revision of the city's fire code, requiring older high-rises to be retrofitted with complete sprinkler systems and other safety features.

For the rest of the 1990s, the stabilized hulk of One Meridian Plaza stood on Penn Square, a scarred testament to the largest high-rise fire in the country to that time. Protracted litigation between the building's owners, insurers, and contractors, along with a slump in downtown office properties, delayed its demolition for seven years. Meanwhile, the adjacent blocks of Chestnut Street withered as stores closed due to lack of business. One of the first images in Jonathan Demme's 1994 Oscar-winning *Philadelphia* was a bird's-eye view of the ruin looming over Center City. In 1998, with legal issues resolved, demolition began on the building, which was dis-

mantled piece by piece over eighteen months because of its proximity to other structures. By then, total costs for settlements, insurance claims, legal fees, building stabilization, and demolition were estimated at well above $500 million.

After years in limbo, one of the choicest, and possibly one of the unluckiest, parcels of Philadelphia real estate is rising from the ashes. In March 2006, following several years of legal disputes with the owner of the adjacent property on Chestnut Street, construction began at the One Meridian Plaza site on a forty-four-story glass tower, the Residences at the Ritz-Carlton.

NewMarket

Location: Area bounded by Pine, Lombard, Second, and Front streets
Completed: 1975
Demolished: 2002
Architect/Builder: Louis Sauer

By the mid-1960s, the redeveloped Society Hill district was flourishing. While some derelict buildings remained, private owners had restored more than 600 historic houses to their original splendor. Population in the once-sleepy area had increased by one-third, and property values had doubled. New residents were flocking not just to the older structures but to I. M. Pei's Society Hill Towers, as well as to modern townhouse complexes like Addison and Bing-

ham Courts. Along the Delaware River, construction was under way on Penns Landing and Interstate 95.

To complement the residential renaissance, a consortium of real estate developers sought to create an upscale shopping district in the area around the New Market on Second Street between Pine and Lombard streets, with its colonial market stalls and 1804 headhouse. The retail-residential development would combine historic houses on both sides of Second Street with a modern complex of buildings in the interior of the square between Second and Front streets.

The $10 million, 100,000-square-foot NewMarket opened in 1975. Its centerpiece, an 80,000-square-foot trilevel glass and steel pavilion, the Glass Palace, extended from behind the older houses on the east side of Second Street to Front Street. Similar in concept to the 1969 Design Research Headquarters in Cambridge, Massachusetts, the Glass Palace was built around a multilevel Water Plaza with a large pool, waterfall, and abstract sculpture. Besides the Glass Palace and the Second Street houses, NewMarket included Old Court, a four-story retail complex at the northeast corner of Second and Lombard, and a 375-car garage at the northwest corner of Second and Lombard. A large sign announcing the center's name in backlit blue letters topped the Glass Palace's Front Street façade.

Despite opposition from neighborhood residents, NewMarket was successful for a short period after its opening. Tourists

In this 1978 photograph, a young couple relaxes near NewMarket's Water Plaza, the Glass Palace in the background. (Temple University Libraries, Urban Archives, Philadelphia.)

bought T-shirts, kites, and souvenirs from its sixty shops. On weekends, young Philadelphians flocked to its restaurants, such as the Rusty Scupper, the Dickens Inn, and Lily's Restaurant. After dinner, they enjoyed the street entertainers who performed for spare change in the Water Plaza, including a skinny young juggler and magician named Penn Jillette, who would later gain fame as the talking half of Penn and Teller.

Within a year of its opening, NewMarket's allure faded, and tenants began to leave because of low volume and sales. The crowds of tourists vanished once summer ended, and NewMarket was too far from downtown to attract office workers for lunch or dinner. Merchants also complained about lack of parking, difficulty of access from Interstate 95, and neighborhood antagonism. Despite a $2.5 million overhaul in 1979, NewMarket became one of Philadelphia's most disappointing business projects.

An attempt to revive the complex with a seventeen-store gourmet food market in Old Court failed within eighteen months of its 1986 opening. Local opposition and lack of financing defeated various plans by the owners to erect a supermarket, townhouses, arts center, or twenty-story condo tower. By 1990, the Glass Palace was completely deserted and barricaded, the NEWMARKET sign overlooking Front Street blacked out. Only a few blocks from bustling South Street, NewMarket had become "a crudely fenced vacant lot on the doorstep of one of the wealthiest neighborhoods in the city," in the words of an *Inquirer* article.[15]

In 2000, Hollywood star and Overbrook native Will Smith purchased the complex for $3.2 million with plans to develop a $35 million, 160-room boutique hotel on the site as part of the W chain. When the local hotel market softened, the decrepit complex was demolished in 2002. In early 2005, Smith sold the parcel for $10.5 million to a Philadelphia developer, who announced plans to build condos and retail stores on the site.

Living History Center

Location: 140 North Sixth Street (southwest corner of Race and Sixth streets)
Completed: 1976
Demolished: 1998
Architect/Builder: Mitchell/Giurgola Associates (architects), Raymond Loewy International Inc. (project designer)

Years before the nation's 200th anniversary, Philadelphia was abuzz with plans for the Bicentennial. City leaders proposed a celebration that would dwarf not only the 1876 Centennial Exposition, but also more recent festivals like the 1964–65 New York World's Fair and Montreal's Expo 67. Architects like Louis I. Kahn, Robert Venturi, and Denise Scott Brown proposed ambitious designs that would go beyond celebrating the United States to redraw the face of Philadelphia.

By 1976, poor planning, political squabbling, and economic recession had burst the city's Bicentennial bubble. Of the many visionary schemes proposed, only a few smaller projects were realized: the Liberty Bell Pavilion, Franklin Court, the Afro-American Historical and Cultural Museum (today the African American Museum in Philadelphia), the Mummers Museum, and the Living History Center, built on the site of short-lived Pennsylvania Hall.

Designed to introduce visitors to the sights and sounds of U.S. history, the Living History Center was the largest and most expensive project developed by the Philadelphia 1976 Bicentennial Corporation (Philadelphia '76), the official planning arm of the Bicentennial. The original design was by Raymond Loewy, creator of the Lucky Strike package and Shell Oil logo. Philadelphia architects Ehrmann Mitchell and Romaldo Giurgola, designers of the Penn Mutual Tower and United Way Building, adapted Loewy's grandiose concept to fit the requirements of the project budget and location at the northern end of Independence Mall.

lion, the center's cost had swelled to $11 million by its completion in early 1976.

The IMAX Theater was the Living History Center's big draw. Developed in the late 1960s, the 3,100-pound IMAX projection system flashed huge, high-resolution images on a seven-story screen. Exhibited at Osaka, Toronto, and San Diego, IMAX made its U.S. East Coast debut at the Living History Center. *American Dreams*, a specially commissioned film by Oscar-winning director Francis Thompson, played on the world's largest movie screen, measuring 6,510 square feet.

The multilevel center was a long, rectangular building divided between exhibit space in the front and an IMAX theater in the rear. Two rounded brick corner towers framed its asymmetrical stone and glass façade, which featured a curved glass canopy over the front entrance. Two smaller wings for offices and a cafeteria extended from its northern side, framing a courtyard along Race Street. A large theater billboard on Sixth Street advertised the center's attractions near a metal statue of a barefoot Revolutionary youth playing a fife. Originally budgeted at an economical $2 mil-

The center's Exhibit Hall offered interactive and multimedia displays that are now common in museums but were then revolutionary. Visitors could enjoy a Birthday Machine, which printed out important events occurring on their birthdays; a Kaleidoscope theater that presented 200 years of American songs "while mirrors reflect an infinity of related images"; *To the New World*, a montage of 2,500 slides projected on sixty-four screens; and Historytoys, giant replicas of historic toys that children could operate on a rooftop playground.

While the Living History Center was popular throughout 1976, attendance plummeted after the Bicentennial. The center was hurt by its remote location at the northern end of Independence Mall, surrounded by the Metropolitan Hospital, Police Headquarters, and unsavory Franklin Square. New exhibits like the Laserium, laser beams projected on the IMAX screen in a variety of designs, failed to draw customers. Efforts to market the complex as a convention center foundered, and the expensive, massive structure was soon in the red.

In May 1978, WHYY, the local PBS station, agreed to rent the Living History Center from the city for a token one dollar per year. The moribund center officially closed in June 1980. Its northern end, including the former playground along Race Street, was sold to the American College of Physicians for their new headquarters building in the mid-1980s.

In 1998, WHYY launched a massive capital campaign to develop a Technology Center on its headquarters site, which would enable it to offer new programs and features in the latest digital and HDTV formats. During the construction of the Burt Hill Kosar Rittelmann Associates structure, much of the original Living History Center was demolished. The main building was stripped down to its bare steel and exterior walls and incorporated into the new Technology Center. The IMAX theater was razed in 1999 and replaced with a two-story office building. (Since 1990, the Tuttleman Theater at the Franklin Institute has been the only IMAX theater in Philadelphia.)

Liberty Bell Pavilion

Location: Independence Mall (south side of Market Street)
Completed: 1976
Demolished: 2006
Architect/Builder: Mitchell/Giurgola Associates

A separate structure for the venerable Liberty Bell—placed on public display in Congress Hall in 1852 and later moved to Independence Hall—was first suggested two years before the Centennial. The idea was revived before the Sesqui-Centennial and again in the 1960s, with no success. In 1969, the National Park Service (NPS) recommended moving the bell to a structure that could accommodate the huge crowds expected for the Bicentennial.

At first, the NPS planned to place the Liberty Bell in the new visitors' center at Chestnut and Second streets. Facing strong public opposition to moving the bell so far from Independence Hall, the NPS selected a site on the first block of Independence Mall, across from the bell's original home. In its specifications, the NPS indicated that the new structure needed to receive and channel large crowds with dignity, allow the Liberty Bell to be viewed after hours by passersby, and express the meaning of the bell without enshrining it. The $1 million budget precluded a monumental or elaborate edifice.

In response, architect Romaldo Giurgola created a long, low, rectangular building of only 2,800 square feet. Situated on the Mall south of Market Street, the Liberty Bell Pavilion stood 500 feet from Independence Hall but on the same axis as the older structure. Despite its modern design, the pavilion was constructed of materials that would have been familiar to the original members of the Carpenters' Company: white granite wall panels, a copper roof, and white oak interior paneling and flooring. Glass walls at the north and south ends allowed those outside the building to see the Liberty Bell by day or by night, when it was dramatically lit.

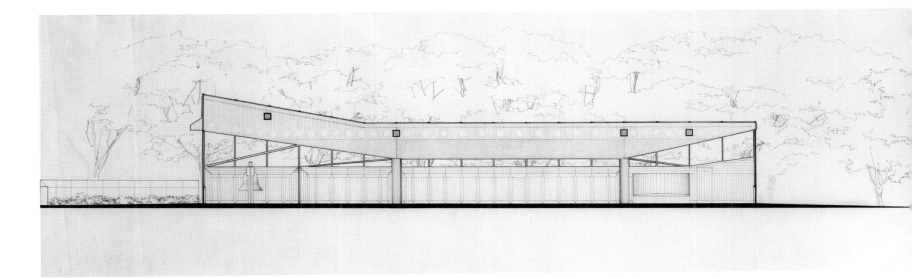

The flat roof flared upward in a winglike formation at the south end, providing greater space and height for the Liberty Bell Chamber. Visitors entered the building at Market Street and proceeded through a narrow, skylit passage to the Bell Chamber, where the bell was framed by Independence Hall in the background.

From the very beginning, public reaction to the Liberty Bell Pavilion was mixed. Some admired its crisp simplicity and the way it connected the Liberty Bell not just to Independence Hall but also to the larger modern buildings lining the mall. Others noted that the bell, supported on steel stanchions at ground level rather than elevated on a platform, was more accessible to visitors in its new setting. A writer in the April 1976 issue of *Progressive Architecture* called the pavilion "a simple, reticent space that does not draw attention to itself, but directs it to the Liberty Bell and Independence Mall which, after all, are what one comes to see."[16]

Less sympathetic observers complained that one of the greatest symbols of American freedom now resided in what was described variously as a bank branch, car wash, or Fotomat. Still others were upset that the most striking sight from the pavilion's south window was not Independence Hall but the Penn Mutual Tower on Walnut Street, also designed by Mitchell/Giurgola.

Just after midnight on January 1, 1976, the Liberty Bell was carefully transferred from the vestibule of Independence Hall to its new home, kicking off the Bicentennial gala. Over the next twenty-seven years, the Liberty Bell Pavilion received more than forty million visitors, until the new plans for Independence Mall rendered it redundant.

On October 9, 2003, the Liberty Bell was transferred to the 13,000-square-foot Liberty Bell Center on the west side of Sixth

The Liberty Bell Pavilion during its dismantling in March 2006, looking north through the original Bell Chamber toward Market Street. The Independence Visitor Center is visible to the left. (Courtesy of Joseph Elliott.)

Street between Chestnut and Market. Designed by Bohlin Cywinski Jackson, the center was meant to correct many of the perceived mistakes of the Mitchell/Giurgola pavilion. The placement of the new structure put the Liberty Bell closer to Independence Hall, creating a more intimate connection between its current and original homes. Unlike the pavilion, which had focused exclusively on the bell, the Liberty Bell Center leads visitors down a long corridor of multimedia exhibits relating the history of the bell and its role in the American consciousness before bringing them to the Bell Chamber. The orientation of the Bell Chamber veers from Sixth Street at an angle, creating a panorama in which Independence Hall frames the Liberty Bell, while the Penn Mutual Tower remains unseen.

After the Liberty Bell Center opened, the fate of the Mitchell/Giurgola pavilion hung in limbo. For two years, the National Park Service used it as the security checkpoint for Independence National Historical Park, where visitors were screened before being granted access to the bell and Independence Hall. The NPS offered to give away the pavilion to anyone who would pay to remove it. In 2004, American College in Bryn Mawr expressed interest in acquiring the building for its campus, home to three structures designed by Romaldo Giurgola. The college later rescinded its offer because it could not raise the $800,000 needed to relocate the building.

In March 2006, the thirty-year-old Liberty Bell Pavilion was dismantled as part of Operation Mall Vista, unblocking the view of Independence Hall along the length of the mall. As a civic gesture, ten local unions contributed $300,000 in labor to demolish the structure. "Sometimes subtraction is a great addition," Mayor John Street announced before he helped union members rip up the pavilion's floorboards.

About 85 percent of the pavilion went to Anchorage, Alaska, where it will become part of a remembrance park commemorating the September 11, 2001, attacks. Among the pieces sent north were forty seven-foot granite slabs, copper covers and cladding, oak flooring and paneling, two sets of double-glass doors, ten three-by-five-foot windows and frames, and the steel bell stanchions, which will support a replica of the Liberty Bell made at the same London foundry that produced the original. The rest of the pavilion was scrapped, and its basement filled in to allow the landscaping of Independence Mall to be completed.

While some critics have praised the new Liberty Bell Center, others have condemned it as a fussy, faux-historical structure that enshrines the bell while hiding it from view. John Andrew Gallery, executive director of the Preservation Alliance, has written: "The loss of openness and transparency—the public visual accessibility—is the key difference between the old and new and why, by comparison, the old is such an exceptionally right approach."[17] To many observers, the Liberty Bell Center symbolizes the National Park Service's dubious efforts to protect the shrines of Independence National Historical Park by placing them beyond public reach.

CHAPTER 7

Projected Philadelphia

What is the city but the seat of Availabilities?
—LOUIS I. KAHN, 1972

Facing page: **A** conception of Penn Center developed in 1925, shortly after the city and the Pennsylvania Railroad signed a contract to demolish the Chinese Wall. Handsome office blocks extend west from a truncated Broad Street Station to the new Beaux-Arts terminal at Thirtieth Street; the Fairmount Parkway extends diagonally to the completed Museum of Art. (Collection of the author.)

Philadelphia may qualify as America's first planned city, which means that it was also the first American city not to turn out as planned. Only a few years after Penn founded his "Greene Countrie Towne," his plan for good-sized houses placed within large, well-shaded plots of land arranged in orderly blocks running inland from both the Delaware and Schuylkill Rivers had given way to the reality of a messy, congested town with houses crowded along the Delaware like thirsty animals at a watering hole. The spacious promenade Penn had envisioned along the waterfront was a thicket of warehouses, vaults, and wharves, over which the masts of harbored ships towered.

Perhaps part of William Penn's visionary legacy is that Philadelphia has always possessed an inner image of itself as a pure and perfect city, regardless of the squalor of its everyday reality. From its inception, order has competed with chaos, civic virtue with greed, and careful planning with entrepreneurial freedom, creating a tension unmatched in most U.S. cities. Since every attempt to realize the perfect Philadelphia falls short, there is always the need to reimagine the city another fifty years or so hence. (And since this timeframe often coincides with major anniversaries of U.S. independence, there is the added incentive of federal funding to help finance the latest dream.) With each attempt at reinvention, there is the hope of capturing the "seat of Availabilities" of which Kahn speaks, the essence of what Philadelphia wants to be, the city of Penn and Franklin updated to meet the needs and realities of the present.

What would this City of Availabilities look like—the Philadelphia that was planned but never built? Would it be a city of towers topped by enameled Beaux-Arts domes and pointed Art Deco spires, reflecting the countless buildings left on the drawing board once the Depression struck? Would these have given way, in turn, to new vistas of endless modernist glass and steel boxes, or to Louis Kahn's organic landscape of cylindrical towers, raised viaducts, and hemistyles?

Visitors to this imaginary city might detrain at the Beaux-Arts Pennsylvania Railroad Station erected at Thirtieth Street as part of

the Philadelphia Improvements, with its huge vaulted roof and immense window looking east down Pennsylvania Boulevard. From there, they could transfer to the second-largest subway system in the nation, extending north to Byberry, west to Upper Darby, and northwest to Roxborough and Chestnut Hill.

Car travelers could cross the Bicentennial Bridge spanning the Delaware River (8,000 feet long by 1,250 feet wide, with forty million square feet of apartments, hotels, and restaurants on four levels below the surface highway) or arrive via the 1,500 miles of expressways interlacing the city and surrounding suburbs, with names like the Crosstown, Cobbs Creek, Northeast, West Chester, and Pulaski. Once in town, they would be forced to leave their cars in one of Louis Kahn's harbors, vast cylindrical parking towers erected on the edges of Center City to ease traffic congestion.

Their cars safely stowed, commuters could walk or take electric trams to the sleek towers of elegant Penn Center, with its roof gardens and sunken terraces, or to the echeloned skyscrapers of the nearby Unicenter, built over the Pennsylvania Railroad tracks north of Thirtieth Street Station. City workers would file into Paul Cret's U-shaped Municipal Services Building on Reyburn Plaza, or into the triangular white concrete and black glass Justice Center looming over the north end of Independence Mall like a storm trooper's helmet from *Star Wars*.

Center City residents could stroll to work from William Johnston's classical townhouses on Summer Street east of Logan Square, built in the 1840s as part of the Loganian Institute near the old Episcopal Cathedral. The wealthiest Philadelphians would descend in express elevators from Sky Alley, a pedestrian street lined with two- and three-story townhouses built atop Academy House, while the less wealthy would leave their nineteenth-century townhouses along a South Street revitalized by Denise Scott Brown's Crosstown Development.

While thousands of Philadelphians headed to work, thousands of tourists and visitors would arrive to sightsee and play. Some would ascend City Hall Tower, the only surviving part of the massive structure, to view the surrounding city. If the World Series–winning Phillies (hey, this *is* an imaginary city) were in town, baseball fans would pack the Thirtieth Street Sports Arena, built in the shadow of the Unicenter. A few hardy souls might hop a monorail and travel south to see the crumbling restoration of King Solomon's Temple and Citadel built for the Sesqui-Centennial, complete with the Ark of the Covenant. Sadly, the pipelines that once pumped in clouds of smoke to simulate the temple's destruction broke down during the Rizzo administration.

Most of the designs just mentioned, along with many of the structures described in this chapter, will never see the light of day. Philadelphia's Episcopal elite will never worship at a cathedral in the hills of Roxborough, and City Hall appears fairly safe from demolition for the moment. Even Louis I. Kahn's most devoted acolyte would probably not want to see Center City ringed by massive parking harbors and boxed in by viaduct expressways.

Surprisingly, however, a number of the projected designs have taken shape in different form after a long gestation period, like the Washington Monument or the Kimmel Center. Whether due to Quaker caution, political corruption, or the absence of a truly ruthless power broker like Robert Moses, Philadelphia often takes decades to create its notable landmarks, including City Hall, Benjamin Franklin Parkway, Penn Center, Vine Street Expressway, and Penn's Landing. Still others appear to be gradually taking shape not as the result of a master plan, but through a confluence of government, business, and individual efforts, such as the development of the Thirtieth Street Station district, and the east and west banks of the Schuylkill.

Who knows? Edmund Bacon's laser beams may yet shine through the portals of City Hall and overhead, broadcasting William Penn's message of diversity and consensus into the night sky.

Washington Monument

Proposed location: Center of Washington Square
Period of origination: 1816
Architect/Builder: George Bridport, William Strickland

In the early 1800s, Philadelphia's citizens began to demand that the city's public squares be used for more attractive purposes than burying paupers and grazing cattle. In 1816, the City Councils moved that the four smaller squares be converted to parks and renamed for George Washington, Benjamin Franklin, William Penn, and Christopher Columbus.

The English painter and decorator George Bridport presented plans for laying out the South-East Square (then known as the Strangers' Burying Ground, the city's largest Potter's Field) as a park called Washington Square. The layout had a central quatrefoil space for a monument, from which eight paths radiated through concentric circles.

Bridport also submitted two designs for a central monument commemorating the square's namesake. One was a square arch topped by a low dome, combining Greco-Roman and Egyptian motifs. The second was a tall Roman triumphal arch sheltering a statue of Washington and topped by an American eagle, with decorative friezes and spandrels. A fund-raising campaign launched for the Washington Monument had raised only $3,500 by 1819. The square was laid out in a simplified version of Bridport's design, but plans for a monument were dropped.

The 1824 visit by the Marquis de Lafayette and the approach of the fiftieth anniversary of U.S. independence renewed interest in honoring the memory of the first president. In 1825, the South-East Square was officially renamed after Washington, while the remaining squares were named Franklin, Logan, and Rittenhouse (the name of Penn was bestowed upon what had formerly been Centre Square). At the urging of the Citizens' Washington Monument Fund, the City Councils authorized the construction of a monument.

Several architects submitted designs for the Washington Monument, including John Haviland and John Abraham Chevalier. The winner of the competition was William Strickland, who offered a 120-foot monument modeled after the Choragic Monument of

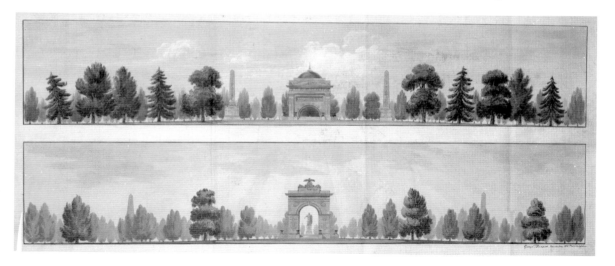

George Bridport's alternative designs for a monument to George Washington in Washington Square, prepared in 1816. (The Library Company of Philadelphia.)

A John Sartain engraving of William Strickland's proposed Washington Monument. To the right, the cupola of John Haviland's First Presbyterian Church, then located at Washington Square's southwest corner, rises above the trees. (The Historical Society of Pennsylvania.)

Thrassylus. The tall, rectangular shaft with a flattened pyramidical roof would have cost $67,000 to build. According to one description, the monument's "square pillars rest upon pedestals of the same form, and that on a terrace, the ascent to which is by a flight of stone steps. On each side the pillars are ornamented with pilasters in panels between faces and other ornaments, the top ornamented with entablature and garlands. The entrance into the interior of the monument [is] from a terrace by a door on each side. The whole may be surmounted by an urn or statue."[1]

Many Philadelphians were opposed to filling up Washington Square with a vast slab that would overshadow buildings like John Haviland's First Presbyterian Church. One newspaper account referred to it as a "massy monument . . . unperforated by a single loophole, to relieve the eye," the sheer bulk of which suggested that "our regard for Washington were to be measured by the square foot."[2] Once again, supporters were unable to raise the needed funds.

In 1832, the centenary of Washington's birth, a new initiative to erect a Washington Monument was undertaken, with

John Cresson Trautwine and Thomas U. Walter submitting designs. This time, supporters were so confident that they laid a marble cornerstone for the monument on February 22, 1833, in a ten-foot hole dug in the central circle of Washington Square, "in the course of which the remains of several of the ancient tenants of that ground were unearthed."[3] For the third time, the birthplace of America was unable to raise sufficient funds to begin construction. The cornerstone was covered over and remained undisturbed for decades.

The small sums collected in 1824 and 1832 were carefully invested, and by 1890 nearly $200,000 had accumulated. The commingled funds were then entrusted to the Society of the Cincinnati of Pennsylvania, which had first proposed a monument to Washington in 1810. The society commissioned German sculptor Rudolf Siemering to create a granite and bronze equestrian statue of Washington, surrounded by allegorical human and animal figures.

Although the society wished to install the monument in Washington Square, it bowed to public and political pressure and placed it at the Green Street entrance to Fairmount Park. In the 1920s, the monument was moved to its current location in front of the nearly completed Museum of Art. A monument to the Washington Grays, a volunteer unit that fought in the Mexican-American War, was placed in Washington Square.

The former South-East Square would have to wait until the 1950s to receive its own Washington Monument. In 1954, a group of local business executives formed a committee to restore the derelict park, which boasted a public lavatory as its central feature. The monument, designed by G. Edwin Brumbaugh, features a bronze replica of Jean Antoine Houdon's standing figure of Washington before a marble wall. In front of the statue are an eternal flame and the Tomb of the Unknown Soldier, a sarcophagus containing the remains of a Revolutionary soldier laid to rest in the Square and recovered in a 1956 archaeological dig. Whether the young soldier was a British or Continental combatant has never been determined.

Philadelphia Public Buildings

Proposed location: Independence Square
Period of origination: ca. 1847
Architect/Builder: John J. McArthur Jr. and Thomas U. Walter

From Philadelphia's birth, William Penn intended the city's most important buildings to be located on the ten-acre square at the intersection of Broad and High streets. The "short advertisement" that accompanied Thomas Holme's 1683 *Portraiture of the City of Philadelphia* specified that "at each angle are to be houses for Publick affairs as a Meeting-house, Assembly or State-House, Market-House, School-House."[4]

Despite this instruction, nineteenth-century Philadelphia was governed from the two federal-era structures that had flanked Independence Hall since its days as the national capital. The former U.S. Supreme Court Building at Chestnut and Sixth became City Hall and also housed the police and fire departments. Congress Hall at Fifth and Chestnut served as Philadelphia's main courthouse throughout the nineteenth century. The criminal courts in Congress Hall had a particular reputation for chaos, filled with noisy crowds of "soaplocks and loafers" into which prisoners had successfully vanished on more than one occasion.[5]

Early efforts to provide new quarters for the city's government and courts were unsuccessful. An act passed in 1838 to erect a new city hall on Penn Square was never realized, nor was an 1847 act authorizing the erection of a courthouse on Independence Square. As part of the competition for the proposed 1847 structure, John Haviland designed a combined city hall–courthouse on the Walnut Street side of Independence Square, with wings extending along Fifth and Sixth streets to Chestnut.

The consolidation of the city in 1854 created a megalopolis of 129 square miles and 565,000 inhabitants, for which the Independence Square structures were inadequate. In 1860, the City Coun-

cils sponsored a fresh competition for two public buildings, a municipal center and a courthouse, to face each other across Broad Street at Penn Square. John McArthur Jr., the competition winner, created two classical structures with pedimented porticoes and monumental domes supported by colonnaded towers, similar to Thomas U. Walter's redesign of the U.S. Capitol. The project was stalled by public opposition to the $1.5 million cost, the move west, and McArthur's being named both architect and contractor even though he was not the low bidder. The outbreak of the Civil War in 1861 effectively killed the new public buildings.

Once the war ended, Philadelphia's politicians were anxious to provide themselves with more spacious and elegant quarters. On December 31, 1868, the City Councils announced plans to erect lavish new public buildings that would trumpet Philadelphia's power and wealth to the world. Recalling earlier objections to locating the buildings on Penn Square, the councils selected Independence Square as the site for the new civic center. All buildings on the square except Independence Hall were to be demolished, including historic Congress Hall, the U. S. Supreme Court Building, and the American Philosophical Society.

A committee advised by Thomas U. Walter held a new competition and once again selected John McArthur Jr. as the winner. With the change in venue, McArthur abandoned his 1860 design, adapting Haviland's earlier concept of a massive U-shaped structure embracing the former State House between its two arms. This time, McArthur eschewed classicism for a modern Second Empire structure strongly resembling the Louvre in Paris. The main façade, on Walnut Street, featured a domed clock tower on the same axis as the lower cupola of Independence Hall. On the Fifth and Sixth street sides, three-story wings extended outward from four-story central pavilions with monumental entrances and elaborate mansard roofs. On the Chestnut Street side, pavilions with two-story colonnaded porticoes framed Independence Hall.

Before ground could be broken, another public outcry arose over the plans to "desecrate the sacred enclosure" of Independence Square.[6] Besides opposition to the destruction of historic structures, many Philadelphians were now upset by the decision to keep the municipal government and courts downtown, instead of following the city's development westward. The City Councils, divided between supporters of Penn Square and Independence Square, were deadlocked.

In response, the state legislature ordered a special referendum in October 1870 to decide between Penn Square and Washington

Square as the site for the new public buildings, leaving Independence Square untouched. The vote was a decisive victory for Penn Square, with 51,623 votes versus 32,825 for Washington. The former Centre Square was finally fulfilling the role William Penn had assigned it nearly two centuries earlier.

McArthur, still the official architect for the public buildings, began to revise his designs once again. This time, he was aided by his former teacher and mentor, Thomas U. Walter. Walter, beggared by the 1873 financial panic, had accepted a position as draftsman in the office of the man he had personally favored as the architect of City Hall. At first, McArthur was instructed to erect four public buildings on Penn Square, leaving the intersection of Broad and Market streets in place. Once construction had begun, it was decided to leave Penn Square intact and erect only one building, creating the traffic obstacle that exists today.

Gradually, the new Public Buildings assumed their current aspect, a four-sided structure around a central courtyard with towered pavilions over massive arched entrances on each side. The domed central tower, topped by a statue of William Penn, grew taller with each successive rendering; city leaders insisted on this elongation to match the height of the District of Columbia's Washington Monument, which was finally being completed after a long hiatus. Hundreds of allegorical statues and carvings, ranging from the crops of Pennsylvania to the massive statue of Penn, became integral elements of the design. Architectural historian Michael J. Lewis has theorized that Walter, who before his financial downfall was instrumental in having McArthur chosen as the City Hall architect, effectively codesigned City Hall as it now stands.[7]

Construction began on the foundations in 1871, and the cornerstone was laid on July 4, 1874, with hopes that City Hall would be finished for the Centennial Exposition. Thanks to cost overruns, graft, and bureaucratic bungling, the "Marble Monster" was not finished until 1901, by which time it had become an architectural fossil and a symbol of political corruption.[8]

Centennial Exposition Main Building

Proposed location: George's Hill, West Fairmount Park
Period of origination: ca. 1873
Architect/Builder: Collins & Autenreith

In 1873, the U.S. Centennial Commission announced a competition for the buildings of the International Exhibition planned for Fairmount Park in 1876. The fair's showpiece was the main exhibit building, expected to cover twenty-five of the exhibition's fifty acres. While most of the building was meant to be temporary, a five-acre section of the structure would remain as a permanent museum and art gallery called Memorial Hall, in memory of the country's founding fathers. From the forty designs received from unknown amateurs and renowned architects, ten preliminary designs were selected for a second competition in October 1873.

The building committee's first choice for the second round, a pavilion by Central Park designer Calvert Vaux and collaborator G. K. Radford, was disqualified because it did not conform to the competition specifications. The top four qualifying designs were all produced by Philadelphians, whose wildly eclectic creations drew on historical models to announce the nation's emergence as a global power. All four were also cathedral-like in appearance, symbolizing the apotheosis of the Revolutionary generation in the country's secular pantheon.

Fourth-place winners H. A. and J. P. Sims produced a church-like building in the shape of a Greek cross, with Romanesque windows and a massive domed tower. John McArthur Jr. and Joseph Wilson, third-prize winners, designed a cruciform Gothic building

Facing page: The Collins & Autenreith design for Memorial Hall (permanent section only), reproduced in the May 7, 1874, edition of the New York *Daily Graphic*. (Collection of the author.)

that resembled both a cathedral and a train shed, while the second-prize winner, Samuel Sloan, also designed an impressive neo-Baroque structure.

First-prize winners Collins & Autenrieth created an elaborate Venetian Renaissance cathedral as the permanent structure, also in the form of a Greek cross, with temporary wings extending from both ends. Its huge central dome, rising to 390 feet, was divided into thirteen segments, decorated by American eagles and lucarnes, and topped by a two-tiered cupola supporting a figure of Liberty. It was surrounded by four smaller domes, also topped by statues, at each corner of the central pavilion. A two-story arched entryway stood on either end of the transept, surmounted by monumental statuary groups. Two tiers of clerestory windows provided additional light for the galleries below.

A tad late, the Centennial Commission realized that its prize-winning design was far too expensive. The projected construction costs were between $8 and $10 million, more than the budget of the entire Centennial. The commission then reconsidered the simpler, more economical design of Vaux and Radford. Even that design proved too extravagant after the financial panic of 1873 shrank the budget for the main building to only $2 million. Faced with unacceptable demands for cost reductions, both Collins & Autenrieth and Vaux & Radford withdrew.

In 1874, the Centennial Commission selected the design of exposition engineers Joseph Wilson and Henry Pettit. Adapted from the Vaux & Radford pavilion design, their utilitarian structure was constructed of wrought-iron columns with brick to a height of seven feet, and topped by a glass and iron frame. The simple design cost only $73,000 per acre, coming in well below budget at $1.4 million. To further simplify planning, the permanent art museum was made a separate structure, designed by Hermann J. Schwarzmann, chief engineer of the Centennial Exposition. Schwarzmann's elaborate Memorial Hall, which at $1.6 million cost more to build than the twenty-acre Main Building, is the only major Centennial building to survive.

Chestnut Hill–Main Line Parkway

Proposed location: Montgomery County, Roxborough, Chestnut Hill
Period of origination: ca. 1885
Architect/Builder: Paul Philippe Cret, others

Plans for a direct connection between Philadelphia's two most upscale residential districts—Chestnut Hill in the northwest, and the Main Line outside the city—date back to the nineteenth century. As early as 1885, Pennsylvania Railroad president Alexander J. Cassatt and Chestnut Hill developer Henry H. Houston recommended a highway between the two areas to connect northwest Philadelphia with the Railroad's Main Line, and to build up the open land in rural Upper Roxborough, much of which was owned by the Houston family.

In the early 1900s, increased automotive traffic and suburban growth revived interest in a Chestnut Hill–Main Line Boulevard, which would reduce the driving distance between the two regions from fourteen miles to seven. With an eye to developing Houston holdings in Upper Roxborough, Henry Houston's son Samuel offered to donate the land on which the boulevard would be built. Houston recommended extending the boulevard north and east from Chestnut Hill to Jenkintown, another upscale suburb. This "social highway," in the words of one newspaper, would serve as "the main avenue of communication between sections whose residents are in the millionaire class."[9]

Fifteen years later, the Chestnut Hill–Main Line Boulevard was still on the drawing board, despite the administration's assertion that "progress has been made towards creation of a Chestnut Hill–Bryn Mawr Road, crossing the Wissahickon Creek and Schuylkill River, and extending through Montgomery County to connect at its western end with the Lincoln Highway."[10] In February 1927, the consolidated City Council passed the necessary legislation for the project and appropriated $1 million for construction.

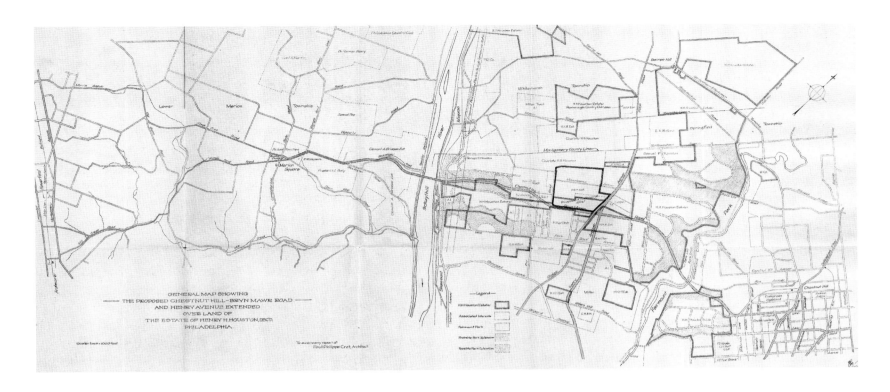

Paul Philippe Cret's proposed 1927 layout for the Bryn Mawr–Chestnut Hill Parkway, originating at Lancaster Avenue in Ardmore (at far left), proceeding northeast across the Schuylkill River and through Roxborough and the Wissahickon Valley, and connecting with Germantown Avenue at Bethlehem Pike in Chestnut Hill. (Collections of the University of Pennsylvania Archives.)

Paul Philippe Cret conducted the preliminary study for the Chestnut Hill–Bryn Mawr Road (also referred to as the Chestnut Hill–Ardmore Boulevard) and prepared designs for the bridges spanning the Schuylkill River and Wissahickon Creek. Cret's proposal had the boulevard following Mill Creek Road from Lancaster Avenue in Ardmore (where Suburban Square now stands), then bearing north on Soapstone Road and crossing the river at what is now the Schuylkill Center for Environmental Education. In Roxborough, the route followed current-day Cathedral Road (skirting the planned Episcopal Cathedral, another Houston family project) and intersected a new traffic artery called Henry Avenue.

The road spanned the Wissahickon Valley and entered Chestnut Hill at Indian Rock in Fairmount Park, skirted the western side of the Houston estate Druim Moir, then followed Gravers' Lane. On the west side of Pastorius Park, the road joined the extension of Lincoln Drive (some alternate designs show Pastorius Park redesigned as a traffic rotary into which the Chestnut Hill–Bryn Mawr Road and Lincoln Drive both merged). From there, the road veered northwest to join the key intersection of Germantown

Avenue and Bethlehem Pike, providing access to northern Montgomery County.

In 1932, the Regional Planning Federation of the Philadelphia Tri-State District, the first interstate planning organization in the Philadelphia region, reworked the Chestnut Hill–Bryn Mawr Road as the Suburban Belt-Line Parkway. Instead of running through Chestnut Hill, the Belt-Line Parkway skirted the city to the west, through lightly developed Springfield and Whitemarsh townships. The Depression and World War II delayed the parkway indefinitely, despite local business owners' periodic efforts to revive it.

After World War II, the Houston estate, still anxious to develop its Upper Roxborough holdings, pressured the city government to revive the Chestnut Hill–Bryn Mawr Road plan. By this time, Chestnut Hill civic groups and even some members of the Houston family opposed the highway, saying it would worsen the increasing congestion in the region. In 1955, the city officially dropped the plan for a new north-south road connecting Northwest Philadelphia with the Main Line. Today, travelers between the two areas must use one of the three prewar options and cross the Schuylkill at East Falls, Manayunk, or Conshohocken.

Schuylkill River Improvements

Proposed location: East and west banks of the Schuylkill River
Period of origination: ca. 1905
Architect/Builder: Paul Philippe Cret, Charles Louis Borie, Clarence Clark Zantzinger, John F. Collins, and others

Despite efforts to protect the city's water supply by establishing Fairmount Park, the Schuylkill River became heavily polluted during the nineteenth century. Outside the park, factories, refineries, and slums lined the river as far south as Point Breeze and as far north as Pottstown. When a typhoid epidemic ravaged Philadelphia in the 1890s, civic leaders took steps to cleanse the Schuylkill by building new water-pumping stations with sand-filtration beds throughout the city. Architects, hoping this action presaged the rebirth of the Schuylkill, drew up plans to make the waterway as beautiful and elegant as the Seine in Paris.

In 1905, Paul Philippe Cret, working with Charles Louis Borie and Clarence Clark Zantzinger, completed a design, "Improvement of the Schuylkill River Embankments with Adjacent Parks and Avenues," for the Fairmount Park Commission. A natural extension of Cret's plans for the proposed Fairmount Parkway (later the Benjamin Franklin Parkway), these improvements were meant to beautify the Schuylkill River from Fairmount Avenue south to Bartram's Garden.

Cret's study transformed dusty East and West River Drives into elegant riverside parkways punctuated by plazas, circles, and bridges. Cret envisioned a boat landing and shelter at the foot of Fairmount Avenue designed to harmonize with the architecture of the adjacent Water Works. Parks and recreational areas would replace the decaying industrial district on both sides of the river below South Street. In congested Center City, Cret and his colleagues proposed reuniting Philadelphia with its river by roofing over the highways and railroad tracks that lined the Schuylkill, providing access via landscaped overpasses and embankments.

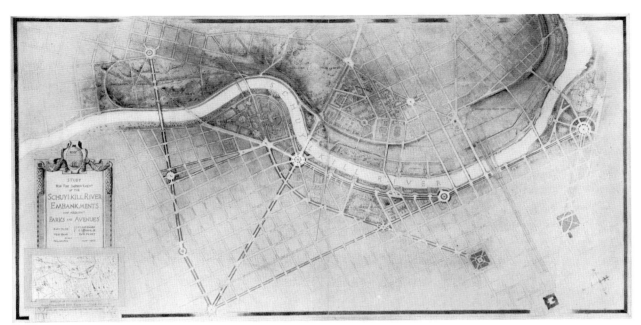

The 1905 proposal, "Improvement of the Schuylkill River Embankments with Adjacent Parks and Avenues." According to the legend at left, Paul Philippe Cret was responsible for the west bank of the Schuylkill, while Charles Louis Borie and Clarence Clark Zantzinger designed the east bank. Besides riverbank improvements, the architects proposed a series of diagonal boulevards cutting through South Philadelphia and crossing into West Philadelphia, an extension of Grays Ferry Avenue to Rittenhouse Square as a parkway, and traffic circles at University Avenue, Locust Street, and the new Art Museum at Fairmount. (Athenaeum of Philadelphia.)

Since the city took no actions against the industries polluting the Schuylkill River, most of Cret's riparian improvements remained unrealized while the city focused on Fairmount Parkway and the Art Museum. During the first two decades of the twentieth century, East River Drive became a busy blacktop highway, a far cry from the stylish boulevard envisioned by Cret.

In 1924, civic activist John Frederick Lewis, author of *The Redemption of the Lower Schuylkill*, launched a crusade to clean up the river and its surrounding area. Lewis proposed developing the east bank of the Schuylkill in Center City as a residential district with leisure and recreation facilities. The completion of the Museum of Art and Fairmount Parkway, along with the Pennsylvania Railroad's plans for a majestic new station at Thirtieth Street, drew Philadelphians' attention to its western river and spurred the creation of the Schuylkill River Development Project. Once again, Cret produced plans for new bridges across the Schuylkill, a "west

embankment drive" stretching north and south from Market Street, and the extension of East River Drive from Fairmount Avenue south to Walnut Street. In addition, the development project planned to upgrade sewage-disposal systems to reduce the river's heavy pollution.

Bridges went up and work began on the River Drives, but most of the Schuylkill River Development Project's agenda was deferred by the Depression and World War II. After the war, with Philadelphia's factories and railroads in decline, Edmund Bacon proposed high-rise luxury apartments on the Schuylkill's east bank. In 1965, landscape architect John F. Collins drew up plans similar to Cret's designs from sixty years earlier, with a stone walking path, formal plazas, and groves of trees. Farther north on East River Drive, the Ellen Phillips Samuel Memorial, first envisioned in 1907, was completed in 1960, with a series of statues tracing an emblematic history of the nation.

BOAT LANDING AND SHELTER
AT THE END OF FAIRMOUNT AVENUE
DEVELOPED ELEVATION AT ONE INCH EQUALS SIXTEEN FEET

PAUL PHILIPPE CRET
Architect

Paul Philippe Cret's design for a boat landing and shelter at the foot of Fairmount Avenue, north of the Water Works (partly visible at far right). (© The Architectural Archives of the University of Pennsylvania.)

Over the past two decades, antipollution measures set in motion in the 1970s have come to fruition, and the Schuylkill is home once again to numerous species of fish, as well as the occasional whale and otter. During the same period, a combination of public and private plans to improve the Schuylkill's east and west banks has gathered steam. The Schuylkill River Trail, extending from the southeastern tip of Fairmount Park at the Art Museum to Spruce Street along the east bank, is nearing completion after more than forty years and $130 million. Luxury apartment buildings on the east bank are mirrored in the reflective glass of the Cira Centre on the west bank. Farther south, the University of Pennsylvania is developing its riverfront property into a Schuylkill Gateway that will serve as the entrance to University City and West Philadelphia.

Meanwhile, the Schuylkill River Development Council (SRDC) has launched an ambitious master plan to develop the Schuylkill south of the Fairmount Water Works dam. Echoing Cret's 1905 study, the SRDC plans an extension of Fairmount Park to the lower banks of the Schuylkill through improved public access, connections to such historic sites as Bartram's Garden, and the acquisition and reclamation of industrial sites.

Episcopal Cathedral

Location: Ridge Avenue at Cathedral Road, Upper Roxborough
Period of origination: ca. 1917
Architect/Builder: Watson, Edkins & Thompson

Episcopalians, though relatively few in number, represented a disproportionately large segment of the country's economic, political, and social elite in the early twentieth century. As the Gilded Age drew to a close, the Episcopal oligarchy seemed obsessed with erecting urban cathedrals that would rival the great Catholic churches of Europe in stature and beauty. In 1892, the cornerstone

was laid for the Cathedral of St. John the Divine in New York City. In 1907, the foundation stone was set atop Mount St. Alban for the Protestant Episcopal Cathedral of the District of Columbia (today Washington National Cathedral).

Philadelphia's early plans for an Episcopal cathedral were deeply rooted in the original concept of the Fairmount Parkway. In 1917, Jacques Gréber's initial design for the parkway featured a domed Romanesque cathedral flanked by a campanile, built on the north side of the parkway between Twenty-first and Twenty-second streets, where the Rodin Museum stands today. While the nineteenth-century Roman Catholic Cathedral of SS. Peter and Paul dominated the parkway's midpoint at Logan Circle, the modern

The architect's model for the Episcopal Cathedral in Upper Roxborough, looking northeast toward Ridge Avenue. Only the apse and the first two bays of the eastern end (the section beyond the second tower, in the upper right-hand corner) were ever erected, along with two side chapels. According to Dr. Thomas McClellan, rector of St. Mary's Church, the model alone cost about $10,000 in the 1920s; its location today is unknown. (Courtesy of St. Mary's at the Cathedral.)

Episcopal cathedral would mark the transition between urban Philadelphia and its affluent, mostly Protestant garden suburbs.

By 1919, the proposed cathedral had become a cruciform Gothic structure located farther south, overlooking the Schuylkill River west of the current Park Towne Place. That summer, Episcopal bishop Philip M. Rhinelander held outdoor services on the site. By this time, support for the parkway location was waning in light of the boulevard's slow progress, the heavily polluted Schuylkill, and the Episcopal elite's accelerating migration to neighborhoods outside Center City.

In 1922, Samuel F. Houston sold the Episcopal Diocese of Pennsylvania a plot of land in rural Roxborough that he had unsuccessfully offered to the city for the Sesqui-Centennial Exposition. The diocese paid $500,000 for more than 100 acres south of Ridge Avenue in Upper Roxborough, near the Montgomery County border. Houston's land, which marked the approximate geographic and population center of the Philadelphia Diocese, stood on one of the highest points in the city.

Buoyed by the booming economy of the 1920s, the diocese made plans to build the largest Gothic cathedral in the world. The cruciform structure designed by ecclesiastical architects Watson, Edkins & Thompson extended nearly 1,000 feet along its east-west axis and boasted both a 300-foot bell tower over the central crossing and a lower tower over the apse. Rising more than 500 feet above sea level, the cathedral's central tower would be visible for miles. The exterior would be constructed of Wissahickon schist, the interior of golden Kasota stone. Vast plazas and ancillary structures would encircle the cathedral, while its immense campus would be dotted with boys' and girls' schools, a home for the aged, an orphans' home, and housing for retired clergy.

By the time ground was broken for the Cathedral Church of Christ in June 1932, the Great Depression had paralyzed the nation. On All Saints' Day 1934, the first Mass was held in the unfinished St. Mary's Chapel. This section, intended to stand in the rear of the apse of the completed cathedral, was paid for by Annie Masden Vaughan Watson as a memorial to her mother, Mary Masden Vaughan. The deepening economic crisis, however, forced the Episcopal diocese to reevaluate its grandiose scheme. In 1935, the Cathedral Building Committee issued a new design reducing the size of the cathedral by nearly one-half. The redesign eliminated the surrounding buildings and apse tower and replaced the square central tower with a lower octagonal lantern modeled on the one at Ely Cathedral.

Despite this retrenchment, construction ground to a halt by 1940, with only the shells of St. Mary's Chapel and two side chapels completed. The western end of the truncated structure was walled in with a "temporary" facing of corrugated metal that would remain in place for four decades. By the time prosperity returned after World War II, the original cathedral builders were either elderly or dead, and the Episcopal Church's priorities had shifted from massive cathedrals to social reform on the parish level. In the 1960s, the Episcopal diocese officially dropped plans to complete the cathedral and even considered abandoning the structure completely, leaving it to decay as a memorial ruin.

After much discussion, the diocese built a $22 million retirement community, Cathedral Village, on the property adjacent to the unfinished cathedral between 1977 and 1981. During the same period, Edward R. Watson of Mirick Pearson Batcheler redesigned St. Mary's Chapel as a parish church, replacing the metal shield on its west end with a glass wall. Watson discovered that in the haste to finish the chapel before money ran out in the 1930s, the last fill stones for the roof had been laid in place with wadded newspapers rather than mortar. For nearly fifty years, St. Mary's congregation had been at risk of being crushed by falling masonry.

Today, St. Mary's Church (its roof stones securely mortared) ministers to the Episcopal community of Upper Roxborough, including its neighbor, Cathedral Village. Meanwhile, the former Church of the Saviour at Thirty-eighth and Chestnut streets in West Philadelphia has served as Pennsylvania's Episcopal cathedral since 1992.

City Hall Tower

Proposed location: City Hall Square
Period of origination: 1924
Architect/Builder: Paul Philippe Cret and Harry Sternfeld;
   Vincent G. Kling

By the time it was completed in 1901, Philadelphia's Second Empire City Hall was not only out of fashion, but also a symbol of the municipal graft, arrogance, and sloth that had led Lincoln Steffens to label the city "corrupt and contented."[11] A deep-seated loathing of City Hall was one of the hallmarks of being progressive: Architect Ernest Flagg saw the building as a monument to bad taste, while essayist Agnes Repplier referred to it as "that perfect miracle of ugliness and inconvenience, that really remarkable combination of bulk and insignificance."[12]

The increase in automotive traffic in Center City, and the resulting traffic jams around City Hall, provided another incentive for either remodeling or removing the structure. In 1913, Thomas Martindale proposed running Market Street through the east-west axis of City Hall, necessitating the widening of its eastern and western arches and the removal of the central tower.

In 1924, Paul Philippe Cret, also seeking to improve traffic flow on Market Street, proposed a redesign for Penn Square. Cret reversed Martindale's plan, removing all of City Hall except its tower, stripped of most of its statuary and ornamentation. Cret's design caught the imagination of Philadelphia's progressive leaders. Several, including *Ladies Home Journal* editor Edward W. Bok and philanthropist Eli Kirk Price, formed the Philadelphia Commission, dedicated to beautifying the city primarily by demolishing City Hall.

This 1927 conception of City Hall Tower, prepared by Paul Philippe Cret and Harry Sternfeld, shows the streamlined tower as it would appear looking north from South Broad Street, with a fountain and reflecting pool at its base. (© The Architectural Archives of the University of Pennsylvania.)

A 1933 view of Cret and Sternfeld's proposed redesign shows the former City Hall Square looking northwest toward the Schuylkill. To the right of City Hall Tower, a U-shaped municipal services building stands on the site of Reyburn Plaza, housing the city offices displaced by the demolition of McArthur's building. (Temple University Libraries, Urban Archives, Philadelphia.)

Under their sponsorship, Cret and his student Harry Sternfeld designed a comprehensive plan for the tower, which they presented to the City Planning Commission in 1929. In Cret and Sternfeld's redesign, the streamlined tower was sheathed in a modern façade, unadorned except for the Calder statue of William Penn at its top and a carving of the city coat of arms near its base. Behind the four clock faces, a hidden carillon sounded the hours. On the south side of the tower's base, a tree-lined fountain and reflecting pool extended toward Broad Street. Automobiles streamed around a Penn Square reshaped into a giant traffic circle reminiscent of the Place de la Concorde, with City Hall Tower as its Obelisk of Luxor. Municipal offices were relocated to a U-shaped building on nearby Reyburn Plaza.

The Depression saved City Hall from possible destruction, giving Philadelphians time to reevaluate McArthur's masterpiece. Even Cret began to think kindly about it, telling the *Bulletin* in 1937 that City Hall "is part of the city's history and tradition. It is a date in the evolution of the city. All we can say is that it has a bad location and if we were building today we would not do it in this way. . . . Nevertheless, we must have some respect for those who have gone on before us. . . . You cannot change permanent edifices to suit the fancy of each generation."[13]

In the early 1950s, during the Penn Center redevelopment campaign, architect Vincent G. Kling and city planner Edmund N. Bacon revived Cret's design. In 1932, as part of his architecture thesis at Cornell University, Bacon had proposed a "New Civic Center for Philadelphia" that adapted Cret's plan of replacing most of City Hall with a public plaza and moving the city offices to newer buildings.[14] Twenty years later, Bacon saw the demolition of the bulk of City Hall as a logical extension of the renewal that would replace Broad Street Station and the Chinese Wall with modern offices. Kling's early models of Penn Center show City Hall once again reduced to a streamlined tower, this time surrounded by a square plaza lined with trees on its western side. A reconnected Market Street extended through Penn Square, while a loop road routed Broad Street traffic around the tower.

The prospect of demolishing City Hall appealed to the new Democratic administration, which saw its destruction as a symbolic exorcism of the ghosts of their corrupt Republican predecessors. However, the city comptroller estimated that it would cost $25 million to destroy the world's largest free-standing masonry structure, leaving the municipal government with insufficient funds for a new home.

By this time, attitudes toward Victorian design were beginning to soften, thanks in part to a 1953 exhibition at the Art Alliance and the subsequent publication of Theodore B. White's *Philadelphia Architecture in the Nineteenth Century*. In 1957, a subcommittee of the American Institute of Architects gave City Hall official recognition as a major architectural monument. Today, City Hall is considered one of the finest Second Empire structures in the nation and a civil engineering landmark, especially now that a multimillion-dollar rehabilitation campaign has restored the original majesty of its exterior and major public spaces.

Original Penn Center

Proposed location: Area bordered by Market Street, Fifteenth Street, JFK Boulevard, and Eighteenth Street
Period of origination: ca. 1925
Architect/Builder: Vincent G. Kling, others

As early as the 1920s, plans were underway to demolish the hated Chinese Wall that carried Pennsylvania Railroad trains between West Philadelphia and Broad Street Station. In 1925, the city government reached an agreement with the Pennsylvania Railroad to remove the Wall and relocate the main railroad station to the west bank of the Schuylkill River. West of Broad Street, narrow Filbert Street would be renamed Pennsylvania Boulevard and widened to a ninety-foot approach to the new train station. Tall office towers would line the eighteen acres covered by Broad Street Station and the Chinese Wall, generating $2 million a year in taxes for the city treasury. In expectation of this imminent improvement, demolition began on the Wall in the late 1920s.

Although the new railroad station (Thirtieth Street Station) was completed by 1934, the Depression and World War II postponed the demolition of Broad Street Station and the remainder of the Wall for twenty years. Their replacement with a modern business complex was an integral element of the Center City redevelopment proposed by the City Planning Commission at the 1947 Better Philadelphia Exhibition. The original plan for the Triangle (the central business district bounded by the Schuylkill River, Market Street, and the Benjamin Franklin Parkway) included contributions from Louis I. Kahn, Oskar Stonorov, and Roy Larson.

When the Pennsylvania Railroad announced definite plans to demolish Broad Street Station and the Chinese Wall in the early 1950s, City Planning Commission executive director Edmund N. Bacon and architect Vincent G. Kling unveiled their concept for what Bacon called Penn Center. Their original design, stretching between Fifteenth and Eighteenth streets, featured seven build-

City Planning Commission executive director Edmund N. Bacon (standing) and two other officials study a model of the Penn Center complex before a presentation luncheon in March 1953. At the right end of the model stands Vincent G. Kling's proposed City Hall Tower, updating Cret and Sternfeld's design from the 1920s. (Temple University Libraries, Urban Archives, Philadelphia.)

ings, including four office towers, a television and radio building, a hotel, and a bus station. Tall, rectangular structures of varying heights were staggered and set back from the street to provide open space and to prevent uniformity. The easternmost and westernmost buildings were placed on a north-south axis to admit light and to mark the borders of the complex.

Using Rockefeller Center as their model, Bacon and Kling designed a diverse, pedestrian-friendly complex with terraces, roof gardens, and a sunken parklike concourse between the structures. According to biographer Gregory Heller, Bacon also drew on his memories of the Forbidden City in Beijing to create Penn Center,

or covering much of the proposed concourse. Facing financial difficulties, the Railroad sold much of the site piecemeal, further undermining the master design. As Penn Center took shape in the 1950s and 1960s, the tall, nondescript office blocks that lined Market Street and Pennsylvania Boulevard (renamed John F. Kennedy Boulevard in 1964) were dubbed the second Chinese Wall.

During the building boom of the 1980s, Penn Center expanded westward to the Schuylkill River with the erection of Eight and Ten Penn Center, Independence Blue Cross Building, Mellon Bank Tower, and Commerce Square. While many of Penn Center's original buildings have been refaced or redeveloped over the past two decades, the overall layout of the complex remains uninviting. Open spaces between buildings are barren, windy corridors, while the sunken terraces remain dank, cramped, shadowy spaces despite repeated makeovers.

Even with the shortsighted alterations to the Bacon-Kling design, Penn Center remains a pioneering model of urban renewal that prevented a wholesale decampment of Philadelphia's businesses to the suburbs in the postwar period.

seeing the buildings as a series of Chinese gates which pedestrians would pass by and under before confronting the Imperial Throne Room in the form of City Hall Tower.[15] Several of the buildings rested on steel columns, enhancing the sense of openness and accessibility. An underground parking garage and shopping concourse kept cars off the street and allowed commuters to access adjacent Suburban Station.

The Pennsylvania Railroad, which still owned the Penn Center site, altered the Bacon-Kling plan to maximize profitability, increasing the size of the buildings, reducing open space, and eliminating

Broad Street Subway
Roosevelt Boulevard Extension

Proposed location: Northeast Philadelphia
Period of origination: ca. 1928
Architect/Builder: Various

For nearly a century, the city government has intended to provide Northeast Philadelphia with rapid transit, first as a means to develop the area, and later as a means to control its explosive growth in population. In 1913, only six years after Philadelphia's first subway-elevated line opened, the city's transit commissioner suggested extending the Frankford Elevated to Bustleton via the ten-year-old Northeast Boulevard (renamed Theodore Roosevelt Boulevard in 1920).

On September 1, 1928, the Broad Street Subway began running the six-mile route between City Hall and Olney Avenue. Shortly after the subway opened, Mayor Harry Mackey called extending it north to Roosevelt Boulevard a "defensive measure" to "keep citizens of this city inside the municipal boundaries and stop the exodus to Mont-

gomery and other suburban counties and to the New Jersey suburbs."[16] In 1931, the City Council proposed extending the Broad Street Subway to Oxford Circle along Roosevelt Boulevard at a cost of $18 million. While the line was extended south to Snyder Avenue by 1933, the worsening Depression stopped the northern extension of the subway.

After World War II, the rapid development of Northeast Philadelphia prompted the city government to reconsider extending the Broad Street Subway farther north. In 1949, city consultants mapped three possible routes for an extended high-speed subway-surface line, including a route branching off at Hunting Park and

The Sears Distribution Center (its tower visible above the construction sign) proudly announces plans for a new parking facility and subway station in May 1967. Finished that year at a cost of $1 million, Sears' subway station, never used, was demolished with the rest of the Distribution Center in 1994. (Temple University Libraries, Urban Archives, Philadelphia.)

following Roosevelt Boulevard to Pennypack Circle. Estimated costs for the subway-surface line ranged between $55 and $59 million.

The subway was extended north to Fern Rock in 1956, where it became an aboveground line that connected to a Regional Rail Station. Once again, expansion of the subway ground to a halt until, in the early 1960s, growing congestion prompted the City Planning Commission to propose a Northeastern Expressway. The four-lane depressed highway would extend along Roosevelt Boulevard from Hunting Park Avenue, then follow Pennway Street to the Delaware River extension of the Pennsylvania Turnpike in Bensalem, Bucks County.

An extension of the Broad Street Subway was proposed as part of the expressway, running on a center median fifty-six feet wide between the northbound and southbound lanes. This time, voters approved an $87.3 million bond issue to pay for the nine-mile extension. In anticipation, the Sears Distribution Center at Adams Avenue and Roosevelt Boulevard built a basement subway station in 1967 at a cost of $1 million.

The Pennsylvania Department of Transportation acquired and demolished a number of houses in preparation for a Northeast Expressway/Broad Street Subway extension. Rather than build a Northeast subway, Mayor Frank Rizzo transferred funds to the Center City rail tunnel and airport rail line. The Northeast Expressway died when PennDOT halted all funding on highway projects in 1977. Lean municipal budgets during the 1970s and 1980s put a northern subway extension on indefinite hold, although money was found to construct new stations at Oregon and Pattison avenues in the south to serve the sports complex. Meanwhile, the unused Adams Avenue subway station was demolished with the rest of the Sears complex in 1994.

In 1999, the City Planning Commission, PennDOT, and the Southeastern Pennsylvania Transportation Authority proposed improving highway and transit access to the Northeast through extending the Roosevelt Expressway, the Broad Street Subway, or both. In 2001, the City Planning Commission gave preliminary approval to a continuation of the Broad Street Subway along Roosevelt Boulevard to Southampton Road, with no expressway extension. At Blue Grass Road, the subway would emerge from underground and continue to Southampton as an elevated or surface-level train in the Roosevelt Boulevard median. A one-mile spur would connect the subway line at the intersection of the boulevard, Bustleton Avenue, and Levick Street with the Market-Frankford Line at the Bridge-Platt station. An estimated 130,000 riders would use the new line daily.

Assuming federal funding can be obtained for the project (the estimated cost ranged between $3 and $4.5 billion in 2002), construction for the Broad Street Subway extension is tentatively scheduled to begin in 2009, with completion in 2018. Meanwhile, thousands of Northeast residents continue their decades-long wait for a rapid transit system that will carry them safely to Center City in twenty minutes and save them the hours they now spend in traffic on one of the deadliest roads in Philadelphia.

Municipal Concert Hall

Proposed location: Block bordered by Logan Circle and Cherry, Eighteenth, and Nineteenth streets
Period of origination: ca. 1930
Architect/Builder: Voorhees, Gmelin & Walker

From its inception, the great parkway between City Hall and Fairmount was designed to be Philadelphia's Avenue of the Arts, a succession of cultural institutions culminating in the new Museum of Art atop its acropolis. Besides the Free Library and the Franklin Institute, city leaders hoped to see the Fairmount Parkway lined with magnificent buildings housing the American Philosophical Society, Pennsylvania Academy of Fine Arts, Episcopal Cathedral, Convention Hall, Municipal Stadium, a victory hall for public celebrations, branches of Temple University and the University of Pennsylvania, and an opera house and concert hall.

In the 1920s, music lovers Cyrus H. K. Curtis and his son-in-law Edward W. Bok, respectively the publisher and editor of the *Ladies Home Journal*, planned a replacement on the parkway for the Academy of Music. In June 1930, Curtis paid $1.1 million for the Wills Eye Hos-

pital, located on the south side of Logan Circle since 1834 in a building originally designed by Thomas U. Walter. Additional property at Nineteenth and Race streets was acquired from the Franklin Institute, which had planned to build on that site before selecting Twentieth Street instead.

When Edward Bok died shortly afterward, his son W. Curtis Bok took up the campaign to build the concert hall. With his mother, Mary Louise Curtis Bok (founder and first president of the Curtis Institute of Music), his grandfather Cyrus Curtis, and Eli Kirk Price, Bok founded the Philadelphia Arts Association to raise $4 million for the new facility.

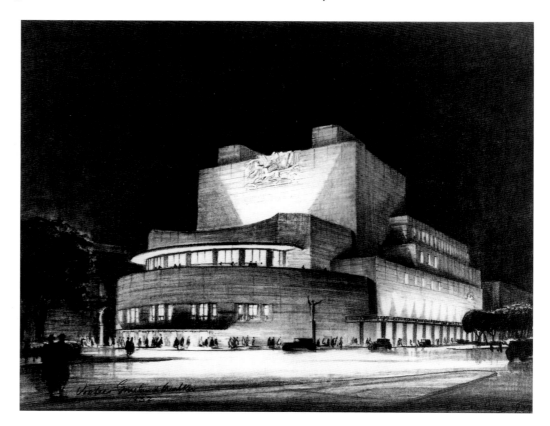

The architect's conception of the Bok-Curtis Concert Hall at night, looking southwest toward the intersection of Race Street, Eighteenth Street, and the parkway. (Athenaeum of Philadelphia.)

The association selected Ralph T. Walker of the New York firm of Voorhees, Gmelin and Walker as the hall's architect. By early 1932, Walker had produced designs for a streamlined building that contained two auditoriums seating 4,000 and 1,500, and a recital hall seating 500. Walker's design placed the two larger halls back-to-back, with a single large fly tower emerging from a rectangular base with setbacks. The hall's decoration was limited to a bas-relief of mythical figures and animals at the top of the fly tower.

The semicircular entrance to the building, topped by a glass-enclosed restaurant, softened the angularity of the overall design. This rounded bow stood where the parkway cut diagonally across Eighteenth Street and looked northeast toward LeBrun and Notman's Roman Catholic cathedral. Sketches of the Art Moderne structure at night resemble an ocean liner cutting through the dark, its bridge and funnels ablaze with lights.

In 1933, the worsening financial crisis and the deaths of board members Cyrus Curtis and Eli Kirk Price made construction of the concert hall impossible. Writing to Walker, who did not even receive his commission, W. Curtis Bok explained: "Because of the recent passage of dividends on all Curtis stock, my family is rapidly heading toward the ranks of the unemployed."[17] After being used as a juvenile court from 1934 to 1938, the old Wills Eye Hospital was demolished in 1944 at the instruction of the Curtis family. The Four Seasons Hotel has stood on the site since 1983.

The Bok-Curtis Concert Hall was one of several parkway projects scuttled by the Depression. Plans for six other proposed institutions were scrapped; others were erected in scaled-back form and facing side streets. During the 1930s, only three new buildings opened along the parkway, followed by two in the 1940s. Large stretches of the parkway remained open and raw well into the 1950s, when the Youth Study Center, the Parkway House, and Park Towne Place filled some of the gaps. Today, the Benjamin Franklin Parkway is still a work in progress, as attested by ongoing studies and recommendations to improve and populate the space.

Center City Redevelopment

Proposed location: Center City
Period of origination: ca. 1939
Architect/Builder: Louis I. Kahn

According to Vincent Scully, Philadelphia was Louis I. Kahn's city; here, as a small boy walking the streets, he discovered "what he wanted to do his whole life."[18] What Kahn wanted to do for much of his professional life was recreate from scratch the city in which he had grown up and studied architecture. Kahn's visionary designs attempted to liberate Philadelphia, especially Center City, from the demons plaguing it during much of the twentieth century: shabby and obsolete Victorian architecture, growing traffic congestion, and lack of decent, affordable housing.

Most of Kahn's early work involved public or subsidized housing, including projects for the newly founded Philadelphia Housing Authority. In 1939, Kahn helped develop an information campaign for the U.S. Housing Authority designed to overcome opposition to public housing. As part of a related exhibition, "Houses and Housing," at the Museum of Modern Art, Kahn contributed a large panel entitled "Housing in the Rational City Plan."

While Kahn's Rational City Plan provided a number of housing solutions for various environments, the one that captured public attention was his plan for Center City, inspired by Le Corbusier's radical scheme for a new Paris. In Kahn's design, most of the existing city is leveled and replaced by symmetrical rows of megalithic high-rises interspersed with raised superhighways. The *Evening Bulletin* published Kahn's design in May 1941 and quoted his opinion of it; the drawing, he said, "shows the ideal use of the Philadelphia site as a functioning metropolis."[19] For most Philadelphians, preoccupied with the spreading global conflict, Kahn's visions seemed as ephemeral and irrelevant as the dismantled Futurama at the defunct World's Fair.

Kahn was employed as a consultant architect for the City Planning Commission from 1946 to 1954. In 1947, he worked with Edmund N. Bacon and Oskar Stonorov on the Better Philadelphia Exhibition, planting the megaliths from his Rational City Plan along the Schuylkill River in the Triangle district to be created by the removal of the Chinese Wall. In Philadelphia's optimistic postwar atmosphere, Kahn's position seemed to offer an opportunity to recreate his city from the ground up. It would soon bring him into direct conflict with Bacon, executive director of the Planning Commission from 1949 to 1970, who sought to build upon Philadelphia's historical framework rather than obliterate it.

Bacon's plans to dismantle most of the McArthur City Hall may have prompted Kahn's design for a new City Tower (1952–57), a network of offset and interlocked polyhedral panels surrounding three circular towers which he developed with Anne Tyng, assisted by the young Robert Venturi. The 616-foot-high structure was to be the heart of a new Civic Center erected on the banks of the Schuylkill River. To his admirers, Kahn's soaring, transparent City Tower was the antithesis of the oppressive, Byzantine bulk of the current structure; to his detractors, it looked like a clumsy child's Tinkertoy contraption.

During the same period, Kahn began a major study of urban circulation patterns. Hoping to relieve Center City of its traffic jams and parking lots, Kahn developed the idea of harbors: large, cylindrical parking towers topped by open parks. Offices and apartments would encircle the garages at irregular levels, suggesting the Coliseum in Rome. In Kahn's designs, these harbors ring Center City, swallowing cars arriving from outlying areas and guarding the core like medieval watchtowers.

Kahn also developed a hierarchical pattern of street movements, with streets designated as "go" (fast movement), "staccato" (slow movement), and "dock" (stop). Cars were banned from shopping streets, which became either pedestrian walkways or public transit corridors. When these imaginative concepts received a cold reception from Bacon, Kahn ended his consultancy with the Plan-

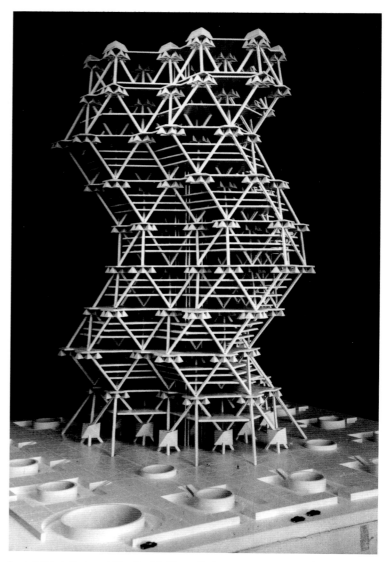

Louis I. Kahn's final model for the City Tower Project, created 1956–57. (© 1977 Louis I. Kahn Collection, University of Pennsylvania and the Pennsylvania Historical and Museum Commission.)

Kahn's sketch of his proposed Civic Center redesign ca. 1955 shows the area between City Hall (at left) and Independence Mall ringed by circular harbors and filled with modern structures. (© 1977 Louis I. Kahn Collection, University of Pennsylvania and the Pennsylvania Historical and Museum Commission.)

ning Commission and focused on such projects as the Richards Medical Research Building at the University of Pennsylvania and the Salk Institute for Biological Studies in La Jolla, California.

In 1961, thanks to a grant from the Graham Foundation for Advanced Studies in the Fine Arts, Kahn was rehired by the City Planning Commission for a redesign of Market Street East, the decaying retail corridor between Independence Mall and City Hall. Kahn expanded the scope of the project to include all of Center City, incorporating features from his earlier designs.

For the Market Street East study, Kahn's system of hierarchical street patterns evolved into Viaduct Architecture, with cars raised on elevated expressways (viaducts) that enclosed much of Center City. Arches supporting the viaduct contained warehouses, bringing to mind the Chinese Wall of the Pennsylvania Railroad.

When asked about the resemblance, Kahn pointed out that the Chinese Wall had divided the city, while his viaducts surrounded and protected it. The enclosed area resembled an urban amusement park, with a circular harbor, reservoir, heliport, fountains, a series of gates leading to the riverfront district, and truncated pyramids called hemistyles. In 1963, Kahn and the City Planning Commission parted ways again.

Kahn went on to design some of his best-known works, including the Phillips Exeter Academy Library, Kimbell Art Museum, Yale Center for British Art, and Sher-e-Bangla Nagar capital complex in Bangladesh, before his sudden death in 1974. While Kahn's physical legacy in Philadelphia may be limited, the memory of his visionary designs was fresh in the mind of his former employer toward the end of Edmund N. Bacon's own life. When Kahn's son Nathaniel interviewed Bacon for the 2003 film *My Architect*, the planner exploded with indignant rage when asked about Kahn's plans to redesign the city: "It would have been an incredible tragedy if they had built one single thing that Lou proposed in downtown Philadelphia. His ideas were all brutal, totally insensitive, and totally impractical."[20]

Crosstown Expressway/Southbridge

Proposed location: Between South and Fitzwater streets
Period of origination: ca. 1947
Architect/Builder: Modjeski and Masters

As early as 1930, the City Planning Commission had proposed a Center City ring road. At the 1947 Better Philadelphia Exhibition, this proposal took shape as a grid of expressways that channeled traffic between local streets and the planned network of parkways in and around Philadelphia. Thanks to the Federal Highway Aid Act of 1956, by 1970 Center City was boxed in on the west by the Schuylkill Expressway (I-76), on the north by the Vine Street Expressway (I-676), and on the east by the Delaware Expressway (I-95). Only the Crosstown Expressway (I-695) on the south side remained unbuilt, delayed by fierce community opposition.

For decades, South Street had been the historic center of Philadelphia's African American community. During the nineteenth century, black civil rights activist Octavius Catto and Underground Railroad conductor William Still lived on South Street. Nearby Mercy Hospital was founded in 1907 as the city's first African American hospital. In the twentieth century, South Street was the African American commercial and entertainment district, home to black jazz clubs

and theaters. Jazz great Thomas "Fats" Waller began his career playing the organ at the Royal Theater at 1524 South Street, while the Inkspots got their start at the Budweiser Tavern at Sixteenth and South. When the redevelopment of Society Hill displaced many of its minority residents in the 1950s, a number relocated to South Street.

By 1959, the City Planning Commission had announced plans for a four-lane sunken highway running along South Street, including it in the 1961 Center City Comprehensive Plan. The Pennsylvania Department of Highways began to purchase rights-of-way on and around South Street, causing many businesses and residents to sell out and leave.

In 1964, the consulting firm of Modjeski and Masters prepared a preliminary engineering report for the Crosstown Expressway, an

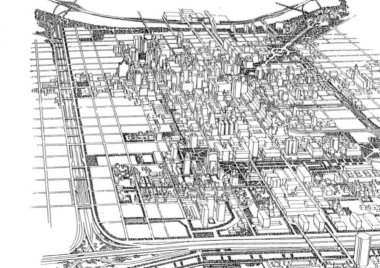

The Crosstown Expressway, running along the left side of this Philadelphia City Planning Commission map, was first proposed in the 1961 Center City Comprehensive Plan. The amended map notes that the Crosstown Expressway was canceled in 1974. (© 1963 City of Philadelphia. All rights reserved.)

eight-lane depressed highway between South and Fitzwater streets. The 2.8-mile highway, connecting the Schuylkill and Delaware Expressways on Center City's southern edge, would eradicate Kater and Bainbridge streets and displace an estimated 2,000 households. At Grays Ferry Avenue, the Crosstown would veer southwest to become the Cobbs Creek Expressway, extending through West Philadelphia and Delaware County to connect with I-95 near the airport.

As the South Street neighborhood decayed, grassroots opposition to the Crosstown Expressway grew among both blacks and whites. George Dukes, president of the South West Central Residents Association, labeled the expressway a "Mason-Dixon Line" that would segregate white neighborhoods in the north from black ones in the south.[21] Local groups like the Citizens Committee to Preserve and Develop the Crosstown Community (headed by citizen activist Alice Lipscomb) and the Delaware Valley Housing Association (headed by future mayor W. Wilson Goode) rallied at City Hall, wearing buttons that read "Houses Not Highways."

Architect Denise Scott Brown, acting as an advocate for the Citizens Committee, called the Crosstown Expressway "an immoral act." With Steven Izenour and David Manker, she prepared a planning study, "The Philadelphia Crosstown Community." Meant as a counterproposal to the expressway, Scott Brown's study recommended stabilization of the South Street community by preserving its nineteenth-century architecture, revitalizing businesses and residential areas, and establishing community service centers. In 1969, Mayor James Tate bowed to community pressure and dropped plans to build the Crosstown, telling Edmund Bacon to "let the people have a victory."[22]

Expressway opponents had only a brief time to relax. In 1972, the Crosstown rose from the grave in the form of Southbridge, a proposal for an underground expressway covered by thousands of new apartments, offices, and a light-rail system. Revived community opposition and the project's hefty price tag ($750 million) prevented Southbridge from getting underway, despite the support of

An artist's illustration for Denise Scott Brown's Crosstown Community project envisions South Street and the adjacent area with rehabilitated older structures, new housing and community facilities, and attractive signage and amenities. (Courtesy of Venturi, Scott Brown and Associates, Inc.)

Mayor Frank Rizzo; PennDOT's 1977 decision to halt all proposed highway projects finally killed it.

By the 1960s, South Street had become a ghost town, filled with derelict buildings sold or abandoned by their owners when the expressway seemed inevitable. As hippies took over its vacant structures or opened shops in its empty storefronts, South Street became Philadelphia's version of Haight-Ashbury or the East Village. Gradually, a vibrant counterculture emerged, with artistic ventures like the Theater of the Living Arts and the Painted Bride, underground newspapers like the *Distant Drummer*, and restaurants like Lickety Split. Once plans for the Crosstown Expressway died, South Street grew more upscale, with an eclectic mixture of boutiques, restaurants, nightclubs, and theaters. Today, despite concerns over violence and rowdyism, South Street remains one of the city's most vibrant shopping and entertainment districts.

Bicentennial Designs

Proposed location: Throughout the city
Period of origination: 1960s–1970s
Architect/Builder: Various architects

During the 1950s, Philadelphia began to lay the groundwork for a great national Bicentennial celebration. For years, however, progress was slow, as nearly a dozen government and citizens' groups bickered over the location, size, and focus of the fair. While the City Planning Commission drew up plans for a traditional World's Fair near the Centennial site in Fairmount Park, the populist group House in Order by 1976 insisted on a socially responsible event that would train the unemployed, create new housing, and channel money to poor neighborhoods.

In 1970, President Nixon selected Philadelphia as the official site for the Bicentennial Exposition, which was duly authorized by the Bureau of International Exhibitions in Paris. Two years later, a group of leaders from government, business, industry, and academia created the Philadelphia 1976 Bicentennial Corporation (Philadelphia '76) as the official planning arm for the celebration. The corporation developed a consortium of the architectural firms Venturi & Rauch; Mitchell/Giurgola; Bower & Fradley; Eshbach, Glass, Kale & Associates; Murphy Levy Wurman; and Louis I. Kahn (who headed the consortium in addition to contributing designs) to prepare a proposal for the American Revolution Bicentennial Commission.

These architects tried to blend the diverse Bicentennial proposals advanced by various groups into one coherent vision. While the

Louis I. Kahn's rough sketch of the Forum of the Availabilities for the Bicentennial, including such features as the Court of Events and the Threshold, where, in Kahn's words, the desire to express would meet the possible. (© 1977 Louis I. Kahn Collection, University of Pennsylvania and the Pennsylvania Historical and Museum Commission.)

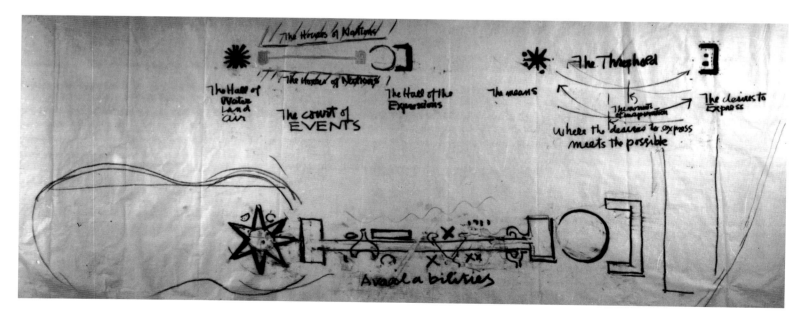

Philadelphia celebration would offer traditional World's Fair attractions, such as a midway and corporate and international exhibits, it would also provide an opportunity to rebuild the city, developing an infrastructure that would benefit not only the anticipated forty-five million visitors, but all Philadelphians long after the Bicentennial had ended.

The consortium submitted a tripartite design for the fair, with three major sites: Penn's Landing/Camden for the national Bicentennial celebration, Thirtieth Street Station for the International Exposition, and North Philadelphia for exhibits on the urban environment and the new model city. The Penn's Landing/Camden site would receive a conference center, along with theaters, restaurants, stores, and hotels. The Thirtieth Street Station district would be developed as a major transportation hub, with a new exhibition center, office towers, and housing. Included in the North Philadelphia site were a community college, conference center, transportation center, and new offices. A system of monorails and enclosed pedestrian walkways would facilitate movement between the various fair locations and Center City.

The Bicentennial allowed planners to turn the entire city into a giant architectural and social laboratory, on a scale far more abstract than that of previous world's fairs. Posing the question, "What is the city but the seat of Availabilities?" Louis Kahn proposed a concourse called the Forum of the Availabilities to connect two giant plazas, the Courts of the Physical Resources and the Courts of the Expressions. For international exhibits, Venturi & Rauch designed a Street of the World, overhung with gigantic multimedia signs and lined with a Potemkin village of simple sheds with facades representing the Taj Mahal, the Kremlin, and other world landmarks.

Shortly after the Bicentennial Corporation submitted its proposal, the Nixon administration, driven primarily by economic constraints, decided against a single-site fair and opted for smaller celebrations across the country. The corporation's price tag of over $1 billion, or roughly $7 million an acre, was unrealistic even by the standards of the go-go sixties, let alone the recessionary seventies.

A 1972 newspaper illustration shows exposition grounds built over the railroad tracks north of Thirtieth Street Station, featuring a dual monorail. (Temple University Libraries, Urban Archives, Philadelphia.)

In the end, Philadelphia received only $50 million in federal funds for the Bicentennial. Instead of a comprehensive redevelopment of the city, Philadelphia '76 was forced to select a few key projects, such as the Living History Center.

Other organizations stepped in to develop Bicentennial projects. The Philadelphia Greater Cultural Alliance asked Venturi & Rauch to reimagine the Benjamin Franklin Parkway as a venue for events and performances. With Steven Izenour as project manager, the firm adapted its proposed Street of the World into a series of temporary buildings and kiosks, supplemented by mobile orchestra shells, performance platforms, and covered exhibit wagons. At night, a dazzling display of moving lights, lasers, projections, and fireworks would turn the parkway into "a Crystal Palace of light,

PRELIMINARY PLANNING FOR BENJAMIN FRANKLIN PARKWAY CELEBRATION FOR '76   Venturi and Rauch, Architects and Planners   Philadelphia   December 1, 1972
PANORAMIC — TRIPTYCH 6   6

A preliminary design by Venturi & Rauch for the Benjamin Franklin Parkway Celebration for '76 shows the parkway at night, with fireworks and projections. (Courtesy of Venturi, Scott Brown and Associates, Inc.)

stretching from the Philadelphia Museum of Art to City Hall," and culminating in a giant Benjamin Franklin floating above the Museum of Art.[23]

Sadly, lack of funding prevented even this truncated fairground from being realized. Financial constraints, combined with municipal opposition, also killed the Venturi & Rauch/Murphy Levy Wurman plan to brighten the city's dingy automobile approaches with colorful, pop-art billboards promoting local attractions, from the Philadelphia Museum of Art to soft pretzels.

A combination of public and private efforts did provide Philadelphia with some lasting improvements, including new attractions like Franklin Court, the Afro-American Museum, and the Mummers Museum; replicas of the Graff House and City Tavern; the refurbishment of Independence National Historical Park; and the restoration of the First and Second Banks of the United States. In the end, Philadelphia's Bicentennial year turned out to be a pleasant affair, even after Mayor Rizzo scared away visitors by demanding federal troops to combat protestors who never materialized. President Gerald R. Ford addressed the nation from Independence Hall on the Fourth of July, there were plenty of fireworks and parades, and six million visitors enjoyed the spruced-up city.

Despite these high points, the modest celebration became one of Philadelphia's most bitter disappointments; in the words of one reporter, "the New Atlantis described in 1965 has become the Big Block Party of 1975."[24] The inability to produce a high-profile Bicentennial after two decades of planning and millions of wasted dollars wounded the city's collective self-confidence and tarnished its national image for years afterward.

Philadelphia Orchestra Hall

Proposed location: 260 South Broad Street
Period of origination: 1987
Architect/Builder: Venturi, Scott Brown and Associates, Inc.

After decades of thwarted attempts to leave the Academy of Music for another home, the board of directors of the Philadelphia Orchestra began a major campaign to build a new hall in the 1980s. While LeBrun and Runge's Academy was an architectural masterpiece, it was too small for the orchestra to share comfortably with its fellow tenants, the Pennsylvania Ballet and the Opera Company of Philadelphia. The Academy's acoustics were also considered a problem, for the ornate hall absorbed sound and diminished orchestral clarity. Land for a new symphony hall was acquired at the southwest corner of Broad and Spruce streets, a block from the Academy.

After a lengthy competition, Philadelphia's foremost architects, Robert Venturi and Denise Scott Brown, were selected to design Philadelphia Orchestra Hall in July 1987. Both architects cautioned that, given the relatively low budget of $60 million, their design would be more a Quaker meetinghouse than the Paris Opera. For a decade, Venturi, Scott Brown and Associates, Inc. (VSBA) produced numerous designs that met the orchestra's budget requirements while providing a suitably august home.

VSBA's final design for the Hall was an elegant yet simple "decorated shed," Venturi and Scott Brown's term for a utilitarian structure whose ornate façade indicates its purpose. (At the opposite end of their architectural spectrum is the "duck," named after a duck-shaped Long Island restaurant, denoting any structure where functionality takes a back seat to sculptural or expressionistic design.)

The brick and steel, 246,000-square-foot Orchestra Hall boasted a main façade composed of colored glass panels in a lively pattern of grids and diagonals. A frieze of oversized musical notation from Beethoven's "Moonlight Sonata," executed in satin-finished steel, ran along the front patio. In keeping with VSBA's environmental

The exterior of the proposed VSBA Orchestra Hall at night. In later designs, the words "Philadelphia Orchestra Hall" were replaced by a frieze of notes from Beethoven's "Moonlight Sonata." (Courtesy of Venturi, Scott Brown and Associates, Inc.)

An architect's conception of the main concert hall shows the four tiers of wraparound balconies. (Courtesy of Panoptic Imaging.)

approach to architecture, the Hall blended in with its neighbors rather than overpowering them: a glass pediment at the top of its façade mirrored the adjacent University of the Arts by John Haviland.

Inside, a ceremonial staircase led to an elegant Grand Lounge overlooking Broad Street, a 2,700-seat concert hall, and a 600-seat recital hall. Four tiers of balconies ran around the concert hall, surrounding the orchestra platform on all sides. The large façade windows on Broad Street could be opened into the Grand Lounge, "allowing the excitement and gala atmosphere of an orchestra evening to be glimpsed from the street," according to VSBA's project description. Besides the performance spaces, the design accommodated a 400-car parking garage, administrative offices, and an automobile arrival area on the south side.

In the mid-1990s, after further revisions, the VSBA design was torpedoed by garment manufacturer Sidney Kimmel, who had contributed a much-needed $12 million to the Hall's capital campaign. Kimmel found the VSBA design too commercial and modest, a sentiment echoed by Mayor Ed Rendell and other backers of the Avenue of the Arts campaign (in Robert Venturi's succinct analysis, "The building was too cheap").[25]

VSBA was dismissed as architect, and the project was rebid as a multipurpose "regional arts center," with a budget of $203 million. Despite their ten years of work on Symphony Hall, Venturi and Scott Brown were summarily rejected from the second competition. Rafael Viñoly, designer of the Tokyo International Forum, was named architect for the performing arts center in 1997.

The Kimmel Center for the Performing Arts, renamed in honor of its leading patron, opened in December 2001 with a price tag of $265 million and debts of $30 million incurred during construction. Viñoly's design, a supersized arts complex covered by an arched steel and glass barrel vault, has been called "incongruous in conception and cheesy in execution" by Martin Filler in the *National Review*[26] and described as "two concert halls nestled under a glass snow globe" by *Inquirer* architecture critic Inga Saffron.[27] Critics are also divided on the acoustics of Verizon Hall, the main auditorium. Despite several years of adjustments, a 2005 report by the original sound designer announced that a complete acoustical remedy for Verizon Hall would entail "enormous technical difficulties (and cost)," including the replacement of more than 100 doors.[28]

In November 2005, the Kimmel Center filed suit against Rafael Viñoly Associates for cost overruns, missed deadlines, and "deficient and defective design work."[29] The suit, settled out of court in March 2006, helped the Kimmel finish its first fiscal year in the black since its opening. Despite this windfall, the direct and indirect costs to the Philadelphia Orchestra of their world-class duck—in the form of larger operating deficits, increased ticket prices, lower attendance, and slashed salaries and staff—continue to mount.

Market Street Redesign

Proposed location: Market Street
Period of origination: ca. 1993
Architect/Builder: Edmund N. Bacon

Between his departure from the City Planning Commission in 1970 and his death in 2005, Edmund N. Bacon maintained a passionate interest in his city, whether raging against what he perceived as the desecration of Independence Mall or mounting a skateboard to protest the city's ban of skateboarders from Love Park.

In 1993, the eighty-two-year-old Bacon proposed a series of landmarks along Market Street between the Delaware and Schuylkill Rivers. His designs, along with those of his students, went on display at the Mellon Bank Center on Market Street as part of an exhibit entitled "New Visions for Philadelphia." Bacon wrote of Market Street in 1967: "This line, moving inland from the seminal point of the riverbank landing from the Old World, is a kind of microcosmic expression of the westerly movement of American development."[30]

Besides commemorating Market Street as Philadelphia's central artery, the "New Visions" exhibit represented a culmination of key themes from Bacon's work. Bacon had an almost mystical reverence for Penn's original design for the city, which his plans for redevelopment sought to reassert rather than erase. Biographer Gregory Heller explains that "Bacon's visions, while new creations, were responses to the history and structure of the city. Everything he built responded to William Penn's plan, and everything that has come since."[31] Penn Center, Market East, and Penn's Landing not only modernized and revitalized downtown Philadelphia, but also reinforced Market Street's position as the city's primary business and retail corridor. Bacon's earliest concept for Penn Center, obliterating all of City Hall except its tower, also rejoined the eastern and western halves of Market Street, severed since 1871.

In time, Bacon came to respect even the Second Empire pile that marked the meeting of Penn's two great boulevards. His fierce enforcement of the "gentlemen's agreement" that no Center City building would rise above the statue of William Penn atop City Hall cowed developers until Willard G. Rouse defied him and built Liberty Place in the 1980s, incurring Bacon's wrath.

Bacon's 1993 exhibit included designs to celebrate Market Street, "the ancient and venerable 1682 axis of William Penn," at three key points: at the Delaware River, which became the heart of Penn's settlement shortly after its founding; at City Hall, Penn's central square and the seat of government; and at the Schuylkill River, Philadelphia's gateway to the west.[32]

At Penn's Landing, a central tower on the axis of Market Street provided a focal point for the sprawling project, just as Pei's Society Hill Towers had done for Society Hill. Bacon hoped to reawaken official interest in his tower, a prominent feature of the original design for Penn's Landing, which had been dropped from the city's most recent plans. In addition to the tower, a sculpture of the ship *Welcome* commemorated the 1682 arrival of William Penn, while an arch facing Market Street framed City Hall, the next stop on the journey westward.

In the City Hall courtyard, a glass gazebo held a globe from which four colored beams of laser light radiated up and down Market and Broad streets through City Hall's arches. A fifth beam rose into the heavens, illustrating William Penn's belief that the interests of all people should rise above the interests of any individual or group. Underneath the gazebo, a compass and astrological calendar marked the convergence of Market and Broad streets at the true heart of Philadelphia.

The west bank of the Schuylkill River, which Bacon saw as the locus of the city's future economic development, was the subject of his most elaborate designs. A public plaza at Thirtieth Street, Universe Square, served as a symbolic entrance to West Philadelphia. Situated west of the train station and post office, Universe Square was framed by twin skyscrapers flanking Market Street, connected by a pedestrian bridge high above the street. A new Thirtieth Street subway station featured two levels of terraces, gardens, and foun-

The east façade of Universe Square, the twin skyscrapers framing Market Street west of Thirtieth Street Station, in a model prepared by Edmund N. Bacon's students at the University of Illinois, Urbana-Champaign. (Photograph by James Carroll, Athenaeum of Philadelphia.)

tains, resembling the sunken concourse in the original Penn Center. Universe Square was the centerpiece of a two-mile row of office towers stretching from Spring Garden Street to South Street in a crescent that mirrored the curve of the Schuylkill River.

Bacon's designs for Universe Square represented his ongoing efforts to integrate the Schuylkill River and West Philadelphia into Center City. In addition to his earlier plans to build luxury apartments along the Schuylkill's east bank, Bacon had proposed the Unicenter at Thirtieth Street, a new business complex with a glass-enclosed core where the Metroliner, airport high-speed line, subway, and commuter rail lines would interconnect. He had also suggested Center City West, a multilevel, multipurpose development that would rise over the railroad tracks north of Thirtieth Street Station.

Bacon hoped to awaken Philadelphia to its potential as the heart of the Northeast transportation corridor. After the gas shortages of the 1970s and 1980s, the former champion of the Crosstown Expressway passionately advocated public transit, electric cars, and other alternatives to gas-powered vehicles. In 1988, Bacon had predicted how Thirtieth Street Station would become a key commercial and transportation hub in a postpetroleum world: "Looking ahead . . . to 2032, the center of Philadelphia will be 16 blocks farther to the west at a highly significant crossing: that of Market Street, William Penn's 1682 axis, and the Metroliner, now the central spine of the northeastern United States."[33]

The completion of the Cira Centre, with its pedestrian bridge to Thirtieth Street Station, has initiated the development of that area as the business center Bacon envisioned and marks its growing absorption into Center City's sphere of activity. Similarly, the University of Pennsylvania's plan for a Schuylkill Gateway is reminiscent of Bacon's proposed Universe Square. The closest that the rest of Bacon's 1993 plan for Market Street ever came to realization, however, was the painting of a large compass rose in City Hall courtyard in 1994, with a silver orb strung overhead to stand in for his laser-beam globe.

NOTES

INTRODUCTION

1. Baltzell, *Philadelphia Gentlemen*, 202.
2. "Broad Street Station Closes."
3. "Clark Pries Off 1st Brick."
4. Tatum, *Penn's Great Town*, 138–139.

CHAPTER 1

1. Penn to William Crispin, John Bezar, and Nathaniel Allen, September 30, 1681, in Jean R. Soderlund, ed., *William Penn and the Founding of Pennsylvania 1680–1684: A Documentary History* (Philadelphia: University of Pennsylvania Press/Historical Society of Pennsylvania, 1983), 85.
2. Roach, "The Planting of Philadelphia."
3. *Charter, By-Laws, Rules and Regulations of the Carpenters' Company of the City and County of Philadelphia*, 1916, cited in American Philosophical Society, *Historic Philadelphia*, 96.
4. Quoted in Myers, *Narratives of Early Pennsylvania*, 405.
5. Quoted in Scharf and Westcott, *History of Philadelphia*, 120.
6. Ibid.
7. See www.russellhooverstudios.com/pimg1.html.
8. Watson, *Annals of Philadelphia, and Pennsylvania, in the Olden Time*, 1:130.
9. Quoted in Jenkins, *The Guide Book to Historic Germantown*, 138.
10. Lossing, *Pictorial Field Book of the Revolution*, 2:4.
11. Quoted in Goodman, *Benjamin Rush*, 335–336.
12. Franklin, *The Autobiography of Benjamin Franklin*, 32.
13. Iwanicki, "The Naglee House."
14. Ibid.
15. "Plan Offered for Preserving Naglee House."
16. Quoted in Watson, *Annals of Philadelphia*, 1:371.
17. Bridenbaugh, *Rebels and Gentlemen*, 260.
18. Quoted in Faris, *The Romance of Old Philadelphia*, 165.
19. Quoted in Webster, *Philadelphia Preserved*, xxiv.
20. American Philosophical Society, *Historic Philadelphia*, 309.
21. Quoted in Avery, "Cannonball House Is Shot."
22. Quoted in Reinberger and McLean, "Isaac Norris's Fairhill," 274.
23. Quoted in Scharf and Westcott, *History of Philadelphia*, 368.
24. Westcott, *The Historic Mansions of Philadelphia*, 493.
25. Quoted in Peterson, Greiff, and Thompson, *Robert Smith*, 71.
26. Weilbacker, *Historic Structures Report*.
27. Eberlein and Hubbard, *Portrait of a Colonial City*, 312.
28. Kieran, Timberlake & Harris, *Assessment of Ten Historic Structures*.
29. Lopez, *Benjamin Franklin's "Good House,"* 24.

CHAPTER 2

1. Christopher Marshall, "Remembrance," June 25, 1778, quoted in Scharf and Westcott, *History of Philadelphia*, 386.
2. Quoted by Scharf and Westcott, *History of Philadelphia*, 907–908.
3. Ibid., 486.
4. Hamlin, *Benjamin Henry Latrobe*, 319.
5. Ibid.,1827.
6. Quoted in Scharf and Westcott, *History of Philadelphia*, 1829.
7. "Germantown Mansion Bows to Progress."
8. Quoted in Tatum, *Penn's Great Town*, 43.
9. Quoted in Watson, *Annals of Philadelphia*, 414.
10. Scharf and Westcott, *History of Philadelphia*, 911.
11. Quoted in Charles S. Peterson, "Library Hall," in American Philosophical Society, *Historic Philadelphia*, 132.
12. Quoted in Tatum, *Penn's Great Town*, 41.
13. Westcott, *Historic Mansions of Philadelphia*, 270.
14. James, *Old Drury of Philadelphia*, 27.
15. Nash, *Forging Freedom*, 1.
16. Rush, *The Autobiography of Benjamin Rush*, 228.
17. Quoted at www.ushistory.org/tour/tour_bethel.htm.
18. Tatum, *Penn's Great Town*, 44.
19. Watson, *Annals of Philadelphia*, 410.
20. Hamlin, *Benjamin Henry Latrobe*, 155.
21. Roberts, "The Water Works."
22. Ibid.
23. Cope, *Philadelphia Merchant*, 207.
24. Westcott, *Historic Mansions of Philadelphia*, 453.
25. Frank H. Goodyear Jr., "A History of The Pennsylvania Academy of the Fine Arts, 1805–1976," in Pennsylvania Academy of the Fine Arts, *In This Academy*, 12.
26. Benjamin Latrobe to Isaac Hazlehurst, July 19, 1806, quoted in Hamlin, *Benjamin Henry Latrobe*, 178.
27. Goodyear, "History," 25.
28. "Special Report to the Directors," PAFA Board Minutes, January 16, 1865, quoted in Pennsylvania Academy of the Fine Arts, *In This Academy*, 31.
29. White, et al., *Philadelphia Architecture in the Nineteenth Century*, 24.

CHAPTER 3

1. Quoted in Agnes Addison Gilchrist, "The Philadelphia Exchange: William Strickland, Architect," in American Philosophical Society, *Historic Philadelphia*, 86.
2. Quoted in Scharf and Westcott, *History of Philadelphia*, 1793.
3. Journal of Nathaniel T. W. Carrington, October 31, 1837, quoted in Thomas, Cohen, and Lewis, *Frank Furness*, 135.
4. "A Walk around Mayfair," www.urban75.org/london/mayfair.html.
5. Scharf and Westcott, *History of Philadelphia*, 618.
6. "Men and Things," *Philadelphia Public Ledger*, July 28, 1909.
7. White et al., *Philadelphia Architecture in the Nineteenth Century*, 26.
8. Croskey, *History of Blockley*, 126.
9. Webster, *Philadelphia Preserved*, 183.
10. "Wreckers Smash 'Old Moko.'"
11. Quoted in Packard and Greim, *Some Account of the Pennsylvania Hospital*, 46.
12. Scharf and Westcott, *History of Philadelphia*, 1672.
13. Quinones, "West Phila.'s Doorway to Nowhere."
14. Notes of Edwin S. Dunkerly, June 1956, Monument Cemetery Collection, Genealogical Society of Pennsylvania, Philadelphia.
15. Quoted in Scharf and Westcott, *History of Philadelphia*, 643.
16. Cuyler, "The Camera Opens Its Eye on America," 73.
17. Mitchell and Giurgola, *Mitchell/Giurgola Architects*, 76.
18. Swarthmore Friends Historical Library, www.Swarthmore.edu/Library/friends/ead/4077paha.xml.
19. *History of Pennsylvania Hall*, 11.
20. Quoted in Warner, *The Private City*, 133.
21. *History of Pennsylvania Hall*, 181.
22. George W. Carpenter, *A Brief Description of Phil-Ellena* (Philadelphia: Privately published, 1844), 28.
23. Ibid., 19.
24. Ibid., 24.
25. "Philadelphia's First Floating Church," *Philadelphia Public Ledger*, n.d.
26. Quoted in Tatum, *Penn's Great Town*, 181.

CHAPTER 4

1. Thomas, Cohen, and Lewis, *Frank Furness*, 60.
2. Quoted in Lewis, *Frank Furness*, 133.
3. Huger Elliott, "Architecture in Philadelphia and a Coming Change," *Architectural Record* 23 (1908): 295; William F. Gray, *Philadelphia's Architecture* (Philadelphia: City History Society of Philadelphia, 1915), 339.
4. Fisher, *A Philadelphia Perspective*, 474.

5. "Old Scott Mansion Being Torn Down," *Philadelphia Telegraph*, February 24, 1913.
6. Quoted in Lewis, *Frank Furness*, 78.
7. Maass, *The Glorious Enterprise*, 63.
8. Guarantee Trust and Safe Deposit Company advertisement, Historical Society of Pennsylvania, Philadelphia, n.d. (ca. 1900).
9. *American Architect and Building News*, September 22, 1877, quoted in Thomas et al., *Frank Furness*, 71.
10. Campbell, "Revitalizing A Marketplace."
11. Wanamaker, *Golden Book of the Wanamaker Stores Jubilee Year*, 70.
12. Henry S. Morais, *The Jews of Philadelphia* (Philadelphia: The Levytype Company, 1894), 382.
13. William P. Harbeson, "Yesteryear in Our Town," in White et al., *Philadelphia Architecture in the Nineteenth Century*, 9.
14. Alexander Woollcott, "Miss Kitty Takes to the Road," *Saturday Evening Post*, August 18, 1934.
15. Elliott, "Architecture in Philadelphia," 301.
16. http://www.brynmawr.edu/cities/archx/04-600/wgh/portfolio.htm.
17. *Friendly Beginnings: The Origins and Growth of Philadelphia's Schools*, 10.
18. Gummere, *Old Penn Charter*, 1.
19. Baltzell, *Philadelphia Gentlemen*, 215.
20. Correspondence dated September 6, 1968, and Lydia Morris, "Last Will and Testament," cited in letter dated June 26, 1961, both in Morris Arboretum Archives.
21. Minutes of the Philadelphia Art Club, 1887, quoted in Thomas, "Frank Miles Day," in Philadelphia Museum of Art, *Philadelphia*, 428.
22. "Open New Store at Broad and Chestnut." *Philadelphia Evening Bulletin*, October 13, 1932.
23. Elliott, "Architecture in Philadelphia," 296.
24. Adrian Lee, "The Library: 130 Years of Yellowing Memories," *Philadelphia Evening Bulletin*, January 29, 1982.
25. Historic American Buildings Survey: Hotel Walton (John Bartram Hotel), 5.
26. Gray, *Philadelphia's Architecture*, 365.
27. Historic American Buildings Survey: Hotel Walton, 8.
28. "Plot Summary for *Woodside Park Trolley Panorama* (1902)," www.imdb.com/title/tt0364753/plot summary.

CHAPTER 5

1. Wister, *Romney and Other New Works*, 102–3.
2. *Philadelphia: Historic, Central, Metropolitan, and Industrial* (Philadelphia: Public Ledger, 1922), n.p.
3. Wister, *Romney and Other New Works*, 6.

4. Kuklick, *To Everything a Season*, 32.
5. Ibid., 73.
6. DeWolf, "The Nixon Theater."
7. "Rescue Reyburn Plaza."
8. Federal Writers' Project, *The WPA Guide to Philadelphia*, 469.
9. Quoted in Morrison, "The Arena."
10. Chanda, "Area's Pride Became Its Eyesore."
11. Photo caption, *Philadelphia Evening Bulletin*, June 15, 1958.
12. Glazer, *Philadelphia Theaters*, 77.
13. Cipriano, "The Buzz in South Philadelphia."

CHAPTER 6

1. Lingenbach, "Historic Philadelphia Redevelopment and Conservation."
2. Ian Nairn, *The American Landscape* (New York: Random House, 1965).
3. "Things That Aren't There Anymore," WHYY-TV, 1993.
4. John F. Morrison, "Latin Casino: Ring A Ding Ding," *Philadelphia Daily News*, May 12, 2004.
5. Donna St. George, "Harry Skinman, One-Time Owner of the Latin Casino on Walnut St.," *Philadelphia Inquirer*, November 5, 1988.
6. Patrick Kerkstra, "Crowds Cheer As Housing Project's Walls Come Down," *Philadelphia Inquirer*, November 25, 2002.
7. Donohue, "Kahn Finds Lesson."
8. Ibid.
9. Ibid.
10. Schedule of Events, Official Opening, Sheraton Hotel, March 3–4–5, 1957.
11. Smart, "In Our Town."
12. "Philadelphia's 515-Room Adam's Mark Hotel Shuts Doors in 60 Days," *Philadelphia Daily News*, December 1, 2004.
13. Jeff Merron, "It's So Hard to Say Goodbye," ESPN Page 2, espn.go.com/page2/s/ball parks/veterans.html.
14. Ibid.
15. Susan Warner, "At New Market, the Theater May Bring a Revival," *Philadelphia Inquirer*, July 20, 1992.
16. Quoted in "Housing the Bell."
17. Gallery, "Cityspace."

CHAPTER 7

1. Quoted in Scharf and Westcott, *History of Philadelphia 1609–1884*, 615.
2. Quoted in Gilchrist, *William Strickland*, 69.
3. Scharf and Westcott, *History of Philadelphia 1609–1884*, 635.

4. Quoted in ibid., 1772.
5. Lewis, "'Silent, Weird, Beautiful,'" 14.
6. Ibid., 14.
7. Ibid.
8. Ibid., 20.
9. "Proposed Boulevard."
10. J. Harvey Gillingham, Chief Engineer and Surveyor, Bureau of Surveys, *1925 Report of W. Freeland Kendrick, Mayor, City of Philadelphia*, 67.
11. Lincoln Steffens, "Philadelphia: Corrupt and Contented," *McClure's Magazine*, July 1903, 249.
12. Agnes Repplier, *Philadelphia: The Place and Its People* (New York: Macmillan, 1898), 356.
13. Quoted in O'Gorman et al., *Drawing toward Building*, 209.
14. Heller, *The Power of an Idea*, 39.
15. Ibid., 79.
16. Quoted in Rose DeWolf, "Safety beneath the Boulevard."
17. Quoted in David B. Brownlee, *Building the City Beautiful: The Benjamin Franklin Parkway and the Philadelphia Museum of Art*, 113.
18. Vincent Scully Jr., *Louis I. Kahn* (New York: George Braziller, 1962), 114.
19. "Imaginative Study of Philadelphia."
20. Edmund N. Bacon, interview, *My Architect*, by Nathaniel Kahn, directed by Nathaniel Kahn, New York Films, 2003.
21. Brownlee, DeLong, and Hiesinger, *Out of the Ordinary*, 47.
22. "Interstate 695—Crosstown Expressway," www.phillyroads.com/roads/crosstown/.
23. Benjamin Franklin Parkway Bicentennial Planning Project, www.vsba.com/projects/archive/bicentennial.html.
24. Mallowe, "How They Blew the Bicentennial."
25. Nicholas Lemann, "Letter from Philadelphia: No Man's Town," *New Yorker*, June 5, 2000, 46.
26. Martin Filler on Architecture: The Spirit of '76, TNR Online, www.tnr.com/070901/filler070901_print.html.
27. Inga Saffron, "In the Kimmel, an Idea That Exceeded Reality," *Philadelphia Inquirer*, December 4, 2005.
28. Peter Dobrin, "Study: Verizon Hall Needs Major Work," *Philadelphia Inquirer*, January 30, 2005.
29. Peter Dobrin and John Shiffman, "Kimmel Suit Cites Architect," *Philadelphia Inquirer*, November 29, 2005.
30. Bacon, *Design of Cities*, 305.
31. Heller, *The Power of an Idea*, 26.
32. "New Visions for Philadelphia," January 15–30, 1993, Mellon Bank Center. Exhibit program.
33. Bacon, "Westward Ho!"

SELECTED BIBLIOGRAPHY

BOOKS

Alberts, Robert C. *The Golden Voyage: The Life and Times of William Bingham 1752–1804.* Boston: Houghton Mifflin, 1969.

Albrecht, Harry P. *Broad Street Station, Pennsylvania Railroad, Philadelphia 1881–1952.* Clifton Heights, Pa: Harry P. Albrecht, 1976.

American Philosophical Society. *Historic Philadelphia: From the Founding until the Early Nineteenth Century. Papers Dealing with Its People and Buildings with an Illustrative Map.* Philadelphia: American Philosophical Society, 1953.

Andrews, Wayne. *Architecture, Ambition, and Americans: A Social History of American Architecture.* Revised edition. New York: Free Press, 1978.

Avery, Nicholas C. *National Register Nomination for the London Coffee Shop, 100 Market Street, Philadelphia, Pa.* (Dissertation.) University of Pennsylvania Graduate Program in Historic Preservation, archived at the Athenaeum of Philadelphia. December 1988.

Bacon, Edmund N. *Design of Cities.* Revised edition. New York: Viking, 1974.

Baltzell, E. Digby. *Philadelphia Gentlemen: The Making of a National Upper Class.* Glencoe, Ill.: The Free Press, 1958.

Barnes, Andrew Wallace. *History of the Philadelphia Stock Exchange, Banks, and Banking Interests.* Philadelphia: Cornelius Baker, 1911.

Belair, Margaret. *Carlton Mansion of Germantown.* (Dissertation.) University of Pennsylvania Graduate Program in Historic Preservation, archived at the Athenaeum of Philadelphia. December 1988.

Binger, Carl. *Revolutionary Doctor: Benjamin Rush, 1746–1913.* New York: W. W. Norton, 1966.

Blumenson, John J.-G. *Identifying American Architecture: A Pictorial Guide to Styles and Terms, 1600-1945.* Nashville, Tenn.: American Association for State and Local History, 1982.

Bond, Earl D. *Dr. Kirkbride and His Mental Hospital.* Philadelphia: J. B. Lippincott, 1947.

Brandt, Francis Burke, and Henry Volkmar Gummere. *Byways and Boulevards in and about Historic Philadelphia.* Philadelphia: Corn Exchange National Bank, 1925.

Brenner, Walter C. *Old Rising Sun Village.* Philadelphia: Privately printed, 1928.

Bridenbaugh, Carl, and Jessica Bridenbaugh. *Rebels and Gentlemen: Philadelphia in the Age of Franklin.* New York: Reynal and Hitchcock, 1942.

Brodsky, Alyn. *Benjamin Rush: Patriot and Physician.* New York: Truman Talley Books/St. Martin's Press, 2004.

Brown, Scott Cameron. *The William Bingham Mansion: A Historic Structure Report.* (Dissertation.) University of Pennsylvania Graduate Program in Historic Preservation, archived at the Athenaeum of Philadelphia. December 1985.

Brownlee, David B., and David G. DeLong. *Louis I. Kahn: In the Realm of Architecture.* Condensed edition. Los Angeles: Universe Publishing (with the Museum of Contemporary Art), 1997.

Brownlee, David B., David G. DeLong, and Kathryn B. Hiesinger. *Out of the Ordinary: Robert Venturi, Denise Scott Brown and Associates.* Philadelphia: Philadelphia Museum of Art, 2001.

Bullitt, William C. *It's Not Done.* New York: Harcourt, Brace, 1926.

Burke, Bobbye, Otto Sperr, Hugh J. McCauley, and Trina Vaux. *Historic Rittenhouse: A Philadelphia Neighborhood.* Philadelphia: University of Pennsylvania Press, 1985.

Childs, C. G. *Views in Philadelphia and Its Environs from Original Drawings Taken in 1827–30.* Philadelphia: C. G. Childs, 1830.

Ching, Francis D. K. *Architecture: Form, Space, and Order.* New York: Van Nostrand Reinhold, 1979.

———. *A Visual Dictionary of Architecture.* New York: John Wiley, 1995.

City of Philadelphia. *The Philadelphia Civic Center, 1962–1972: A Decade of Progress.* Philadelphia: City of Philadelphia, 1971.

Cohen, Charles J. *Rittenhouse Square Past and Present.* Philadelphia: Privately printed, 1922.

Contosta, David R. *A Philadelphia Family: The Houstons and Woodwards of Chestnut Hill.* Philadelphia: University of Pennsylvania Press, 1988.

———. *Suburb in the City: Chestnut Hill, Philadelphia, 1850–1990.* Columbus: Ohio State University Press, 1992.

Cook, Kathleen Kurtz. *The Creation of Independence National Historical Park and Independence Mall.* (Master's thesis.) University of Pennsylvania, 1989.

Cooledge Jr., Harold N. *Samuel Sloan: Architect of Philadelphia, 1815–1884.* Philadelphia: University of Pennsylvania Press, 1986.

Cope, Thomas P. *Philadelphia Merchant: The Diary of Thomas P. Cope, 1800–1851.* Edited by Eliza Cope Harrison. South Bend, Ind.: Gateway Editions, 1978.

Cotter, John L., Roger W. Moss, Bruce C. Gill, and Jiyul Kim. *The Walnut Street Prison Workshop: A Test Study in Historical Archaeology Based on Field Investigation in the Garden Area of the Athenaeum of Philadelphia.* Philadelphia: The Athenaeum of Philadelphia, 1988.

Cotter, John L., Daniel G. Roberts, and Michael Parrington. *The Buried Past: An Archaeological History of Philadelphia.* Philadelphia: University of Pennsylvania Press, 1992.

Croskey, John Welsh. *History of Blockley: A History of the Philadelphia General Hospital from Its Inception, 1731–1928.* Philadelphia: F. A. Davis, 1929.

Cutler, William W., III, and Howard Gillette Jr., eds. *The Divided Metropolis: Social and Spatial Dimensions of Philadelphia, 1800–1975.* Westport, Conn.: Greenwood Press, 1980.

Dallett, Francis James. *An Architectural View of Washington Square.* Philadelphia: Athenaeum of Philadelphia, 1964.

Davis, Allen F., and Mark H. Haller. *The Peoples of Philadelphia: A History of Ethnic Groups and Lower-Class Life, 1790–1940.* Philadelphia: Temple University Press, 1973.

Dorwart, Jeffery M., with Jean K. Wolf. *The Philadelphia Navy Yard: From the Birth of the U.S. Navy to the Nuclear Age.* Philadelphia: University of Pennsylvania Press, 2001.

Drexel and Company. *A New Home for an Old House.* Philadelphia: Drexel, 1927.

Dubin, Murray. *South Philadelphia: Mummers, Memories, and the Melrose Diner.* Philadelphia: Temple University Press, 1996.

Eberlein, Harold Donaldson, and Cortlandt Van Dyke Hubbard. *Portrait of a Colonial City: Philadelphia, 1670–1838.* Philadelphia: J. B. Lippincott, 1939.

Eberlein, Harold Donaldson, and Horace Mather Lippincott. *The Colonial Homes of Philadelphia and Its Neighbourhood.* Philadelphia: J. B. Lippincott, 1912.

Eckhardt, Joseph P. *The King of the Movies: Film Pioneer Siegmund Lubin.* Madison, N.J.: Fairleigh Dickinson University Press, 1997.

Episcopal Diocese of Pennsylvania. *Spanning Four Centuries: Pages of Parish Histories of the Episcopal Diocese of Pennsylvania.* Philadelphia: Episcopal Diocese of Pennsylvania, 1997.

Fairmount Park Art Association. *Fairmount Park Art Association: An Account of Its Origin and Activities from Its Foundation in 1871.* Philadelphia, Pa.: Fairmount Park Art Association, 1922.

Faris, John T. *Old Churches and Meeting Houses in and around Philadelphia.* Philadelphia: J. B. Lippincott, 1926.

———. *Old Roads out of Philadelphia.* Philadelphia: J. B. Lippincott, 1917.

———. *The Romance of Old Philadelphia.* Philadelphia: J. B. Lippincott, 1918.

Federal Writers' Project of the Works Progress Administration for the Commonwealth of Pennsylvania. *The WPA Guide to Philadelphia.* Philadelphia: University of Pennsylvania Press, 1991.

Finkel, Kenneth, with contemporary photographs by Susan Oyama. *Philadelphia Then and Now: 60 Sites Photographed in the Past and Present.* New York: Dover Publications (with the Library Company of Philadelphia), 1988.

Fisher, Sidney George. *A Philadelphia Perspective: The Diary of Sidney George Fisher Covering the Years 1834–1871.* Edited by Nicholas B. Wainwright. Philadelphia: Historical Society of Pennsylvania, 1967.

Fitzgerald, Kimberli. *Fairhill Mansion.* (Dissertation.) University of Pennsylvania Graduate Program in Historic Preservation, archived at the Athenaeum of Philadelphia. Fall 1992.

Franklin, Benjamin. *The Autobiography of Benjamin Franklin.* New York: Grosset and Dunlap, n.d.

Freedman, Ellen. *The Slate Roof House: Historic Structure Report.* (Dissertation.) University of Pennsylvania Graduate Program in Historic Preservation, archived at the Athenaeum of Philadelphia. HSTPV SM 632. December 1985.

Frey, Carroll. *Philadelphia's Washington Square.* Philadelphia: Penn Mutual Insurance Company, 1952.

Friedman, Murray, ed. *Jewish Life in Philadelphia, 1830–1940.* Philadelphia: Institute for the Study of Human Issues, 1983.

Friendly Beginnings: The Origins and Growth of Philadelphia's Schools 1683–1836. Philadelphia: William Penn Charter School, 1982.

Gallagher, H. M. Pierce. *Robert Mills: Architect of the Washington Monument, 1781–1855.* New York: AMS Press, 1966.

Gallery, John Andrew, gen. ed. *Philadelphia Architecture: A Guide to the City.* Prepared for the Foundation for Architecture, Philadelphia, Pa., by the Group for Environmental Education. Cambridge, Mass.: MIT Press, 1984.

Gallman, J. Matthew. *Mastering Wartime: A Social History of Philadelphia during the Civil War.* Cambridge: Cambridge University Press, 1990.

Garvan, Anthony N. B., and Carol A. Wojtowicz. *Catalogue of the Green Tree Collection.* Philadelphia: Mutual Assurance Company, 1977.

Garvan, Beatrice B. *Federal Philadelphia, 1785–1825: The Athens of the Western World.* Philadelphia: Philadelphia Museum of Art, 1987.

Gilchrist, Agnes Addison. *William Strickland: Architect and Engineer, 1788–1854.* Philadelphia: University of Pennsylvania Press, 1950.

Glazer, Irvin R. *Philadelphia Theaters: A Pictorial Architectural History.* New York: Dover Publications/Athenaeum of Philadelphia, 1994.

Golden, Janet, and Charles E. Rosenberg. *Pictures of Health: A Photographic History of Health Care in Philadelphia, 1860–1945.* Philadelphia: University of Pennsylvania Press, 1991.

Goodman, Nathan G. *Benjamin Rush: Physician and Citizen, 1746–1813.* Philadelphia: University of Pennsylvania Press, 1934.

Gowans, Alan. *Images of American Living: Four Centuries of Architecture and Furniture as Cultural Expression.* Philadelphia: J. B. Lippincott, 1964.

Gummere, John F. *Old Penn Charter.* Philadelphia: William Penn Charter School, 1973.

Hamlin, Talbot. *Benjamin Henry Latrobe.* New York: Oxford University Press, 1955.

Heller, Gregory. *The Power of an Idea: Edmund Bacon's Planning Method Inspiring Consensus and Living in the Future.* (Bachelor's thesis.) Wesleyan University, 2004.

History of the Baldwin Locomotive Works, 1831–1923. Philadelphia: Bingham, 1923.

History of Pennsylvania Hall, Which Was Destroyed by a Mob, on the 17th of May, 1838. Originally published 1838 by Merrihew and Gunn, Philadelphia. New York: Negro Universities Press, 1969.

Hunter, Robert J. *The Origin of the Philadelphia General Hospital, Blockley Division*. Philadelphia: Rittenhouse Press, 1955.

Hunter, Ruth H. *The Trade and Convention Center of Philadelphia: Its Birth and Renascence*. Philadelphia: City of Philadelphia, 1962.

Jacobs, Jane. *The Death and Life of Great American Cities*. New York: Vintage Books, 1992.

James, Reese Davis. *Cradle of Culture: 1800–1810, The Philadelphia Stage*. Philadelphia: University of Pennsylvania Press, 1957.

———. *Old Drury of Philadelphia: A History of the Philadelphia Stage, 1800–1835. . . .* Philadelphia: University of Pennsylvania Press, 1932.

Jenkins, Charles F. *The Guide Book to Historic Germantown*. Germantown, Pa.: Site and Relic Society, 1902.

Kauffman, James Laurence. *Philadelphia's Navy Yards (1801–1948)*. New York: Newcomen Society of England, 1948.

Kennedy, Roger G. *American Churches*. New York: Stewart, Tabori, and Chang, 1982.

Keyser, Naaman H., C. Henry Kain, John Palmer Garber, and Horace F. McCann. *History of Old Germantown*. Philadelphia: Horace F. McCann, 1907.

Kieran, Timberlake & Harris Architects. *Assessment of Ten Historic Structures in Fairmount Park*. Harrisburg: Pennsylvania Historical and Museum Commission, 1987.

King, Moses. *Philadelphia and Notable Philadelphians*. New York: Moses King, 1901.

Kocher, Donald Roth. *The Mother of Us All: First Presbyterian Church in Philadelphia, 1698–1998*. Woodbine, N.J.: Quinn Woodbine, 1998.

Kuklick, Bruce. *To Everything a Season: Shibe Park and Urban Philadelphia, 1909–1976*. Princeton, N.J.: Princeton University Press, 1991.

Lewis, Michael J. *Frank Furness: Architecture and the Violent Mind*. New York: Norton, 2001.

Library Company of Philadelphia. *At the Instance of Benjamin Franklin: A Brief History of the Library Company of Philadelphia*. Philadelphia: Library Company of Philadelphia, 1995.

Lopez, Claude-Anne. *Benjamin Franklin's "Good House": The Story of Franklin Court*. Washington, D.C.: National Park Service Division of Publications, 1981.

Lossing, Benson J. *Pictorial Field Book of the Revolution*. 2 vols. New York: Harper and Brothers, 1850.

Maass, John. *The Glorious Enterprise: The Centennial Exhibition of 1876 and H. J. Schwartzmann, Architect-in-Chief*. Watkins Glen, N.Y.: American Life Foundation, 1973.

Malcomson, William J. *Official Souvenir Programme, 81st Annual Communication of the Sovereign Grand Lodge I.O.O.F, September 18th to 23rd, 1905*. Philadelphia, 1905.

Maynard, W. Barksdale. *Architecture in the United States, 1800–1850*. New Haven, Conn.: Yale University Press, 2002.

McCosker, M. J. *The Historical Collection of Insurance Company of North America, 1792–1967*. Philadelphia: Insurance Company of North America, 1967.

McGlinn, Frank C. P. *Philadelphia: The Almost Hollywood and Its Lost Movie Palaces*. Philadelphia: Privately published, 1968.

McVarish, Douglas C., and Richard Meyer. *Warships and Yardbirds: An Illustrated History of the Philadelphia Naval Shipyard*. Philadelphia: Kvaerner Philadelphia Shipyard, 2000.

McVey, Lorraine. *The Cliffs*. (Dissertation.) University of Pennsylvania Graduate Program in Historic Preservation, archived at the Athenaeum of Philadelphia. December 1994.

Millar, John Fitzhugh. *The Architects of the American Colonies or Vitruvius Americanus*. Barre, Mass.: Barre, 1968.

Miller, Fredric M., Morris J. Vogel, and Allen F. Davis. *Still Philadelphia: A Photographic History, 1890–1940*. Philadelphia, Pa.: Temple University Press, 1983.

———. *Philadelphia Stories: A Photographic History, 1920–1960*. Philadelphia, Pa.: Temple University Press, 1988.

Mitchell, Ehrman B., and Romaldo Giurgola. *Mitchell/Giurgola Architects*. New York: Rizzoli International, 1983.

Moore, Edwin Coutant. *The House of Excellence: The History of Philadelphia's Own Market Place*. Philadelphia, William B. Margerum, 1931.

Morrone, Francis. *An Architectural Guide to Philadelphia*. Layton, Utah: Gibbs Smith, 1999.

Moss, Roger W. *Historic Houses of Philadelphia*. Philadelphia: University of Pennsylvania Press, 1998.

———. *Historic Sacred Places of Philadelphia*. Philadelphia: University of Pennsylvania Press, 2005.

Myers, Albert Cook, ed. *Narratives of Early Pennsylvania, West New Jersey, and Delaware, 1630–1707*. New York: Barnes and Noble, 1959.

Nash, Gary B. *First City: Philadelphia and the Forging of Historical Memory*. Philadelphia: University of Pennsylvania Press, 2002.

———. *Forging Freedom: The Formation of Philadelphia's Black Community, 1720–1840*. Cambridge, Mass.: Harvard University Press, 1988.

Nickels, Thom. *Philadelphia Architecture*. Charleston, S.C.: Arcadia, 2005.

Northeast Philadelphia Chamber of Commerce. *Northeast Philadelphia—And Why*. Philadelphia: Northeast Philadelphia Chamber of Commerce, 1928.

O'Donnell, Donna Gentile. *Provider of Last Resort: The Story of the Closure of Philadelphia General Hospital*. Philadelphia: Camino Books, 2005.

O'Gorman, James F., Jeffrey A. Cohen, George E. Thomas, and G. Holmes Perkins. *Drawing toward Building: Philadelphia Architectural Graphics, 1732–1986.* Philadelphia: University of Pennsylvania Press for The Pennsylvania Academy of the Fine Arts, 1986.

Oliver Evans Chapter of the Society for Industrial Archaeology. *Workshop of the World: A Selective Guide to the Industrial Archaeology of Philadelphia.* Philadelphia: Oliver Evans Press, 1990.

One Hundred Years in Philadelphia: The Evening Bulletin's *Anniversary Book, 1847–1947.* Philadelphia: Evening Bulletin, 1947.

Packard, Francis R., and Florence M. Greim. *Some Account of the Pennsylvania Hospital of Philadelphia from 1751 to 1938, with a Continuation of the Account to the Year 1956.* Philadelphia: Pennsylvania Hospital, 1957.

Pennsylvania Academy of the Fine Arts. *In This Academy: The Pennsylvania Academy of the Fine Arts, 1805–1976.* Philadelphia: Pennsylvania Academy of the Fine Arts, 1976.

Peterson, Charles E., Constance M. Greiff, and Maria M. Thompson. *Robert Smith: Architect, Builder, Patriot, 1722–1777.* Philadelphia: Athenaeum of Philadelphia, 2000.

Philadelphia 1976 Bicentennial Corporation. *Development Program Report.* Philadelphia: The Corporation, 1969.

Philadelphia Museum of Art. *Philadelphia: Three Centuries of American Art. Bicentennial Exhibition, April 11–October 10, 1976.* Philadelphia: Philadelphia Museum of Art, 1976.

Rabzak, Denise R. *Washington Square: A Site Plan Chronology, 1683–1984.* Philadelphia: National Park Service, 1987.

Regional Planning Federation of the Philadelphia Tri-State District. *Regional Plan of the Philadelphia Tri-State District.* Philadelphia: The Federation, 1932.

Riley, Edward M., et al. *Historic Philadelphia: From the Founding until the Early Nineteenth Century.* Philadelphia: American Philosophical Society, 1953.

Rottenberg, Dan. *The Man Who Made Wall Street: Anthony J. Drexel and the Rise of Modern Finance.* Philadelphia: University of Pennsylvania Press, 2001.

Rules of Work of the Carpenters' Company of the City and County of Philadelphia. Annotated, with an introduction, by Charles E. Peterson, F.A.I.A. New York: Bell, 1971.

Rush, Benjamin. *The Autobiography of Benjamin Rush: His "Travels through Life" Together with His Commonplace Book for 1789–1813.* Princeton, N.J.: Princeton University Press for the American Philosophical Society, 1948.

Scharf, J. Thomas, and Thompson Westcott. *History of Philadelphia 1609–1884, in Three Volumes.* Philadelphia: L. H. Everts, 1884.

Scranton, Philip, and Walter Licht. *Work Sights: Industrial Philadelphia, 1890–1950.* Philadelphia: Temple University Press, 1986.

Skaler, Robert Morris. *Images of America: Society Hill and Old City.* Charleston, S.C.: Arcadia, 2005.

Sky, Alison, and Michelle Stone. *Unbuilt America: Forgotten Architecture in the United States from Thomas Jefferson to the Space Age.* New York: McGraw-Hill, 1976.

Smith, Philip Chadwick Foster. *Philadelphia on the River.* Philadelphia: Philadelphia Maritime Museum, 1986.

Snyder, Martin P. *City of Independence: Views of Philadelphia before 1800.* New York: Praeger, 1975.

Soderlund, Jean R., ed. *William Penn and the Founding of Pennsylvania, 1680–1684: A Documentary History.* Philadelphia: University of Pennsylvania Press/Historical Society of Pennsylvania, 1983.

Sudjic, Deyan. *The Edifice Complex: How the Rich and Powerful Shape the World.* New York: Penguin Press, 2005.

Stewart, Frank H. *History of the First United States Mint, Its People, and Its Operations.* Philadelphia: Frank H. Stewart Electric, 1924.

Tatum, George B. *Penn's Great Town: 250 Years of Philadelphia Architecture.* Philadelphia: University of Pennsylvania Press, 1961.

Taylor, Frank H. *Philadelphia in the Civil War, 1861–1865.* Philadelphia: The City, 1913.

Teeters, Negley K. *The Cradle of the Penitentiary: The Walnut Street Jail at Philadelphia, 1773–1835.* Philadelphia: Pennsylvania Prison Society, 1955.

———. *They Were in Prison: A History of the Pennsylvania Prison Society, 1787–1937.* Philadelphia: John C. Winston, 1937.

Teeters, Negley K., and John D. Shearer. *The Prison at Philadelphia: Cherry Hill. The Separate System of Penal Discipline: 1829–1913.* New York: Columbia University Press (for Temple University Publications), 1957.

Teitelman, S. Robert. *Birch's Views of Philadelphia with Photographs of the Sites in 1960 and 1982.* Philadelphia: Free Library of Philadelphia/University of Pennsylvania Press, 1983.

Teitelman, S. Robert, and Richard W. Longstreth. *Architecture in Philadelphia: A Guide.* Cambridge, Mass.: MIT Press, 1974.

Thomas, George E., and David B. Brownlee. *Building America's First University: An Historical and Architectural Guide to the University of Pennsylvania.* Philadelphia: University of Pennsylvania Press, 2000.

Thomas, George E., Jeffrey A. Cohen, and Michael J. Lewis. *Frank Furness: The Complete Works.* Revised edition. New York: Princeton Architectural Press, 1996.

Tinkcom, Harry M., and Margaret B. Tinkcom. *Historic Germantown: From the Founding to the Early Part of the Nineteenth Century.* Philadelphia: American Philosophical Society, 1955.

Venturi, Robert. *Complexity and Contradiction in Architecture.* New York: Museum of Modern Art, 2002.

Venturi, Robert, Denise Scott Brown, and Steven Izenour. *Learning from Las Vegas: The Forgotten Symbolism of Architectural Form.* Revised edition. Cambridge, Mass.: MIT Press, 1977.

Von Moos, Stanislaus. *Venturi, Rauch and Scott Brown: Buildings and Projects.* New York: Rizzoli International, 1987.

Wainwright, Nicholas B. *Philadelphia in the Romantic Age of Lithography.* Philadelphia: Historical Society of Pennsylvania, 1958.

Waite, Diana S., ed. *Architectural Elements: The Technological Revolution.* Princeton, N.J.: Pyne Press, 1973.

Walther, Rudolph J. *Happenings in Ye Olde Philadelphia, 1680–1900.* Philadelphia: Walther, 1925.

Wanamaker, John. *Golden Book of the Wanamaker Stores Jubilee Year, 1861–1911.* Philadelphia: Privately published, 1911.

Warner, N. Thomas. *Anthony Benezet House, c. 1700–1818.* (Dissertation.) University of Pennsylvania Graduate Program in Historic Preservation, archived at the Athenaeum of Philadelphia. HSTPV 632. December 1988.

Warner, Sam Bass. *The Private City: Philadelphia in Three Periods of Its Growth.* Philadelphia: University of Pennsylvania Press, 1991.

Watson, John F. *Annals of Philadelphia, and Pennsylvania, in the Olden Time. Enlarged, with many revisions and additions, by Willis P. Hazard.* Philadelphia: J. M. Stoddart, 1877.

Webster, Richard. *Philadelphia Preserved: Catalog of the Historic American Buildings Survey.* Philadelphia: Temple University Press, 1976.

Weigley, Russell F., et al. *Philadelphia: A 300-Year History.* New York: W. W. Norton, 1982.

Weilbacker, Lisa. *Historic Structures Report on John Krider's Gun Shop, 135 Walnut Street.* (Dissertation.) University of Pennsylvania Graduate Program in Historic Preservation, archived at the Athenaeum of Philadelphia. December 1987.

Westcott, Rich. *Philadelphia's Old Ballparks.* Philadelphia: Temple University Press, 1996.

Westcott, Thompson. *The Historic Mansions and Buildings of Philadelphia, with Some Notice of Their Owners and Occupants.* Philadelphia: Porter and Coates, 1877.

White, Theodore B., et al. *Philadelphia Architecture in the Nineteenth Century.* Philadelphia: University of Pennsylvania Press for the Philadelphia Art Alliance, 1953.

Wilson, Robert H. *Philadelphia Quakers, 1681–1981.* Philadelphia: Philadelphia Yearly Meeting of the Religious Society of Friends, 1981.

Wister, Owen. *Romney and Other New Works about Philadelphia.* Edited by James A. Butler. University Park: Pennsylvania State University Press, 2001.

Wolf, Edwin. *Philadelphia: Portrait of an American City.* Harrisburg, Pa.: Stackpole Books, 1975.

Wolf, Edwin, II, and Maxwell Whiteman. *The History of the Jews of Philadelphia from Colonial Times to the Age of Jackson.* Philadelphia: Jewish Publication Society of America, 1957.

Wright, Robert E. *The First Wall Street: Chestnut Street, Philadelphia, and the Birth of American Finance.* Chicago: University of Chicago Press, 2005.

Wurman, Richard Saul, and John Andrew Gallery. *Man-Made Philadelphia: A Guide to Its Physical and Cultural Environment.* Cambridge, Mass.: MIT Press, 1972.

PAMPHLETS/MAGAZINES/NEWSPAPER ARTICLES

Avery, Ron. "Cannonball House Is Shot: Neglect Threatens 'Oldest Building' in City." *Philadelphia Daily News,* February 15, 1993

———. "Farewell to Farmhouse: Cannonball House Taken Down by City." *Philadelphia Daily News,* November 21, 1996.

———. "Historic Pasts, Uncertain Futures: 2 of 3 Buildings in Bad Shape." *Philadelphia Daily News.* April 12, 1995.

———. "Neglect of Historical Building May Cost City." *Philadelphia Daily News,* December 18, 1997.

Bacon, Edmund N. "Clean Air, No Gangs, No Private Cars." *Philadelphia Daily News,* April 14, 1975.

———. "Westward Ho!" *Philadelphia Magazine* 79, 9 (September 1988): 124–27.

Barrett, Jean. "200-Year-Old Gun Shop at 2nd and Walnut Falls Under Hammers of Demolition Crew." *Philadelphia Sunday Bulletin,* May 29, 1955.

Bauman, John F. "The Expressway 'Motorists Loved to Hate': Philadelphia and the First Era of Postwar Highway Planning, 1943–1956." *Pennsylvania Magazine of History and Biography* 115, 4 (October 1991: 503–34.

Bernstein, Mark F. "Notes from the Underground." *Philadelphia Magazine* 89, 11 (November 1998): 150–55.

Berson, Lenora. "The South Street Insurrection." *Philadelphia Magazine* 11 (November 1969): 87–92.

Brandow, James C. "Notes and Documents: A Barbados Planter's Visit to Philadelphia in 1837: The Journal of Nathaniel T. W. Carrington." *Pennsylvania Magazine of History and Biography* 106, 3 (July 1982): 411–22.

"Broad Street Station Closes: A New Era Begins." *Philadelphia Inquirer,* April 27, 1952.

Byrd, Dorothy S. "Razing of Historic Home Opposed by Park Officials." *Philadelphia Evening Bulletin,* July 6, 1971.

Campbell, Roy H. "Revitalizing a Marketplace and a Neighborhood As Well." *Philadelphia Inquirer,* August 19, 1988.

Chanda, Harriet. "Area's Pride Became Its Eyesore: The Mayfair Is No One's Home, No One's Welcome Neighbor." *Philadelphia Inquirer,* September 19, 1993.

Cipriano, Ralph. "The Buzz in South Philadelphia: Palumbo's Soon May Close." *Philadelphia Inquirer,* May 12, 1994.

"Clark Pries Off 1st Brick in Razing of Terminal," *Philadelphia Inquirer,* April 29, 1952.

Cochran, Thomas C. "Philadelphia: The American Industrial Center, 1750–1850." *Pennsylvania Magazine of History and Biography* 106, 3 (July 1982): 323–40.

Crompton, Robert D. "Franklin's House off High Street in Philadelphia." *Antiques Magazine* 92, 4 (October 1972): 680–83.

Cuyler, D. Jay. "The Camera Opens Its Eye on America." *American Heritage* 8, 1 (December 1956): 49–64.

Daughen, Joseph R. "Palumbo's: South Philly Gem." *Philadelphia Daily News,* March 17, 2004.

DeWolf, Rose. "Aquarama—Theater of the Sea." *Philadelphia Daily News,* March 18, 2004.

———. "The Nixon Theater." *Philadelphia Daily News,* March 21, 2004.

———. "Resident Wants Boulevard Tunnel Reopened." *Philadelphia Daily News,* July 2, 2003.

———. "Safety beneath the Boulevard," *Philadelphia Daily News,* August 26, 2002.

———. "Sears on the Boulevard," *Philadelphia Daily News,* March 19, 2004.

Donohue, Victoria. "Kahn Finds Lesson in Ruins of His Work," *Philadelphia Inquirer,* August 27, 1973.

Dunkerly, Edwin S. Notes of. Monument Cemetery Collection, Genealogical Society of Pennsylvania, Philadelphia.

Evers, Charles A. "A List of Philadelphia's Modern Monuments." *Philadelphia Architect,* May 1997. Article accessed through web site: http://www.brynmawr.edu/iconog/modern.html.

Farmer, John J. "It Was the Best of Times, the Worst of Times." *Philadelphia Evening Bulletin,* January 29, 1982.

Ferrick, Thomas, Jr. "House Beat Cannon Balls . . . But Falls to the Wrecking Ball." *Philadelphia Inquirer,* December 6, 1996.

Fried, Daisy. "Blasting the Past." *CityPaper,* September 4–11, 1997.

———. "You Win Some and Lose Some in the Preservation Game." *CityPaper,* September 4–11, 1997.

Gallery, John Andrew. "Bell's Hell." *CityPaper,* June 12–18, 2003.

"Germantown Mansion Bows to March of Progress." *Philadelphia Evening Bulletin,* February 7, 1948.

Haas, Al. "'Tear It Down' Is Historic Pastime." *Philadelphia Inquirer,* July 8, 1971.

Higgins, Dennis M. "Naglee House Yields to Gas Station." *Philadelphia Inquirer,* April 26, 1965.

Hine, Thomas. "Just How Good Was Ed Bacon, Really?" *Philadelphia Magazine* 90, 3 (March 1990): 84–93.

———. "Welcome Park's Exposed Look Overshadows Its Tribute to Penn." *Philadelphia Inquirer,* January 14, 1983.

Historic American Buildings Survey: Hotel Walton (John Bartram Hotel), HABS No. PA-1091, July 1964.

Horn, Patricia. "Franklin's 300th: Libraries Turn the Next Page." *Philadelphia Inquirer,* October 10, 2005.

"Housing the Bell: 150 Years of Exhibiting an American Icon." Exhibit brochure, Kroiz Gallery of the Architectural Archives of the University of Pennsylvania, April 19–August 18, 2006.

Hughes, Samuel. "Treasures and Travesties." *University of Pennsylvania Gazette,* August 24, 2004.

Hutchins, Dexter C. "Plan Offered for Preserving Naglee House." *Philadelphia Inquirer,* September 17, 1964.

"Imaginative Study of Philadelphia Done Over on Modernistic Planning Principles," *Philadelphia Evening Bulletin,* May 17, 1941.

Iwanicki, Edwin. "The Naglee House." *Germantown Crier* 17, 3 (September 1965): 85–93.

Kurjack, Dennis C. "The 'President's House' in Philadelphia." *Pennsylvania History* 20, 4 (October 1953): 380–94.

Labs, Kenneth B. *The Southeast Square of Philadelphia: An Evolutionary History.* Pamphlet. Philadelphia: Published by the author, May 1973.

Larson, Roy F., et al. *Independence Hall and Adjacent Historic Buildings: A Plan for Their Preservation and the Improvement of Their Surroundings.* Pamphlet. Philadelphia: Fairmount Park Art Association in Collaboration with the Independence Hall Association, 1944.

Lawler, Edward, Jr. "The President's House in Philadelphia: The Rediscovery of a Lost Landmark." *Pennsylvania Magazine of History and Biography* 126, 1 (January 2002): 5–92.

Layne, Elizabeth N. "A Question of Values." *American Heritage* 21, 5 (August 1970): 119.

Lewis, Michael J. "'Silent, Weird, Beautiful': Philadelphia City Hall," *Nineteenth Century* 11, 3–4 (1992): 13–21.

Lingenbach, William E. "Historic Philadelphia Redevelopment and Conservation." Pamphlet. In *The Independence National Park and Independence Mall in Historic Philadelphia.* Philadelphia: Independence Hall Association, 1951.

Mallowe, Mike. "How They Blew the Bicentennial." *Philadelphia Magazine,* June 1975.

"Men and Things," *Philadelphia Public Ledger,* July 28, 1909.

Miller, Karen E. Quinones. "West Phila.'s Doorway to Nowhere Has a History Shrouded in Mystery." *Philadelphia Inquirer,* February 18, 1998.

Morrison, John F. "The Arena." *Philadelphia Daily News,* March 8, 2004.

O'Gorman, James F. "A New York Architect Visits Philadelphia in 1822." *Pennsylvania Magazine of History and Biography* 117, 3 (July 1993): 153–76.

"Old Landmarks in Philadelphia." *Scribner's Monthly* 12, 2 (June 1876): 145–167.

"Open New Store at Broad and Chestnut," *Philadelphia Evening Bulletin,* October 13, 1932.

Philadelphia Chamber of Commerce Aviation Committee. "Philadelphia: Aeronautical Center of the East." Pamphlet. Philadelphia: Philadelphia Chamber of Commerce, May 1930.

"Philadelphia's First Floating Church," *Philadelphia Public Ledger,* n.d.

"Phil-Ellena into Pelham: A Country Seat Becomes 'a Bit of Country in the City.' *Germantown Crier* 38, 4 (Fall 1986): 83–90.

"Proposed Boulevard to Link Chestnut Hill with the Main Line." *Public Ledger,* March 26, 1911.

"Reburying the Past." *University of Pennsylvania Gazette,* April 28, 2002.

Reinberger, Mark, and Elizabeth McLean. "Isaac Norris's Fairhill: Architecture, Landscape, and Quaker Ideals in a Philadelphia Country Seat." *Winterthur Portfolio* 32, 4 (Winter 1997): 243–74.

"Rescue Reyburn Plaza." *Philadelphia Evening Bulletin,* April 29, 1952.

Richardson, Edgar P. "Centennial City." *American Heritage* 26, 2 (December 1971): 17–32.

Riley, Edward M. "Philadelphia, the Nation's Capital, 1790–1800." *Pennsylvania History* 20, 4 (October 1953): 357–379.

Roach, Hannah Benner. "The Planting of Philadelphia: A Seventeenth Century Real Estate Development." *Pennsylvania Magazine of History and Biography* 92, 1 (1968): 29–38.

Roberts, Christopher. "The Water Works: A Place Wondrous to Behold." www.state.nj.us/drbc/edweb/waterworks.htm.

Romano, Carlin. "Finally, a Memorial to Penn." *Philadelphia Inquirer,* October 29, 1982.

Saffron, Inga. "Echoes of Slavery at Liberty Bell Site." *Philadelphia Inquirer,* March 24, 2002.

———. "Presidents' House Site Marginalized . . . Again." *Philadelphia Inquirer,* March 31, 2002.

Schedule of Events, Official Opening, Sheraton Hotel, March 3–4–5, 1957. Urban Archives, Temple University, Philadelphia.

"The Schuylkill River Crossing at Market Street in Philadelphia: Commemorating the Construction of the Bridge and Subway Tunnel, November 18, 1932." Pamphlet. Philadelphia: Dravo Contracting Company, 1932.

Schwartz, Joel. "To Every Mans Door": Railroads and Use of the Streets in Jacksonian Philadelphia. *Pennsylvania Magazine of History and Biography* 128, 1 (January 2004): 35–62.

Shaffer, Gwen. "Boning Up." *CityPaper,* September 3–10, 1998.

Siegel, Richard D. "Naglee House Razing Haunts Plan to Create National Historic Area." *Philadelphia Inquirer,* June 27, 1965.

Skaler, Robert M. "Broad Way of Life." *CityPaper,* September 25–October 1, 2003.

Smart, James. "Another Historic Structure Is Saved—for Demolition." *Philadelphia Evening Bulletin,* June 21, 1971.

———. "In Our Town: Aquarama Sold for Motel after Years of Floundering." *Philadelphia Bulletin,* March 5, 1969.

Stitt, Susan. "The 'Fireproof': The Society's Building." *Pennsylvania Magazine of History and Biography* 124, 1/2 (January/April 2000): 43–101.

Tangires, Helen. "Public Markets and Civic Culture in Nineteenth-Century America." Speech to the Culinary Historians of Washington, D.C., February 8, 2004.

Taylor, George Rogers. "Philadelphia in Slices." *Pennsylvania Magazine of History and Biography* 93, 1 (January 1969): 23–72.

Thomas, George E. "From 'Frontier' to Center City: The Evolution of the Neighborhood of the Historical Society of Pennsylvania." *Pennsylvania Magazine of History and Biography* 124, 1/2 (January/April 2000): 7–42.

Thompson, Peter. "The Friendly Glass": Drink and Gentility in Colonial Philadelphia. *Pennsylvania Magazine of History and Biography* 113, 4 (October 1989): 549–74.

Ward, Townsend. "The Germantown Road and Its Associations, Part First." *Pennsylvania Magazine of History and Biography* 5, 1 (1881): 1–18.

Webb, Amy L. "Philly's Most Endangered Bldgs." *CityPaper,* December 12–17, 2003.

"Wreckers Smash 'Old Moko' as Democrats Plug Tate." *Philadelphia Evening Bulletin,* November 3, 1967.

INDEX

Page numbers in *italics* indicate illustrations or information found in captions.

THOMAS H. KEELS is a local writer and historian. He is the author of *Philadelphia Graveyards and Cemeteries* and co-author (with Elizabeth Farmer Jarvis) of *Chestnut Hill*.